Leader
of the
Band

Leader

of the

Band

The Life of Woody Herman

Gene Lees

OXFORD UNIVERSITY PRESS

New York   Oxford

Oxford University Press

Oxford   New York
Athens   Auckland   Bangkok   Bogota   Bombay
Buenos Aires   Calcutta   Cape Town   Dar es Salaam
Delhi   Florence   Hong Kong   Istanbul   Karachi
Kuala Lumpur   Madras   Madrid   Melbourne
Mexico City   Nairobi   Paris   Singapore
Taipei   Tokyo   Toronto

and associated companies in
Berlin   Ibadan

Library of Congress Cataloging-in-Publication Data
Lees, Gene.
Leader of the Band: The life of Woody Herman / Gene Lees.
p. cm.   Includes bibliographical references and index.
ISBN 0-19-505671-X
ISBN 0-19-511574-0 (Pbk.)
1. Herman, Woody, 1913–1987.   2. Jazz musicians—United States—
Biography.   I. Title.
ML419.H375L4   1995
781.65'092—dc20   [B]   95-5567

1 3 5 7 9 10 8 6 4 2

Printed in the United States of America
on acid-free paper

For Charlotte

IN MEMORIAM

FOREWORD

On the evening of July 16, 1986, in the Hollywood Bowl, Woody Herman and his current band and some of his alumni played a concert in celebration of his fiftieth anniversary as a bandleader. The true anniversary was in the following November, but the July date was the only one available at the Bowl.

Woody was old and ill and should not have been working at all. But the Internal Revenue Service left him no choice. It had been hounding him for more than twenty years in what many lawyers and other observers consider the most egregious case of IRS persecution in the history of that branch of government. Often seizing gate receipts at the end of performances, they had left him utterly destitute.

Afterwards there was a party at Woody's house in the hills of West Hollywood, a property the IRS was even then trying to take from him, and, ultimately, would.

The house was crowded. Woody found me in the living room. He said, "Listen, I have to talk to you about something. I want you to write my biography." A truly humble man under his show-biz bravura, he nonetheless knew who he was and understood his place in history. He knew he had been one of the great bandleaders of his era and that the era itself was great. As he said of jazz of that period, "It was the popular music of the land."

"But Wood," I said, "Stuart Troup is working on a book, and a lot of people will probably do biographies on you."

"I don't care," Woody said, "I want you to do it. You will do the definitive biography, because . . . "—and he was emphatic about this—" . . . you knew Charlotte. Promise me!"

And he held my forearm, pressing his fingers into it, almost hurting me. In view of how feeble he was, I was surprised by the strength of his hand.

"All right, Wood, I promise."

His daughter, Ingrid, told me later, "He always wanted you to write it—I thought you knew that."

Later, various persons confirmed that he wanted me to do this book, Bill Byrne, his road manager for more than twenty years, Charlotte's cousin and friend, Shirley Mancuso, and Jack Siefert, one of Woody's closest friends, among them.

Woody had, among his quirks, this one: He praised people behind their backs, never to their faces. Often they did not know how much he liked or respected them, although I'm sure they intuitively sensed it. This resulted, I think, from a surprisingly shy facet of his character, a certain perhaps Germanic reticence.

Bill Byrne said Sal Nistico died without ever knowing how Woody loved him.

Jack Siefert told me wistfully, "I never really knew how highly Woody thought of me until he was gone."

And Woody never mentioned to me that he wanted me to do this book until that party, when he was well aware that his days were dwindling away and there was no time left to talk about it. He just mentioned it to seemingly everyone else.

I told Bill Byrne, "You know, Woody not only knew what his people could do. He knew what they would do."

He knew that if he told me to do this book, I *would* do it.

And he was right.

I never saw him again.

G. L.

ACKNOWLEDGMENTS

Stuart Troup started work with Woody on an autobiography, but time ran out, and Stuart completed it with quotations from Woody's friends. It was published in 1990 by E. P. Dutton with the title *The Woodchopper's Ball*. Though it is inevitably incomplete, it was a valuable guide for my own research, and I am grateful to the publisher and especially Stuart for permission to quote from it.

In 1957 the late Ralph J. Gleason did a series of interviews with Woody with the intent of developing an autobiography. But Ralph died in 1975 with the book unwritten and his wife, Jean, donated the transcripts of the interviews with Ralph to Ingrid, who granted me permission to quote from them.

In December, 1978, and January, 1979, Dr. Herb Wong did four interviews with Woody for the oral history-of-jazz series commissioned by the Smithsonian Institution on a grant from the National Endowment for the Arts. Later, the project was transferred to the Institute of Jazz Studies at Rutgers University, where the transcript now rests. I thank the Institute for access to this material and to its file of newspaper and magazine clippings. And everyone owes gratitude to the late Marshall Stearns and to James T. Maher, who established the Institute. It is hard to imagine what researchers in jazz would do without the files, books, and memorabilia at Rutgers.

Further, I am grateful to Jim Maher for his direct and generous advice and help, particularly for his precise recollections of the Isham Jones band. Jim's memory is a national treasure. He also read the manuscript of this book at one stage of its development and gave wise counsel. So too Bill Kirchner from whose essay on Gregory Herbert I have quoted. Terry Teachout's essay on travels with Woody, in *The American Scholar*, is superb, and I thank him for permission to quote from it at length.

I thank Ray and Gen Sherman and the Reverend Dan Sherman not only for their information about Woody's childhood and youth but for their hospitality when I visited them in Milwaukee, and, similarly, Jack and Mary Siefert when I visited them in Lower Gwynedd, Pennsylvania. Ray Sherman and Jack Siefert between them collected the archives of Woody's career that he never bothered to keep himself. It takes only a little time in the homes of the Shermans and Sieferts to reveal why these two families were Woody's lifelong closest friends.

In addition to the Shermans and Sieferts, I interviewed Nat Adderley, Kenny Ascher, Alan Broadbent, Les Brown, Ralph Burns, Tom Cassidy, Donald Erb, Midge Ellis, Leonard Garment, Terry Gibbs, Dick Hafer, Fred Hall, Neal Hefti, Jake Hanna, Ingrid Herman, Chubby Jackson, Milt Jackson, Red Kelly, Peggy Lee, Lou Levy, Dr. Stanley Levy, Tommy Littlefield, Artie Malvin, Shirley Mancuso, Johnny Mandel, Tony Martin, Nelson Hatt, Gene Norman, Red Norvo, Kirk Pasich, Flip Phillips, Polly Podewell, Jimmy Raney, Howie Richmond, Marvin Stamm, Richard Stoltzman, George Wein, and Phil Wilson, some of them many times, and I thank them for their patience. Some of them did me the further kindness of reading the manuscript, particularly Ralph Burns, who read it several times in the course of its evolution.

In earlier years, I interviewed Bill Chase, Al Cohn, Nat Pierce, Abe Turchen, and Woody Herman, and I drew on this material. I interviewed Woody many times over a period of nearly four decades, and we had countless informal conversations as well.

I apologize to many persons I did not interview. But the number of witnesses to Woody's life, including the alumni of his bands, is all but endless, and it simply wasn't feasible to interview all of them.

Bill Byrne gave me enormous help. Through his gift of the band's uninterrupted itinerary from 1965 until 1987, when Woody died, he made it possible to date events with certainty.

Members of the Turchen family, including Abe's cousin, Mayer Kanter; his nephew, Dick Turchen; his daughter-in-law, Marty; and his son Steve, were helpful beyond anything I might have hoped for.

Clarinetist Tad Calcara expanded my understanding of the instrument and led me to Donald Erb.

I also drew on the memory of conversations and interviews with Dave Brubeck, Paul Fontaine, Gerry Mulligan, Alvino Rey, Zoot Sims, and Artie Shaw.

In Bedford, England, author and critic Richard Palmer obtained documents not easily found on the western side of the Atlantic, including his book on Stan Getz. In Adelaide, Australia, H. R. (Kym) Bonython, race-car driver, speedboat racer, adventurer, impresario, jazz lover, and former Mosquito bomber pilot (DFC), went to considerable trouble to gather documentation of Woody's Australian tour. And from Warsaw, Pawel Brodowski, editor of *Jazz Forum*, sent me material on Woody's trips to his country. My especially dear friends Adam Makowicz, the great jazz pianist born of Polish parents in Czechoslovakia, and his wife, Irena Chalecka, expended similar effort to help me document Woody's Polish trips, and Irena translated newspaper articles and other materials for me.

Willis Conover of the Voice of America gave me the benefit of his memories, as well as tapes of the Warsaw concerts of 1976 and '77.

Without all these persons, this book could not have been written.

CONTENTS

Leader
of the
Band

He was born with a gift of laughter and a sense that the world was mad.

RAPHAEL SABATINI, *Scaramouche*

1

Milwaukee

In the glory days of the big bands, little more than the decade between 1935 and 1945, the leaders of these orchestras were public heroes. Scores of name bands toured the North American continent. While the names of these famous groups still ring in the collective memory, it is generally forgotten that there were also what were known as territory bands, regional orchestras many of which were of almost legendary excellence. Even small cities, cities of 35,000 or so, could support three or four bands of part-time musicians. Sometimes the musicians in these local bands graduated to the name bands.

The instrumentation was fairly standard: a rhythm section comprising piano, bass, drums, and possibly guitar; a saxophone section consisting of two altos, two tenors, and, later in the era, baritone; and a brass section of three or four trumpets and two or three trombones. The era was the first in history in which the saxophone was put to extensive and serious musical use.

The leaders of the "name" bands were celebrities. So were their sidemen, and the fans knew their names as baseball, hockey, football, and basketball fans know the names of the athletes. Changes in personnel were reported in *Down Beat* magazine and followed avidly by the admirers of the music. The more dedicated fans could rattle off the names of the players in the major bands—all of them.

To those of us who took this music seriously, there were two kinds of band, the bad and the good, the "sweet" bands and the swing bands. A list of the greatest bands, anybody's list, would have to include those of Duke Ellington, Count Basie, Tommy Dorsey, Benny Goodman, and Woody Herman. And what made the bands great was that, while they did indeed play for dances, everything they played, including the ballads, was inflected with jazz and provided long stretches of time for improvised solos by the brilliant young musicians who manned them. We must not forget how young these men were. Many of them reached formidable heights of creative brilliance before they were twenty. The world never had known anything like this sunburst of extensive collective artistic genius and certainly has known nothing like it in the half-century since the gradual ending of that era.

There were three great clarinet-playing bandleaders in the big-band era, Woody, Benny Goodman, and Artie Shaw. One of the reasons they chose the instrument, rather than saxophone, according to Shaw, was that with its higher pitch, the clarinet could cut through the sound of the band and the poor amplification systems of the time the way a saxophone could not.

Throughout his life, writers reiterated that his full name was Woodrow Wilson Herman. It was Woodrow Charles Thomas Herrmann. Since he was born May 16, 1913, in the second year of the Wilson administration, it seems likely that he was named after the President. In later years, many of those who loved him called him simply Wood.

The oldest of his relationships was that with the family of John and Julia Sherman. It passed beyond friendship, this intimate connection with people whose name rhymed with his own. Woody was an only child, and he looked on Julia Sherman as his aunt and on her three sons—Erwin, usually called Erv; Ray; and Dan—and her daughter, Joyce, as his brothers and sister. So intimate was the relationship that Ray talks like Woody. He drops the g in gerunds in the same way Woody did, saying, for example, goin'. Ray says "avenoo" the way Woody did, and a tune is a toon. The vowels are very distinctive, with flat midwestern a's, and the cadence is identical to Woody's. Unexpected words get sudden emphasis, and Ray, like Woody, sometimes breaks words in the middle, saying, for instance, "lime (slight pause) light" for "limelight." But the similarity passes beyond pronunciation. Although one would certainly be able to tell whether one was listening to Ray or Woody on a tape, even Ray's voice is much like Woody's, resonating from the mask area of the face. I could understand this if they had been blood relatives. So striking is this resemblance that when I first met Ray, I found it a little unsettling, four years after Woody died.

If his death had the elements of tragedy, his life was anything but that.

There was a slight quaver in Woody's voice, like that of someone on the verge of tears. To the contrary, he was on the verge of laughter.

Ray Sherman, a good-looking man with a full head of white hair, in his seventies when I met him, told me: "My people came from Poland about the middle eighteen hundreds. My father was a tool-and-die maker. The family name was Stachowski. They changed it to Sherman about 1920 or even earlier. If people knew you were Polish, you were looked down upon, the way the Irish and the Italians were browbeaten when they came to this country. Lots of people did it. It was much easier."

Woody's mother, Myrtle, was born of Polish parents in Germany on September 5, 1888. Her name was Bartoszewicz, pronounced Bar-toe-she-veech. Her parents emigrated to the United States when she was a year or so old and became part of the German-Polish ethnic mix common in Milwaukee. Woody's father, Otto Herrmann, was born in Milwaukee of German parentage on November 25, 1886.

"My folks and Woody's folks were friends from the neighborhood before they were married," Ray Sherman said. "My dad went with my mother, and Woody's dad was going with his mother. They were dating, whatever terms they used back in those days. My folks were married in 1910 and Woody's parents around the same time. Woody's father worked for the United Shoe Machine Corporation. They sold shoemaking machinery to the shoe factories and serviced the machines. When they'd get a new machine, Otto would help install it in the factory and teach the workers how to use it.

"My brother Erv is the oldest in our family. When he was a year old, my mother walked, with Erv in a buggy, from Locust and Humboldt Avenue over on the east side of Milwaukee, to Racine Avenue, where the Herrmanns lived, probably a mile and a half or so, down in the Third Ward, to call for Woody's mother. They were going to go to an afternoon tea at a Welsh church downtown. And when my mother got to their house, Woody's mother was in labor. Woody was born. The doctor handed Woody to my mother. Erv slept through it all in the buggy."[1]

The night before that birth, in Paris, Nijinsky danced to Debussy's *Jeux* in the ballet company of Sergei Diaghilev. Debussy was fifty, Maurice Ravel was thirty-eight, the Russians Sergei Rachmaninoff and Igor Stravinsky were thirty. Stravinsky had already written *Petrouchka* and *The Firebird* for Diaghilev, and his *Le Sacre du printemps* was in rehearsal for presentation in Paris May 29, 1913, when Woody was thirteen days old. Earl Hines was nine, Bix Beiderbecke was ten, Louis Armstrong was twelve, Will Marion Cook was forty-four, Duke Ellington was fourteen, and William Basie was eight. Geronimo had died only four years earlier, at the age of seventy. The main streets of Milwaukee were paved with cedar cobbles, and the sidewalks were made of planks. Bread and dairy products and green groceries were delivered in horse-drawn wagons. In winter, workmen cut blocks of ice from the rivers and stored them in insulated warehouses for delivery in the summer on flat-bed wagons, also drawn by horses. The iceman, as he was called, a leather-aproned figure with strong arms, was popular with children in the hot-weather months. As he cut the big rectangles into the smaller blocks he would carry to his customers with big tongs, the rapid strokes of his pick sent silver shards flying, leaving chips of ice on the wet wooden wagon bed. Kids would scramble to get them and suck on them happily as they ran away. Radio broadcasting did not exist, although the theory of it was understood, as, for that matter, was the theory that would lead to television. The Victrolas, as they were called, on which phonograph records were played, were not electrical. They were wound with cranks and produced through flower-shaped horns a distorted kind of music that was nonetheless thrilling in its time. Telephones were not yet common. And the word *jazz* had not come into general use.

Ray Sherman said, "I always called Woody's father Uncle Otto. My folks were Uncle John and Aunt Julia to Woody. To his dying day, he called her Aunt Julia. There were three of us boys in my family. I was two years younger than Woody, and my brother Dan came along in 1919. And there was my sister Joyce.

"When Woody's mother and dad were first married, they rented from my mother and dad. We lived just west of the Locust Street viaduct. My grandfather owned an entire block, and he had a grocery store on one corner, and at the other corner of the block he had a saloon. Next to the saloon there was a small flat with a cottage in the rear, and the Herrmanns rented one of those units before they moved over to the place on Racine Street. When they were first married, the families lived next door to each other. And later on the Herrmanns moved to the Lower East Side. There were a lot of Polish people and Italian people in that area.

"The house where Woody was born was a frame flat. It's been torn down. There's an apartment building there now. The Herrmanns moved around a lot. They never owned a home in their lifetime. They always rented."[2]

No one seems to know why the Herrmanns moved so much. Woody said his mother was always trying to get closer to Lake Michigan. At one point the Herrmanns lived above a music store. "And I could try anything I wanted to down there," Woody said, "check the reeds out and so on. Another time we lived above a grocery store, and I used to do a little part-time gigging there, filling five-pound sacks of sugar and things of that nature. I was early into playing gigs in high school. I also doubled at one of the better men's clothing stores during the holiday season . . . and they would give me great deals on clothes."[3]

He remembered with affection a summer home rented from the Uihlein family, who owned the Schlitz brewing company. The Herrmanns shared this house in a northern suburb with a family named Reuter. The land, which Woody remembered as lavishly covered in summer by wild violets, extended for more than half a mile to the shore of the Milwaukee River, one of three rivers that divide the city. The winters were bitterly cold, and the boys would skate on the river. The house had a tower reached by three or four flights of winding stairs. Woody used to sleep in that tower, which he found romantic. From its height he could see the great green crowns of the trees that covered the property and, in the distance, on the river's edge, a small boat landing. In the deep, humid, midwestern heat, he would leap from that landing into the waters and swim.

According to Ray, the house was in the style of a German castle; it had turrets with leaded stained-glass windows. "One time we caught hell," Ray said, "because we got a hold of a BB gun and shot out all the windows. All that we *could* shoot out, anyway.

"There were empty stables at the back. We used to play in the stables. The yard went all the way down to the river. We used to run down to the river and jump in. You could swim any place in the Milwaukee River in those days. It wasn't polluted.

"Up the riverbank a way, there was a swimming pool. It was called Pleasant Valley. We'd go swimming over there too. They had a roped-off area, and once in a while they'd have a lifeguard. They'd give you a basket for a nickel and you could leave your clothes in a little tin locker, and that's where we swam a lot.

"Woody's mother liked to swim. She almost lived in the water. In later years she'd go to the natatorium once or twice a week for exercise. She was a very good swimmer. Woody was a good swimmer too.

"Woody was always interested in sports, especially race driving. When we were in high school, and even after he had his band, when he'd come home, we'd go to the midget car races and big car races. Milwaukee was always a pretty good town for automobile racing. He just loved it, and he knew a lot of the race drivers." Woody was known in his later years for his love of automobile races; Ray's testimony shows that it began in his childhood. He loved to drive, too, and said that he started driving the family car when he was only twelve.[4]

According to Ray, Woody also loved riding horses. Ray said, "Across the street from the house he was born in was the Owen Roberts family. They were Welsh people. They had relatives who had a farm out in Wales, Wisconsin. Woody used to go out there and ride the horses. I've got a picture of him with jodhpurs on.

"He liked to ice skate. Not roller skate. We used to ride our bikes a lot. We had three-quarter-size bikes. His was a Roosevelt. One bike was called a Lincoln, another was a Ranger."

The childhood of Woody Herman seems unremarkably normal, except for the early initiation into vaudeville. He and the Sherman boys played marbles, spun tops, flew kites, pretended to be streetcar motormen, and had fights with slingshots, firing hickory nuts. The two families spent summer vacations together, and would travel north to a farm owned by relatives of the Shermans, where they would have tomato fights and jump into the haystacks.

"My father had a brother and a sister, a small family," Woody said. "And my mother came from a family of, I think, about nine or ten." He said he and his parents would get together with the Herrmann relatives, but not often with his mother's family. "Not many of them spoke English at all. They spoke Polish or, sometimes, German."[5]

The Herrmanns, according to American pattern, aspired to more. Otto Herrmann next went to work for the Nunn Bush shoe company. Woody said, "He worked himself up over a period of forty years to being an executive of that company. He was in charge of quality and design, to some degree—styling. And my mother, in order to help the family income, and in their desire to live better, worked part of the time at the same place, on a machine. And never thought anything about it. When they were able to get into a better financial position, she quit."[6] The housing improved, Woody said, but her absence at work made him what we now call a latchkey kid, and he felt anxiety about coming home from school to an empty house. His formal education began at Fratney Street School, which he attended with Erv Sherman.

Ray Sherman said Milwaukee has always been a very conservative city, and Woody never had the following there that he did in the rest of America, although he ultimately was given an honorary degree by Marquette University. Ray said, "Whether he actually got it, I don't know. Because Woody never saved anything. I could have kept his three Grammys. I had them for about a year. He didn't care. It was over and done with." That is a key to Woody's character: he didn't keep souvenirs. Ray, fortunately, did: he has all sorts of souvenirs, photos, and other memorabilia dating back to Woody's days as a child star in Milwaukee vaudeville and before. There were about ten vaudeville theaters in Milwaukee alone, such was the prevalence of live entertainment in America.

Milwaukee, a pragmatic and workaday city and important Great Lakes port on the west shore of Lake Michigan eighty-five miles north of Chicago, is best known for beer. Indeed, its first brewery was established in 1840, the year the first German immigrants arrived. By the dawn of the twentieth century 72 percent of its population was of German origin. Later there was a small influx of Irish and Scandinavian populace and, around the turn of the century, an immigration from Poland. It was at that time that Woody's mother arrived there. It is not known when Otto Herrmann's people first came from Germany.

I met Otto Herrmann once. Some time in late 1962 or perhaps it was early 1963, Woody asked me to drive out to the airport to pick up his father. Otto was a rotund and rather self-important little man, almost universally called Otsie in Milwaukee. I delivered him to Woody's New York City office at 57th and 7th. Otto Herrmann's son, by then fifty years old, the man who had been an idol to millions of young people in the 1940s, greeted him affectionately amidst the general disarray of the office's three small rooms: an outer office designed for a receptionist and two smaller offices whose windows overlooked 57th Street.

Ray Sherman says Otto Herrmann was a flirtatious man with an eye for beautiful girls. He says Otto had a hot temper, in contrast to Myrtle, a patient woman. Woody combined both qualities. Normally, he was patient and long-suffering with the young musicians who filled his bands, but he could explode with anger.

Woody's mother, being Polish, was Catholic. Otto became a convert. He sang in various groups, those sentimental and novelty songs popular at the turn of the century. Otto had a collection of recordings and loved to sing along with them. He acquired an electric grand piano that played piano rolls, including semi-classics and classical pieces, performed by outstanding pianists. "I heard a lot of music I would not have heard," Woody said. From the time he could walk and talk, there was music in his home. He said of his parents, "They were kind and beautiful. They let me try to do anything I wanted, and if it didn't work out, they were sympathetic."

But there's evidence that Otto Herrmann was sometimes hard on him. Ray Sherman said Myrtle was nervous, made that way by Otto. At some point in their life, Ray said, Otto got the odd idea that he could save money by turning off their electric refrigerator at night. Woody's daughter, Ingrid, says, "He came from a traditional Germanic background. His father was as German as German could be. Autocratic."

Ray said, "For six months or something like that, Woody's dad had an Indian motorcycle with a sidecar. We used to go for rides in that thing. Uncle Otto would put on the helmet and the goggles and away we'd go.

"My mother played piano when she was young. My dad had studied violin. They sang in the church choirs. Woody's dad, I imagine, sang in church choirs too. But he was more into barbershop trios or quartets. He sang harmony. He had a very good ear, and he played one-finger piano. And he knew two or three chords on the black keys. He loved music, just loved it. And my folks loved music too." Erv Sherman learned to play piano, Ray studied violin, Dan sang professionally by the age of four, and their sister, Joyce—the youngest of the family, born in 1926—took a degree in music and sang in the Chicago Lyric Opera.

"In fact," Ray continued, "when we'd go for a ride on Sunday or go on vacation, we'd sing. You had no car radios in those days. You made your own entertainment, and when we were kids we all knew the words to all the popular songs. They were mostly novelty songs. *I Miss My Swiss; My Swiss Miss Misses Me.* One of Woody's favorites was *Oh Gee, Say Gee, You Ought to See My Gigi from the Fiji Isles,* 'she wears a little bit here and a little bit there, just enough to protect her from the air.'

"The Herrmanns didn't have a car in the early days. My folks had a 1921 Buick touring car. And we used to do a lot of riding around together. They all liked to go for a ride on Sunday and stop at some roadside tavern. The men would have beer and the women would have soda water, the kids would have ice cream. And that's the way we spent our Sundays, many times."

One of the groups with which Otto Herrmann sang was called the Cream City Four. "But they never really got too far," Woody said, "because they would become disengaged, going to the engagement. They'd stop at a few taverns, roadhouses, on the way to the state fair that they were supposed to be working." Always his main love was show business, and he projected this passion into his son, getting Woody club appearances when the boy was only six.

When Woody was nine, Otto took him to audition for a revue in which six or seven children performed with an old actress—Woody could never remember her name—in the role of a schoolmarm. Woody passed the audition and joined the show, some sort of prologue to a movie based on a Booth Tarkington story, *School Days,* starring Wesley Barry. In ways that

Woody never made clear, he played the part of the freckle-faced boy Barry played in the movie.

A surviving newspaper clipping reports:

> A Milwaukee boy is traveling over the state playing as Wesley Barry in a prologue to *School Days* at motion picture theaters in many Wisconsin cities. He is Woodrow Herrmann, 9, son of Mr. and Mrs. Otto Herrmann, 1460 Humboldt av. He is said to be the youngest juvenile actor in the state. He will tour the state for eight weeks and will then return to Milwaukee to appear at the Strand, where he has been seen on previous occasions in the prologue to *Penrod*. He has appeared also on club programs and at other entertainments."[7]

The reference to *Penrod*, a popular novel by Booth Tarkington, presents a minor puzzle. Woody never mentioned it to anyone I know of; yet the newspaper item says he was in such a show before *School Days*. Certainly it was murky in Woody's memory. He said, "All I knew was that I had to sing and dance, along with other kids."

In 1954, when Woody was about to play an engagement at a local ballroom for Edward J. Weisfeldt, its manager, the *Milwaukee Journal* printed a photo of the young cast of *School Days*. Woody is in the forefront among the seven youngsters, dancing. The photo's caption says the picture was taken in 1922. It also says that Edward J. Weisfeldt had written and directed the *School Days* skit when he was production manager of the Saxe theaters, staging prologues to movies.

The group performed that summer in northern Wisconsin and Michigan, never more than a hundred miles from home. Woody earned forty dollars a week, much of which he saved toward the purchase of a saxophone.

The relatives of Woody's mother disapproved of his show business activities. Ray Sherman said, "Woody had lots of cousins on his mother's side and one cousin on his father's side. Woody's uncle, John Herrmann, had one boy, Bill Herrmann, a very good legit trumpet player. He died quite young, in his thirties or so. Woody's Aunt Lilly on his father's side was a good pianist and she had a fine voice. But Woody's cousins from his mother's side never came to see him when he worked. They just thought it was evil or something to be performing in front of people. They were very hard-nosed Polacks.

"Woody was very proud of being Polish. If you asked him about being German and Polish, he favored the Polish side." It seems likely that this was at least in part because the Shermans, the family to whom he was closest, were Polish.

Woody had two nicknames. His mother called him Putsey. The Shermans and other friends called him Vietzek, pronounced veet-sek. Ray has no idea where it originated or what it meant; he presumes it is of Polish origin. But for years Ray would receive cards and letters from Woody signed *Vietzek*.

Woody took the usual childhood piano lessons and at one time was given a violin, which he disliked intensely. He thought it was a sissy instrument. He studied piano with two or three women teachers and then with a priest named Tony Mack who, he said, was an excellent jazz pianist. Mack was an admirer of Earl Hines and introduced Woody to the music of Louis Armstrong.

It is common for jazz musicians to recall that they tried several instruments before finding the one that suited them. In Woody's case, it was an E-flat alto sax, "silver with a gold belt," that he purchased with his savings from that first summer's tour.

If Woody was then nine, as he told me, that purchase was made in 1922, the year Mussolini marched on Rome, Alexander Graham Bell and Lillian Russell died, and Louis Armstrong joined King Oliver's small band at Lincoln Gardens in Chicago, making it a mecca to many young white midwestern musicians.

The saxophone was coming into widespread use in American dance music and in jazz, a word that was being heard with increasing frequency. Woody's first saxophone teacher, a man named Art Buech, told him, "You're going to have to play clarinet too. It's much more difficult, but you'd better get one so we can start working on it." Woody described Buech as "an old German fellow who would take nothing but hard work. This was the answer to everything. Practice until you turn blue and your lip is numb and your teeth hurt and you may accomplish something. But he was very good and I was very fortunate in starting with someone like that."[8]

When he was twelve or thirteen, he took a lesson from Rudy Wiedoeft, a virtuoso of the instrument who was then quite famous. Though Wiedoeft was not a jazz musician, many of the better jazz saxophonists later would testify to his influence on them, because of his outstanding technical command of the instrument. Wiedoeft was touring and happened to be in Milwaukee. Woody spent an hour or two with him and thought later that he had derived a great deal from the encounter.

Woody also studied dance, first at a school run by a woman named Rosalie Edwards, a friend of his parents. She once got him to play a rooster in a children's ballet recital. He wore a feathered costume that he hated. Later he went to other teachers to study tap dancing. Woody's dancing experience probably was the reason for his grace and ease on a stage. All his life he looked perfectly at home there. And he was unintimidated by audiences. It was as if he were inured to them.

"The vaudevillians," he once said to me, "had one expression for all audiences. They called them the Great Unwashed. And that's where I gained my first philosophy of the business, at nine years of age."9

This is deceptive: it seems to suggest that he thought of himself as far above them. But that is not so. He was too much the populist, and he despised pretense. The remark did, however, reflect his long experience in show business and his lack of illusion about the general public taste.

2

School Days

Woody's teachers and the school administration thought there was something amiss in his parents' allowing him to be in show business. "And I was having difficulty getting permission from juvenile court to have working papers," he said. "I was performing only while school was out. But the school officials were nonetheless annoyed with the idea and were delaying the court's approval of my papers. Their negativity bugged me even after the working papers came through, and I decided to do something about it." Here, already, was evidence of a free, independent, and strong spirit.

"I was only ten, and in the fifth grade, but I managed on my own to transfer to St. John's Cathedral Grade School in downtown Milwaukee, where I had heard the administration and teachers were more interested in individuals."[1] Another student, a year or two ahead of Woody, played piano duets with her sister. She later became famous as the singer Hildegarde.

Ray Sherman still has a court order issued when Woody was fourteen. It reads:

State of Wisconsin, Milwaukee County, in the Juvenile Court, Milwaukee County.

In the matter of the application for a special permit for Woodrow Herman, a

minor, to participate in musical and theatrical performances. Upon the peti-
tion of Mrs. Myrtle Herman, 894 Hubbard Street, filed herein, this day, pray-
ing that a permit be issued enabling Woodrow Herman, a minor, to take part in
certain musical and theatrical performances, and it appearing satisfactorily
that the said Woodrow Herman is a regular attendant of St. John's Cathedral
High School, in the City of Milwaukee, County of Milwaukee, and that the
appearance of said minor at such musical and theatrical performances will not
interfere with his general health or education: NOW THEREFORE, permission is hereby granted that the said Woodrow Herman, a minor, take part in
certain musical and theatrical exhibitions or performances to be held in the
City of Milwaukee, Wisconsin, 3 evenings a week, not later than 10:30 o'clock,
during the ensuing year from the date of this permit, said minor to be accompanied, however, at each of said exhibitions or performances by his mother,
Mrs. Myrtle Herman, dated this 2nd day of March, A.D. 1928.
   Signed: John C. Karel, Judge of the Juvenile Court.

We should note that Woody by now spelled his name Herman. "Already an
editor," he said later. And his mother's name also has that spelling on the
court order.
   Dan Sherman also sang in vaudeville, and often worked on the same bill
with Woody. Ray said, "Dan started when he was four years old. Woody and
Dan were hoofin' together. Woody danced more than my brother Dan. Dan
was small, and he usually led the orchestra. My mother was a dressmaker.
She made him a tuxedo with black satin lapels. She made a lot of the
clothes that the kids wore on the stage. She made Woody shirts and pants
and the outfits that my brother Dan wore." There seems to have been a
division of labor between Julia Sherman and Myrtle Herman. Julia, as a
talented seamstress, made the children's clothes and Woody's mother,
skilled in the kitchen, cooked a great deal for both families.[2]
   "Some of Dan's specialty numbers," Ray said, "were *Barney Google* with
the great big googly eyes, and *Why Did I Kiss That Girl?* Dan and Woody
each had an act. They'd do a show in the north end of town and then go to
the south end and put another show on. And lots of times you'd have to
carry the movie film along. After that was over, you had time to get back
while they were showing a film to the north end of town and you did
another performance. There were only certain nights of the week when
they had vaudeville in these houses.
   "They would have maybe three or four young girls in a chorus line. And
then they'd have a juggler or a comedian. These guys wore outrageous
clothes, like some of the rock stars of today. This stuff wasn't flashy, but it

was funny. They'd wear a pair of pants with the waist line like ninety-six inches around. Big balloon pants.

"They'd wind up with every one onstage in an ensemble.

"My mother or my dad or Uncle Otto would take Dan and Woody around."

Later on the Hermans had a Chevrolet. Woody's mother never drove. When Woody's dad couldn't make it, Woody would drive the car, sitting on two pillows. The round trips with Woody at the wheel sometimes amounted to two hundred miles. Woody was rather small; as an adult he was only five-foot-eight. He also was self-conscious about his nose, which he thought was too big.

The saxophone was eventually incorporated into Woody's song-and-dance act. "I never really liked working in theaters or this vaudeville-type operation," he said. "As a matter of fact, when I got to be eleven or twelve, I couldn't stomach it. But I was still being booked. I was in Chicago . . . out on the South Side in the Capitol Theater . . . . They hired me for a week or two. I think it was the second day or the first day and I was on the side of the stage and they had these two big fountains. These were those deluxe, million-dollar theaters they used to build . . . . And I wore some kind of navy-type uniform and I played my saxophone solo and did my song and dance. And I was now bowing myself into oblivion when I did a back-type header into this fountain on the end, and, well, they couldn't get me to go on for the next two shows, I was so embarrassed."[3]

But, as he said on another occasion, "Being in show business gave me some kind of glow. I tried not to be too self-impressed, but it was a gas to walk by a theater and see my name in lights, and to collect as much as fifty dollars a week—a powerful income in the early twenties. My parents held the salary for me in a bank account and saw that I had spending money."

Woody now was working all year long as a single. He would play local jobs on school nights and travel to other centers on weekends, accompanied as a rule by his mother. His billing was "The Boy Wonder." About that same period, the young Buddy Rich, four years Woody's junior and some day to be his friend, was also touring in vaudeville, billed as "Traps, the Drum Wonder." He played drums in his act and, like Woody, sang and danced.

A photo from the period shows Woody in a military jacket, cap at an angle, pants smoothly pressed, shoes brightly shone, holding his alto. It was taken when he was performing *Nola* at the Wisconsin Theater in Milwaukee. Another shows the marquee of the Oshkosh Theater. The billing reads:

WOODROW HERMAN
BOY WONDER
SAXOPHONIST

One of Woody's specialties was an imitation, in top hat and carrying a clarinet, of bandleader Ted Lewis singing *Me and My Shadow*. The boy who played the shadow was Dan Sherman. Woody by then was twelve, Dan was six and billed as Danny the Boy Wonder. But even then, Dan told me, he was drawn to the priesthood, and would lead the other children in—highly illicit—versions of the Mass.

By his freshman year in high school, Woody said, "I was now to the point, as I remember, of being completely bored and not finding this amusing any more. It was fun in the very early stages. I suppose any kid likes attention, and it did give me lots of attention. But as I started to grow up and mature, I decided I really didn't like all that, and I wanted to have more time to play with other kids.

"I became truly interested in (jazz) via some early jazz records. Some of the things that were influencing me were pieces played by such groups as the Indiana Five, Red Nichols, because I liked all the soloists . . . . One of the earliest records I had was Duke Ellington, when he had an eight-piece group known as the Washingtonians. And it sounded to me like jungle music. And I guess at some point it was even called a jungle band." Woody was also impressed by the bands of Don Redman, some of whose records he had, and Andy Kirk and his Twelve Clouds of Joy. But all his life, Woody said Ellington was his chief inspiration.

"Woody and I had crystal sets before the regular radios came out," Ray Sherman said. "We used to listen, when we were nine, ten, eleven years old, to Jean Goldkette from Detroit, and to Paul Whiteman, and whatever came over the radio. I remember KDKA in East Pittsburgh. We had headphones and the little crystal sets with the cat's whisker. You'd find the loudest place on the crystal. And of course we had phonographs." Later Woody had one of the early Atwater Kent radios in his bedroom, and would stay awake late into the night listening to his favorite musicians. Ray, as a violinist, was enamored of the playing of Joe Venuti and Eddie South.[4]

By now Woody was studying with a teacher named Arthur Krueger, a clarinetist and saxophonist who had a taste for jazz and would transcribe solos from records for him. Krueger, born July 27, 1897, in Burlington, Wisconsin, settled in Milwaukee, where he led a band in the Badger Room of the Wisconsin Hotel for twelve years. His was the first Milwaukee band to make "remote" radio broadcasts, and for a time was heard on the Co-

▼

lumbia network all over America. He would have been in his middle twenties when Woody studied with him.[5]

Jazz, though still in its formative period, was beginning to sweep America, catching the fancy of the young people on the one hand and, on the other, impressing intellectuals and opinion-makers, such persons as composer John Alden Carpenter, Chicago music educator Felix Borowski, dramatist John Luther Long, and Carl Engel. Engel, head of the music division of the Library of Congress, a composer by training who in 1922—the year Woody was on the road with that first "kiddie revue"—wrote an article for the *Atlantic* in praise of the new music. Articles about jazz appeared in publications both small and large, including the *New York Times*, which printed at least a hundred of them in the decade from 1918 to 1928.

Woody had gathered a collection of brochures issued by various booking agencies, particularly Music Corporation of America, which was then simply a band-booking company but would evolve into a huge entertainment conglomerate. "They had marvelous photos," he said, "of all these bands they handled, in full regalia and uniforms and thousands of instruments in front of each player.

"And this was very impressive to me, and I think right then and there—I had to be still in grade school—[I knew] that was what I wanted to do. That was bigger than being a ball player or anything else."

By the time he was twelve, Woody had made up his mind that he wanted a career in jazz. He told his parents "that I was retiring from show business and, in the vernacular of the day, I was going to be a hot player." Otto and Myrtle Herman were shocked. Yet they encouraged him to try it.

By now he was listening to Red McKenzie, who sang hot solos through tissue paper over a comb, and the Mound City Blue Blowers. Such was the growing enthusiasm for jazz that the group's first recording, *Arkansaw Blues*, made in 1924, sold a million copies. At various times McKenzie recorded with Eddie Condon, Gene Krupa, Glenn Miller, Pee Wee Russell, Muggsy Spanier, and Coleman Hawkins. Woody found the Hawkins solos a revelation and studied them avidly. He was listening as well to Frank Trumbauer, the half-Indian C-melody saxophone player whose influence on jazz through Lester Young, Benny Carter, and others has been largely ignored by critics and jazz historians. Woody was cognizant of Trumbauer's influence.

"He had to be a big influence on some other people," he said, "because he was the first one to use the glissando as a means of making his feelings known, and I think Johnny Hodges would have to feel pretty much the same way as I did."

Erv Sherman would come over to Woody's house, wind up the Victrola, and listen to records with him. Woody struggled to replicate solos by Hawkins and Trumbauer. He was also listening to Jack Teagarden, the Texas trombonist who did much to revolutionize the instrument, demonstrating for everyone who came after him that the trombone could be played with a flexibility approaching that of trumpet. Woody first heard Teagarden on a Red Nichols record. He said, "And I never could get over it. It just gave me the feeling that this man had never made a mistake in his whole life and didn't plan on making any . . . .

"I realized then what a great feeling of relaxation and assurance it gives your audience if you're that kind of player . . . ."

In high school he had made friends with Al Mack, brother of the piano-playing priest Tony Mack. Al Mack would later be well known as an arranger for MGM musicals. Tony Mack would become a monsignor and join the staff of the Vatican. Al Mack was a year older than Woody. The two formed a small band that played jobs around Milwaukee. They expanded it in their high school years and performed daily after school on radio station WTMJ. These were Woody's first radio broadcasts and the first signs of his prowess as a bandleader.

Woody liked the Dominican nuns who taught him, but one of them would have a far-reaching influence in his life, and he would never forget it. He would refer to her in later reminiscences as "an angel." Sister Fabian Riley was his science and mathematics teacher.

Woody was behind in his school work because of his night jobs, even falling asleep in class, but the nun believed that a musician "was a good thing to be" and when he was sent to the principal's office, Sister Fabian would intercede in his behalf.

"I'd just get to my desk in school in the morning and I'd conk out," he remembered. "A lot of days I never made it to school at all and I'd be in hot water with all the teachers but Sister Fabian."[6]

Woody for a time considered becoming a cartoonist; Ray Sherman has preserved a number of his drawings and cartoons, which are quite good. But Sister Fabian counseled him: "Just stick to your music. It's the best thing for you." Woody left high school without graduating to enter the music world. According to Ray Sherman, he eventually got his high school diploma—through the efforts of Sister Fabian. "She knew I was only interested in music," Woody said. "Without her defending me all the time and encouraging me in my music, who knows what might have become of me?"[7]

3

On the Road

Woody worked in a circuit of roadhouses around Milwaukee. One was the Blue Heaven, probably named for *My Blue Heaven*, which was new: the song came out when Woody was eleven. Others were Pick's Club Madrid and the Modernistic, set in the fairgrounds on the west side of the city. On weekends he would travel to jobs as far away as Oshkosh and Waupaca. For a brief time he led his own band. Then he joined the ten-piece band of Joie Lichter.

Despite the spelling, which is that of the French word for "joy," the name was pronounced Joey. Lichter was a native Milwaukeean who led the house orchestra at the Strand Theater. During the period when Woody was with him, it made radio broadcasts on radio station WTMJ, and Lichter made records for the Gennett, Paramount, and Puritan labels under the name Joie Lichter's Strand Symphonists.[1] Woody apparently did not record with that band.

Lichter had hired Woody on the recommendation of some of his other musicians. The band's instrumentation was two, sometimes three, trumpets, two trombones, two altos and a tenor, and rhythm section, the standard configuration at the time. Woody joined the band on tenor and clarinet, and Lichter featured him singing as well.

"I had some major weaknesses," Woody said. "Like, my reading was very poor. Because I was never really in a position to read. I would practice and play the exercises and the chords and scales, and I would play and I would perform. So I had never really gotten around to having to read. And it was kind of a challenge the first few months, but the older people in the band, particularly the saxophone players, were kind enough to work with me and help me."

Lichter would bring "stocks"—commercial arrangements of the latest hits, published mostly in New York and sold in music stores everywhere, so common were bands in America—and require his musicians to read them down. Because Woody read so poorly, Lichter would hit him with his violin bow, sing a passage over for him, and even kick him. But Woody remained grateful that Lichter had tolerated him and even extended a comparative patience while he learned.

The band wore morning coats with gray vests, black trousers, black patent-leather shoes, and white linen spats. And Woody, by his own later statement, had become highly clothes conscious; he would remain so all his life. Lichter was a fine musician, but by no stretch of the imagination a jazz musician. Yet he had what Woody described years later as an "out-and-out jazz band."

It worked five nights a week and a matinee at the Eagles Ballroom. Woody said, "It was for dancing and they had two big bands, the house band and all the hit bands, people like Coon-Sanders and Austin Wiley, would come in . . . . I got to hear a lot of players that I ordinarily would not have heard." One of the bands he heard was that of Paul Whiteman, whose phenomenal success foreshadowed the big-band era. Woody said, "I got to meet a lot of these people whom I had been hearing only on records and on the radio . . . . These were important times for me, very important."

"When Woody was about sixteen," Erv Sherman recalled, "his car broke down west of Madison, about a hundred and fifty miles from Milwaukee, on the way back from a gig with Joie Lichter. He called me, because he couldn't get his folks, who were out for the evening. I kept calling his house all evening, and I finally got Uncle Otto. We went out there together—me driving and him sleeping all the way. We got there at three in the morning, and we had to tow Woody's car—it was a Whippet—all the way back to Milwaukee. After the car was repaired in a couple of weeks, he was on the road again with Lichter."[2]

The band ranged fairly far, playing jobs in such places as Joyland Park in Lexington, Kentucky, and in Toledo, Ohio, where Woody encountered Andy Kirk and His Twelve Clouds of Joy, a new band he admired.

Lichter played an engagement in Kansas City, Missouri, a cradle of jazz at the time. According to Woody, this was in 1929. He remembered hearing a very good band there; years later, Count Basie told Woody he had been in that band at the time. This could have been Walter Page's Blue

Devils, but was more likely the Bennie Moten band, which Basie joined early in 1929.

The Lichter band went on to Tulsa, Oklahoma, for a summer job at a place called the Coliseum. Woody had found marijuana—in which he had no personal interest, then or later—in wide use among Kansas City musicians, as well as some of those in the Lichter band. One of these was a trumpeter from Kansas City, whom they'd picked up on the way, named Roy. Woody couldn't remember his last name. He was perhaps fifteen years Woody's elder, and small, about five feet tall. He and Woody roomed together at the Alvin Hotel in Tulsa. The prairie weather was hot, and Woody was consuming great quantities of Dr Pepper and Coca-Cola, lining up his empties on a window sill. Roy, meanwhile, was smoking his pot.

"He kept pretty numb day and night," Woody said, laughing. "I used to come from seeing a picture or taking a walk and he'd be seated because of his small stature in the sink bowl in the bathroom, with a tweezer taking out little blackheads and things from his puss, his face right up to the mirror, and giggling. You know the state he was in."

Marijuana produces keen paranoia in some users—what jazz musicians have sometimes called the horrors. And apparently Roy was one of them. Woody said, "He used to hit panics when he would go to sleep. All of a sudden he'd leap up, straight up, and this was very unnerving, especially when I had just fallen asleep. And this one morning was unbearable. I had just fallen asleep and probably an hour had passed, and he leaped up and started screaming 'fire' because these bottles were lined up on the window and there was a red neon sign across the street reflecting in them. And he was getting everyone up out of the building, and calling on the phone. Oh it was miserable."[3]

Woody remembered that in Tulsa the musicians and high school students alike "were all high on grass."[4] Also in use was a drink called "chalk," made from the mash left over from home-brewed beer. "It was pretty drastic stuff," he said with his dry chuckle, "and they would serve it up in tin cups. A little of this went a long way, and we'd go out then and listen to the oil pumps. And we'd get some beautiful sounds. Deep, throbbing, beautiful kah-booms. And bombs were being thrown everywhere. You know, if you liked lows in sound, it was beautiful, and for the guys that liked highs, they could always listen to a cement mixer."[5]

Woody had some sort of an affair with a local girl. "One of the rich oilmen's daughters liked me," he said, "and used her father's car to drive us around town. I found out her boyfriend, an Indian, was mad and was after me with a bunch of his friends. I left in a hurry."[6]

One of the most significant events of that summer trip was Woody's first encounter with the saxophone of Coleman Hawkins. He picked up *Hello, Lola*, a record by the Mound City Blue Blowers. He was immediately enthralled by Hawkins, began a struggle to imitate him, and would listen avidly to radio broadcasts from New York by the Fletcher Henderson band, in which the great tenor master was playing.

Meanwhile, in Newton, Massachusetts, Ralph Burns was coming up to the age of eight. In Philadelphia, Willard Palmer Harris, later to be known as Bill Harris, was fourteen, and Stan Getz, four. In Hawthorn, California, John Haley Sims was five. In Cheraw, South Carolina, Dizzy Gillespie was thirteen. In New York, Benny Goodman was a twenty-two-year-old studio musician, playing saxophone and clarinet—sometimes in sections that included Artie Shaw—in radio orchestras. The country was on the verge of the Swing Era, the fruition of musical and social forces that had been converging for some time.

The ragtime phenomenon, one of the major black developments in American music, came and went early in the century, but not without leaving its influence on popular music. Irving Berlin had a huge hit in 1911 with *Alexander's Ragtime Band*. While writers often point out that the song is not a rag—it is closer to being a march—they seldom put the title under scrutiny.

The name "Alexander" turns up in many songs of the century's first decade. It was considered funny when applied to a black man. The name's putative dignity made it incongruous, implying that the man was putting on airs. The musicians in *Alexander's Ragtime Band*, then, were black, although when the song became a hit, the faces on the cover of the sheet music had faded to white.

A craze for various new dances swept the United States between 1907 and 1914. Like the music to which they were performed, the new steps were derived from the black subculture. They were energetic, abandoned, done face to face, belly to belly, and knee to crotch. They bore names such as the rag, turkey trot, monkey, maxixe, Gotham gobble, humpback, and bunny hug, and they shocked polite society.

Repeatedly in America white performers have taken the music of black models and toned it down to make it acceptable to white audiences. The classic case is the rise of rock and roll, with white singers such as Elvis Presley recording material by black originators whose records were, as a matter of tacit policy, barred from radio. This also happened in dancing. The dance team Vernon and Irene Castle brought about the change. Laurence Bergreen, in *As Thousands Cheer*, a biography of Irving Berlin, wrote that "the Castles, Berlin's counterparts in dance, appeared on the scene and tamed the outrageous dances and their precarious dives, pelvic thrusts, and violent rhythms. The Castles slowed the tempos, simplified the rhythms, restrained the gestures, and made the movements seem altogether healthy."

This attractive young couple, who achieved an extraordinary popularity, traveled with a fourteen-piece band called the Syncopated Society Orchestra. Most of its members were black. The conductor was James Reese Europe. In 1912, Europe became the first black to perform in Carnegie Hall, conducting an orchestra of 125 musicians, all black. In 1913, his was the first black group to make records, and during World War I, he took his music to Europe with his 369th Infantry Band, which became famous. (Big Jim Europe, as he was sometimes called, died in 1919 of a stab wound inflicted by one of his sidemen in a petty dispute. He was thirty-eight.)

The Castles became an industry unto themselves, owning ballrooms and a dance school. Meanwhile, the form of the orchestra used to accompany this vast new clientele of dancers was changing. Violins gradually disappeared. During the 1920s, arrangers, as we have noted, tried to find out how to write for these new orchestras of brass, saxophones, and rhythm section. They had no models to go on. The classical orchestration books were of no use, because they did not treat this instrumentation. Several arrangers were chiefly responsible for working out the ways of writing for this new formation, particularly Ferde Grofé, Bill Challis, Don Redman, and, later, Fletcher Henderson and Benny Carter. By that spring of 1931 when Woody Herman joined the Tom Gerun band, the essential problems had been solved.

The image of jazz as a music played in whorehouses has been exaggerated. But later on it was played in the nightclubs of gangsters, including Owney Madden, the owner of the Cotton Club in Harlem, where Duke Ellington's band was making the "jungle music" that so impressed the young Woody Herman. It is ironic that the early patrons of this great art were gangsters. Or perhaps it is not ironic: the more respectable patrons of art, with English or Dutch rather than Italian and Jewish names, are often descended from men the moral equivalent of gangsters and as fully capable of interring opponents.

All of this was in the air when the band of Tom Gerun, born Gerunovich, arrived to play at the Schroeder Hotel, the best location in Milwaukee. He pronounced Gerun with a hard g and emphasis on the second syllable. Some of the musicians from the Joie Lichter orchestra told Gerun about Woody. Gerun sent for him and asked him to join the band not on alto but on tenor and baritone. Gerun obtained permission from Otto and Myrtle Herman for Woody to go with him on the road, telling them he would treat Woody like a son. He left for Chicago and Woody followed him in his Whippet Four, a convertible manufactured by Willys, joining the band at the Grenada Cafe on January 3, 1931. The Great Depression was well under way, and unemployment in the United States had passed four million.

Woody, full of youthful enthusiasm, expected the others in the Gerun band to want to go out and blow after work. He found instead, he recalled, a group of musicians who looked like businessmen in striped trousers and black coats. The band was musically good but a little stiff.

The Gerun band had followed the Paul Whiteman band into the Grenada Cafe, sometimes called Al Quadback's. It was a front for the Al Capone mob, but then every nightclub in Chicago was a mob front. A few years earlier, Guy Lombardo had been playing the Grenada when gangsters entered with machine guns and shot the place to pieces, sending Lombardo and his musicians diving for cover. Woody said the place was always "infested" with hoods, which in Chicago they pronounce to rhyme with "foods."

On the bill with Gerun was Fuzzy Knight, a comedian who would make a name in movies. When they finished work at three in the morning, some of the musicians from the band would go, still in their band tuxedos, to the Grand Terrace Ballroom to hear the Earl Hines band, which worked later than they did.

"One night," Woody told me, "we were in the Grand Terrace, feeling no pain. Fuzzy and I were with Steve Bowers, the bass player with Gerun. Somebody spotted that Fuzzy had a big diamond on his finger. And we were tipping everybody like it was going out of style. So they figured us for live ones. It was winter, and when we came out of there at five or six o'clock in the morning, it was still dark. We got into my little car and headed back to our hotel. We got about a block when we were stopped by a traffic light. A big black sedan drove up, and when that happened in those days, you thought something was going to happen to you. Three guys jumped out. One of them had a gun, the other two had blackjacks. And they kept opening the door of my car. It was a roadster, and the side curtains weren't up. So they were scuffling with us, and they wanted us to get into the big car. Well that was the thing that put us in shock, man. We weren't going to go for a ride, right? So everybody starts flailing around with their arms."

"You were fighting them in the car?"

"Yeah, which is the hard way. And finally, seeing that nothing was happening, these guys figured it was taking too much time, and so the one with the gun shot into the floorboards, and the calf of my leg happened to be in the way."

"Which one?" I said.

"The *right* one," he said, with a furrowed brow as if impatient that anyone could ask so pedantic a question.

"Do you still have the scar?"

"Yeah, where it went in and where it came out."

"It went right through?"

"Yeah."

"Then what happened?"

"We got out of the car, and they started to frisk Fuzzy. The only reason I didn't get knocked out is that I was wearing a black bearskin fur coat and a Homburg hat. They kept hitting me with something, and the Homburg saved my head. A crowd began to gather. And I began to get bored with the whole thing and I walked off."

"With a bullet wound?"

"Well I was dragging the leg a little. And I ran into this big black cop. He said to me, 'What's the matter with you, boy?' I told him what was happening and said that if he looked he could still see them. He said, 'You're drunk, boy.' But by then the crowd was growing, and those guys took off."[7]

Fuzzy Knight and Steve Bowers took Woody back to their hotel and sent for a doctor, who put him in a South Side hospital. He was released the next day. When Woody showed up with a cane at the Grenada, Al Quadback, the owner, said, "Look, punk, put your hands up next time."[8]

Woody's mother became almost hysterical when she heard about the incident, but for some reason Woody was allowed to remain with the Gerun band.

"Tom Gerun was a very important influence on me," Woody said, "because I think he taught me a great deal about music as a business. Tom was a businessman, and he was not in any sense of the word a musician you would look up to as an incentive to play better. But he did have a good sense of logic and he had a feeling for what the public would like. The truth is that the majority of the bands . . . were really built on a pattern to find favor with an audience. The quality of music really was secondary. . . .

"I learned a great deal from Tom not because it was the best musical band I worked in but because it was a great entertainment band. He had some very important people in the band. . . . It was an entertainment unit . . . with some reasonably good music being played because we had a good arranger and a good musical director by the name of Gary Nottingham."

The Gerun band played Pittsburgh, where it made a radio broadcast on February 9, 1931, which Ray Sherman heard in Milwaukee. On March 22, the band left Pittsburgh for San Francisco. On Woody's first night there, some of the local musicians took a tour of bars and then went to a Chinese restaurant. When the musicians emerged, the restaurant was surrounded by police: there was a tong war under way, and the police wanted to know what these Occidentals were doing there. They were questioned and released.

The band worked at a San Francisco spot called the Noon Club and then settled in for a long stay at the Bal Tabarin, owned by Gerun and a partner named Frank Martinelli. The building still stands, housing a place called Bimbo's. Woody had his eighteenth birthday at the Bal Tabarin. The band played shows with people such as Harry Richman and Sophie Tucker. San Francisco musicians and listeners were impressed by Woody's tenor playing. What they did not know, he said, was that he was emulating Coleman Hawkins, whom few of them had heard. "I was completely gassed by him," he once told me. He also admired Bud Freeman and Eddie Miller. Woody's singing was influenced by Russ Columbo, Red McKenzie, Jack Teagarden, Harold Arlen—who had recorded a number of his own songs—and, later, Lee Wiley. He was also listening to some avant-garde records from Paris, probably to music of Edgard Varèse, possibly *Ionisation*, since he remembered what sounded like sirens.

Woody had affectionate memories of San Francisco, which is of course one of the spectacular cities of the world with its endlessly interesting vistas of hills and its glorious bay. He recalled the city in those Prohibition cum Depression days as wild and wide open, with personal delivery service of liquor and any number of blind pigs where musicians hung out. One in particular, on Broadway, was called Gaby's, and musicians used to store their clothes there. Some of these places hired pianists or trios, and other musicians would sit in with them.

Two of Woody's friends during this period were drummer Phil Harris, later a prominent bandleader and comedian, and Bob Crosby, younger brother of Bing Crosby, who arrived from Spokane, Washington, and sang with the Anson Weeks band. He was two years younger than Woody. Crosby and Woody were for a time roommates in the basement of the old Fairmont Hotel. Woody paid his share of the rent to Crosby, who, he assumed was paying the hotel. Crosby went to Los Angeles for a few days, and Woody found himself locked out of the room; the rent hadn't been paid in weeks. Woody slept in the furnace room in his tuxedo for a night or two.[9]

Crosby, as Woody put it, was still living "Pacific Northwest style," up early every morning to play tennis and pursue the healthy life. "I thought he was completely insane," Woody said. In due course, however, Woody resumed his interest in riding and felt healthier for it. With a musician friend, he would get up at nine in the morning, drive down the peninsula on which San Francisco stands, and, when he reached open country, ride a rented horse until late afternoon, get an hour or two of sleep, and go to work. Woody even considered buying a horse, but found that his spending in bars and on clothes left little from his salary for anything as exotic and expensive as a horse.

One evening a young xylophone and marimba player, five years Woody's elder, dropped in to hear the Gerun band and was sufficiently impressed by Woody to remember him. "He played saxophone and sang a little," he said in April, 1993. "I thought he was talented."

Born Kenneth Norville in Beardstown, Illinois, on March 31, 1908, the young man inevitably bore the nickname Red for his bright, almost orange, hair and eyelashes, a legacy of his Scottish ancestors. His father was a railway dispatcher who played piano and sang, a common avocation in that time before widespread music reproduction. Beardstown is in central western Illinois on the Illinois River, which empties into the Mississippi twenty-odd miles above St. Louis. The town was regularly visited by showboats, which presented dance bands and such melodramas as *The Drunkard*. Red said that he heard Bix Beiderbecke and Frank Trumbauer on one of the showboats and was captivated by Trumbauer. It was on a showboat that Red first heard Louis Armstrong.

Red became intrigued by the xylophone and worked and saved up until he had enough money to buy a table-model instrument. He taught himself to play it and read music. At nineteen he went into vaudeville and toured with a marimba band and then joined Paul Whiteman.

In 1927, the Deagan company, until then makers of xylophones and marimbas, unveiled its first vibraharp, as they named it, and Red became one of its first players. He was thus the first musician to play jazz on the instrument. Whitney Balliett wrote of him:

> Norvo is the father of his instrument, and, like many originators, he is a visionary. In 1933, he made a startling avant-garde recording on xylophone that had Benny Goodman on bass clarinet, Dick McDonough on guitar, and Artie Bernstein on bass. One side was Bix Beiderbecke's *In a Mist*, and the other was Norvo's *Dance of the Octopus*. Both numbers are full of odd harmonies and notes and arrhythmic collective passages that suggest free jazz.[10]

He had acquired the nickname Red early and inevitably, but he bore the name Norville until a master of ceremonies mispronounced his name, calling him Red Norvo, on the very evening he was to get his first review in *Variety*. The paper spelled it "Norvo" and since this was important early publicity, he kept the name. He and Woody did not actually meet that night in San Francisco; they would meet in New York, and Red Norvo would play an important role in Woody's life.[11]

Woody was responsible for the hiring of a young saxophone player named Al Morris, who would change his name to Tony Martin and go on to fame as a singer and movie star. It is apparent from Tony's testimony that Woody functioned as a sort of second-in-command in the Gerun band. "Woody was very close to Tom Gerunovich, or Tom Gerun," Tony said. "I was born in San Francisco and grew up in Oakland. I was playing with Tom Coakley's orchestra at the Oakland Athletic Club on weekends while I was going to St. Mary's College. One night they told me that Woody Herman was sitting there with Tom Gerun, and they'd come to hear me. I told Tom Coakley, 'Tom, these people apparently want to hear me.' He said, 'Yes, and they're going to. Do you want to be a professional, or do you want to go on in college?'

"Well, at that time, in the Depression, my father had lost his store and my mother was working. Woody liked the way I played and sang. Tom Gerun needed a fourth saxophone. They offered me $92.50 a week. I almost fell down. I couldn't believe it! I took the job.

"After I joined the band, Woody used to bear down on me to read my parts better and play better. He was always after me. I resented it, but now I know what he was trying to do.

"We even shared clothes. He wore great clothes. His father made beautiful shoes, and my father was a tailor. We had nice clothes!"

Woody said that Tony—then still Al Morris—played good alto and better clarinet. He also sang well, but in the style of whomever he'd just heard. Tony said, "I played all right, but I sang better than I played. Woody was responsible for me trying to find some way to sound like myself. If I listened to Harry Richman, I'd sing like him. I'd sing like Bing Crosby one night and the next like Russ Columbo. I even tried Rudy Vallee. Woody used to say, 'Who are you tonight?' We played one show when the regular singer took sick. Tom Gerun asked me if I wanted to sing. Woody said, 'If you're going to sing, sing like yourself, so at least if they don't like what you're doing, it's you. You've got a good quality. Why don't you sing like yourself?' I tried, and it worked. Woody was responsible for a lot in my life.

"We used to tease each other. Woody had great qualities. I admired

Woody very much. He played eastern style saxophone, that real wonderful, sharp, tenor style. He used to woodshed all the time. He'd practice, practice, practice. I'd say, 'Come on, let's go somewhere; let's go to a movie." He'd say, 'No, I've got to practice another hour.' He was really into it.

"Woody was responsible for me joining that orchestra, so he was responsible for what I became. He did this kind of thing for people all his life."[12]

What Tony Martin became, of course, was one of the biggest singers of the 1940s and a major movie star. He married dancer Cyd Charisse. Thus his was the first major musical career launched by Woody Herman.

Woody, whose Whippet was gone—he was very hard on cars—by now owned a little red Pontiac roadster. One night he was driving down one of the perilously steep San Francisco streets when he shifted into second, without first pushing the clutch in. "And I dropped the whole transmission right on the hill," he said long afterwards, "and as far as I know it's still there. On Sutter Street or someplace. Never took time to go and seek it out again."

Woody liked to take a ferry boat across San Francisco Bay to Oakland. The ferries had small diners aboard whose food he found excellent, and some people took the trip early in the morning to watch the sun come up.

A new musical, *The Nine O'Clock Revue*, was in rehearsal to open at the Curran Theater. After the opening night show, the entire cast went to the Bal Tabarin to hear the Gerun band, dance, and celebrate. Woody immediately noticed a beautiful dancer, escorted by a friend of his, a San Francisco bandleader named Bunny Burson. Woody arranged an introduction. Her name was Charlotte Neste, and her origins were Norwegian.

Tony Martin said, "He fell in love that night, and that was it. Charlotte was redheaded and beautiful. She had an extremely beautiful figure, and a charming smile. I think she fell in love with Woody in five minutes, and after that I didn't see much of him. He was with her all the time."[13]

Charlotte Neste had been born in North Dakota, but her family, unlike Woody's, kept moving around, to Oregon and other places, and finally settling in the San Francisco Bay Area. Charlotte's mother was from a large family. One of her grandmother's sisters, Minnie, had a daughter, Shirley, who grew up in Canada and then, when she married an aeronautical draftsman named Vincent Mancuso, lived in Cleveland. In the early 1950s, she and her husband moved to California (where he died in 1993) and she and Charlotte immediately became close friends. "Vince and Shirley became our extended family," said Woody and Charlotte's daughter, Ingrid.

In 1994, Shirley said, "Charlotte and I used to wonder who was the dominating force among the grandparents, and we decided it was the old man, Nels Hedalen, our grandfather. He was very bright. He taught himself English when he came from Norway at the age of sixteen. His wife, Carrie, died at the age of forty-four. She'd had fifteen kids. He was a politician. He would leave his two young kids, six and eight years old, alone on a farm for weeks at a time in the winter. He was a member of the state legislature and would go off and do his politicking in the capital of North Dakota, Bismarck. I think it all started with him. He had a terrible conceit. It was either conceit or a cover-up.

"My Aunt Inga married Martin Neste. She was about sixteen years old at the time and she always talked about her eighteen-inch waist when she was married. They were the most conceited bunch, particularly my grandmother and my Aunt Inga."[14]

Why Charlotte's mother didn't have a large family, as her parents did, can't be determined now, but Ingrid suspects it was because her great-grandmother had borne so many children and died young of exhaustion. According to Shirley, Charlotte's father, Martin, "was just a gentle man who didn't want to make waves." The propensity of Charlotte's mother for dominance was already fully developed when Woody met the family, and she almost certainly instilled in Charlotte a hatred of farm life.

Martin Neste loved the saxophone and perhaps in part for that reason was immediately empathetic to Woody. Ingrid said, "My grandfather was a fiddle player and sax player. He played with Ole Rasmussen, who was a west coast Bob Wills–type band."

After the meeting with Woody, Charlotte's show went on to Los Angeles. Woody made a trip down from San Francisco to visit her. Tom Gerun had asked him to find a new girl singer while he was there. Woody described the auditions he held:

"There was a guy who worked for a publisher, by the name of Lucky Wilbur. His wife, Hazel, played the piano. They demonstrated songs together. Hazel and Lucky. And in those days, the picture companies were still pretty fresh in the publishing business as far as songs were concerned. And their office was right on the lot on Sunset Boulevard. I can't remember the name of the studio. Now it's a bowling alley. I called Lucky.

"And the first day I stopped by at some given hour in the afternoon and he had maybe fifteen chicks sing. The next day some more. Fantastic! Just one call from this [movie] lot, you know, and all the aspiring movie actresses would show up. Anything was better than not working, you know.

"If a girl looked good, if she looked like a car hop, if she was beautiful, she couldn't sing. And the ones who sounded possible looked like Lincoln. And the second day we were going through these gals, and Ginny Simms was among them."[15]

Simms was then a high-school girl. Woody, back in San Francisco, told Tom Gerun about her. Gerun called Simms and hired her over the telephone. Her mother drove her to San Francisco, and she started singing with the band at the Bal Tabarin. Later she remembered watching Woody play clarinet, tap dance, and sing *I'm a Curbstone Cutie, Mama's Pride and Beauty, They Call Me Jelly Bean.* He wore a straw hat for these routines. In the chorus line of the Bal Tabarin show was a dancer named Ann Miller who, like Tony Martin, would later star in movie musicals.

Simms went with the Gerun band to an engagement in Chicago, and then on Gerun's recommendation joined the new band going into the Bal Tabarin, of which he was a co-owner. The band was that of Kay Kyser, with which she would become famous. If Tony Martin's was the first of the major musical careers initiated by Woody Herman, hers was the second. Still only eighteen, he had that eye and ear for talent that was one of the most significant of his abilities. As many persons would learn over the years, he was never wrong about talent, and he was unfailingly generous and supportive to those who had it.

"After *The Nine O'Clock Revue*," Woody said, "Charlotte was in another show, which traveled across the country from San Francisco to New York, with Barbara Stanwyck and her husband, Frank Fay, who was a funny man. But he wanted to take a show back to New York, to prove he was a great director and producer, I suppose. And of course, Miss Stanwyck paid the tab. They finally got to New York and the show lasted a week or so."[16]

Woody was playing tenor and baritone saxophones with the band, and occasionally alto, as well as jazz clarinet. A number of the musicians in the Gerun band were from San Francisco, and decided when they reached that city, to stay there. Woody began to agitate Gerun to replace them with hotter players, more attuned to jazz. Gerun often took his advice.

After approximately a year's sojourn in San Francisco, the band went on the road. It was now, in Woody's later opinion, a much better band, though what it had gained in quality it had lost in commercial appeal.

The band was booked for a double engagement in Chicago. Tony Martin remembers the trip vividly: "That was a thrill to me, to go east. I had a favorite uncle in Oakland. He promised me that if I ever got to go east, he'd lend me the money to buy a car. I bought a Chevrolet, a wonderful little car. Woody and I put our saxophones in the back and set off for Chicago. We drove to Reno, Nevada, and decided that instead of stopping overnight we were going to make it all the way to Salt Lake City and save the money. We'd been given expenses, and we were going to keep the expenses.

"We got into Utah. We were just outside of Salt Lake City. It was a new highway, with soft shoulders—they hadn't completed the highway on the side. We made a turn in the dusk, and the wheel of my car caught. I was driving, and when I felt us going over, I held Woody by the head so that he wouldn't go into the glass. We turned over four times, broke the window, did a total on the car. I was bleeding and so was Woody. I'd fractured my hand. Woody jumped out of the car and opened the back and took his saxophone out to see if it worked. Then he checked our liquor supply. Then he fainted.

"We hitchhiked into town. We went to a hotel. We called ahead. We were supposed to have a meeting in Nebraska. We told Tom we were all right. We waited two days and got another car and drove all the way to Chicago."

In the afternoons, the band performed at the 1932 Chicago World's Fair. Tony said,"We played at the Pabst Blue Ribbon Casino. There were four orchestras, Guy Lombardo, Ben Bernie, Tom Gerun, and Ted Weems. There was a revolving stage and we'd each do fifteen minutes an hour. We were both punk kids. I was twenty years old, and Woody was nineteen."[17]

In the evenings the band performed at the Chez Paree on a bill with Helen Morgan. A poster of the time bills the band as "Tom Gerun And His Californians" right under "$2.00 dinner de luxe from 5:30 to 10 p.m."

Woody took an apartment in Chicago and brought his mother down from Milwaukee. Ray Sherman, who was seventeen, joined them for a month, and Charlotte, on her way from New York to California, stopped off to spend two weeks with them. Ray would escort Charlotte to the Chez Paree to pick Woody up after work.

Woody said, "Charlotte and I had been romancing over the telephone and by letter. She finished a radio show or something in New York and she stopped in Chicago, where the band was playing, and I arranged for her to meet my mother, because I was trying to prepare her. I was going to ask her to marry me. I was doing my midwestern-type family business."[18]

The Chez Paree's house band was the Ben Pollack group, whose personnel at the time included Jack Teagarden, Sterling Bose, Charlie Spivak, Ray Bauduc, Harry Goodman (Benny's bassist brother), Nappy Lamare, Matty Matlock, and Eddie Miller. One of its arrangers was David Rose. Woody was profoundly impressed by the band, which he described as a "very clean, very good blues band."

After Chicago the Gerun band played an engagement at the William

Penn Hotel in Pittsburgh, then played a gambling club called the Club Forest in New Orleans. The stay in that city gave Woody a chance to hear a number of New Orleans musicians he admired, including the clarinetists Irving Fazola and Sidney Arodin. Arodin would take Woody in a small rented motorboat on the bayou, or crabbing on Lake Charles. As the afternoon waned, they would cook the crabs on a beach and then return to the city. Though Prohibition was the law of the land, New Orleans remained a roaring town with bootleggers doing business twenty-four hours a day, unimpeded by the authorities. Woody had now spent time in the three of the cities accounted the most important in the development of jazz up to that time, Chicago, Kansas City, and New Orleans.

The band then moved to New York and played five weeks at the New Yorker Hotel. By contrast with Chicago and New Orleans, Woody found Manhattan sedate. He and a few other musicians went up to Harlem, but there seemed to be little action even there in 1932. He did, however, meet another clarinet player he admired, Pee Wee Russell, who was living in the Bronx in an armory that had been condemned. Russell opened the door wearing a tattered bathrobe. The quarters were shabby and poor, lighted by a single bulb. This glimpse into deprivation made him re-evaluate a vague intention to stay in New York. He was making excellent money with Gerun.

"Tom kind of put up with me," Woody said, "because I was a first-rate ham, and show biz-type kid and he knew he could always get me to leap up and do three numbers that would break it up." He was singing a good deal of novelty material such as *Curbstone Cutie, Old Man Mose, I'll Be Glad When You're Dead You Rascal You*, and *Stick Out Your Can*. Ballads, presumably, were the domain of Tony Martin.

Woody's first recorded vocals were made with Gerun in New York City on August 1, 1932—*Lonesome Me* and *My Heart's at Ease*. On August 19, he again recorded with Gerun, singing *Sentimental Gentleman from Georgia*. Victor Young, later a prominent film composer, was what would now be called the A and R—for artists and repertoire—man of the sessions. They were done for the Brunswick label, which was headed by Jack Kapp. Woody could not understand why the band was not allowed to record its stronger jazz pieces, and without consulting Gerun he went directly to Kapp's office and complained. Kapp informed him acidly that the label already had Red Nichols to handle the jazz chores, and from then on Woody recorded what he was told to.

Woody was considering starting his own band; indeed, he had harbored this intention at least since he was a boy. That is another of the curious qualities about Woody Herman: While other boys might think of being cowboys or firemen and soldiers or policeman, Woodrow Herman apparently, from the time he bought his first saxophone at the age of nine, never considered any career other than that of musician and bandleader. He had a remarkable singleness of purpose.

The courtship of Charlotte grew more protracted because both of them were on the road, Charlotte with various theatrical companies. Woody did not intend to marry her until he had his own band. He had made up his mind about that, too.

Woody always remembered Tom Gerun as a kind and gentle man and a thoughtful employer. Gerun treated the personal problems of his musicians with patience and understanding—exactly as Woody did in later years. Gerun and Joie Lichter, then, seem to have been important models for Woody's attitudes and behavior as a bandleader in later years.

Though Woody was capable of sulphurous bursts of anger, he had a remarkable ability to handle emergencies well. I asked him about it once.

Woody said, "I think I learned it from Tom Gerun. It was during the Depression, the end of the Wall Street crash. One night in Pittsburgh he got a telegram, right while we were on the bandstand, telling him that he had been wiped out financially. He went white, and said, 'Boys, tonight we're going to have a party.' And we had a band party. I think that had something to do with shaping my philosophy."[19]

4

Life with Isham

Hoping to form his own band, Woody left Gerun in July, 1934, in Denver. In what seems a formidable feat of travel for that age before freeways, his mother, Aunt Julia Sherman, and Joyce and Erv Sherman drove from Milwaukee to Colorado to pick him up and bring him home with his instruments and clothes. Why he no longer had a car and why he didn't simply take a train are unexplained, but the information about this curious odyssey is contained in Ray Sherman's private diary. Woody spent the last half of July and all of August at home in Milwaukee. On September 1, Ray Sherman and Woody went to the Modernistic Ballroom to hear McKinney's Cotton Pickers. Meanwhile, Woody's friend and sometime roommate on the road, Tony Martin, had received a call from Dick Stabile, then a sideman with Ben Bernie, and had joined that band.

But Woody was unable to interest the major band-booking agencies in a Woody Herman orchestra, and as the leaves turned autumn colors in Milwaukee, he joined Harry Sosnick's orchestra, a well-known band that made radio broadcasts from the Chase Hotel in St. Louis and the Cosmopolitan in Denver. He stayed with the band nearly a year, though it was what musicians have long called a Mickey Mouse band—obvious, superficial, and saccharine. The band played mostly hotels. When it moved on to Los Angeles for an engagement at the old Palomar Ballroom, Woody warned Sosnick that the crowd there wouldn't long tolerate this kind of music, what Woody called "waterfall music." The prediction proved accurate. The opening night was a disaster, and Sosnick called a rehearsal at which he told the men to pull out a lot of David Rose jazz arrangements that they did not normally play. The band rehearsed all day and that night sufficiently redeemed itself with Palomar dancers that the booking lasted more than a month.

In October, 1934, the upstart new magazine *Down Beat* reported:

> After making a few changes in his band, Harry Sosnick played a very success-ful week at the Palace Theater here in Chicago. The orchestra seems to have improved with the change. He has a new chap in the band, Woody Herman of Milwaukee, formerly with Tom Gerun on the West Coast. This boy is plenty fast on the sax and clarinet, and he can step out and do a song and dance that is something to talk about. Harry, you'll have to watch this boy, or some day he'll blossom out with a band of his own; he's clever enough to handle a band.

Woody stayed with Sosnick only a few months and then joined Gus Arnheim, whose orchestra gave employment to a number of future jazz-men. Stan Kenton had left the band's piano chair. Woody did featured solo spots, singing and then going into his dance. He said, "I was a right-footed dancer. The left one was always a little late. But I used to run into people who really were dancers. They said I was one of the greatest fakers they had ever seen. It looked all right from the front but they knew that what I was doing was all wrong."

He did little playing. "You'd turn blue if you tried to blow after that," he said.

For a time Arnheim paired him with a harpist named Adele Girard, who was a head taller than Woody. They did a soft-shoe dance at the end of the act. Woody said, "Adele took a header one night and landed right on her can in the middle of the show." Woody laughed so hard she didn't speak to him for weeks.

Woody was doing well. His salary rose to $125 a week. But, he said later, the importance to him of his job with Arnheim was that on the band's eastward tour that year it crossed trails in Pittsburgh with the Isham Jones orchestra, a large band—it carried eighteen men.

Isham Jones was born on January 31, 1894, in Coalton, Ohio, the son of a mine boss; grew up in Saginaw, Michigan, and trained as a pianist. For a few years in his youth, he worked in a mine, driving a mule that pulled a string of coal cars. This doubtless was the major factor in shaping a charac-teristic that Woody and others, no matter how much they admired him, always noted: his frugality.[1]

There is no rhyme in the English language for his first name. The "i" is pronounced as that in "ice," and those who knew him pronounced the abbreviation, Ish, with that same vowel sound—not as a rhyme for "dish." He had a horseshoe of dark hair around a bald pate. He was an irascible man with a trigger temper and an utter contempt for his audience. In photos there is a certain austerity about him. Yet he was a felicitous writer of gracious melodies, who, working mostly with lyricist Gus Kahn, turned out a large body of songs that became standards, among them *On the Alamo* (1922), *Swinging Down the Lane, Indiana Moon* (both 1923), *It Had to Be You, I'll See You in My Dreams, Spain, The One I Love Belongs to Somebody Else* (all 1924), *You've Got Me Crying Again* (1933), *There Is No Greater Love* (1936), and *It's Funny to Everyone but Me*.

The ability to write distinctive and distinguished melody is not common: some highly trained composers lack it, and some untrained composers, like Irving Berlin, have it. Isham Jones was one of those who had it. Yet this ability to write romantic ballads seems at odds with his temperament. According to one story, he was lining up a shot in a pool game with Gus Kahn when the latter said Isham's cue had touched the ball. Jones hotly denied it and didn't speak to Kahn again for several years.

Along with his touchy temper, Jones had an astute sense of business. He told Woody that when he came out of the army after World War I, he took up the saxophone, still a novelty instrument, and joined a small group that auditioned for the Sherman House hotel. He was told by the management to stand in front of the band, since he played that strange-looking horn, the saxophone. This propelled him into the role of bandleader.

The author James T. Maher, who knew Jones and Woody, in a liner note for an RCA Victor LP reissue of sixteen of the band's records, wrote:

> Isham Jones was a unique figure in the world of dance music. No other individual during the era that took shape in the anxious years after the First World War and foundered during the Second—the big band epoch—matched the range of his excellence.
>
> In the period from 1919 to the mid-1930s, his career as a dance orchestra leader reached a level of success matched by few others: Paul Whiteman in New York and Art Hickman in San Francisco (and New York), Vincent Lopez, Ted Lewis, Ben Bernie. A few others, perhaps, but the lists of the great leaders is short, and it is spotted with names more famous as "presentation artists" than as dance men (Whiteman, Lewis, Bernie). The Jones orchestra flourished in the shuffle of dancing feet in Chicago, a city that built and supported (before 1923) such vast pleasure domes as the Rainbow Gardens and the Trianon Ballroom, each of which cost more than a million dollars . . . .[2]

Jones played the College Inn from about 1920 to 1925. He made a hugely successful tour of theaters, nightclubs, ballrooms, and hotels in the United States and in England that reportedly netted him $6000 a week, a considerable sum in those days. He broke house attendance records at every engagement and then returned to Chicago to play the summer at the Marigold Gardens. In 1923, the Brunswick label announced that it had paid Jones more than a half million dollars in royalties.

Maher wrote:

> Jones was one of the critical innovators in dance-band music. He probably ranks with Art Hickman as a major influence in determining the instrumentation, the aural character, the voicings, the blend of rhythmic pulse and melodic smoothness that marked the best bands during the years when dance music shifted from the traditional Viennese violin ensembles—the potted palm music of the early century—to the modern dance orchestra. Hickman and Jones arrived at a very nearly identical instrumentation at the same time: Jones, a saxophone player, leaned heavily on that instrument in pairs (adding a third by 1922), and Hickman (the composer of *Rose Room*) early discovered an outstanding pair of sax men who made clear, during the band's New York triumphs at the Biltmore Roof and the *Ziegfeld Midnight Frolic and Follies*, that the instrument was more than a loud substitute for the violin as the melody instrument for dancing.[3]

The instrumentation that became the norm for both the big dance bands and jazz bands, from Sammy Kaye and Kay Kyser to Count Basie and Dizzy Gillespie, was largely the work of a well-trained young violinist, pianist, composer, and arranger named Ferde Grofé, who was born in New York City and grew up in California, where he had worked in the Los Angeles Symphony.

"In 1915 or thereabouts," James Lincoln Collier wrote in *Jazz: The American Theme Song*:

> Ferde Grofé was probably the only person anywhere who was well versed in both jazz and classical music. At some point it occurred to him that he could improve on the very limited dance music being offered if he brought to it some of the ordinary devices of formal music, such as grouping the instruments in choirs to provide harmonized melody lines, adding countervoices, alternating solos with polyphony, and so forth. None of this was very complicated: the very popular military and concert bands of the day had been utilizing these devices as a matter of course for decades. The significance was that Grofé was apply-

ing these more interesting and musically sophisticated devices to dance music, hitherto a stepchild in the world of music.

The Art Hickman band at first was known only in San Francisco, although it was a huge success there. Its leader was a drummer and pianist. Collier recounts:

At some point Hickman became aware of Grofé's new approach to dance music, and brought Grofé into the group as pianist and arranger. Exactly what sort of arrangements Grofé was giving the band and how it sounded at this point is, once again, difficult to say. The critical moment came in 1918 when somebody heard a vaudeville saxophone team, Bert Ralton and Clyde Doerr. To this point, the saxophone had been seen as an unusual or even eccentric instrument, and it was mainly used in vaudeville for its novelty effect. Hickman no doubt was aware of the novelty value of the saxophone, but Grofé saw that saxophones could be used as a small "choir" in the dance band. Doerr and Ralton were hired. This was the beginning of the modern dance orchestra.

The band was a sensation in San Francisco. Collier continues:

In 1919 the band was brought to the Biltmore Hotel in new York, where it also created a minor sensation, and a boom for the saxophone began. According to Abel Green, dance band correspondent of the *New York Clipper*, Hickman, with his New York exposure, was the start of the new dance band . . . .
    The great success of the Hickman orchestra encouraged others to follow his lead. One of the first to jump in was another classically trained musician who was working around San Francisco, Paul Whiteman. He was something of a fast liver, and like Grofé and Hickman, he spent a lot of time in the Barbary Coast, where he heard the new jazz music. Whiteman's first step was to hire away Ferde Grofé to play piano and arrange for his group. The Whiteman band, with Grofé's arrangements, was an even greater success than the Hickman group. By 1920 it was playing in New York, and soon its Victor records were selling in the millions. By 1923 it had become the most famous popular-music organization in the United States and probably the world.

Hickman hired Doerr and Ralton in 1918, just about the time Isham Jones was getting out of the army.
    Fresh out of high school, James T. Maher, born in Cleveland on January 27, 1917, was a seventeen-year-old junior newspaper reporter when he first knew Isham Jones. In 1994, Maher told me: "The important thing to remember about Isham was that he became Mr. Chicago. He was *the* dance orchestra. In my view, his was the best dance orchestra we've ever

had. He played saxophone, and he played the piano, although he didn't perform on piano. He came to Chicago before World War I, from Saginaw, Michigan, and apparently went to a music school. He was in the army during the war. Bert Kelly, a banjo player who came to Chicago from San Francisco during the Pan American Exposition, and then founded Kelly's Stables in Chicago and later in New York, told me that he got Isham his first job. He had a little band in the Sherman Hotel, then called the Sherman House. Bert said that in 1917, he got this kid Isham Jones his first job in a little band at the Sherman House before World War I."[4]

For Canada and the nations of Europe, of course, World War I began in 1914. But in 1917 the United States was about to enter the war, and Jones was about to enter the army. "Isham wrote arrangements and really led the band," Maher said. "He was a very serious leader, a phenomenon that doesn't exist very often in jazz music, though there are lots of people standing up in front of bands. But there have been few true conductors."

Much has always been made in jazz histories about the young white musicians of the Midwest who traveled to the South Side of Chicago to hear Louis Armstrong. But according to information Jim Maher accumulated from his many contacts, cornetist Louis Panico and other members of the Jones band went there to listen to King Oliver. Isham Jones demanded that they do so.

"Louis Armstrong was the second cornet, but Oliver was their man," Maher said. "You read Max Kaminsky, you read Bud Freeman, you read all these white guys talking about going down there. They never mention all the white dancers who were there, a hundred or more every night to dance to Joe Oliver. In Isham Jones' mind, Joe Oliver had as good a dance band as there was. Isham always understood what was happening in jazz but never pretended to be doing it himself, despite the wonderful blues recordings he made. So he managed this perspective. Buster Bailey is the only witness I know who describes accurately the fact that Isham Jones used to come down frequently with the whole band. I think Louis Armstrong also mentions it in one of the biographical books.

"So here are the two black cats recognizing that Isham is there with his band, knows what is going on, appreciates it, and praises it.

"The bandleader Art Landry had a brief career with good recordings at Gennett and some very good recordings for Victor. Then he just sort of disappeared. Art took his own first dance orchestra into Chicago about 1922 or '23. He was on a vaudeville tour. One of the first things he did was go to see Isham Jones at the Sherman. He sent a little handwritten note up, saying he wanted to meet him. Isham came around very courteously,

and Landry told him that he wanted to have a band as good as Isham's
some day. Isham told him, 'If you want to know what dance music is all
about and what it's becoming, you'd better go down and listen to Joe
Oliver.

"When Art Landry first mentioned Joe Oliver, I said, 'How did you ever
hear of Joe Oliver?' He said, 'What do you mean, hear of him? I *knew* him.'
Landry went down with his whole band and got to know him and even used
Joe Oliver on a Gennett recording with his band. The record has been
completely lost, and, believe me, I've tried to find it. There were recordings
made of *Ripsaw Blues* that were never released.

"But there was this connection, this very strong connection, of dance-
band leaders to Joe Oliver, particularly Isham Jones. Landry said, 'Everybody in Chicago knew the King.' He constantly used the phrase 'the King.'
He never stopped praising him till the day he died. Joe was it.

"I met an old gentleman who had grown up on the North Side. He told
me that on his prom night, he and his girl had sneaked out of the prom and
gone down to dance to Joe Oliver. He said, 'Every night, the place was full
of white people dancing. He played such beautiful music. He'd play a
waltz, and it would go on for eight or ten minutes. He gave me an impression of a man playing dance music and being successful.

"Till he died, Isham had that feeling about the jazz musicians."[5]

As many writers have noted, jazz didn't just go up the river to Chicago, as
the simplified mythology would imply. It dispersed throughout the United
States. "What kind of music the [Hickman] group was playing," James
Lincoln Collier writes, "is difficult to know, but by 1913 New Orleans
blacks had been playing in San Francisco for at least five years, and it is
probable that the Hickman people were playing some sort of raggy version
of New Orleans jazz."[6]

Thus the New Orleans influence entered mainstream American popular
and dance music through several doors. The instrumentation of the big
bands was largely the inspiration of Ferde Grofé, followed by that of Bill
Challis, a young saxophonist who was writing arrangements using a smaller version of the big-band instrumentation (three saxophones) in Wilkes-
Barre, Pennsylvania. Challis later wrote for the Jean Goldkette band in
Detroit and then for Paul Whiteman. I have examined scores that Challis
wrote in 1920. They are on commercial score paper that was already set up
for the trumpet-trombone-saxophone choirs. This is an indication of how
quickly and widely that concept of a dance band had been disseminated. It
was the instrumentation that Fletcher Henderson, Don Redman, Benny
Carter, and others would utilize brilliantly to highly expressive personal

ends, helping to launch the Swing Era. If Grofé was the arranging influence, Joe Oliver was the phrasing influence, in James T. Maher's view. The
overstriding image of Louis Armstrong, who defined the art of the solo
while he was with Oliver in Chicago, has tended to pale the direct influence of Oliver himself.

Jim Maher wrote:

> During the years that dance orchestras were groping their way toward some
> musical rationale, some grammar of harmony, rhythms, and instrumental col-
> orations, the role of the arranger was undefined. Isham Jones wrote his own
> arrangements. "They were good, and they were tough to play," according to
> Metronome magazine. Arriving on the heels of the first white "jazz bands" with
> their often frenzied sounds and tempos, the Jones orchestra moved toward a
> more relaxed, smoother kind of dance music. His early arrangements of blues
> (his library always had a heavy representation of blues) such as *Aunt Hagar's
> Blues* flowed with far more felicity than the performances of almost all of his
> contemporaries.

Jones was offered a recording contract, with a proviso: The company
told him he could receive a straight scale payment or a royalty on records
sold. He advised the musicians of the offer. They didn't want a royalty in
the future, they wanted scale now. Scale at that time was probably about
$10 a session. After pondering the possibilities, Jones borrowed enough
money to pay the musicians and reserved the royalty for himself. The first
record sold about 3 million copies, and Isham was at once an established
bandleader and a prosperous man. "Good gambler," Woody said drily.

If the Jones band fell into the category later known as "sweet bands," he
retained his respect for jazz feeling, and its personnel sometimes included
jazz players such as Pee Wee Erwin, Jack Jenney, Maynard (Saxie) Mansfield, Joe Bishop, and Walt Yoder. It was noted for its big, round sound. It
made use of a clarinet section in ballads in a way that would turn up later
in the Tommy Dorsey orchestra, which I mentioned once to Woody. "Oh,
yes," he said, "I think you heard that with Tommy's band. Our chief arranger when I was with Isham was Gordon Jenkins." Also writing for the
band were Jiggs Noble and Joe Bishop, and Jones bought ten arrangements
from Fletcher Henderson in 1935.

Trumpeter Ziggy Elman told the writer Dave Dexter Jr. that Isham Jones
"had the greatest sound of any of the dance orchestras. No one else came
close." One of the factors in that sound was the way Jones used the tuba.
The instrument was used for bass lines during the early and middle 1920s,
but by the end of the decade, string bass was replacing it.

Said Jim Maher: "Isham had an Indian named John Kuhn on tuba, undoubtedly the finest tuba player in jazz or dance music at that time. When it was obvious toward 1928, '29, that string bass was taking over, Isham brought in string bass, but unlike the other people, he didn't dismiss the tuba. He moved it into the brass section, and put a bottom on it. There was no sound like it. It's odd that nobody else had the good sense to do that. Isham was the first to have that kind of ears."[7]

One of the few writers to take an accurate measure of Isham Jones is the composer, conductor, and educator Gunther Schuller, president from 1967 to 1977 of the New England Conservatory of Music. In his major study of the big bands, *The Swing Era*, Schuller wrote:

> Isham Jones, like his contemporary Paul Whiteman, led one of the finest dance bands of all time—some would argue *the* finest—for some 17 years (from 1919 to 1936). Jones managed to combine the highest musicianship with a desire to present the best popular repertory in the most pleasurably danceable form. To that end, like Woody Herman after him, he always surrounded himself with the finest musicians available, thereby according dance music a professionalism and class it rarely enjoyed, especially in the 1920s . . . .
>
> Jones was, in addition, a first-rate arranger, as witness his outstanding work with his early 1920s band. From the very outset Jones brought a sophisticated sense of variety (of orchestration, timbre, texture, and dynamics) to his dance band, literally unheard of in those days. One can listen to virtually any of the two-hundred-odd sides Jones recorded, for example, between 1920 and 1927, and scarcely discover any repetition of instrumental combinations and devices. Unlike other bandleaders, both then and later, who searched for a formula or gimmick and then rigidly held on to it for the rest of their days, Jones eschewed formularization. His first criterion—that a piece be perfect for dancing—was combined with a high degree of creativity and resourcefulness in exploiting the necessarily limited instrumentation at his command (originally ten players, then enlarged to 11 and in the 1930s to 15 and 16).
>
> Indeed, Isham Jones was, along with Art Hickman and Paul Whiteman, one of the three prime innovators in determining the basic instrumentation and character of the modern dance orchestra.[8]

If, as Bud Freeman argued, Chicago was the birthplace of jazz as we know it, a good case can be made that the big-band or Swing Era began in Detroit.

Detroit was the home base of the Jean Goldkette organization. Goldkette, who was born in France in 1899, had been trained on piano as a child. His family moved to the United States when he was eleven, and he played piano in Chicago until he formed a band of his own in 1924, hiring good arrangers such as Russ Morgan and Bill Challis.

Prohibition caused the entertainment industry to flourish in Detroit. It was not illegal to manufacture liquor in Canada, nor was it against Canadian law to export it. It was against U.S. law to import it. On the Ontario side of the Detroit River, all sorts of slips and small canals were cut into the land to house and hide the countless fast motorboats used to transport the "good stuff" to the U.S. side. Many of them are still there.

Only two large industrial American cities sat right on the Canadian border, Buffalo and Detroit, and Detroit was far the more important. For one thing, by the 1920s, it had a burgeoning automobile industry. And, from the vantage point of the importers of illegal liquor, it was the gateway to the Midwest. Taken off the speedboats, packed into trucks or even under the floorboards of cars, the liquor was shipped out to the various cities of the region. Its underworld was dominated by Jewish gangsters who collectively came to be known as the Purple Gang, just as Chicago was dominated by Italian hoods. And, movie legend notwithstanding, they did not hate each other: they operated in an *entente cordiale*. And Prohibition, even perhaps as much as the automobile industry, was making Detroit a rich city with a taste for entertainment. As the argot of a later time would put it, it was a swinging town.

Goldkette must have made some sort of accommodation with the Purple Gang and its allies, for he not only had several bands that bore his own name, but he also owned the National Amusement Corporation, which at one point controlled more than twenty bands in the region. When the owner of the Graystone Ballroom could not meet his payroll, Goldkette took it over.

Goldkette was never a jazz musician, but he hired excellent young jazz players, including Tommy and Jimmy Dorsey, Eddie Lang, Joe Venuti, Frank Trumbauer, and Bix Beiderbecke. When, in 1927, business for his band faltered, he closed it down and a number of his best people joined Whiteman.

One of the bands Goldkette controlled was McKinney's Cotton Pickers, which used the Graystone Ballroom as a base. Goldkette hired the arranger and saxophonist Don Redman as its music director in 1927. This all-black orchestra, under Redman, became a superb organization whose records sound remarkably fresh to this day. Another group that Goldkette set up was a white band called the Orange Blossoms, which evolved into the Casa Loma orchestra, directed by Glen Gray. Because so much is made of Benny Goodman's role in launching the Swing Era, the part played by the Casa Loma, with its excellent Gene Gifford arrangements, usually is overlooked.

To cite Gunther Schuller again:

> The Casa Loma Orchestra is generally cited as the band that set the stage for the Swing Era, the first white band consistently to feature jazz instrumental and pursue a deliberate jazz policy, and thus the most influential white big band of the early 1930s until Benny Goodman's breakthrough success of 1935. There is much truth to these claims, even if they require some qualification. How strange it is, therefore, that the Casa Lomans have been so skimped in jazz histories and—in many cases—dealt with quite disparagingly or ignored completely . . . .
>
> It seems to me that the many questions the work of the Casa Loma band raises are of vital enough interest to be seriously addressed, particularly considering the band's chronologically pivotal position in the history of jazz . . . .
>
> The band first recorded in 1929 . . . originally called the Orange Blossoms . . . . In 1929 the Orange Blossoms band was scheduled to inaugurate a new nightclub in Toronto, the Casa Loma, and when the club failed, the players decided to rename their group the Casa Loma Orchestra—in the club's memory, as it were. Soon thereafter the band dismissed frontman (Henry) Giagnini and reorganized as a co-operative orchestra and a corporation—the first of its kind—with one of its saxophone players, Glen Gray, as its president and the rest of the band as its board of directors and stockholders.[9]

The Casa Loma was not a nightclub but a huge old castle built by a Scottish millionaire for his bride. By the 1920s, dances were held in its large, handsome ballroom. The Casa Loma is still there, a wonderful red-brick-and-stone manse that stands on a hill, and dances are still held there. Whether the Orange Blossoms actually did play there is unknown. Artie Shaw has always cited the Casa Loma orchestra as the group that set the stage for the Swing Era.

The Goldkette bands, including McKinney's and the Orange Blossoms, were based in Detroit. Still another important band began there: Red Norvo always had been fascinated by mathematics, and during this period he decided to study with a noted mathematician at the University of Detroit. He settled in the city and formed a band, which played at the Mirror, one of the many ballrooms thriving there at the time.

Having grown rich on his songs, Isham Jones had left the band business. But with the rise of network radio and the exposure he saw various bands getting through "air play," he decided to get back into the business, which he did in 1929. He would use the new medium to plug his own songs and make them hits. That at least is what Red was told.

"I had three eight o'clock classes, and worked this ballroom five days a week," Red told me in 1993. "The office in Chicago that had booked me into the Mirror called me and said, 'Isham Jones is coming back into the business, and he wants to get a band that's already organized.' So Isham Jones came to Detroit and heard the band and liked it. He bought the band from me, and all the guys went with him.'[10]

During the engagement Woody had played at Joyland Park in Lexington, Kentucky, with Joie Lichter, he had met a young bassist, still in high school, named Walt Yoder. They became friends. Yoder had worked for Joe Haymes as well as Tommy and Jimmy Dorsey before joining Isham Jones in 1934. "He was the one who really steamed Isham up into hiring me," Woody said. "And when I went over to meet Isham at the theater, the only conversation we had was, 'Yoder says that you sing, dance, and play saxophone. Is that right?' I says, 'Yeah.' He says, 'OK.'"

Jones told him to join the band in Denver, the same city in which Woody had left Tom Gerun. When he arrived, Jones had forgotten hiring him. But Jones gave the tenor player Woody was to replace an extra two weeks' pay and dismissed him. Woody started with the band at $125 a week, the same pay he had been getting from Arnheim. Out of that he had to pay his travel expenses, but transportation was cheap then, and so were hotels, sometimes as little as $1.50 a night. This was, after all, 1934, and North America was in the depths of the Great Depression.[11]

After the Gerun band with its neat uniforms and impressive onstage presence, and Gerun's gentle manner, Isham Jones came as a shock to Woody. He said, "I was pretty much impressed with a band that looked keen on the stand and so forth. And with Isham it didn't matter if you had the wrong suit, or brown shoes with a black suit, as long as you showed up in your right mind and, after you got there, didn't ever miss a note. Even an eighth note. Because this was death. He stood in front of the band with a complete score of every tune. We played those tunes night after night, seven nights a week, and he still had the score out there. And if a customer annoyed him by pulling his coat to say, 'Mr. Jones, would you play *Stardust?*' or something, he'd say, 'Get the hell out of here.' Warm personality on the stand.'"[12]

Jones's manager was James Breyley, whom James T. Maher had known when he was growing up in Lakewood, Ohio. Maher went down to Columbus, Ohio, in September, to enroll at Ohio State University. Breyley tele-

phoned him. The Jones band was playing an engagement at the Valley
Dale, a well-known Columbus ballroom. Breyley invited Jim to meet him
there and hear the band. When he arrived, Breyley told him, "We've got a
new clarinet player in the band. A guy from Milwaukee. He's a young
guy—you'll like him." That night Jim heard Woody for the first time.

Jones featured him prominently. Maher noticed immediately that he was
not only an interesting musician but an astute entertainer as well; Jim did
not know, of course, about the young man's extensive experience in vaudeville. That night Woody sang a satirical version of *Brother, Can You Spare a
Dime?* At the end of it, he drew out a pocket handkerchief and, with limp
wrist, waved it at the crowd. Today this 1932 song, with music by Jay
Gorney and lyrics by E.Y. (Yip) Harburg, seems a stark evocation of the
Depression. But according to Maher, it seemed lugubrious to the point of
the risible to the "in" crowd of that time. That is why Woody made fun of it,
and Isham Jones allowed it. One cannot help wondering if Harburg, who
was quite proud of the lyric, ever heard Woody do it.

Trade-press accounts document a long summer contract for the Jones
band at Elitch's Gardens in Denver. This probably filled July and August,
and it was during this time that Woody apparently joined the band. Certainly he had settled into the band by the time of the September engagement in Columbus. The band continued east, reaching New York by Tuesday, October 1, 1935. On that date, it began a new radio show on the
Mutual Broadcasting System, sponsored by the United Cigar Stores and
titled *Good Evening Serenade*. The next night it opened a "winter engagement" at the Blue Room of the Hotel Lincoln in New York.

Woody at first sang only novelty songs with the band, never ballads, and
evidently he thought he was suited only to such songs. All his life, he
manifested a dismissive attitude toward his own singing. Then Jones assigned Woody the 1935 Dorothy Fields-Jimmy McHugh ballad *I'm in the
Mood for Love*. Woody said, "I can't sing that kind of song."

Jones said, "Sing it." And Woody began singing ballads. The next year,
Jones assigned Woody one of his own tunes, *There Is No Greater Love*,
which would go on to become one of Jones' most popular tunes. Woody
introduced it to the public and kept it in his repertoire when he had his
own band.

The Jones band was, in Woody's view, almost a swing band. In the spring
of 1934, Benny Goodman formed his big band, commissioning arrangements from Deane Kincaide, Will Hudson, and Benny Carter, and in November of that year he was contracted for the National Broadcasting Company's network radio show *Let's Dance*. He purchased arrangements from

Fletcher Henderson and hired Gene Krupa as his drummer. The Goodman band was not, however, an immediate success. That same year, Tommy and Jimmy Dorsey formed their short-lived orchestra. But so far, the national and ultimately international craze for big jazz-oriented bands had not happened: the Swing Era was still in gestation.

The Jones band, Woody said, "gave me a chance to prove what I wanted to do musically." He recorded with the Isham Jones band. "I did some (recordings) earlier with Tom Gerun's band," he said, "but they were once again entertainment-quality records. And this was my first (somewhat) more musical experience. Our first jazz date was done as a small combo, the Isham Jones Juniors. It was really my group, along with the rhythm section and maybe a trumpet, and Joe Bishop on fluegelhorn or something."[13]

Jim Maher remembers it this way: "Jim Breyley was courting a girl named Virginia Verrell. She was briefly successful as a singer on a CBS network show called *Saturday Night Swing Club* and on a forgotten but hip network show called *Uncle Walter's Dog House*. Jim arranged with Decca for a group to be taken out of the Isham Jones band. He called them the Isham Jones Juniors. He had two purposes in mind: to showcase Woody and to showcase Virginia. They recorded on March 25 and March 31, 1936."[14]

The personnel was Chelsea Quealey, trumpet; Sonny Lee, trombone; Woody Herman, clarinet, baritone, and vocal; Saxie Mansfield, tenor; Howard Smith, piano; George Wartner, guitar; Walt Yoder, string bass; Walter Lageson, drums; Virginia Verrell, vocals. Woody's memory notwithstanding, Joe Bishop was not on the date.

One of the tunes the Juniors recorded was *Nola*, with an arrangement by Howard Smith and featuring him on piano. Smith later joined Tommy Dorsey, who recorded the chart. The other songs on the first session were *Home Cookin'* and *Slappin' the Bass*, both featuring Verrell; and *I've Had the Blues So Long*, vocal by Woody. *Home Cookin'* was rejected, but the other three sides were issued. On the second session the group recorded *Tormented*, with Verrell, *Hollow Hole in the Ground*, *Take It Easy*, and *Fan It*, all with vocals by Woody. *Hole* was rejected.

This idea of a small jazz band within a band went back at least to Paul Specht, whose orchestra contained a group called the Georgians. The example would be followed by Benny Goodman with his trio, quartet, and sextet; Tommy Dorsey's Clambake Seven; Artie Shaw with his several small groups, all named after New York City telephone exchanges such as Gramercy Five; and eventually Woody with his Woodchoppers.

Fan It was a hit. Woody would re-record it with his own band and keep it in the book, along with other tunes that came into his repertoire during his time with that band. One way or the other, Isham Jones, like Tom Gerun, influenced Woody all his life. He even had Jones's quality of acerbity on the bandstand when a fan annoyed him.

"One summer just before Woody joined the band," Jim Maher recalled, "Isham was playing at the Public Auditorium in Cleveland. I went down to visit Jim Breyley that evening. I was seventeen, just starting out as a sports reporter at the *Cleveland Plain Dealer*. It was just after midnight. I looked at the band, and Isham wasn't there. I looked at Jim and said, 'Where's the old man?' Jim laughed and said, 'He does this all the time. He leaves the stand a half hour or forty-five minutes early, and the guys can then play what they want to.'"15

Woody would follow that practice.

Woody continued listening to the other bands, particularly those that were bringing jazz into dance music and featuring great soloists. Armstrong had established the pattern and now, instead of playing mostly ensemble, bands were permitting improvised solos.

The band recorded for Decca, a new company with limited finances. This gave Woody an entree to the company, and he was doing a certain amount of studio work, being paid twenty dollars scale for a record date. The musicians often had trouble collecting even this amount. He worked on a number of recordings with a singer named Dick Robertson, usually at bright tempos with a Dixieland feel. Occasionally cornetist Bobby Hackett played on the sessions.

During this period, the Isham Jones band was making frequent network broadcasts. Jones was writing arrangements for it, playing a little piano, and once in a while, to amuse the musicians, he would play tenor. Woody said, "And he could get a sound out of it that was unbelievable."

All his life Woody retained his respect for Isham Jones and that band. He said it was an excellent dance band. "He would never sacrifice anything for commercialism at all," he said. "So this actually was my first big change in music. All the other bands had been more or less entertaining bands. And this was the first one I worked in that was strictly a musical unit. And that's all, brother. You couldn't budge this man about anything else. He kind of hated all audiences. It was a concession if he turned around once or twice a night and looked at them. I should say glared at them . . . .

"It was a better caliber of guys, and the music was better. And it was a band that was respected by most all of the musicians around the country, and that way I made a lot of acquaintances and friends I probably wouldn't have had the opportunity to meet if I hadn't been in that group. It was the kind of band musicians came to hear.

"Ish had a very good name, and even though it was near the end of his career, we still did very good business. Our jumps weren't ordinarily bad. You could stay in one territory for weeks on end. New England, the middle west. The band traveled in cars."

Isham Jones, according to Woody Herman, had the essential elements for a great swing band, but he would not be a part of the era. He would quit the business instead.

5

The Band That Plays the Blues

For some time a series of historic developments had been converging to produce social and economic conditions that would change the lives of Woody Herman, Artie Shaw, Jimmie Lunceford, William (Count) Basie, and many other men who ventured out as bandleaders, as well as the lives of the singers and musicians who worked for them, and the entire American entertainment industry. One of these was the craze for a newer and freer kind of dancing, led by Vernon and Irene Castle. Another was the establishment of countless ballrooms and outdoor dance pavilions, many of them strung like pearls on the trolley lines that connected the communities of America.

Most important of all, network radio broadcasting in the United States was approaching a maturity that would last, alas, only a few years.

The theory of wireless transmission of sound was understood as far back as 1820, and by 1899 British battleships were using equipment developed by the Italian Guglielmo Marconi for communications up to seventy-five miles. In 1901, at Saint John's, Newfoundland, Marconi successfully received a trans-Atlantic broadcast from England. Much of his pioneering work was done in Canada, which for a long time was in the forefront of the development of broadcasting. In Massachusetts, on Christmas Eve, 1906, R. S. Fessenden, a Canadian, broadcast the first known North American radio program, comprising two musical pieces, a poetry reading, and a short talk. In 1910, Lee de Forest, using a 500-watt transmitter, made a broadcast from the Metropolitan Opera House in

New York; Enrico Caruso sang. By 1916, David Sarnoff, then employed by the Marconi Wireless Telegraph Company of America, was proposing the development of a "radio music box" to be sold for home reception of programs. In 1918, in Montreal, the Canadian division of Marconi's company established the first regularly operated broadcasting station in the world, licensed the following year as CFCF. In May, 1920, CFCF made a broadcast with a full orchestra, which was received by men on ships in the St. Lawrence River and a few others. The station has been on the air ever since.

That same year, KDKA was established in East Pittsburgh, Pennsylvania, by the Westinghouse Electric and Manufacturing Company. On the evening of November 2, 1920, it went on the air to broadcast the results of the Harding-Cox election campaign, and it stayed on the air to broadcast music and entertainment. By the end of 1921, there were eight radio stations operating in the United States, and such was their success that by November 1, 1922, there were 524 stations licensed to operate. At first they were heard only through headphones by amateurs who had acquired or built primitive crystal sets, but Sarnoff's vision of the radio music box was rapidly being fulfilled, with consequent expansion of the popularity of the new communications medium.

Soon stations were being linked by long-distance telephone lines, so that a single program could be heard in several cities at once. In 1926, the National Broadcasting Company was established by Sarnoff as a network of stations, some of which it owned and some of which it contracted with as affiliates, to originate and broadcast daily programs. The Mutual network and the Columbia Broadcasting System soon followed. These networks grew rapidly in power, scope, and influence.

Until that time, the phonograph record and player piano were the two means of reproduction of music. These were mechanical devices; radio was electronic. With the stock market crash of 1929 and the onset of the Great Depression, the sale of records plummeted, and it was highly unlikely that Isham Jones or anyone else could have experienced a record sale of three million in those dark years. Several record companies came to the edge of collapse. But radio only increased in popularity; financed by advertising, it was "free."

With the expansion of broadcasting, the owners of the new medium turned to whatever was available in the entertainment world for program material. The stations and networks aired the music of established performers and conversely created stars of their own.

It is difficult for anyone born after 1945 to grasp the cultural influence of radio broadcasting, particularly network broadcasting, in that era. After the 1950s, U.S. radio broadcasting became almost totally parasitical on another industry, the recording industry, and the two are today locked in an unwholesome symbiosis. But in the early days, recorded music was not the main fare of broadcasting; for a long time radio stations were enjoined from playing records. Radio originated music: CBS and NBC both employed full-time symphony orchestras on staff, and sponsored commercial broadcasts employed uncounted dance and jazz bands.

Franklin D. Roosevelt, perhaps the first American political figure to understand the power of the new medium, used it for direct communication with the people to help pull the nation slowly out of economic disaster—just as, in Germany, Adolf Hitler was using it to stir a nation to war.

Even small-town radio stations employed singers, pianists, and little orchestras. Broadcasts from the Cotton Club in New York established Duke Ellington as a major American musical figure before the 1930s began. The networks brought America *Grand Ol' Opry* from Nashville, Tennessee, and grand opera as well, with broadcasts from the Metropolitan in New York City on Saturday afternoons. Arturo Toscanini's NBC Symphony was heard weekly, as was the CBS Symphony conducted by Howard Barlow. The networks aired a great many weekly programs devoted to "light classical" music, sponsored by Firestone, Bell Telephone, Cities Service (a gasoline company), and others. Anyone who simply turned on a network station and left it playing effortlessly acquired exposure to a broad range of music. It was almost impossible not to know such names as Toscanini, John Charles Thomas, James Melton, Albert Spalding, Vivian della Chiesa, Lily Pons, Jessica Dragonette, André Kostelanetz, Leopold Stokowski, and other figures of the classical music world.

Meanwhile, late at night, there were so-called remote broadcasts of dance bands from hotels and dance pavilions across the country, which were steadily building interest in this kind of music. The dance craze inspired by Vernon and Irene Castle, evolving constantly more athletic forms to brighter and faster music, and the locations in which to do them, was bringing an interest in bands to a kind of critical mass, which the booking agents clearly did not understand. A cultural explosion was about to occur. Benny Goodman was its fuse.

Goodman's *Let's Dance* broadcasts on NBC, on the air since November, 1934, came to an end in May, 1935. The band played an engagement at the Roosevelt Hotel in New York. Attendance was poor, and the band's morale was waning. Willard Alexander, an agent with Music Corporation of America, who would emerge as the most important booking agent of the big-band era, put together a tour of the country.

"In the mythology of jazz," James Lincoln Collier wrote in his book *Benny Goodman and the Swing Era*, "the trip by the Goodman band across the country in 1935 was an unmitigated disaster." In fact, Collier points out, it was not nearly as horrendous as has usually been said. The Goodman band was fairly successful in Woody's home town, Milwaukee, with a strong attendance of musicians who had come up from Chicago to hear it. It did well in Salt Lake City but badly at Elitch's Gardens in Denver, Colorado. From there the band went to Los Angeles and an engagement at the Palomar Ballroom at Vermont and Second Avenue.

Collier in his research encountered disparate reports about what happened at the Palomar. One musician said the crowds grew steadily through the week. Another and more dramatic version holds that on opening night the band encountered a large audience of young people who, because of the difference in time zones between New York and the west coast, had been hearing it three hours earlier in the evening.

Goodman wrote in *The Kingdom of Swing* that at first he played the milder arrangements he thought the audience wanted. When the response to this music was weak, he said something like "The hell with it—if we're going to sink, we may as well go down swinging" and called up the stirring Fletcher Henderson arrangement of *King Porter Stomp*. Still another musician said that the great trumpeter Bunny Berigan, who was planning to leave the band anyway, yelled to Goodman, "Let's cut this shit; let's get out *Bugle Call Rag*," a Dean Kincaide arrangement.

Whatever happened, there was an enormous convulsive reaction of young Los Angeles audiences to the Goodman band, and they soon were packing the Palomar. It is significant that Woody's instincts for audiences were sufficiently astute that he had warned Harry Sosnick against playing "waterfall music" at the Palomar. Sosnick's success with jazz-flavored arrangements tends to give the lie to the tale that Goodman's New York *Let's Dance* broadcasts had created an audience for his band in California. The Sosnick experience suggests that there was a growing audience for all jazz-inflected music in California, which then as now was the land of origin of all sorts of national fads and fashions.

Whatever the circumstances and cultural ambience that caused the change in its fortunes, the Goodman band had an enormous success at the Palomar and went on to another successful engagement at the Congress

Hotel in Chicago, where it remained for six months. Collier wrote: "The details, then, are not certain, but it is clear enough that there was an audience for what would come to be called 'swing' on the West Coast."[1]

▼   ▼   ▼

For all his success, according to Woody, Isham Jones was always talking about "quitting the business." There have been any number of musicians—and other artists, for that matter—who have abandoned careers at their peak, including Rossini, Sibelius, and later, another clarinet-playing bandleader, Artie Shaw. We can only speculate that Jones, who, like Shaw, hated audiences, simply had had enough of the business. Aside from the money he had already accumulated, there was much more that would come willy-nilly in royalties from his considerable catalogue of songs. The ASCAP logging of radio performances of his songs alone assured him a life of ease.

Woody always insisted that, for all his musical sophistication, Jones was essentially a country boy. Woody said, "He bought this ranch a few miles outside of Denver, and, oh, he had books of instruction, and he set up a great plant for turkey raising, and I don't know how many eggs he bought. It takes a fantastic amount of care, particularly in a climate of that sort. He sent a brother out there to oversee it and hire people and run it."

Thus, a year after the Goodman breakthrough at the Palomar, in the summer of 1936, while the band was in Texas, Isham Jones, only forty years old, gave his musicians notice. In 1940, when his memory of the incident was comparatively fresh, Woody described how Jones did it:

"It was in Knoxville, Tennessee, that he called us all into his room. He was very simple and straightforward about it. 'I've got a ranch near Denver,' he said. 'I'm going there to write music and take it easy. We've had a good outfit, and it was nice while it lasted, but I'm retiring. We're breaking up.' He paid us off, rather nicely, too, shook us all by the hand and wished us luck. And we were in Knoxville without jobs.

"Most of us were ready to pack it in and look for other jobs, but there were those of us who felt that we were a pretty good outfit, and that we ought to stick together and keep on being a pretty good outfit. It takes a long time for musicians to 'work into' each other, and it seemed a crime to break up our now-excellent outfit."

A small group of the musicians, comprising Woody, Saxie Mansfield, fluegelhorn player and arranger Joe Bishop, bassist Walt Yoder, arranger Jiggs Noble, and a violinist and arranger named Nick Hupfer, whom

Woody had known in Milwaukee, held a series of meetings. Woody had always admired the Ben Pollack band. When Pollack retired, some of the men from his band decided to stay together in a co-operative, with singer Bob Crosby, Woody's erstwhile San Francisco roommate, as their elected leader. There was another precedent for a co-operative in the Casa Loma orchestra. Woody and his friends decided to follow the pattern, forming their own group, with members holding shares in the band. The Isham Jones Juniors had recorded for the Decca label, and Woody had been doing studio work for the company. He quickly arranged a contract with Decca.

Two or three of the other musicians joined the Ray Noble band at the Rainbow Room atop Rockefeller Center in New York. The remaining six men—Yoder, Mansfield, Bishop, Herman, Hupfer, and arranger Gordon Jenkins—discussed which of them should be the leader. Jenkins said in later years that the discussion centered on himself and Woody, but Jenkins got an assignment to orchestrate a Broadway show and finally the men elected Woody their nominal leader because of his wide show-business background, though he was the youngest among them—twenty-two years old. Jenkins contributed a number of arrangements, which, Woody said, "were more or less gifts, because we couldn't afford them."

Where the discussion that led to Woody's election as leader occurred is unclear. Woody said in a 1940 interview, "We argued about it all the way from Knoxville to New York, and by the time we hit the big town, we were Woody Herman and the Band That Plays the Blues."

In New York, the men began auditions to find seven more musicians to make up a complement of twelve. Woody at last had his own band, even if he was only an elected leader. He telephoned Charlotte, who at the time was visiting her parents in California, and asked her to come to New York to marry him.

Woody was always careless about detail. He ran a band on a very loose leash, which, according to Al Cohn and others who worked in it, was one of the reasons for its incredible fire, no matter who was in its personnel. But this let-it-slide attitude would some day cause him anguish. By his own testimony, when Charlotte arrived in New York, he bungled everything.

Charlotte arrived exhausted by the long train trip. He took her out to Harrison, New York, to a justice of the peace, who slammed the door in their faces because it was almost 11 p.m. Woody and his fellow bandsmen Walt Yoder and Nick Hupfer drove with Charlotte to Armonk, where, at approximately 2 a.m., they found a j.p. who would marry them. He told them, yawning, that he was going fishing in the morning and hurried them through the ceremony. The date was September 27, 1936.[2]

That day the rebels in Spain took Toledo, and Francisco Franco was named their chief. A rehearsal for another world war was under way. That year the big songs included *Goodbye*, by Woody's bandmate and friend Gordon Jenkins, *Easy to Love, Goody Goody, I Wished on the Moon, I'm an Old Cowhand, Is It True What They Say About Dixie?, It's a Sin to Tell a Lie, I've Got a Feeling You're Fooling, I've Got You Under My Skin, Let Yourself Go, Let's Face the Music and Dance, The Night Is Young and You're so Beautiful, Pennies from Heaven, There's a Small Hotel, These Foolish Things, The Touch of Your Lips, Twilight on the Trail, Until the Real Thing Comes Along, The Way You Look Tonight*, and *When Did You Leave Heaven?* Despite the Depression—or possibly because of it, for the dream of love is free—it was a very romantic era.

Woody often said in reminiscences that he and Charlotte spent their honeymoon on 52nd Street, a ferment of jazz with great musicians playing in one room after another. "It was a great street, along about '36 and '37," he said. "That was a fabulous street. You'd go from door to door, run in and catch a set that was a gas and leave for the next one, hear John Kirby for a while . . . .

"A group of musicians bought a place on the street and named it the Famous Door. Lennie Hayton and a bunch of guys were stockholders in this little club. And they brought Bunny Berigan in. The clubs along the street included the Onyx, the Famous Door, Leon and Eddie's, and Jack White's."

Berigan was a fellow native of Wisconsin, five years Woody's senior. Woody called him the greatest jazz musician to come out of that state. He met Berigan, however, not in Wisconsin but in New York. Berigan had just left the Goodman band. "And later Bunny found little Joe Bushkin, who was then about fifteen," Woody said. He was wrong about that. Bushkin, an excellent pianist who later was with the Tommy Dorsey band, was twenty-one, only a year younger than Woody. "In the intermission they had Teddy Wilson and then later [they] brought in Billie Holiday, this kid who sang tunes. It was a wonderful place. And Red McKenzie sang and handled the room, kept it alive and warm."

Backing Billie Holiday was a group led by Red Norvo, who was married to singer Mildred Bailey, whom he had met when they were both with the Paul Whiteman band. Bailey was by then a big star, able to make a hit for a songwriter with a single network broadcast. Norvo, too, was a star, and the two of them were known as Mr. and Mrs. Swing. Bailey had been the principal discoverer of Holiday.

"Woody and Charlotte would come in to hear Billie and our group all the time," Red said.[3]

It is likely that Woody met the pioneering jazz violinist Joe Venuti about that time. Red Norvo had met Venuti, too, with Whiteman. "Joe was my best friend," Red said. "A lot of the stories they tell about him came from me. I was there." Venuti was the author of countless practical jokes, such as pouring white sand a few spoonsful at a time into the instrument of Whiteman's bassist, who could not understand why his bass seemed to be growing heavier.

Years later Woody told me one of the Venuti stories—probably the most infamous—which Red may have told to him in those early days of their friendship. This, Red said, is what really happened: "Benny Goodman's brother Harry Goodman had a restaurant in New York called Pick a Rib. There was a gangster speakeasy next door. You walked down the steps, and there was a bar. The second floor was a dining room, and on the third floor there was gambling. Joe Venuti and I were drinking at the bar. The guy next to us was drunk. He was a pin-stripe advertising guy from Madison Avenue. And he kept sliding down the bar, and he knocked Joe's drink over. Joe knew the bartender, so he ordered another. The guy said, 'No, I'll buy the drinks here.' This went on. He spilled three of Joe's drinks. Finally Joe shoved him over. So then the guy got kind of smart alecky. He stood up and mumbled and said, 'What are you going to do about it?'

"Joe said, 'What am I going to do about it? Look down, and you'll see what I'm doing about it.'

"He'd opened his fly, and he was pissing on the guy's leg."[4]

With friends such as Berigan, Venuti, and Norvo, there may have been companionship and laughter for Woody at that time, but there was no work.

"I never was much for sitting in any place unless it was a session or something. I thought it was kind of overbearing on a guy's part to want to blow with a set group. I think once or twice I did when I was invited to. One night Fats Waller came in, and Bunny was blowing and they asked me if I cared to. I was usually pretty backward about trying to prove anything. I just kind of joined up.

"No job in sight. I cashed in an insurance policy and we were swinging."

Ingrid recalls that her mother told her Woody had wanted her to sing with the band but Charlotte wasn't interested. Charlotte and Woody began their married life in a fifth floor Bleecker Street walkup apartment for which Charlotte made curtains. They acquired a wire-haired terrier puppy and, as Woody put it, taking it out for walks several times a day kept them in prime physical condition. "Charlotte was heart-broken when the pup died of distemper that first year," he said, "and I began shopping for

another one right away. From that point on, we had a cocker spaniel."[5]
Babied by Charlotte, the spaniel lived eighteen years and traveled with
Charlotte and Woody back and forth across America on trains.

Red McKenzie, a happily married man, took Woody and Charlotte in
charge as "kind of a fatherly adviser in our new marriage. I was so intrigued
by this guy's ability and then too as a person. Anything he said was the law."
Woody admired the way McKenzie sang: "The way he phrased was the
freshest thing I'd ever heard and very musical . . . ."[6]

The new band began rehearsals in a ballroom of the Capitol Hotel,
which the hotel's management allowed them to use without charge. "We
didn't know what we were rehearsing for, but we were rehearsing," Woody
said.

The personnel of the first Woody Herman orchestra eventually included
Clarence Willard, Kermit Simmons, and Joe Bishop, trumpets; Neal Reid,
trombone; Murray Williams and Don Watt, alto saxophones; Saxie Mansfield and Bruce Wilkins, tenor saxophones, Nick Harper (formerly
Hupfer), violin; Norman Sherman, piano; Walt Yoder, bass; Chick Reeves,
guitar; and Frankie Carlson, drums. The baritone saxophone was not yet
generally used in bands, except Ellington's, which is the reason bands then
lacked bottom. And the brass section—three trumpets and one
trombone—was notably light.

With no specific engagements in view, many musicians dropped in and
then out of the band. "It wasn't easy to find them, with nothing to offer a
player besides stock in an orchestra without a gig," Woody said. "But if a
guy was nutty enough, he would join us."[7]

His own money rapidly dwindled. "I got so broke, having just gotten
married," Woody said, "and I started to take casual dates and wound up
with, I think it was, the Meyer Davis outfit. A couple of Saturday nights
were beautiful jobs because they paid forty bucks but were what they
called a continuous, for about eight hours.

"But the music and the whole thing was so horrible that, as broke as I
was, after the second one I reneged. I wouldn't do it any more. The last day,
Joe Marsala and I were in the saxophone section. Joe couldn't read at all,
and I was never a fast reader. And we loused up the whole thing. We got
glares and nudges from these guys . . . . We were ostracized."

Meanwhile, the new co-operative band growing out of the remnants of
the Isham Jones orchestra struggled along, rehearsing. Every decision was
taken in committee, a process Woody would eventually find crippling. But
they were determined to be a jazz band.

At last they got an engagement. With perhaps twenty arrangements in the book, the band opened at the Roseland Ballroom at Fulton Street and Flatbush Avenue in Brooklyn—not to be confused with the more famous Roseland in Manhattan. The date is usually given as the evening of election day, Tuesday, November 3, 1936, as polls all over the United States were closing and the counting of ballots was under way in the election that Franklin D. Roosevelt would win by a huge majority. That seems unlikely. A ballroom's owner would be disinclined to open a new and untried band on election day. It seems more plausible that the band opened the previous night, Monday, November 2.

Whatever the date, the other band members were paid fifty dollars a week, Woody seventy-five for acting as leader. "Big deal—leader," he said. "It was a job I couldn't afford.

"The main thing is that we were a hit. After three weeks there, Lou Brecker, who owned both ballrooms, moved us into the Roseland in Manhattan. The blues were the best thing we knew how to play, but we had to do a lot of fighting to play them. The management preferred that we play mostly . . . fox-trots, rumbas, and waltzes . . . to satisfy the dancers."

George Simon recalled: "Woody had both a loud band and high musical ideals. The ballroom manager, a man named Joe Belford, who looked like a Green Bay lineman, used to bellow to the band to play waltzes, rumbas, tangos, and sambas, none of which it had in its book and none of which it would have played on principle anyway. Woody handled Joe beautifully. He'd just bust out in a grin, bellow back kiddingly at Belford, telling him to get lost and quit bothering him. And he'd continue playing what he wanted to. So good-natured was Woody's approach, and yet so firm and so positive, that Belford not only took it but became one of the band's biggest fans."[8]

The band's stay at Roseland in New York was extended. At one point a new band arrived in town from Kansas City to play opposite them: Count Basie's. The Herman band already had the feel of the ballroom and its dancers. Basie did not, and at first the Herman band had the advantage. But Basie, known throughout his life for his astute sense of the audience, soon caught on, and meanwhile his band was having a considerable impact and influence on the Herman group. Woody was impressed by the tenor playing of Herschel Evans, and Frankie Carlson was absorbing the high-hat work of Basie's great drummer, Jo Jones. The members of the two bands were becoming close friends.

George T. Simon reviewed the two bands in *Metronome* in January, 1937. "I gave the Herman band a higher rating than the Basie band," he recalled, "for which John Hammond never forgave me. But Bill Basie, and Buck Clayton especially, said that I was absolutely right."[9] Basie agreed.

"The only band that ever cut my band was that Woody Herman band," he said. Basie and Woody would remain friends for life.

The Herman group had decided on the billing the Band That Plays the Blues and signed a booking contract with General Artists Corporation. Despite the band's success at Roseland, Willard Alexander and GAC's other executives told them the agency could do little for them. Woody remembered hours of patient waiting in GAC's outer offices.

Meanwhile, the Isham Jones turkey farm near Denver had failed. Woody said: "I don't know exactly how it happened but they had a hail storm and it blew thousands of turkeys, small turkeys, away. Ish had a terrible temper anyway. He was really shook up about it. Goddamn turkeys."

Jones then apparently opened a general store thirty or so miles outside Denver. Woody said: "And in conjunction he put up a little hamburger stand and made hamburgers, and people told me they were driving through and, holy smoke! who did they run into but Isham.

"And the man was always wealthy. But this was something he probably always wanted to do, and he stayed out there for three years, I guess, and he got tired of that, got rid of the ranch, and moved out to California."[10]

In California he opened a music store. Woody told me Jones would go into Hollywood and visit music publishers and get free professional copies of the sheet music of new songs. Then he would sell them in the store. "With all his money!" Woody said in amazement. He opened a second store, then sold both of them for a profit and moved to Florida. He would live out the rest of his life there, dying at the age of sixty-two in Hollywood, Florida, on October 19, 1956.

6

The Summer of '37

There were advantages to the co-operative band, because Woody did not bear sole responsibility for it. Everyone who lived through the experience—Woody, drummer Frankie Carlson, pianist Tommy Linehan among them—said it was a family affair, with even the wives of the musicians sharing the worries and pooling resources. At times they encountered humiliation. After the Roseland engagement, the band toured New England, played in Mississippi, returned to New York. When GAC booked it into a location for two weeks or more, the band might find itself fired on the second night, even though it had a firm contract. Its contracts simply could not be enforced.

When the band went to Milwaukee, the *Milwaukee Sentinel* reported:

WOODROW HERRMANN HERE WITH BRIDE

Woodrow Herrmann, a Milwaukee boy who made good in the orchestra field, dropped in with his bride last night on a surprise visit to his parents, Mrs. and Mrs. Otto C. Herrmann, 2545 North Third Street. The parents were not to be outdone in surprises, as was indicated an hour later when 75 couples, home-town friends of Woodrow's, trooped through the front door. Surreptitious telephoning had assembled the party. Herrmann, known as "Woody Herman" in the orchestra world, has taken over Isham Jones' band, and the members are accompanying him on a cross-country trip. The band stopped at the Schroeder Hotel last night. The young musician recently married Miss Charlotte Neste, an actress, of Los Angeles. "Woody" will leave today with the band, but she plans to remain here for a week or more.

What the paper did not say is that the band had a contract to play two weeks at the Schroeder (where Tom Gerun first heard about Woody from musicians in the Joie Lichter band) but had been told on arriving that the management liked the band it had and was holding it over. A number of members of the Band That Plays the Blues had to eat at the home of Woody's parents. Woody was humiliated to fail in his home town, although a redeeming moment came with a successful afternoon jazz concert. If Charlotte stayed with his parents when the band moved on, it was no doubt because Woody was so short of money.

For a while longer, Woody and Charlotte lived in their fifth floor Greenwich Village walkup, sometimes surviving on White Tower hamburgers and oatmeal. Yet some of the band members remembered that she was on occasion able to entertain with style, setting out memorable meals. Evidently she already was revealing some remarkable characteristics that endeared her through the years to everyone who worked in one of Woody's bands. Bandleaders' wives were notorious for interfering in the band's affairs, sometimes to the extent of hiring or firing of personnel and the making of musical decisions. Charlotte was never that way. She was gracious to the musicians but never obtrusive. She had some sense of how close to let Woody's associates get to her. And it was appreciated.

Woody and Charlotte moved to a ground-floor apartment on 35th Street in Jackson Heights on Long Island, and a number of members of the band moved into the building. Woody remembered that the manager, "a little Jewish man," was extraordinarily kind to them all. The musicians were always behind in their rent, but despite pressure from the owner of the building, the manager never passed that pressure along to the musicians and indeed sometimes lent them money.

On the Fourth of July weekend in 1937, the band played Ocean Pier in Wildwood, New Jersey, one of the countless dance pavilions of America in that simpler time when the bathing suits worn by the girls looked like little dresses and those worn by the men, usually black, covered the upper body. Some of the men's bathing wear had detachable tops, with belts at the waist, and a few men even had the daring to remove these tops and swim bare-chested in "trunks."

Ocean Pier and much of the peripheral amusement area was operated by Guy Hunt, an astute businessman and by all accounts a decent and likable human being. Woody immediately liked Ocean Pier and the broad sandy beach. All his life, he considered the South Jersey beaches the finest he had ever seen. The ton-and-a-half instrument truck, with the Band That Plays the Blues on its side panels, was parked at the rear of Ocean Pier, and the band went to work.

One night a day or two into the engagement, just before the band was to start, a tall and good-looking young man approached Woody. He was from Philadelphia, ninety miles away. The boy was Jacob William Siefert, always to be called Jack Siefert, born on December 30, 1918. He was German by ancestry and freshly graduated from high school. He and Woody would often have occasion to recall this encounter as the years went by. Jack Siefert was nineteen, Woody had just turned twenty-four. Age differences shrink as we grow older, but at that early time a five-year difference is a wide one. When I think about that encounter in the summer of '37, I remember the young man in Conrad's *Youth*, desperate for his ship to leave the harbor on his journey of life. Neither Woody nor Jack Siefert had even an inkling that evening that the other would be one of his closest friends for life.

"I had been listening to him on a radio show coming out of Chicago—it could have been the Harry Sosnick band," Jack said in the autumn of 1994, when Woody was dead and Jack was a retired, white-haired grandfather about to turn seventy-six. "Woody had an Aunt Pauline. She wasn't actually his aunt, but he called her that. Her name was Pauline Traub. I lived in northeast Philadelphia. She moved there from Milwaukee and became a neighbor of ours. She heard me playing my one record much too loud. She said, 'Oh you like music! My nephew's a musician. His name is Woody Herman.'

"So I felt I knew him. I walked up to the bandstand and said, 'Mr. Herman, my name's Jack Siefert and I'm a friend of your Aunt Pauline's.'"

Woody said, shaking his hand, "Oh, how's she doing?"

"Fine," Jack said.

"Stick around, kid—we'll have a milk shake at intermission," Woody said and went to work. Fifty years later, as Jack put it, they were still having milk shakes together.

The engagement, as Jack remembered long afterwards, lasted two weeks. Money was scarce, and few of the young people in Jack's neighborhood had access to cars, but they were desperate to get to the Jersey shore on the weekends and somehow managed to do it. Jack came back the next weekend to hear the band and Woody. "I just fell in love with the man," he said. "So warm." They would watch their children and grandchildren grow up together.

The Ocean Pier engagement was drawing to a close. The owner, Guy Hunt, apparently also had fallen in love with Woody. He asked him, "Where are you going after this?"

"No place," Woody said.

"How about playing another week?"

"Love it!" Woody said.

Hunt hired a biplane to fly up and down the Jersey shore trailing a streamer that read: *Woody Herman held over by popular demand*. Hunt laid out a plywood platform on the sand where the band would play on Sunday afternoons, and he leased a "wire" for these performances to be broadcast on a station in Philadelphia. Thus he built up the band's name and his own business.

The Ocean Pier would be an important locale in the band's career. "From the summer of '37 on," Jack said, "any time Woody had an opening, Guy Hunt would book him in there because he liked him so much. Woody could dance, he would sing, he could entertain, he could mimic, he could be a comedian. He could do anything, and Guy Hunt loved him."

Woody remembered that the young Siefert would dress like the band members, emulate their manners, and pester the radio stations of the Philadelphia area to play their records. Jack said, "I had a corduroy jacket just like Woody's." Afternoons, Woody and Jack would sit on the beach and talk. Sometimes the band played softball on the sand against Jack and his young friends.

The Ocean Pier is no longer there. It burned down during World War II, at a time of stringent rationing, particularly of gasoline. Woody was playing the Adams Theater in Newark at the time. Jack Siefert, backstage, showed Woody a newspaper clipping about the fire. Woody sent Hunt a telegram saying, "Dear Guy. Sorry to hear about your fire. But where the hell did you get the gasoline?"

▼   ▼   ▼

The band continued to function as a sort of house band for Decca Records, grinding out "covers" of recordings by other groups and backing singers signed to the label, among them Mary Martin and the Andrews Sisters. Decca, which was run and partly owned by Jack and Dave Kapp, was a new company but the only real alternative to the two major labels, RCA Victor and Columbia. Woody always retained respect for the Kapp brothers. To understand why, one must consider what had happened to the record industry when he first encountered Jack Kapp.

In 1929, phonograph records were a major medium of entertainment; they had helped make Isham Jones rich. With the crash of October, 1929, sales of records and the machines to play them plummeted. Shortly thereafter—on November 1—Thomas A. Edison, Inc., announced that it would cease making both. Brunswick Records suspended production of classical music and relied on imported material from Deutsche

Grammophon-Polydor. RCA executives held the view that the phonograph record was a thing of the past: radio, they believed, was the medium of the future. Contracts with classical artists were allowed to lapse. As the 1930s began, the fortunes of the phonograph and recordings continued to decline. In 1927, some 104 million records were sold; in 1932, the figure was down to six million. Production of phonographs had fallen from 987,000 to 40,000. By the following year, the record industry of the United States had almost ceased to exist. With banks foundering and the soup-kitchen lines growing longer and young men aimlessly riding the country on freight trains, and with, furthermore, a wealth of classical and popular music to be heard "free" from the increasingly powerful radio networks, who needed to spend sparse cash on records?[1]

Then, slowly, the industry began to find its way back. Sales of RCA Victor's records rose in 1933, though they were still only a tenth of the company's 1927 sales. But there was a problem. Roland Gelatt wrote in *The Fabulous Phonograph*:

> Since 1930, the manufacture of phonographs in America had all but ceased. Those that survived were obsolete—and usually in the attic. On the other hand, twenty million American homes had one or more radio sets to which a record player could easily be hooked up. RCA's sales department began to merchandise one, selling it at cost for $16.50. Columbia put one on the market at $55.
>
> At the very time when RCA introduced its little player a bold new record company made a significant debut. Its guiding genius was Jack Kapp, [an] ex-employee of Brunswick with an unshaken faith in the phonograph record, and its financial backer was E. R. Lewis, a canny London stockbroker who had taken over the management of the English Decca Company. The new American company was also called Decca.

Kapp believed that records were too expensive. As Gelatt put it, "With coffee selling for twenty cents a pound, seventy-five cents was plainly too much to spend for a couple of evanescent dance tunes." Executives at other companies also saw the need to market a cheaper record, but Kapp was the pioneer. He moved quickly to sign up some of the major performers in popular music to his new company, luring away from Brunswick Bing Crosby, the Dorsey Brothers, Guy Lombardo, Glen Gray, Fletcher Henderson, the Mills Brothers, and Arthur Tracy, known as the Street Singer, all of whom had been with his former employer, Brunswick. And he lowered the price of records to thirty-five cents. By 1938, record sales had risen to 33 million a year, with 75 percent of that figure coming from just two companies, RCA and Jack Kapp's Decca.

And then a new gadget came into prominence: the jukebox. These dumpy, rounded, garish machines on which you could play a song for a nickel proliferated in bars and diners and drugstores everywhere. And a good many of the records now being produced were being sold to that industry. Jukeboxes became wildly popular with teen-agers. By 1939, there would be 225,000 of them, consuming 13 million discs a year.

Kapp's first roster of performers comprised established artists, but he began investing in performers no one had ever heard of, including Ella Fitzgerald and two bands that had met at the Roseland Ballroom: Count Basie and Woody Herman. In 1938, he had a huge hit with Fitzgerald's *A-Tisket A-Tasket*. Only five years old, Decca was the second-ranking record company in America, selling 19 million records a year.

Woody's respect for Jack Kapp, then, was well founded. And although the band in itself was not yet a success, Kapp kept them working. They would get a call to come in the next day for a session with one of the Decca artists, and sometimes would have to work out impromptu arrangements collectively improvised in the studio—what musicians call "head arrangements." Some of the arrangements were written, of course, the work of the band's sole violinist, Nick Harper, who, Woody said, was a skilled jazz writer. Fluegelhorn player Joe Bishop, who with Gordon Jenkins had written *Blue Prelude* for the Isham Jones band, continued to contribute to the band's book, which was gradually getting better. Aside from his arrangements, his compositions included *Indian Boogie Woogie*—a feature for pianist Tommy Linehan—and *Be Not Disencouraged*.

Decca was a straitened operation. "They had to buy used equipment," Woody said, "and some of the wax that they put on it looked like it had been reused about eighty times. We used to cut the master on this heavy wax thing, wheel them in in boxes, and every time you finished one tune you had to go out for a fresh batch. It was all pretty basic. Some of the other companies were going ahead, and developing, particularly RCA and Columbia with all their massive appliances and scientists and people on their staffs working on sound and everything. We were just working on trying to make a record that wasn't warped before it was pressed. Jimmy Dorsey used to say, 'For God's sake, when are you going to put the hole in the middle?' They were always off center.

"In spite of it, Decca became probably the outstanding record label on the market and did more to revive the big record-sale business than anyone else. And it was always done the cheapest way possible. It had to be, because they put out a thirty-five-cent product when the rest of the world was selling a seventy-five-cent product."

One of the influences on the band and on Woody was Dave Kapp. "I learned a great deal from their operation," Woody said. "Dave was the guy that used to take the sound truck out and go into the South and try to discover folk and blues (material) and do it right on the spot. And he had a goodly supply and an unlimited kind of repertoire to offer me to record. This led to such things as *Trouble in Mind* and *Dupree Blues* . . . .

"So they were very helpful in a lot of ways. They knew what they were seeking and I was still finding where I wanted to go. So a lot of times I did feel—and so did the guys in the band—we were being maneuvered. But it was probably best for us in the long run."

This explains why that band did not have a distinctive personality, and assuredly not a Woody Herman personality. Red Norvo said, "I never went by to hear the Band That Plays the Blues. I really didn't like the band. I liked a lot of the guys in the band. When I'd see them in bars, like the White Rose around Fifty-second Street, where everybody drank, they'd say, 'Well, you know, it's an idea. Maybe we can make a buck.'"[2]

Woody continued to form professional relationships and personal friendships that would endure through his lifetime. One of these was with a young man named Howie Richmond, a native of New York City who, at six-foot-two, towered over him. One day Howard S. Richmond would be an important music publisher, but when Woody met him he was a neophyte press agent.

Before the turn of the century, Howie's father, Maurice Richmond, had been what used to be called a "music man." He traveled, mostly in Connecticut and Massachusetts, setting up sheet music sales in stores for a publisher in Springfield, Massachusetts, that specialized in marches. Howie said: "My dad got married in 1903, and came down to New York to work for his company. Dad was in the business in New York in those first years of the century when guys like Irving Berlin were starting and when ASCAP was established in 1914. He knew all of those fellows.

"Irving Berlin wanted him to go with him, but my dad started Richmond Music. He brought his little nephew from Worcester, who was Jack Robbins. He was Jack Rabinowitz." (Jack Robbins, too, would become a publisher and Robbins Music one of the important music houses.)

"In 1937," Howie said, "I was just a young kid press agent in New York. I'd done a couple of years at the University of Pennsylvania at the Wharton School, but I wasn't really that interested. I took a course in public relations, and when I came home at the Christmas holidays, I looked around New York and got a job in a publicity office.

"Woody was around New York. I had Larry Clinton and Glenn Miller as clients. The Band That Plays the Blues was rehearsing. Because it was a co-operative, Woody didn't have much authority. He would try to pacify everybody. They hired me and I worked for the band for about a year on publicity, trying to get the band mentioned in the papers, getting reviews by George Simon, that kind of thing.

"And Woody was a sort of a hero of mine. I loved the band.

"Part of my job was trying to get Woody bookings. Larry Clinton had played the Glen Island Casino and did very well. The Dorsey Brothers had come before. Woody was being booked by Rockwell-O'Keefe." The agency run by Tom Rockwell and Francis C. O'Keefe, called Cork O'Keefe, was famous at the time. "Cork O'Keefe," Howie said, "was a wonderful, loyal Irishman. A unique man. Tommy Rockwell moved around, hung out, drank, a Broadway guy. But Cork was a really, really noble man. He loved the bands and he wanted them all to be happy.

"The band wanted to play the blues. Everybody told them not to. They'd get a booking and have to play dinner music. It was very tough, because even Benny Goodman couldn't really cut loose and play before 11 o'clock at night.

"Charlotte was a wonderful wife and not typical of the band wives. They wanted to have a little baby and a home life. Woody just had his nose to music.

"At the time Woody's band owed me twelve or fifteen hundred dollars. I had Gene Krupa and Larry Clinton as clients. Larry had hit big by then. I really wanted to be around the more creative guys, and Woody would let the musicians play more than two bars of solo. The band had soloists and musicians in it. Because I had Larry and Gene, I wasn't exactly starving, but I did need the money Woody's guys owed me. I mentioned it to Woody. He said, 'If those guys don't pay you, Howie, I would leave.'

"I said, 'But I love the band!'

"He said, 'We'll get you back. That's the way to make 'em pay.'

"I went to California, and they sent me, I think it was, a hundred bucks a month. I lived out there for about a year. When it was paid off, I had a different relationship with Woody. It was just that of a loving friend."[3]

The band continued to struggle, borrowing money to survive. At one point during an engagement in Cincinnati, several of the musicians pooled their funds and gave the money to Nick Harper to take across the river to Newport, Kentucky, where gambling went unhindered by the police, to see if he could increase it. Instead, he lost it.

When he was in New York, Woody would visit the offices of GAC, looking for bookings, and most of the time was left to sit and fret in the waiting room. Often sitting next to him, sharing this intangible and debilitating mist of indifference, was another midwesterner, then thirty-three years old, a trombone player and arranger born in Iowa, brought up in Fort Morgan, Colorado, and educated in part at the University of Colorado at Boulder, where his horn rests now in a glass case in the music building. He had worked in the bands of Tommy and Jimmy Dorsey, Ray Noble, Ozzie Nelson, and the Casa Loma orchestra. He too was trying to get a band off the ground. He and Woody became friends. His name was Alton Glenn Miller, and neither he nor Woody would ever be a sideman again.

"I was twenty-four years old and optimistic," Woody told Stuart Troup. "Glenn was a little older and sour. He had already blown a ton of money with three bands and he was full of sad stories. GAC apparently didn't think much of either of us at that point."

Miller by then was living on money borrowed from his own parents and his wife's. In 1937, Miller organized a band that recorded for Decca, but it failed, and he disbanded. What is fascinating in both young men—and Tommy Dorsey and Harry James and many more—is that they had such faith in this form of dance music, this comparatively new instrumentation, that they would ignore rejection, humiliation, and defeat to return to the struggle. Most of them, Woody once pointed out to me, failed. It is rarely remembered, for example, that Coleman Hawkins and others tried in vain to launch big bands.

Another year passed. By the fall of 1938, when it turned two years old, the Band That Plays the Blues might better have been called the Band That Sings the Blues. Nick Harper had left the band. A young Boston guitarist named Hy White had joined it. For all the hardships, he found the band thrilling. And he wrote *Riverbed Blues*, which the band would record. On December 22, 1938, the band recorded a King Oliver piece, *Doctor Jazz*, with a vocal by Woody that seemed to echo the version of it made by Jelly Roll Morton in 1926. It got rave reviews in the trade press.

About this time, the band began to get help from the Shribman brothers of Boston. Cy and Charlie Shribman were personal managers who also owned ballrooms throughout New England. According to Red Norvo, it was almost impossible to get booked in New England without their co-operation. Even the major booking agents dealt with the Shribmans in seeking engagements for their clients. Refreshingly, the Shribmans had a reputation for decency in their dealings. George Simon said, "Cy Shribman was completely honest. I never heard a bandleader ever say a word against him."

The Shribmans were instrumental in finally launching Glenn Miller, in whose band they invested not only effort but money. Someone suggested to Woody that he get in touch with the brothers, who booked rising bands into hotels and ballrooms that didn't pay them enough to survive but that had network broadcasting connections. The broadcasts gave the bands the exposure they needed to build an audience and assure bookings. The Shribmans would underwrite these engagements out of their own money, even paying for the air time. The Shribmans decided to help Woody, and the band settled in Boston to do what musicians call "run-outs"—trips from a central location to engagements in the area. The Band That Plays the Blues was playing throughout New England, thanks to the Shribman brothers.

"People fought desperately to get hotel locations," Woody said, "because you'd be on the air coast to coast on one of the networks or another. That way, when you came out and went on the road, your audience was bigger, and you'd start to do business.

"Without the Shribmans, I don't think the whole era could have happened . . . . After a few weeks, that air time would make the audience aware of you and, when you went on the road, you started to earn some money on percentages, getting X amount of dollars as a guarantee and then maybe 50 or 60 percent of the gross.

"The Shribman brothers started way back with some of the earliest bands. In their stable at one time or another were people like Artie Shaw and Glenn Miller. They helped Tommy Dorsey in the beginning, they helped us, and any new band that had any potential at all."[4] They also helped Duke Ellington.

George Simon recalled: "I knew Cy better than Charlie, because he was always on the scene. Charlie Shribman was the quieter of the two, a kindly sort of guy. Cy was sort of a big gruff guy. He would just barge ahead and do what he thought was right. He apparently had a tremendous instinct to do the right thing. The guys told me that he would go around at night to the various places in the Boston area, collecting money for bookings. His pockets would be bulging with cash. Then he'd take what he got in one place and use it to pay a band in another place. It was unbelievable."[5]

Bandleaders were even willing to lose money to get "remote" broadcasts. Woody said, "The band became more important via records, and then all of a sudden we started to get much better air time and a lot more. That's when we started playing major hotels in New York or whatever, and if we had to lose $2,000 or $3,000 a week, it didn't matter because we were getting the right kind of air time."[6]

Sometimes the Shribmans would have the men of two or three bands living at the Avery Hotel in Copley Square at the same time, several of them to a room. The manager of the hotel, named Phil Young, was a man of enormous tolerance who would even lend the bands gasoline money to get to engagements. In this permissive atmosphere, some wild parties occurred, one of them by the combined personnel of the Woody Herman and Glenn Miller bands.

"Glenn," Woody said, "was an excellent arranger and was one of the people that I respected and admired, along with a lot of other guys, because he had written for the Ben Pollack band, which was a great band; he also had written for Ray Noble. He had this innate ability. And a lot of times he was called in on a jazz date, by Red Nichols or somebody, because there might be something to fix where there wouldn't be any charts. For instance, he wrote that little introduction and exit thing on *Basin Street Blues* . . . .

"He was a fixer on a lot of dates. So, consequently, he got in on dates where he otherwise might not have been; his prowess on trombone was not too heavy.

"Glenn had made a pact with his wife that he was through drinking. He couldn't drink, and he knew it. He would turn crazy. While he was on the wagon, breaking in his band around Boston, he and I got into drinking one night, and pretty soon some of the guys started wandering in. It got to be a real roaring party. We locked one of my guys out on the fire escape in his underwear, and it was snowing like hell. We were doing numbers like that.

"Anyway, everybody just passed out or went to bed. And someone rang Glenn very early to remind him that he had to go three hundred miles in this snowstorm to play a one-nighter. So he was damn mad. He got up and started beating on everybody's door. Then he came to my room with a bellman who was carrying a big tray of ice and a bottle of booze. Glenn slapped me awake. Then he handed me the bottle of booze and said, 'Either you drink the booze or I give you the ice.'

"I just lay there drunk and helpless and said, 'Give me the ice, man.' And he poured it over me and stomped out. I was covered with ice, but after the night we had, it felt good."[7]

The Shribmans did so effective a job in getting the Band That Plays the Blues work in New England that its members voted him into their corporation as an owner. Red Norvo, one of those whom the Shribmans helped, told me that the Shribmans owned a large share of the Glenn Miller band, in consequence of their investment and efforts. "But Glenn cut them 'way down," Red said, "which I didn't think was fair."[8]

7

Woodchopper's Ball

Cy Shribman would urge Woody to get a girl singer. "He put it very nicely," Woody said. "He'd say, 'Get a blonde broad. It doesn't matter what she does. If she's got big tits, she'll make it.'" Tom Gerun had once called him in Chicago, saying, "Get a broad. You know. We don't care if she sings. Just get a sexy-looking broad."

"It's a very thankless profession, being a girl singer," Woody said in his characteristically dry fashion. And he was, in fact, interested in those who really could sing. In April, 1939, Mary Ann McCall, a nineteen-year-old singer who had been with Tommy Dorsey and Charlie Barnet, joined the Herman group. She stayed seven months. Her talent had not matured, but Woody had an uncanny flair for detecting ability early.

On April 12, 1939, the band went into the studio and recorded four tunes, including *Blues Downstairs* and *Woodchopper's Ball*, both of which are listed in catalogues as compositions by Joe Bishop, the latter a collaboration with Woody. Actually *Woodchopper's Ball* was a head arrangement on a blues pattern that the band had developed at the Roseland Ballroom, its simple one-note theme a riff by the brass section behind one of the soloists. Bishop organized it and put it on paper.

The title was not a play on Woody's name. On the contrary, from the title of the tune he became known as the Woodchopper. Bassist Walt Yoder had seen a woodchopping contest at the Sportsmen's Show in Boston Garden and suggested the title. The tune was thrown into the record date at the last minute. The band found a good tempo for it at the session, and the record was issued without thought to its possible commercial success. The notes to the reissue of some of the Decca recordings of that period (GRP Records) give the date as May 24, 1939; Woody said it was April 12.

Woodchopper's Ball was released with *Big Wig in the Wigwam*, vocal by Mary Ann McCall, on the other side. The thirty-one-year-old English professor Marshall Stearns, an avid jazz collector and contributor to magazines, reviewed the record in the July issue of a magazine called *Tempo*. He wrote:

> Woody Herman has finally hit the wax with what it takes. *Woodchopper's Ball* and *Big Wig in the Wigwam* and *Blues Upstairs* and *Blues Downstairs* make history on Decca. *Woodchopper's* cops the tops with straightforward swing that is fresh and mellow with a wacky tenor solo by Saxie Mansfield who felt sultry, and a gang of fine clarinet and trumpet. Wood takes a dog-eared vocal on *Blues Upstairs* after a fine guitar passage and the band makes a simple series of riffs swing on out. This band doesn't need plugs from this column. Man, they're on their way!

But *Woodchopper's Ball* was not an immediate hit.

"Decca had [a] good system, which would be wonderful if somebody picked up on it today," Woody said. "If they thought a thing had something but never really got off to a flying start, they wouldn't just discard it. Every once in a while they would try it again. And that's what happened with *Woodchopper's Ball*. It must have been out three different times. And over a period of several years, it became a giant."

Ultimately the record sold 5 million copies, becoming the biggest hit of Woody's career. And it followed Woody forever after. In time he came to hate it, but it was requested so often that he gradually became resigned to it, playing it almost every night for the rest of his life. It was not, however, a hit with ballroom owners, who still demanded a softer and more commercial dance music. Woody wanted to take the band more in directions being pursued by Duke Ellington, Count Basie, and Benny Goodman. At the Trianon Ballroom in Boston, the management told him firmly not to play *Woodchopper's Ball*, and during a hotel rooftop engagement in Texas, Woody recalled, the management sent him a note saying, "Would you please stop playing that nigger music?"

Glenn Miller, Woody's colleague of the outer offices, had organized a second band in 1938. It began to record for Bluebird, RCA Victor's lower-priced popular music label, but the records did not sell well. On March 7, 1939, the band opened at Frank Dailey's Meadowbrook with a four-week contract, which was extended to seven after their first week. On Wednesday, May 17, the band opened at the Glen Island Casino, where it would remain until August 24. Both locations had what the trade called "a wire," meaning a network radio linkup that offered national exposure by means of these "remote" broadcasts. A ballroom paid a hundred dollars a week for a wire; the band members got three dollars each per broadcast on top of their regular pay.[1]

Their power can be seen in the fact that by the middle of that summer of 1939, the Miller band had a national following, and in the autumn of that year, when it left the Glen Island Casino to begin broadcasting regularly for Chesterfield cigarettes, it had become one of the most popular bands of the whole Swing Era.

Miller did not play out the full summer at the Glen Island Casino. He asked permission to leave a week early, to take advantage of the band's newfound popularity by going on a road tour. The management booked the Band That Plays the Blues to replace Miller. As Woody put it, it was "following the World War to follow Glenn." One night the place was packed to capacity, with fans standing in lines outside, waiting to get in. The next night, when Woody opened, the place was all but deserted. "It was pretty heart-breaking," he said later. But having endured those long waits in offices with Miller, he did not begrudge his colleague this sudden success. Woody and his partners went on, sustained by courage and a collective sense of humor.

Though Woody's 1945 band became known as the First Herd, the term actually dates from August, 1939, when it was used in *Metronome* by the magazine's editor, George T. Simon, a drummer manqué who was of the Simon and Schuster publishing family. Simon used the word "Herd" in a headline and in the story.

Three months after that mention, the band went into the Famous Door on 52nd Street—following Charlie Barnet, according to Woody's later recollection. He said in 1940, however, that they had followed Count Basie.

The significance of the engagement was its publicity value, for the money wasn't very good. Among Woody's friends by now were the young songwriters Saul Chaplin and Sammy Cahn, whose careers were being managed by yet another young man, Lou Levy, later the president of Leeds Music, an important publishing house. Cahn would borrow money from Levy to lend to the band for gasoline to get to its engagements, and in gratitude Woody assigned the publishing rights to *Woodchopper's Ball* and some other tunes to Lou Levy, whose company became a substantial power in music publishing. Levy ultimately sold his publishing interests to MCA, the booking agency that grew into one of the largest entertainment conglomerates in the world. MCA still owns those tunes, as well as Decca Records and thus all the early Herman masters.

The band's trumpet section now numbered three. In September, 1939, Clarence Willard left it, to be replaced by Carroll (Cappy) Lewis, born May 18, 1917, in Brillion, Wisconsin, a town fifty or sixty miles north of Milwaukee. One of his idols was yet another Wisconsin native, Bunny Berigan. Lewis had worked for violinist and arranger Nick Harper, who'd been with the Band That Plays the Blues, but Woody first heard about Lewis from Ray Sherman.

Ray said, "I heard him at the Wisconsin Roof. They had a ballroom up there. Cappy played in a band up there. The fiddle player, Nick Harper, had the band. I told Woody about Cappy, and then a couple of other guys told him. When Woody'd need somebody, he'd say, 'Do you know somebody?' He trusted me. I don't know why. Cappy could play any style. He played mouth organ too."[2]

Lewis played cornet at the time, an instrument he liked—as do many trumpet players—for its soft, warm tone, but he soon found that with the Herman band he needed the greater power and penetration, and so like Louis Armstrong and others before him, he switched instruments. When I at last met Cappy Lewis, in 1991, he had been slowed by a stroke and spoke to me through an anguish of impaired speech, periodically saying "God damn!" when he was unable to articulate a memory. But even then, with his ability to walk impaired, he was a tall, handsome, rather elegant man with a sweet, gentle, and open manner, and those who were in the band with him always remembered him that way. He was an extraordinary trumpet player who never got the full recognition he deserved, except from musicians.

The band had also taken on a new trombonist, Toby Tyler, who wrote for the band something called, for no known reason, *Blues on Parade*, derived from Rossini's *Stabat Mater*. It was recorded September 13, 1939, with Cappy Lewis playing the fiery trumpet. It was the month German armies rolled into Poland. Woody's roots were in both countries.

The original shareholders still owned the band; new members were on salary. When time came to divide the spoils, Lewis remembered, there was a certain amount of friction. But the difference was not enough to spoil the spirit of the band, which was gradually growing more distinctive. The problems of running a co-operative were mentioned in passing in a *Down*

Beat story by Dave Dexter Jr., printed in the January 15, 1940, issue. The story was yet another assertion that the Woody Herman band at last had arrived. Dexter wrote:

> Woody Herman has been over a tough road. For years he went along blowing his head off, singing, leading and dancing on bandstands throughout the land. Nothing happened. The trade papers occasionally printed a rave, and some of the critics who weren't always on a Basie-Ellington-Goodman kick often mentioned Woody's work, but the public never let on. It was too busy with other bands to see Herman's gang. Part of the trouble, you are convinced, was the band itself. Every man in it is a part owner and you recall how Woody's group messed up several good bookings, record dates and other opportunities because everyone in the band had to vote on each proposition instead of letting Woody spiel a fast "yes" or "no" and get things started.
>
> But tough breaks are just that. And they can't go on forever, not if a band has the stuff, and the guts to stick together until the break hits it and the gravy train pulls into sight. Which is exactly what happened to Woody, you recall, about a month ago.
>
> Things are different today. Not that Woody and his boys are set, or are in the plum dough yet, but you know as well as they do that 1940 will be their year. Those dates in Boston and at the Famous Door panned out right, and radio carried the Herman music everywhere.

Dexter's story praised pianist Linehan, fluegelhorn player Bishop, and drummer Carlson, who played, he says, "with a sureness and lift that no other ofay in the business has today." It's curious to read that term now. "Ofay" was a black term for whites, adopted by whites eager to prove how inside they were with blacks. The theory of its etymology is that it is Pig Latin for "foe." It became quite common for a while but has disappeared completely; not even blacks, except older ones, now know what it means. In any case, this bit of journalistic optimism about the band's fortunes once again proved premature.

On April 18, 1940 (according to MCA archives), the band recorded its theme song, *Blue Prelude*, with a vocal by Woody. It would not long remain the band's theme, for ASCAP, the American Society of Composers, Authors, and Publishers, after a strained effort to negotiate a higher pay rate from the broadcasting industry, instituted what amounted to a strike: it refused to allow any ASCAP songs to be played on radio, which in effect meant the entire American song repertoire, except songs whose copyrights had expired, leaving them in what is known in law as the public domain. In other words, nobody owned them. The broadcasting industry, in retaliation, set up its own licensing agency, Broadcast Music Incorporated (BMI), a move that in the opinion of many industry observers contributed to if it did not begin the decline of American popular music.

One of the ban's immediate effects was that many bands changed their theme songs, since they wanted and needed identifying exposure on radio. *Blue Prelude* was registered with ASCAP, since Joe Bishop and Gordon Jenkins were members. To replace it, Bishop quickly wrote a new one, based on a piece already in the book, *Casbah Blues*, calling it *Blue Flame*. Curiously, both the Decca and Columbia record-label credits identify it as the work of James (Jiggs) Noble, another of the band's arrangers, but Woody attested that the piece was Bishop's, and it is so identified in the logging department at ASCAP. A possible explanation is that Bishop, as an ASCAP member, could not at the time claim the work as his own, and Noble, who was not an ASCAP member, was perhaps assigned temporary credit for it so that it could be played on radio as a non-ASCAP composition. The record companies perpetuate the evasion to this day. In any case, *Blue Flame* would remain Woody's theme, earning royalties for Bishop for the rest of his life. Woody recorded it for the first time on March 11, 1941.

The band had previously filmed a musical short for Warner Brothers in Brooklyn, and in July, 1941, the band went to Los Angeles to appear in a Universal picture called *What's Cookin'*? "It was a typical wartime musical," Woody said. "The Andrews Sisters were in it. Donald O'Connor was making his comeback from being a child performer; he was now a teenager." It was a film of such towering insignificance that it isn't even listed in the thick guides to those movies that turn up on television at eldritch hours of the night.

In August, 1941, the band recorded *Woodsheddin' with Woody*. The band was playing the Palladium, and Charlotte was in the last phase of pregnancy. Though they maintained their apartment in Jackson Heights on Long Island, they had taken a house in Los Angeles in July. Indeed, her doctor said the baby was overdue. Friends and dancers at the Palladium kept asking Woody about Charlotte, and he would tell them, "No, the baby isn't here yet."

One night he went home and fixed a drink. Charlotte told him the pains were coming about fifteen minutes apart. Woody called the doctor, who advised him to get some sleep and call back when the spasms were closer together. When at last they were, Woody frantically drove Charlotte to the hospital. As he waited through a long labor, a drunk in the waiting room, as in a bad scene in a movie, said, "What're you worrying about? This is my eighth."

Woody's lawyer invited him to come over to his place, a few blocks from the hospital, to get a little sleep. Hardly had he arrived when Charlotte's mother telephoned to say, "Don't you want to see your baby?"[3]

She was born September 3, 1941, at Cedars of Lebanon Hospital, and given the name Ingrid after her grandmother, Inga, and in order not to slight Woody's mother, they gave her the second name Myrtle. "That shows their devotion to their parents," Ingrid said, "that they would saddle their child with such a ridiculous name. For years I wouldn't even tell anyone my middle name."[4] *Down Beat* ran a picture of the three of them, saying she was "the Hermans' first child." Like Woody and Charlotte, she was destined to be an only child, and Woody would say in later years that the boys he had were the kids who passed through his bands.

In September, the band went back into the studio to record two songs by Harold Arlen and Johnny Mercer, both written for the film *Blues in the Night*, starring Richard Whorf, Betty Field, and Priscilla Lane—one of Hollywood's periodic peculiar and gauche attempts at portraying jazz musicians. The first piece recorded was a production number on *This Time the Dream's on Me*, which was expected to be the hit song from the picture. Arlen attended the recording session and expressed his pleasure at the performance, which must have given Woody a quiet satisfaction, since he always said Arlen's singing was a big influence on his own. Toward the end of the session, the band recorded *Blues in the Night*, with a vocal by Woody. It would turn out to be a hit for the band.

Later that month Woody was admitted to Cedars of Lebanon Hospital in Los Angeles for surgery to correct a hernia. A story in *Down Beat* makes clear that the band was now firmly known as the Herman Herd, well before the so-called First Herd. George Simon's sobriquet had stuck.

> Herman Herd rests at home as Woody rests in hospital, following an operation September 21 . . . Most of the fellows have gone home. Not to return to the Herd, however, are trumpeter Steady Nelson, who has gone back to Houston, and vocalist Muriel Lane. Newcomers are trumpeter George Seaberg and songstress Carolyn Grey, both of whom Woody picked up in San Francisco.

Just that closely did *Down Beat* monitor the changes of personnel in the name bands. Grey was lucky to have the magazine refer to her as a songstress rather than as a chirp or a canary. The magazine was noted in those days for flamboyance and a kind of sophomoric irreverence.

The next month, Woody did something that was virtually unprecedented. Linda Dahl, in a book titled *Stormy Weather*, chronicles the taboo

against women musicians—as opposed to singers—in jazz. Though pianists Lil Hardin Armstrong and Mary Lou Williams had managed to have
careers, the wall maintained against women in jazz was almost impenetra-
ble. Woody broke the taboo. In October, 1941, Woody hired the twenty-
two-year-old trumpeter Billie Rogers, born in Missoula, Montana, and
brought up in the state of Washington. She had then played in vaudeville
and dance bands. She would stay with Woody two years, carrying her full
share of the section work and playing some very fine solos. The musicians
did not at first make it easy for her. One trumpet player expressed embarrassment at being seen on a bandstand with a woman and tendered his
resignation. Woody let him go. Eventually the musicians got used to her,
but Rogers always gave Woody credit for courage in hiring her and opening
the way for other women to follow. Today the prejudice against women in
jazz has diminished but not vanished.

Thirty-odd years later, Woody still talked of her with admiration. He told
trumpeter Nelson Hatt that when the band was playing five or six theater
shows a day, she was the only one who could still play on the last one. The
other guys, he said, were too loaded or had been blown out.

Hatt asked: "Was she any good?"

Woody said, "Hell yes! She'd be playing lead by the end of the day."

▼   ▼   ▼

In the meantime, events in Europe grew constantly more ominous, and it
became increasingly doubtful that the United States could stay out of the
war that had been raging for two years. It is often forgotten that a German
submarine torpedoed the USS *Kearney* in the Atlantic, killing eleven, and
on October 30—a little more than five weeks before Pearl Harbor—
another German sub actually sank the destroyer USS *Reuben James*, which
was on convoy duty west of Iceland. Seventy-six men were lost.

Artie Shaw had, like Glenn Miller, attained a success that still eluded
Woody, who by now was twenty-eight. Shaw had had several hit records,
including *Begin the Beguine* and *Stardust. Stardust* sold two million copies.
Shaw remembered that his band was playing a theater in Newport, Rhode
Island, when he was asked to make an announcement following the December 7 bombing of Pearl Harbor. He stepped up to the microphone and
told servicemen in the audience to report back to their bases. "It seemed
like half the audience got up and left," he said. And suddenly he realized
the nation had been mobilizing for some time. "With the world in flames,"
he said, "playing another chorus of *Stardust* seemed pretty pointless."[5]

Shaw went backstage and gave all his musicians two weeks' notice, and early in 1942, he joined the navy and organized a band to entertain troops. Glenn Miller joined the Army Air Corps and similarly formed a band, made up of some of the finest musicians the big-band era had produced. Sam Donahue, an outstanding saxophonist, was drafted and became a member of Shaw's navy band, along with drummer Dave Tough. The Band That Plays the Blues, too, began to lose musicians as the draft notices arrived, though Woody was exempted because of a second hernia. Bassist Walt Yoder and trumpeter Chuck Peterson got their calls, and in 1943 trombonist Neal Reid went into the Marine Corps.

The band boy also was called up, and Woody pressed his young friend Ray Sherman into his job. Ray traveled with the band, supervising the setup each night and breaking it down after the job, making sure the music stands and music were not lost. "Then I was drafted too," Ray said.

Woody had been generous in giving raises to Cappy Lewis, but in 1943 Cappy hit him for a large one. He told Woody that Tommy Dorsey had offered him fifty dollars a week more than his current salary. Woody said, "Join Tommy then." But Lewis didn't get the chance to go with Dorsey; he got drafted.

Woody's press-agent friend Howie Richmond also got his draft notice. Howie said, "I went into the Signal Corps and then the Army Air Corps in celestial navigation, and I became an instructor. I saw the band at the Sherman in Chicago, and they were getting hot. By then I felt part of the family." The feeling was one that Woody somehow instilled in everyone who ever worked for him.

The band traveled to Hollywood to appear in another movie, *Wintertime*, starring Cesar Romero and the skating star Sonja Henie. It inevitably contained a scene with the band in sleighs wrapped in furs and heavy coats—after all, the Glenn Miller band had done just such a scene in *Sun Valley Serenade*, another film starring Henie.

In 1943 Woody and Charlotte, who had been dividing their residential time between the west and east coasts, took an apartment at the Garden of Allah on Sunset Boulevard at Crescent Heights Avenue in Hollywood. Built twenty-two years earlier, its name reflecting the American fascination with things seemingly alien and particularly Arabic in that age of Valentino, this complex of buildings—a group of "villas" around a large swimming pool—had a certain ersatz and by then fading exoticism. It had long been a favorite of celebrities passing through or newly arrived in Hollywood or temporarily homeless during spats with spouses or after divorces. Writers, actors, actresses, and other members of the unacknowledged world fraternity of gypsies, jugglers, and clowns were its primary patrons, and it was legendary for liaisons both *dangereuses* and otherwise, for drunken parties, and indeed for generalized debauchery. It was also very expensive. One of the friends Woody made there was the wit, writer, and occasional actor Robert Benchley. Also living there were Perry Como and a struggling young singer who worked part time in a defense plant, Frankie Laine.

"Charlotte was wonderful and mercurial," Woody said, "with a mad sense of humor that was sometimes sparked by jealousy." Woody and Charlotte, with Ingrid, who was then about three, spent three days at the home of friends in Malibu, then still a small community. It certainly was not the drab and crowded seaside slum for the rich that it is now. Still beautiful then, it had the vast expanse of the Pacific in front of it and unpopulated coastal mountains at its back. As they prepared to return to Hollywood, Woody thanked their hostess and made the mistake of kissing her.

He and Charlotte got into their car, an aging Cadillac, and started back to Hollywood. But a heavy fog rolled in, and Woody stopped. He got out of the car to wipe the windshield. Charlotte slipped into the driver's seat, floored the gas pedal, and left him there by the deserted highway. Woody sat down on the base of a lamp post and lit a cigarette. It was a long way to the nearest habitation in Santa Monica, and there wasn't a car in sight. It was probably forty miles to the Garden of Allah. Then, inexplicably, a taxi appeared out of the fog. Woody flagged it down. "It must have been like the appearance of a UFO," Ingrid said. "What amazes me is that he had the presence of mind to come up with an evil scheme to get to the Garden of Allah before my mother did." Woody paid the driver ten dollars to get him to the Garden of Allah in quick time. The cab reached its parking lot before Charlotte did. Woody paid the driver and went to the bar. "When my mother got there," Ingrid said, "she had to put me to bed. You know, I still remember it." Charlotte then went to the bar and was astounded to see Woody sitting there sipping a martini.

Once, Woody said, while the band was playing at the Sherman Hotel in Chicago, he and Charlotte stopped for a drink and a late meal at a nightclub on the Near North Side, as they say in Chicago. A woman approached Woody from behind, put her hands over his eyes, and said, "Hello, Woodsy!"

Charlotte began throwing things, glasses, ashtrays, anything that came to hand. She destroyed much of the liquor stock behind the bar and smashed a mirror. Woody, with an equanimity that would have done credit to Tom Gerun, sat quietly, sipping his drink, declining to be engaged in the fray. This let-it-slide detachment that Woody had was a remarkable quality that one day would be his downfall. Finally, he recounted, a heavy-set man whom they knew slightly said, "Charlotte, you're such a lovely gal; why are you doing this?"

Charlotte gave him a punch in the midriff that sank him to his knees.

For several years, Charlotte and Woody would live for six months or so in Jackson Heights, New York, and the rest of the time at the Garden of Allah in Los Angeles.

▼ ▼ ▼

The co-operative structure of the band had always been unsatisfactory to Woody, for all the *esprit de corps*. Every decision required a meeting—often in men's rooms, as he was fond of recalling. Even the wives of the musicians had something to say about many minor matters, such as travel arrangements.

"There was a certain tenor man who insisted that he should be blowing at all times," Woody said. "And we insisted he should be blowing very little. Finally, when we decided we had to make a change for the betterment of the band, we didn't know how to buy him out and give him his notice. Finally one guy came up with a brilliant idea. We would buy him a beautiful embossed shotgun because he dug things like this. We did and he was almost happy to leave to get the shotgun.

"That was Neal Reid's suggestion, and he was loaded with suggestions like this. We had guys like Neal Reid, who is six foot four or five, a handsome young man with a booming voice and less like a jazz musician, if you'd just met him, than anyone you would imagine.

"We had a guy who played tenor and baritone who later went into the real estate business. He lived down south for years and he had the sun-bleached blond hair and he was six-two-and-a-half and a typical playboy type, very casual, at ease with the world, a ladies' man.

"And having guys like this in the band when we arrived at a local joint, they always thought I was the band boy or something. I would have trouble getting in ballrooms and in theaters and in joints, because I always looked like a little creep . . . ."[6] Woody was five-foot-eight and weighed 130 pounds.

His lack of authority bothered Woody more and more. He wanted to be in command of his own band. He said, "As each member was drafted—I don't think anybody enlisted—I bought his stock in the band, and eventually I had all of it. I wanted to do something different with the band. I loved the voicings of the Duke Ellington band, and I got Dave Matthews to write for us." Matthews arranged *Four or Five Times, Do Nothin' Till You Hear from Me*, and *Perdido*, among other pieces, for the band.

"And I got Dizzy Gillespie to write for us," Woody said. "He wrote one piece called *Down Under* and another called *Swing Shift*. Dizzy also played with us for a short time. I think it was a week we did at the Apollo Theater."[7]

Woody was fond of saying in later years that he was so taken by Dizzy's writing that he urged him to give up the trumpet. "I'm glad he ignored me," Woody would say. And Dizzy in turn would say that Woody was the first person to pay him a hundred dollars for an arrangement.

Dizzy also wrote *Woody'n You* for the band. Woody didn't record it at the time, but finally did in 1979. *Down Under* was recorded July 24, 1942, seven months into U.S. participation in World War II and just before the recording ban, which began in August. Gillespie had met Charlie Parker in Kansas City in 1940, when Parker was already moving toward the radical harmonic and rhythmic style that would be known as bebop. But he was still comparatively unknown, even among musicians. *Down Under* is hot, fierce, and for its time, radical. The brass is hotter, the sax section darker and deeper. It presages the Woody Herman bands to come.

The personnel on that date included Chuck Peterson, George Seaberg, Billie Rogers, and Cappy Lewis, trumpets; Neal Reid, Tommy Farr, and Walter Nimms, trombones; Jimmy Horvath and Sam Rubinwich, alto saxophones; Mickey Folus and Pete Mondello, tenors; Skippy DeSair, baritone; Tommy Linehan, piano; Hy White, guitar; Walt Yoder, bass; and Frankie Carlson, drums. The brass section had grown to four, the trombones to three, the saxes to five. This is the configuration of the so-called First Herd.

Also contributing three charts to the band in 1942 was Gerald Wilson, a former Jimmie Lunceford sideman who was now in a navy band stationed in Chicago. One was titled *Spruce Juice*, and the other two, reflecting the state of war, *Terrific in the Pacific* and *Frantic in the Atlantic*. In September, 1942, saxophonists Folus and Rubinwich went into military service. In November, when the band was playing the Paramount in New York, pianist Linehan left the band, to be replaced by Jimmy Rowles, and was drafted the next June.

Woody used Ellington sidemen on sessions. "I had Johnny Hodges come in and do a couple of our record dates, and Ben Webster and a lot of other people," he said. "It was one of those periods with Duke's band where the boys were getting nervous. They were complaining that Duke was taking their backgrounds and making tunes out of them, and [there was] a lot of internal strife . . . . I would hear from them if I didn't call them about doing some record dates with us. And so we would add them to the band.

"They knew what we were into, and they felt the band was trying something. And whether they agreed that what we were doing was the greatest or not, they also knew that there was some bread to be gotten, plus the fact that they wouldn't be asked to do something that was foreign to their nature musically.

"So I think it worked out very well. The very first person out of Duke's band that came with us had already left the band. That was Juan Tizol."[8]

The Band That Plays the Blues had lasted nine years. It had struggled for survival most of that time, and now it was finished. Thenceforth it would be the Woody Herman band, no questions asked, and though Woody was always the most tolerant of leaders, allowing his men tremendous latitude, the band nonetheless would reflect his thinking.

The turnover in personnel continued as one musician after another went into military service. Trumpeter Peterson was one of the draftees. In 1943, the trumpet section acquired Ray Wetzel and Nick (Travascio) Travis; the latter would become known as one of the great lead trumpet players in the history of jazz. Yet the band always sounded like Woody.

As Phil Wilson, who played trombone in one of the later Herds, put it:

"Nobody does what Woody does as well as he does. If we could only figure out what it is he does . . . ."

8

Birth of the Herd

The Swing Era cannot be dated precisely, since its roots go back to the Paul Whiteman band in the 1920s. It is generally considered to have lasted from the time of Benny Goodman's first big success in 1935 through to the late 1940s, a little more than ten years. Before Goodman, however, there were the Casa Loma orchestra, McKinney's Cotton Pickers, the Dorsey Brothers orchestra, and the bands of Duke Ellington, Bennie Moten, Jimmie Lunceford, Cab Calloway, and Fletcher Henderson. But Goodman set a national fashion, lofting the fortunes of those whose bands had existed before his was born, excepting that of Fletcher Henderson, who failed as a leader and became Goodman's most valuable arranger. Soon the booking agencies, slow at first to recognize the trend, were signing up seemingly anyone who could front a band that purported to "swing." Three sidemen from the Goodman band alone became successful bandleaders, vibraharpist-drummer Lionel Hampton, drummer Gene Krupa, and trumpeter Harry James. Trumpeter Sonny Dunham left the Casa Loma orchestra to form his own band.

Eventually there were scores of these bands making records, playing on radio, and touring North America, among them those of Georgie Auld, Charlie Barnet, Count Basie, Will Bradley, Les Brown, Benny Carter, Bob Chester, Larry Clinton, Bob Crosby, Sam Donahue, Tommy Dorsey, Jimmy Dorsey, Jan Garber, Glen Gray, Erskine Hawkins, Earl Hines, Hal Kemp, Stan Kenton, Ray McKinley, Lucky Millinder, Teddy Powell, Boyd Raeburn, Alvino Rey, Jan Savitt, Artie Shaw, Bobby Sherwood, Claude Thornhill,

Jerry Wald, and Chick Webb, all of which were of what we might call the jazz persuasion and featured excellent soloists. Then there were what the hip (in those days hep) fans called the "sweet" bands, despised by the jazz fans as "corny," a term reputedly coined by Bix Beiderbecke to suggest the backward and bucolic. These included Blue Barron, Gray Gordon, Eddy Duchin, Shep Fields, Freddy Martin, Vaughn Monroe, Dick Stabile, Tommy Tucker, Horace Heidt, Richard Himber, Art Kassel, Wayne King, Johnny Long, and Lawrence Welk.

Guy Lombardo repeatedly won the *Down Beat* readers' poll in the King of Corn category. This was a little unfair. What the Lombardo orchestra was until its leader's death was a museum piece, an unaltered 1920s tuba-bass dance band, quite good at what it did and admired by such unlikely persons as Louis Armstrong and Gerry Mulligan. Usually included in the corn category were the orchestras of Kay Kyser, Sammy Kaye, and Ozzie Nelson, though all three were capable of playing creditable big-band jazz, and the Nelson orchestra was a very good band, again one that Mulligan admires. Trombonist Russ Morgan led what was considered one of the corny bands, and few fans realized he had been a pioneering jazz arranger.

The "big-band era," probably a better term than "swing era," since a lot of successful bands not only didn't swing but didn't even aspire to, reached its peak during World War II, despite the problems bandleaders had in finding personnel when so many young musicians were in military service. As we have noted, the fortunes of the bandleaders and their sidemen and singers were followed avidly in *Down Beat* and *Metronome*, but even the lay press got into it when the sequential polygamy of Artie Shaw and Charlie Barnet made news, along with the marriages of Harry James to actress Betty Grable and of Woody's old friend Phil Harris to Alice Faye. These bandleaders were not only treated as movie stars, but sometimes were movie stars—Tommy Dorsey, Artie Shaw, Glenn Miller, Harry James, and Woody among them—appearing in feature films. Almost all of them were at least in short subjects. In some cases, the movies were about the band business, including *Second Chorus*, in which Shaw uncomfortably portrayed a bandleader named Artie Shaw, and *Orchestra Wives*, in which the Miller band was prominently featured.

The jazz bands were substantially supported by dedicated young dancers referred to condescendingly if not contemptuously as jitterbugs. Shaw, whose aspirations to high culture were never disguised, particularly despised them, and said so publicly. Newsreels of the period—the movie theaters each week featured short news films, precursors of television news broadcasts—from time to time would show the gyrations of the participants in dance contests. There was a patronizing tone about these observations, particularly when they showed black dancers in Harlem, as if the camera and commentator were examining the rites of a primitive tribe. The inference was inescapable. But the best of these dancers were remarkable, and their athleticism—the men spinning the women at arm's length, throwing them into the air and catching them or slinging them under their legs and over their shoulders, the gyrations wild but controlled—was imaginative and skilled. Combining elements of gymnastics and ballet, this kind of dance was also risky, and we can only imagine how many sprained shoulders and broken ankles were suffered when dancers botched some of their most hazardous maneuvers. Today only a handful of trained professional dancers can do what seemingly half the adolescent populace of North America did as a matter of course in the 1940s.

In his biography *Lorenz Hart*, Frederick Nolan writes that in the years immediately before World War II, the United States "was big-band swing mad." He continued:

And Manhattan! You could hardly walk a block without seeing one of the famous names: Benny Goodman, the man who started it all, playing his own brand of hard-driving swing in the Madhattan Room of the Hotel Pennsylvania on Seventh Avenue at 33rd; Jimmy Dorsey at the Terrace Room of the Hotel New Yorker, Eighth and 34th; Artie Shaw at the Blue Room of the Hotel Lincoln, Eighth and 44th; Red Norvo at the Palm Room of the Commodore, Lexington and 42nd; saccharin-smooth Guy Lombardo at the Roosevelt Grill, Madison and 45th; Les Brown and His Band of Renown at the Edison's Green Room on West 47th; Bob Crosby and his Bobcats, with their forceful Dixieland, at the Lexington on 48th.

  And the ballrooms: Woody Herman at Roseland, 51st and Broadway; Chick Webb stompin' at the Savoy, Lenox and 140th; Duke Ellington at the Cotton Club, which had moved south from Harlem into Times Square. And movie show-houses like the Paramount, standing on the Seventh Avenue site of what had once between Shanley's Restaurant between 43rd and 44th streets, where you could hear Tommy Dorsey, or Loew's State at Broadway and 45th, where Jimmie Lunceford was playing his relaxed brand of swing, or the Strand two blocks up for Latin music by Xavier Cugat.

Nostalgic fans will tell you that the jazz connoisseurs crowded close to the bandstand to listen with enraptured concentration to the bands and their soloists, while the superficial admirers danced in the back of the ballroom, but the division was not that strict. Some fans alternated the two activities. Nor was the line clear between the "sweet" and the "swing"

bands. All bands played for dancers, including those of Duke Ellington and
Count Basie, and Basie, who probably never gave a thought to whether jazz
was an art form, was considered something of a genius for his anticipation
of what dancers desired. Even some of the "sweet" bands allowed space for
improvised solos. The Les Brown band, generally considered a dance band,
featured intelligent and subtle arrangements by writers such as Ben
Homer and Frank Comstock and some first-rate jazz soloists.

And so they traveled, platoons of musical gypsies, unpacking their instruments and music stands and setting up camp in hotel ballrooms in the
cities or in the open-air pavilions of small towns and lakeside and riverside
amusement parks, even in armories, churches, and skating rinks, bringing
evenings of glamour, romanticism, and excitement to audiences, and then
packing up and piling into cars or buses at evening's end to travel the two-
lane highways of America for yet another in a string of jobs. It must have
been a lonely life, but I have never met a musician who regretted having
lived it. These men were musical pioneers, as were a few women, like
trumpeter Billie Rogers and the vibraharpist Marjorie Hyams, both of
whom played in the Herman band.

Once upon a time it was doubted that track athletes would ever run a
four-minute mile. Now it is so routine that one has to be able to do it even
to qualify for some events. Thus it was with brass and saxophone playing in
those dance bands. Trumpet and trombone players, particularly lead players, were called on to play sustained difficult material and to keep it up for
hours on end. No symphony woodwind players have ever been required to
show the kind of endurance a jazz or dance band demands of saxophone
players. This was exploratory music, and Tommy Dorsey, for one, altered
the tessitura of trombone forever; now even some symphony players have
that kind of technique. Louis Armstrong irreversibly altered trumpet playing, but many symphony players even now cannot do what Harry James,
Dizzy Gillespie, and Maynard Ferguson established as norms for that instrument. Symphony trumpet players are not called on to produce the
sustained evening-long power of the great lead trumpet players such as the
late Conrad Gozzo, or to play the high notes routinely called for by jazz
arrangers, notes once considered off the top of the instrument. Harry
James with Goodman pushed the instrument higher than it had been
before.

The form of the orchestra by then had been defined. In later years some
writers would add French horns—Claude Thornhill was the first to do
this—and expect the saxophone players to double flutes or other woodwinds. But the basic form had been set, a classic musical unit, like the

string quartet or the symphony orchestra, and Woody had built the Band
That Plays the Blues up to that configuration as it entered its last days to
create the first true Woody Herman band. He also, before the end of those
days with Decca, hired a young arranger named Ralph Burns.

Burns was born in Newton, Massachusetts, on June 29, 1922, of Irish
descent. The family's name was originally Byrnes, but such was the prejudice against the Irish that his grandfather changed it to the Scottish spelling. Ralph's family was, and for that matter still is, in real estate. "I was the
black sheep," he said. He began playing club dates with older musicians, at
which time he discovered marijuana. "That was the time when only musicians smoked grass," Ralph said. "But nobody else in the high school did.
The high schools were clean." Ralph attended Newton High School, another of whose students was Serge Chaloff. "I knew him in high school,
but I never used to pay any attention to him then, because he was kind of
like a nutty kid," Ralph said.

Ralph attended the New England Conservatory but, perhaps more significantly, he studied piano with Margaret Chaloff, Serge's mother. One of
those "classical" musicians who have had a significant but unsung influence on jazz, she trained a lot of excellent pianists, including—after
Ralph's time—Michael Renzi, Steve Kuhn, and Dave Mackay. A charac-
teristic of all her former students is a warm, golden tone. Kuhn says that a
lot of established major jazz pianists would consult her when they passed
through Boston. "She was wonderful," Ralph said. "I loved her. She was a
great teacher and a wonderful woman, a lot of fun."

Ralph left the Conservatory after only a year to play in a band led by a
young man named Nick Jerret, whose real name was Bertocci. He had a
sister, Chiarina Francesca Bertocci, who had changed it to Frances Wayne.
Later, when she was with Woody, a critic wrote of her "sultry" voice.
Frances didn't have a sultry voice, she had an Italian voice. There are
national characteristics in some voices, as there are in shape of head and
hair color. There are Japanese voices, which are high and light, and African
voices, which are often soft and airy, like Nat Cole's, and there are Italian voices, warmly woody or sandy-textured, like those of Anne Bancroft,
Brenda Vaccaro, Peter Rodino, Aldo Ray, Julius LaRosa, Frank Sinatra,
and Tony Bennett. Frances Wayne had one of those voices. It was the gift
of nature and genetics.

In April, 1993, Ralph—by now a strikingly handsome man with a full
head of white hair, a white mustache, and dark-rimmed glasses—recalled
those early days, saying: "We had a job in the Mayfair nightclub in Boston,
which was the big nightclub then. We had six pieces, and Frances was the

singer. I moved in with her family. They lived in Somerville. I loved that family. They were like my own family. I was very close to all the brothers, Vinnie and Cosmo and little Louis and the mother and father. I had a wonderful time living there. Vinnie used to manage us.

"We went down to New York and auditioned at Kelly's Stables one weekend and got the job. I was eighteen, I believe. A week or so later we all took the bus down and started work. We were there off and on at least a year. We were the relief band, a little jazz band patterned after a John Kirby style, a bit more modern, I think. I started writing for that band. What a thing to be thrown in with! It was great. Art Tatum and his trio and Coleman Hawkins and his group and Thelma Carpenter. Wow! I just used to wait to get through work so I could sit and listen.

"They flew Nat Cole and his trio in from California, the King Cole Trio. Their first record had come out, *Straighten Up and Fly Right*. I'll never forget. Nat never *let* me forget. He was a wonderful guy. There were two separate unions in New York. They made thirty-two dollars a week, the black union scale. We were white, so we made thirty-five dollars a week. After he was a big star, Nat would see me and yell across the street, 'Hey, Ralph, I remember when!'"

The job at Kelly's Stables was intermittent. When Ralph wasn't working there, he'd pick up jobs along Fifty-second Street. One of these was with Red Norvo.

Ralph said, "Frances Wayne went with Charlie Barnet. Charlie needed a piano player and she got me the job. That's when I started writing for big bands. After that I went with Red Norvo. This was World War II. Red got together a group. We were going to go overseas and play for the troops. We never went.

"Frances then went with Woody. In those days the big bands used to trade off musicians. Chubby Jackson was with Charlie Barnet. Woody offered Chubby a job. Dave Matthews, who wrote Duke Ellington style arrangements for Charlie Barnet, wrote some for Woody. Woody wanted to change the sound of his band. So Frances and Chubby said, 'Why don't you get Ralph? He writes and he plays piano.' On their recommendation, Woody called me up, and I was hired."[1]

Ralph, a slim and sensitive-looking young man when he first wrote for Woody, became an essential element in the evolution of what came to be known, accurately or not, as the First Herd, for a series of brilliant arrangements of popular songs and original compositions, most of which were to remain in the band's book permanently.

Woody said, "I was constantly seeking other colors, you know, as to what it could be and still be able to get a good swinging thing going. And that's why in those years I guess we were starting to use the sound of vibes, clarinet, guitar, and piano. And Ralph had the great ability of writing for these odd instrumentations—odd at the time—and making it happen . . . . Ralph was heavily influenced by Sweetpea . . ."—the nickname of Duke Ellington's arranger and sometime co-composer Billy Strayhorn—". . . and Duke, so we were all shooting for the same thing. We didn't want to be like Duke, but we sure wanted to be good like him. Charlie Barnet . . . did an actual copy of Duke's music, and that to me would have been very distasteful and dishonoring a great man and a great group of musicians. But what we did was try to capture the feeling, warmth, and enthusiasm, and if we could outswing Duke, then we'd figure we'd won the game."[2]

Once Woody invited Ellington over to his house. Duke said he could come for an hour or so. Woody remembered that he liked ice cream and served him some. Ellington stayed for two days of long, warm conversations. Indeed, Woody maintained friendships with most of the other bandleaders, including Guy Lombardo, and commanded the admiration of apparently all of them. "What a wonderful band he had!" Les Brown said as we reminisced about Woody in March, 1993.

Woody was fond of saying "I'm just an editor," as if this were not a singular and excellent ability in itself. "I concern myself with being a fair editor. I may take letter B and put it where letter A is and put letter C somewhere else. And I may change solos, because it will suit that particular chart better.

"The reason I got that, in the early days, was Ralph, who I thought was one of the greatest talents of all, ever. And the first chart he brought in to me, which was about 1944, was *I've Got the World on a String*." (Woody was not quite right about that, since Burns had already written for the Decca band.) "Ralph said, 'Here's this thing I made for you to sing.' It was a tune that I liked and used to sing anyway. Ralph said, 'If there's anything you don't like or anything you feel could be changed, go right ahead' He said, 'I've done the best I can, but if you can make it better, great.' I didn't even touch that one, nor did I very often with Ralph, but it gave me the courage so that if I could make something better—mostly by pacing—I would do it. Ralph had given me this freedom to do that, and if *he* did that, then I believed I could do it as well as anyone else. It was Ralph who encouraged me, and he was much younger than I."[3]

Ralph had never heard that comment of Woody's when I quoted it to him. He laughed and said: "Because I didn't complain." Then he added,

"Woody's big thing was simplicity. As a writer, you'd get carried away. I used to make things complicated and Woody would say, 'Let's simplify it.' And it came out better. I didn't get peeved."[4]

▼   ▼   ▼

Woody began picking up players who for one reason or another felt they were not being fully utilized in other bands, particularly Barnet's.

Willard Palmer Harris, called Bill Harris, was born in Philadelphia on October 28, 1916, and played piano, tenor saxophone, and trumpet before taking up trombone. He had traveled with Gene Krupa, Ray McKinley, Bob Chester, Benny Goodman, and then Charlie Barnet before joining Woody in 1944. He was a dramatic player who could go from soft, lyrical utterance to sudden brassy bursts. He was an extremely good technician with a vibrato that was all his own. He was a notorious practical joker whose temperament was not at all like his bespectacled, professorial mien. His clowning was notorious, and he had no hesitation about dropping his pants to get a laugh or express disapproval of something. Every trombonist who later played with Woody knew that he was being measured against Bill Harris.

Vido Musso, born in Carrini, Sicily, on January 13, 1913, and brought up in Providence, Rhode Island, was in the Herman sax section during the band's transitional period, 1942-43, playing in a rough-and-ready powerful style.

Woody replaced him with a young man who would last only two weeks—and then would re-enter the story much later in Woody's life. Leonard Garment played tenor saxophone in the band led by Henry Jerome in New York. Among the other young players was Johnny Mandel on bass trumpet and trombone, Al Cohn on tenor, and Gene DiNovi on piano. Another of the tenor players was Alan Greenspan, who became an economist and chairman of the Federal Reserve Board.

The story about Garment's sojourn with Woody has been distorted and deserves to be clarified. In 1994, Garment recalled: "I was playing with Henry Jerome at the Lookout House in Covington, Kentucky. Across the river in Cincinnati, at the RKO Albee, Woody Herman was playing. They had movies and a stage show, like the Paramount. It was before the First Herd. Well, let's say it was the First Herd in its third trimester. A lot of the guys were already with the band. They came out to the Lookout House. There was a session after hours. I played and had one of the better nights I've had in my whole life. Chubby Jackson took my name.

"Some weeks later, Vido Musso was drafted. They needed a saxophonist to fill in. Chubby Jackson called me. When he had heard me play some months earlier, it was sort of imitation Ben Webster. What had happened in between is that I had studiously applied myself to becoming one of eight million Lester Young impersonators. I came with the band, and it was an inappropriate style for the band and for the audience. In Providence, Rhode Island, they had a sign out front saying 'Featuring Vido Musso.' Vido Musso was a son of Providence. Instead, here's this pale-faced boy. I got up to play, my saxophone was broken and the neck squeaked, and there was a lot of yelling and booing. It was a total horror story.

"But it was great sitting in with that band. I made a very good friendship with Billy Bauer. It was a wonderful band. But I was just not good. I was lousy, I was disappointed, but I was with the band about two weeks, and played the arrangements, and it was a great moment. My public zenith and private nadir."

Woody let him go, apparently as softly as possible, saying he didn't need yet another Lester Young disciple. "I was supposed to join Teddy Powell's band, but I got drafted," Garment said. "That was the summer of 1944. I remained friends with Al Cohn all his life, and I'm still friends with Johnny Mandel."[5]

At the end of the war, Garment became an attorney. One day he would be very well known. He would become White House counsel to President Richard M. Nixon. He has, I think it should be noted in passing, a soaring, comprehensive, kind, forgiving, and humane vision of life.

Garment's brief sojourn with the band falls between the tenures of Vido Musso and Flip Phillips. Joseph Edward Filipelli was one of many Italian jazzmen to Anglicize their names, in his case to Flip Phillips. Phillips was born in Brooklyn, New York, on February 26, 1915. He was in the Russ Morgan band when Woody approached him and reluctant to leave it. For one thing, commercial or square band or not, the Morgan band represented security.

"Russ liked me and I liked Russ." Flip told me in October, 1994, when he was seventy-nine and still playing superbly, indeed perhaps better than ever before. "I've reached the age where I don't buy green bananas," he said, laughing. And then: "Woody tried to get me away from Russ. I said, 'Well jeez, I don't know.' I didn't want to leave town. Woody said, 'I want to write the book around you.' Which he *did*, at the beginning. We had nothing in the book. We had things like *Who Dat Up Dere?* and *Golden Wedding*. Woody said, 'Do you speak Italian?' I said, 'Sure I speak Italian.' He said, 'Say something in Italian.' I said, 'Vido Musso.' "[6]

Woody's blandishments prevailed and Flip left Morgan. This corporate raiding went on constantly in the band business, and Woody was good at it and ruthless about getting the men he wanted. It caused no resentment, and musicians bargained with their leaders on the grounds that someone else was after them anyway. Woody pillaged no band more than Charlie Barnet's, but they remained friends and Barnet was one of his admirers.

The transition period in the Herman band's history is not documented on record, because of the extraordinary obstinacy of James Caesar Petrillo, the obstreperous president of the American Federation of Musicians. Petrillo had commissioned Ben Selvin to make a study to determine whether the playing of records in jukeboxes and on radio was costing musicians jobs. Selvin was a professional who had conducted recording orchestras under his name and pseudonyms (a not uncommon practice then), had worked for the radio networks, and had also been a recording executive. He read his report to the AFM convention of 1941. Selvin told the union that the record industry actually made work for musicians, paying them millions of dollars every year, and said that it would be "unwise, if at all possible, to curtail the industry when such large amounts are spent on musicians. There are remedies for the unemployment caused by the mechanization of music, but a knockout blow, which could not be delivered, is not the answer."

The convention's delegates gave Selvin a standing ovation. All the major bandleaders agreed with him. Petrillo ignored him, and by imperious edict halted all recording by musicians on August 1, 1942. Singers, however, were not bound by his ukase, and Columbia, RCA, and the little upstart label Capitol rushed them into the studio to make records with choral accompaniment. It served to make many of them stars, in competition with the bands with which many of them had sung. From that August until November, 1944, few instrumental records were made in the United States.[7]

One of the peculiar effects of the ban was that when Woody began to record again, it seemed as if the band had changed almost overnight. The process was actually more evolutionary. The band simply hadn't been recorded during the period when it was undergoing its development into the kind of band Woody wanted, one whose free spirit reflected his own. V discs (V for Victory) were made by the military for performance on the armed forces radio network, heard by servicemen around the world. There is quite a bit of documentation of the Herman band on those discs, material from which occasionally turns up on illicit labels, and a little on Decca, which settled the strike with the AFM before the other labels. The Joyce label has issued thirty of Woody's V discs.

During the period of the record ban, Woody was assimilating into the band elements of the new music eventually to be known as bebop. But just as the Herman band's evolution at that time went largely undocumented on records, so did that of bebop itself.

Bebop was in the air before it acquired its name—an unfortunate one in that its humorous connotation vitiated the seriousness and brilliance of this music in the collective mind of the public and, more seriously, writers on jazz who lacked theoretical understanding or knowledge of the general history of Western music. Most were well-meaning fans who all along mistook for original that which jazz musicians had adapted or merely rediscovered. (Before bebop, Jerome Kern's harmonic practices in "popular music" were far in advance of those of most jazz players.) The two salient figures in the bop movement were, as has been recounted endlessly, Charlie Parker and Dizzy Gillespie, with Thelonious Monk and Kenny Clarke heavily involved.

Jazz simply was not an academic music; on the contrary, it represented a rebellion against the academic and a restoration of the element of spontaneity—improvisation—that had gradually been filtered out of music in the evolution of nineteenth-century Romanticism. Jazz was a music of exuberant iconoclasm. That this witty music was also serious in no way diminished its inner spirit of fun. As Dizzy, expressing his caveat with the terms "jazz" and "serious" music as if they were mutually exclusive, once said, "Men have died for this music. You can't get no more serious than that." Woody, in turn, would in his later years remind young players that jazz was supposed to be fun. Given his own distinct sense of humor and of the incongruous, it was inevitable that Woody, never a minion of respectability even in his childhood, would be drawn to the developments of bebop.

When Charlie Parker was asked by an interviewer what the bebop players were rebelling against, he immediately denied that they were rebelling at all. He said that bebop was simply the direction in which he and Gillespie and others thought the music ought to go.

And in its single components, it was not in the least revolutionary. Frequent use of the flatted-fifth chord was one characteristic of bop. This is a dominant seventh chord in which the fifth has been lowered a half step. Any dominant seventh contains a tritone, known as the tonal tritone. The tritone divides the octave evenly and gives a feeling of instability; Leonard Bernstein used it extensively in the score to *West Side Story*: the first two notes of the song *Maria* are a tritone. Lowering the fifth of a dominant seventh chord establishes another tritone. So the flat-five chord contains two tritones, crossed like swords. It's a very interesting sound. Dizzy gave Monk credit for discovery of the chord. It was not, however, new; Stravinsky used it early in the century. And it wasn't new then.

Composer Hale Smith taught composition at the University of Connecticut, is considered one of the three or four major scholars of black music in America as well as a scholar of Bach, and once played piano with Dizzy. He said, "Even though it has become identified with bebop, that chord has been around. Bach used it. Mozart used it. The difference is that when Monk first came upon it, it was a sheer act of discovery. He didn't know about any of this other stuff. He came across this sound, and they saw this thing as an isolated entity." Another chord to which the boppers were partial was the minor seventh flat-five, which Monk aptly termed half-diminished. It is a very pretty, wistful chord, but it is, like the dominant seventh with a flat five, chromatic. But again, it was not new. Hale Smith said, "There's an example of it in the very first string quartet that Mozart wrote when he was a child. It is in the fourth measure."[8]

But the flat five was not used only as a chord form. Parker and Gillespie would use it as a melody note. Until bebop, harmonic practice in jazz was essentially that of the eighteenth century. Bop brought it up as far as the practice of, say, Wagner in the nineteenth century and not as far as Debussy and Ravel. That came later, with Bill Evans.

The more radical departure of bebop was rhythmic. Jazz phrases, before bebop, had been played in duple and compounds of duple meter: that is, two-, four-, and eight-bar phrases. Parker and Gillespie would play phrases of all sorts of odd lengths, such as five measures, or even five and a half. Again, this goes back as far as Mozart. The boppers further pushed the music into asymmetry by accenting notes in unexpected places. Finally, they moved away from the strong accentuation that earlier jazz had used in patterns of eighth-notes. The earlier players divided the beat into two uneven lengths, the first note long, the second brief, creating the DOO-ba-DOO-ba style of phrase. The boppers divided the beat more evenly, putting equal or almost equal stress on each note in an eighth-note pattern.

Further, they did this with dazzling bravura technique, exceeding what had gone before. This was unsettling to many fans of the music, as well as some of the critics, who got into an acrimonious battle over it, with the traditionalists being called moldy figs by those such as Leonard Feather who admired the new music. The British critic Stanley Dance still was deploring Parker and Gillespie a half century after the bebop "revolution."

By the summer of that year, the band had expanded to four trumpets, three trombones, and five saxophones, with Skippy DeSair playing baritone. The sound was already turning into that of what would be called the First Herd. But it was Dizzy Gillespie's chart on *Down Under* that marked the real departure. It was radical for its time, incorporating elements of what soon would be known as bebop.

Meanwhile, the musicians who were coming into the Herman band were also becoming Gillespie devotees. If they couldn't hear him on records, they could listen to him in nightclubs, including those on Fifty-second Street. Neal Hefti, Shorty Rogers, and Pete Candoli were paying open-eared attention. So was the young Conte Candoli, who would later become one of the most respected soloists in the Gillespie tradition.

Woody began recording for Columbia Records in February, 1945. The band, which would come to be known as the First Herd, had come a long way from the one that played the blues. Ellington and Basie had set their styles by 1940 and continued to work within them. The Herman band of 1945 was the most advanced, innovative, and adventurous of its time. Many admirers, musicians and laymen alike, also thought it was the best.

9

Wild Root

In June, 1944, while the band was playing a four-week engagement in the Panther Room of Chicago's Sherman Hotel, Woody signed a two-month contract for a series of Wednesday night broadcasts for Old Gold cigarettes. Operetta tenor Allan Jones, star of such musical films as *The Firefly* (1937) and *The Boys from Syracuse* (1940), would be featured with the band, though this was an improbable musical pairing, made more so by the presence of sportscaster Red Barber as master of ceremonies. These broadcasts, which began in July and ran for a half-hour starting at prime-time 8 p.m., made the band still more popular.

In the 1980s and '90s, cigarette manufacturers repeatedly denied that their advertising was designed to addict the young to tobacco. But the denial seems something less than honest when historically that is precisely their general policy. Cigarette companies were the primary sponsors of shows by the bands and singers of the 1940s because they had huge followings of young people. Camel cigarettes presented Benny Goodman on a show called *The Camel Caravan*. (There was in those days no Federal Communications Commission prohibition of the use of a product name in the title of a show. Hence Bing Crosby's show for Kraft foods was called *The Kraft Music Hall.*) Lucky Strike cigarettes sponsored *Your Hit Parade* and *Kay Kyser's Kollege of Musical Knowledge*, a quiz show featuring the Kyser band and singer Ginny Simms, whom Woody had discovered. Kool cigarettes sponsored Tommy Dorsey's radio show. Dorsey also did a show for Raleigh cigarettes. Artie Shaw was on the air for Old Gold cigarettes. Woody said to Jack Siefert years later, when he had broken a heavy smoking habit (as had Artie Shaw), "To think, we were all selling cancer."

Cigarettes were thus associated with glamour in the minds of young listeners: smoking was portrayed as giving a person poise, sophistication, the air of maturity.

Leonard Feather gave Woody's Old Gold show a strong review in the August issue of *Metronome*, saying, "Seldom do you hear live music on the air of the kind Herman has been playing. Even more rarely do you hear a coast-to-coast commercial in which the band is given adequate opportunities to display its ability strictly in the field of real jazz." Feather praised the arrangers—Ralph Burns, Eddie Sauter, and Dave Matthews—and said, "May these two months be extended into years."

They weren't. But the show did lead to the composition of *Apple Honey*—named for an ingredient the advertiser claimed enhanced the flavor of Old Gold cigarettes. Ralph said: "I wrote the introduction to *Apple Honey*. It's taken from a Duke Ellington thing. Flip Phillips did the first part, Neal did the bridge. It was a head arrangement. But it all came together. The only written part was the introduction."

Flip said: "*Northwest Passage*. Woody and I used to play that together. I'd show the saxes the lines. The trumpets would make something up, the trombones would make something up. It became a big arrangement. A lot of the tunes were made that way. *Caldonia* was made that way. All the riffs in the saxophones were mine. *Goosey Gander*. All the sections would contribute, and when it came out, it was beautiful. Neal Hefti would make up something. Pete Candoli would make up something. Bill Harris would make up something. There were nights it was just wonderful!"

Flip's relationship with Harris was a close personal one; in later years they co-led a group in Florida. "Bill Harris was my buddy," Flip said. "I think Bill was the greatest trombone player. If he was alive today, we'd be together yet. He knew when I was going to breathe, and I knew when he was going to breathe. He was great. He could play any which way."

Documentation of what the band sounded like that year is found on a two-CD issue by a British label called Hep. Under the heading the Metronome Series, the CDs include material recorded August 2 during a rehearsal for one of the early Old Gold shows, as well as V disc material recorded for the armed forces. The band had been playing much of this material for at least a year. By now the personnel of the First Herd was essentially in place.

The contract with Old Gold expired that fall, but it led directly to a second radio show for Woody. He went on the air for another product aimed at an audience of dating age, Wild Root Cream Oil, largely because two young executives in the company's head office were fans of the band. On September 8, 1945, the band recorded *Wild Root*, listed as a co-composition by Woody and Neal Hefti. A month earlier it had recorded Hefti's *The Good Earth*.

Hefti had joined the band on trumpet. Neal, who was thought to look somewhat like actor Alan Ladd, was born in Hastings, Nebraska, on October 29, 1922, which made him five months younger than Ralph Burns. His father was an indentured servant. It is little realized that a form of peonage existed in the United States into the 1920s. Neal said: "My father's father and mother were from Germany. My father was born in Dayton, Ohio, in the 1890s. He was placed in an orphanage at the age of four when his parents died a few months apart. In those days you could come into an orphanage and say, 'I need someone to work for me.' A family named Hefti took him as an indentured servant. I have the indenture papers. The wording says 'will be bound over to Adam and Sophia Hefti of Plankinton, South Dakota, where he shall live until he reaches the lawful age of twenty-one, at which time he will receive his freedom, a hundred and fifty dollars, two suits of clothing, preferably new, and a Bible.'

"He was educated to the age of ten. By law they could then take him out of school. The papers said he was to learn 'the art of farming.' He was in servitude for seventeen years. I understand he was really mistreated.

"After he got his freedom he became a semi-pro baseball player in the leagues around the Midwest. They would go in these rickety cars from one town to another, like barnstorming, playing sandlot ball.

"He met my mother, who was the daughter of a newspaper editor and publisher in Norton, Kansas. They were married shortly after that and moved to Nebraska. They moved around a lot.

"My mother played a little piano. My parents told me music was the best thing to get out of the poverty of the dust bowl. They sent me to a trumpet teacher. I am sure it was the barter system, and we paid with corn or eggs or something. We had a sort of community farm. We traded with adjacent farms. It was Depression and dust bowl. I joined the union at sixteen. It was a German, Polish, Czechoslovakian area, and I played polkas and German and Polish weddings. I'd practice outside in the summertime and we'd get requests. The neighbors would call up and say, 'Do you think Neal knows *Stars Fell on Alabama*'? And I was listening to the bands on the radio."[1]

Besides Neal, the Herd's trumpet section included Billy Robbins, Ray

Wetzel, and Pete Candoli and Conte Candoli. Conte had joined the band in the summer of 1943, when he was a sixteen-year-old high school student. He wanted to stay but his mother, brother, and Woody sent him back to finish school. Bill Harris, Ralph Pfeffner, and Ed Kiefer were the trombones; Sam Marowitz and Bill Shine, altos; Flip Phillips and Pete Mondello, tenors; Skippy DeSair, baritone; Ralph Burns, piano; Billy Bauer, guitar; Chubby Jackson, bass; and Dave Tough, drums. There were only two holdovers from the old band: DeSair and Mondello. The singer by then was Frances Wayne.

Among the earliest arrangements credited to Burns is *Flying Home*, a co-composition of Benny Goodman, Lionel Hampton, and guitarist Charlie Christian. It probably began life as a head. It had then become a hit in a Decca recording by Hampton's big band, formed in 1940. Woody's version was recorded during a rehearsal for one of the Old Gold radio shows.

From the opening vamp pattern, with the melody stated in unison by Woody on clarinet and Flip Phillips on tenor over that distinctive Dave Tough–Chubby Jackson rhythm section, the spirit is totally different from that of the old band. The pianist is Burns. Neal Hefti said, "I thought Ralph was one of the better piano players I have heard in my whole life and hands down probably did more for Woody than any one person."

Dave Tough was a particularly important addition to the band, as Woody well knew. Born in Oak Park, Illinois, in 1907, Tough was the youngest of the four children of parents born in Aberdeen, Scotland. In his adolescence he became a member of the Austin High Gang, a formative influence in what became known as the Chicago style of jazz played by young whites, many of whom had attended Austin High School. This group included Jimmy McPartland, Jim Lanigan, Bud Freeman, and Frank Teschemacher, but other Chicagoans from other high schools were loosely affiliated with them, including Benny Goodman, Mezz Mezzrow, Muggsy Spanier, and Gene Krupa. Tough was a true pioneer on drums, partly for his ride patterns on cymbals and unorthodox accents on the bass drum, all of which are evident in his recordings with Herman. Tough had continued to evolve, and was one of the few drummers able to adapt to bebop. A small, slight man with sharp features—he weighed a little under a hundred pounds—he also is remembered for his high intellect and an unfulfilled ambition to be a writer. He had introduced the members of the Austin High Gang to H. L. Mencken's *American Mercury* and later wrote a column for *Down Beat*. Even in adolescence, Tough was an omnivorous reader who took language and literature courses and did some drawing and painting. Bud Freeman remembered that Tough took him to see a Cézanne showing at the Art Institute of Chicago. According to Whitney Balliett, he hung out at a nightclub called the Green Mask, where he accompanied poetry readings by Max Bodenheim, Langston Hughes, and Kenneth Rexroth.

By the age of twenty, he was living in Paris, where, Bud Freeman said, he wrote limericks with F. Scott Fitzgerald. He returned to the United States in 1929, played with Red Nichols and then returned to Chicago where, for about five years, he was a derelict. Pianist Jess Stacy told Balliett:

> He'd always had trouble with drinking. I used to see him all the time before I joined Benny Goodman, in 1935, and he was in terrible shape. He looked like a bum and he hung out with bums. He'd go along Randolph Street and panhandle, and then he'd buy canned heat and strain off the alcohol and drink it—this being during Prohibition. I played with him in Goodman's band in 1938, right after Krupa left, and Goodman was running through drummers a mile a minute. Goodman said to Tough one day just before show time, "Hey, Davey, I want you to send me," and Tough replied, "Where do you want to be sent?"
>
> He was a brilliant little guy, and I always wondered if he wasn't torn between being a writer and being a drummer.[2]

Tough moved to New York in 1935 and would sit in with Bunny Berigan's group at the Famous Door. Since Woody used to frequent the place to listen to Berigan, it seems likely that he first heard and perhaps met Tough there. Joe Bushkin, who was in the Berigan group, said: "It was the fashion to take the Benzedrine strip out of an inhaler and put it in a Coke, and he'd do that for courage. When he drank too much, he was gone. He was totally out of body. Sometimes, when I was still batching it, I'd take him home with me. He weighed less than I did. I've always been around a hundred and twenty-eight, but he must have been close to a hundred pounds. He was so much of an artist that having a bank account would have been appalling to him. He was a natural musician who did things effortlessly, and that always made you uncomfortable."

Whitney Balliett wrote:

> He certainly had helped inspire the great rhythmic drive of the Chicago players, and he must have helped shape whatever subtlety they had. He had worked his way through the styles of the New Orleans drummers Baby Dodds and Zutty Singleton and, by ceaselessly experimenting, had become a first-rate, original drummer. He knew books and art, and this added stature and class to the popular image of the jazz musician as an uncouth primitive.

Tough went through the bands of Tommy Dorsey, Bunny Berigan, Benny Goodman, and Jack Teagarden. He played with Joe Marsala and, briefly, was a member of the Band That Plays the Blues. Then he went into Artie Shaw's World War II navy band and played under difficult conditions in forward areas on South Pacific islands. They were often under sniper fire and played one show under ponchos in torrential rain for GIs also under ponchos. At times they were bombed almost nightly by Japanese aircraft. During one of these attacks, Shaw lost the hearing of one ear; it would never return. The band was sent home sick and exhausted. Shaw told me, "Davey Tough was just a ghost."

Fragile to begin with, Tough never fully recovered his health. But there is no evidence of his fragility on the Herman records or in those Old Gold broadcasts.

The other members of the band at first didn't want him. Bebop was in the air, Tough was associated with the Chicago school of playing, and they told Woody, "Man, he's a Dixieland drummer!" He was not only older than they were; he was six years older than Woody.

Woody told the band, "I don't know what kind of drummer he is. The only thing I know is that he'll keep better time than anybody in the world, and this thing will swing like you've never felt it or heard it."

Woody hired him despite the protests. When the band first rehearsed with him, they were "embalmed," Woody said. They had never in their lives heard anything like Dave Tough, nor, for that matter, Woody often said, had he.

Tough owned an idiosyncratic drum kit that included a huge Chinese cymbal with loose rivets around its edge. That cymbal set up an incredible roar, and the sound of it is one of the defining characteristics of that First Herd. The new, smaller bass drums were coming into the market and many drummers adopted them, but Tough refused to use one. Tough had an ability to play a straight-four rhythm that sounded like eight beats to the bar, in effect a shuffle-rhythm sound. The only other drummer I ever heard get that effect was, later on, Mel Lewis, and I was never quite able to figure out how Mel did it. Nor, for that matter, was Woody able to tell me how Tough got it.

"He just did it," Woody said. "And it always swung so hard.

"He was a dynamic time-keeper. There was never one quite like him. He took great pride in his cymbals, the sound of each one, the heads on his drums. He was a very musical person without realizing it. He didn't read or any of that stuff, but he was a meticulous musician as far as taste and ability. He kept you straight, he kept you musically straight. Time-wise you were at home, no matter where you were. It taught a great deal to people. Some of the younger people were forced to take on a different discipline than they were used to. This made for a very tight big band."[3]

The very musicians who had not wanted him in the band now idolized him. Chubby Jackson, Woody said, "thought he had invented Davey." In 1994 Jackson, by now seventy-six, remembered the experience like Saul of Tarsus recalling what happened on the road to Damascus: "We were all twenty-one, twenty-three, and here comes a guy who's nearly forty. We were saying, 'No! We've got to get some other kind of spark in here! Because the band is looking to grow.' I used to do a lot of the suggestive hiring. I figured, 'Hiring a guy who's that age and who's been around all these years? He's coming into this band?' And all of a sudden I started to find out where he was coming from.

"Davey Tough taught me how to play bass. He would be sitting next to me on the bus, with advice *coming out of his nostrils*, and telling me that I should think and at what level to play. Where there's a tenor, get onto this, go down underneath him, and then come up to me and stay there for a while. Or, you want to get on top and just walk down to him? And then, when the ensemble comes in, get right in the middle of things. He was giving me fantastic thinking.

"One time at the Paramount, I was doing my number out front, and all of a sudden, in the last two choruses, with Pete Candoli screaming, the band had dropped down about two pegs in tempo. And I swear, I was listening to a sixty-five-piece band. Like, twenty trumpets . . . . I couldn't believe what was happening.

"I said to him, 'Dave, excuse me, man, I didn't mean to drop the tempo.'

"He used to call me Snuggy. He said, 'Snuggy, didn't you dig that? I brought the tempo down to give it another kind of approach. Didn't it sound bigger, and fatter, and stronger? From now on, recognize the fact that non-metronomical time is the answer to jazz.'

"Like, Sonny Berman used to lay behind the beat. Flip Phillips, right in the middle. Bill Harris was ahead. Dave said, 'Go with them! And then when it comes into the ensemble, look at me, and I'll look at you and we'll settle it right where it should go.'

"And I thought, 'Oh, my God!' Like, I knew where the damn notes were on the fingerboard, but all of a sudden I was learning where to put my fingers.

"I can't tell how long it was from the time I objected to Dave Tough coming into the band, until I was thinking, 'Oooooh, this man *is a genius*.' But it wasn't long. I became his biggest fan and disciple. Woody would look at me and say, 'Aaah, now what do you think?'

"Dave made that band. And he insisted that I play on the same level with him, so that we could look at each other and feel our accents together.

"Dave tuned his drums C, E, and G. He had a cymbal for when the tenor sax played. The ensemble cymbal was one of those rivet cymbals, but he'd taken out all the rivets but two. And then he had sliced a V-cut into it. It looked like something that should be thrown out. But instead, it had a sound that blended, a take-over sound. It had a human warmth to it. All of a sudden the band started to get that fury.

"The trick is to get time going and be in the right slot as to where the orchestra is. And if you do that, then you *own* the band. The majority of the big bands never got that lovely, cookin' swing.

"The co-ordination he had, and the love he had of music, and of us youngsters. He made all of us soloists, so sure of ourselves. I started to find something I felt was my own sound, and it was due to Davey."[4]

There was one thing about Dave Tough that Woody at the time did not know: Tough was epileptic and lived in constant fear of a seizure. The fear was one of the underlying causes of his drinking.

▼   ▼   ▼

One of the most interesting musicians in the 1944–45 band was vibra-harpist Marjorie Hyams. Jack Siefert introduced Woody to her.

"She was working at the Renault Tavern on the boardwalk in Atlantic City," Jack said. "One night after Woody finished playing at the Steel Pier, we were walking back to his hotel when I suggested we stop and hear Marjorie Hyams play." Woody was impressed and hired her.

The prejudice against, the condescension toward, women jazz musicians has faded considerably in the half-century since then. But Hyams, who was born in New York City in 1923 and was twenty-one when she joined Woody, had to contend with it constantly. "In a sense," she told Chris Albertson in an interview for *Stereo Review*, "you weren't really looked upon as a musician, especially in clubs. There was more interest in what you were going to wear or how your hair was fixed—they just wanted you to look attractive, ultra-feminine, largely because you were doing something they didn't consider feminine. Only in retrospect, when you start looking back and analyzing, you can see the obstacles that were put in front of you. I just thought at the time that I was too young to handle it. But now I see it was really rampant chauvinism."

Woody's lack of prejudice against women in music extended into management. His road manager for the First Herd was, for some time, a woman named Dorothy Stewart. Woody said she did "fantastically well."

He said, "It was amazing how a woman, particularly if she was an attractive young lady who was always well groomed, would get things done that probably a guy couldn't in a hundred years." One of Stewart's feats of magic was to hold a crack express train in Chicago for fifteen minutes for a tardy Neal Hefti.

To be sure, the life of show business occasionally got to her. Once when Woody was home in Jackson Heights, off sick for three days, she phoned him from the State Theater in Hartford, Connecticut, to say that the young comic on the bill with the band insisted on walking around backstage wearing only a jock strap. "I wish you would talk to him," she said.

Woody said, "Put the bum on the phone." And when the comic got on the line, Woody said, "Put some pants on, you jerk. This is a regular life. Straight life. There is nothing different here."

Woody said of her, "A very sweet, charming girl and a little on the straitlaced side about certain things, language and everything. The guys got so they were perfect gentlemen at all times and didn't know why they were doing it. It was just that they didn't have the courage to use cuss words in front of Stewart.

"But I had to break her up once in a while. She and Frances Wayne would change gowns and stuff. They were in the theater, and it was very boring and I sent out and got a set of long underwear and, like a ballet dancer, leaped into their dressing room, and poor Stewart went straight up.

"The guys were pretty hacked with me because every so often I would hire a girl musician. And then, when I hired a girl manager, this was the crack-up of all time. But the truth of the matter is that they all got to like her very much and she was very efficient. When she said she would do something, it was done immediately. Real businesswoman."

▼   ▼   ▼

At the end of 1944, just after the end of the record ban, Woody signed a contract with Columbia Records. He said later that he liked the sound the company's engineers got in Liederkranz Hall in New York City, a favorite studio of many performers. It was a former church and had a very high ceiling.

On February 19, 1945, as soon after the record ban was lifted as the band could get into the studio, it recorded *Apple Honey, Laura*, and *I Wonder* for Columbia. The personnel had evolved further. It was now Sonny Berman, Pete Candoli, Chuck Frankhauser, Carl Warwick, and Ray Wetzel, trumpets; Harris, Kiefer, and Pfeffner, trombones; Marowitz and John LaPorta, altos; Mondello and Phillips, tenors; DeSair, baritone; Jackson, bass; Billy Bauer, guitar; Tough, drums; and Burns, piano. The V disc version of *Apple Honey* had been recorded five months earlier. The difference between the two is subtle but powerful: the band now had incredible fire and passion. It had evolved even in those few months. The tempo had risen slightly and the band, very simply, was hotter.

"Those were thrilling times," Ralph said. "There was no tape splicing. You'd go in and you'd make a take. We were so proud of the band, and we went into that session and did *Apple Honey*."[5]

A week later, on February 26, 1945, Woody took them back into the studio to record *Caldonia*, with a frivolous vocal by Woody and silly screams by the whole band. It featured a trombone solo by Harris that startled the fans, who thought you just couldn't play a slide trombone with that kind of speed and facility. (Harris was actually playing a valve trombone on that solo.) But the most amazing thing on the record was a soaring passage by trumpets near the end. It would be a huge hit.

It has often been said, and written, that this was a transcription of part of a Dizzy Gillespie solo. This is not so. It was from a solo by Neal Hefti. Billy Taylor has pointed out that Art Tatum and other founding masters of jazz often played memorized solos, the same notes night after night, the mystique of improvisation notwithstanding. And after a band recorded a piece, the audiences expected the solos to be the same as those on the record. Otherwise, Hefti said, they thought they were victims of a sort of fraud, that the "real" band was not playing the engagement.

Solos on records were short, since the recording engineers of the time wanted tunes to run something like three minutes or less, because the closer the grooves got to the center of the disc, the greater the distortion.

Neal said, "You'd polish your solo to its optimum. You were only playing twelve bars, three bars, two bars, fill-ins. I would play it the same way every time, which was the way of doing it of all the bandleaders and trumpet players I read about, including Harry James and Louis Armstrong. That way the audience would always get their best performance.

"I had worked out a solo for *Woodchopper's Ball*, which is in D-flat. And as would always happen, within two to three weeks, the trumpet players would surprise me by standing up and playing it in unison with me.

"I was in the band twice, once for about a year and a half. Then I left for six months to get my Local 47 union card in Los Angeles. When I returned, they had recorded *Caldonia*. Woody had told them, 'Use that trumpet solo of Neal's that you're playing anyway.' *Caldonia* is in B-flat. Woody told them, 'Go up to D-flat,' which put it in the right register for trumpet. 'Then go back to B-flat and I'll sing it out.'

"So it wasn't a Dizzy Gillespie solo. But it certainly was Dizzy Gillespie-inspired. Dizzy was my hero from way before that.

"A lot of unison things in Woody's band were little things that I used to play as solos and the other trumpet players would learn—those trumpet parts in *Happiness Is a Thing Called Joe*, for example. Ralph didn't even write trumpet parts for that chart. He wrote it for saxophones and trombones. Then it progressed. Every trumpet part in there was my noodling behind the vocal. Ralph said, like, 'Neal, fill it.'"[6]

Such was the nature of the collaboration that a good many pieces are catalogued as Hefti-Burns collaborations. One passage in the band's book was transcribed indeed from a recorded solo. Ralph said, "On *I've Got News for You*, I took a passage note for note off a Charlie Parker record and harmonized it for the saxes. When I did a thing for Ray Charles later on, he asked me to write the same sax chorus." The passage, eight bars long, derived from Parker's solo on *Dark Shadows*, occurs right after Woody's vocal. It anticipates Supersax by nearly thirty years. Med Flory, one of the founders of Supersax, said that it was the memory of the Parker passage in *I've Got News for You* that inspired the formation of Supersax.

This was the definitive First Herd that burst upon the public in those last days of World War II, helped considerably by a heavy promotion campaign from Columbia Records. One of the reasons Woody had signed with Columbia is that he liked the sound they got on bands. Equally important was an unusual business agreement he had reached with the company, one he considered among the few shrewd business arrangements he ever made.

Woody knew only too well that the wartime shortage of shellac limited the number of records a company could make. Indeed the War Manpower and Production Board limited the production of any one record to 350,000 copies. Woody knew this. There would be no point, therefore, in complaining about Columbia's failing to ship enough records. Nor was he primarily interested in the size of the advances the company would pay him. What he wanted was promotion, publicity, and advertising. And so he extracted from Columbia, as a condition of his contract, the promise to give him the same kind of exploitation the company was applying to its two top artists, Frank Sinatra and Dinah Shore.

He mused in later years that every time an ad or a news story about the band turned up in *Billboard, Variety, Down Beat*, or any other publication, Les Brown, Harry James, and other bandleaders who recorded for that company must have been wondering, as Woody put it, "What the hell was going on?"

▼   ▼   ▼

In September of 1945, the band suffered a severe personnel loss. Dave Tough left. Drinking heavily again, he returned to the Joe Marsala group, helped Eddie Condon open his nightclub in Greenwich Village, worked on Fifty-second Street with Bill Harris and Charlie Ventura, and returned to Chicago for a time.

Whitney Balliett wrote:

> He was deteriorating physically, and he was worried by bebop, whose rhythmic intricacies he was certain (wrongly) he could never absorb. He was losing his saturnine good looks. He had a long, wandering, bony face, a high, domed forehead, and black hair with a widow's peak—it was a face, perched on his tiny shoulders, of a bigger man.[7]

Jack Siefert said, "Sometimes I think he was unfairly called a drunk when he was actually an epileptic. Epileptics at that time in our history were not understood as they are today."[8]

Dave Tough spent time in a Veterans Administration Hospital in New Jersey. He left it in the late afternoon of December 8, 1948, with the apparent intent of going to the apartment he shared with his wife in Newark. Somewhere along the way he got drunk and, in the darkness, fell and hit his head on a curb. He evidently was carrying no personal papers, for when he died the next morning in a hospital, he was taken to the morgue as an unidentified body. His wife found him there three days later. He was forty-one.

10

Making It

 On March 1, 1945, *Down Beat* ran a two-column headline:

HERMAN'S IS FINEST
OFAY SWING BAND

The story, by Frank Stacy, began:

Woody Herman has the greatest ofay swing band in the country—bar none! That's what all the band popularity contests said this year and that's just the way I feel about it. Out of 1,606 swing fans who named the Herman Herd their favorite dispenser of jive in *Down Beat*'s annual contest, undoubtedly some (the bobby soxers) cast their votes that way because they go for the snappy corduroy jackets that Woody sports on the stand. Most fans, however, pick Woody's crew for its crack over-all musicianship, for its up-to-the-minute presentation of advanced big band orchestrations, for Woody's superior talents as an instrumentalist, singer, showmanly stick-waver, and, above all, for his grasp of the *right* band ideas.

The girls may have noticed corduroy jackets; Woody's clothes were always superb, and the band itself reflected his clothes-horse tastes. What a good many of the fans, particularly noticed, were his shoes. Woody wore exquisite shoes. His father made them himself by hand at Nunn Bush and sent them to him from Milwaukee. Dave Dexter once wrote that he was the best-dressed man in the music business.

Later that year, at the end of a long tour, the band played an engagement in Boston. Frances Wayne and Neal Hefti had announced plans to be married, and her family said that the band's proximity to Boston offered them the only opportunity to see their daughter married.

"The marriage was sprung on me in two days," Neal said. "It was a surprise marriage. We weren't supposed to be married for about three weeks, in New York, by a justice of the peace. And then we got to Boston on the end of a road trip. Frances's family wanted a church wedding. So they arranged it without my knowing it. I don't know if Frances knew it, but if she did, she was sworn to their secrecy. I didn't have anything to wear except my band uniform, and in those days we were wearing band uniforms without lapels. That was during the war years, and it was to save cloth. They made pants without cuffs. So I borrowed a suit from Woody. Actually it was too big for me, when I look at my wedding pictures. It had droopy shoulders."[1]

In Somerville, Massachusetts, where Frances had grown up and where Ralph had lived with her family, almost like her brother, at midnight on November 3, 1945, with Woody and the whole band in attendance, Frances and Neal were married in the rites of the Catholic church.

The band continued to record throughout 1945: *Goosey Gander, A Kiss Goodnight, I've Got the World on a String*, and *Northwest Passage* on March 1; *The Good Earth, Put That Ring on My Finger*, and *Northwest Passage*, August 10; *Bijou*, August 20; *Your Father's Mustache*, September 5; *Wild Root; Let It Snow, Let It Snow, Let It Snow*, and *Blowin' up a Storm*, December 10. It even turned out an "album" of four ten-inch records by the Woodchoppers, with Sonny Berman and Shorty Rogers, trumpets; Bill Harris trombone, Woody, clarinet, alto, and vocals; Flip Phillips, tenor; Jimmy Rowles, piano; Billy Bauer, guitar; Chubby Jackson, bass; and Don Lamond, drums. The tunes included *Steps*, a title taken from the nickname for Woody's beloved Barney Bigard; *Igor*, in obvious tribute to Stravinsky; and *Pam*, a tune by Bauer named for his daughter. Non-reissue record "albums," in those days before the LP, were not common, except in the classical music field, and collections by small jazz groups were almost unprecedented. This one, most of it recorded in mid-May in Chicago, was a great critical success.

A number of the musicians in the band were alumni of Red Norvo's groups, and Red recalled: "Woody was after me to leave Benny Goodman and come with his band. He said, 'Why don't you come on? Half your guys are here.' And he kept raising the price to me. And Benny's band was getting dull as hell. It was a good band. But Benny started to get funny with

Morey Feld, who played perfect for Benny. He knew how to play drums with the sextet, he knew how to play with the big band." Norvo was referring to Goodman's quirky and sometimes cruel treatment of musicians. Finally, Marjorie Hyams, offered a good job in New York, tired of life on the road, which was even harder on women than on men, gave Woody her notice. By now vibraharp was part of the band's book and sound. Again Woody approached Red.

"So I went to Benny," Red continued, "and I said, knowing him as I did for so long, 'Benny, I need a change. I'm not playing good.' And that went right down his alley. I left him in Jersey City and joined Woody at the Paramount.

"It was wonderful. Ralph was arranging, and Flip was in the saxophone section. I always liked Bill Harris. Things were working out. We were doing the Wild Root show. It was a great radio show. God, Woody did a hell of a job on it. That band was the most exciting thing in the world, and more so after he got Conrad Gozzo and Pete Candoli."[2]

Red alerted Woody that another fine musician was about to get out of military service, Shorty Rogers, born Milton Rajonsky in Great Barrington, Massachusetts, on April 14, 1924, and yet another Norvo alumnus. Woody took note and hired Rogers. Red, long divorced from Mildred Bailey, was dating Shorty's sister, Eve, and while he was with Woody, Red and Eve were married. Shorty Rogers thus became Red's brother-in-law.

Shorty had gone to work for Norvo before he got out of high school. Ralph Burns and several others in the band had also worked for Norvo. And of course Woody's friendship with Red went back to the founding days of the Band That Plays the Blues. Ralph said, "God. I was scared to death. But it was a great feeling. Chubby Jackson was a wonderful spirit in the band. Chubby just made you feel at home. At one time we had Oscar Pettiford in the band, two bass players who hated each other. It was unbelievable! And poor Dave Tough, caught in the middle. We were never sure whether Davey was going to go off and get loaded anyway! Dave was Mr. Solidity. With these two bass players fighting each other, I don't know how we managed to get through. But when that rhythm section went, it really went."

Woody's amused tolerance of human foible, particularly that of the musicians in his band, is manifest in stories he told about Chubby Jackson, the most frenetic member of the band. He said Chubby at one point had decided to leave the band because his nerves had become so bad. Chubby's mother, who was an old vaudevillian and a pianist of a sort—Woody said she played the same chord changes on every tune; Chubby said she knew a thousand tunes but never their releases—came to see Woody. Woody told her, "Look, all that's wrong with this boy, the reason he's frothing at the mouth at the first show in the morning and a few other small scenes, is that he hasn't been to bed in seven days and he's been like smoking pot continuously, and it's bound to catch up with you."

Mrs. Jackson said, "Oh, Chubby just likes to get high. It doesn't mean anything."

Later, Woody said, "We were in the Indianapolis Theater, and I saw Chubby Jackson backstage in a little hallway with a pay telephone, and he's chuckling and laughing and scratching and I stopped by and I said, 'Who are you talking to?'

"And he said, 'Mom.'

"I said, 'Hello, hiya, Mom!'

"So right at the end of the conversation, she said, 'Chub?'

"He said, 'Yeah, Mom.'

"She said, 'Are you high, Chub?'

"He said, 'Yeah, Mom.'

"She said, 'That's good. Have a good time.'"

Woody said that some time later, the band was playing an engagement at the pavilion at Pleasure Beach in Bridgeport, Connecticut, a one-nighter at the end of a long road tour. The next engagement was in New York City. Woody was told that Mom Jackson wanted him on the telephone immediately. She'd said it was an emergency. Woody ran to the phone.

Mom Jackson said, "Wood?"

"Yes."

"The heat's on in New York. Tell the boys to dump all the shit."

Presumably they did so before heading into New York for an engagement at the Hotel Pennsylvania.[3]

(Years after he left the band, Chubby encountered Woody in Chicago one night. He said, "I went into a restaurant at two o'clock in the morning, and who should be sitting there but Woody. We began reminiscing. He said, 'You know, Chubby, that was my band.' I said, 'Yeah, I know.' He said, 'There's a couple of things I could tell you here, young fella'. Do you remember you got all those raises?' I said, 'Yeah, of course.' He said, 'Your mother did it.' I said, 'What?' He said, 'She used to get all dressed up and she'd come into Sardi's and say, "Do you know that Chubby is the reason for this band being as great as it is? He's a bad businessman, but you should take care of him because he idolizes you and will work twenty-five hours a day for you. But don't ever dare tell him that I was responsible for raises.' And until then, Woody never did tell me.

("When we were working the Wild Root Cream Oil show, I got a $125 raise. I joined the band at a $175 and my last salary was about eight hundred.")

Chubby was by no means the only member of the band to smoke marijuana. Ralph Burns had discovered it while still in high school, playing club dates with older musicians. "None of us does it now, but we did then," he said. "We used to get high and listen to Stravinsky records." His great loves were Debussy, Ravel, Stravinsky, and Ellington. "Who else was there?" he asked, laughing.[4]

Woody's friend and early champion, writer George T. Simon, by now was in the army. He was transferred to New York and assigned to produce V discs—for the armed forces. The V symbol was everywhere. It originated with Winston Churchill, who in the most ominous days of the war made his cigar and his middle and index fingers upheld in a letter V—for Victory—two of the most memorable visual symbols of the time. The first four notes of the Beethoven Fifth Symphony also were associated with the letter V, since the sound for it in Morse code is three dots and a dash, like the opening notes of the symphony. The name V disc, then, had a rich set of associations. A captain in over-all charge of their production told Simon, "You know a lot of people in the business. So go ahead and record anybody and anything you want."

The Herman band came into New York. Woody offered to record some V discs. The band was scheduled to play the Paramount Theater and Frank Dailey's Meadowbrook. Simon asked Woody, "When would you rather do it, while you're at the Paramount or at Meadowbrook?"

"Both times," Woody said. "It's the least we can do." Performers were not paid for recording V discs, but the band, and Woody, were more than willing to make them.

On September 5, the band went into the RCA studios to record several pieces, among them the Ralph Burns arrangement of *Happiness Is a Thing Called Joe*, with vocal by Frances Wayne. Ralph said, "I had written it for Charlie Barnet. Charlie never really forgave me! He was good natured about it. I wrote it originally for Mary Ann McCall. Then Frances sang it, then Woody hired her and she wanted to do it. I wrote the exact same arrangement for Woody. It became Frances's big hit."

Another tune from that date is *Red Top*, an up-tempo number whose composer is listed as Woody, although it has no main theme and sounds like a head arrangement. It features a churning figure by unison trumpets right out of Dizzy Gillespie—it will turn up later in *Caldonia*—and superb solos by Flip Phillips and Bill Harris that run longer than one was accustomed to hearing on the ten-inch 78-r.p.m. records of the period. V discs were twelve inches wide. Also on the session were *Jones Beachhead*, a composition by Hefti, and another Frances Wayne vocal on *I Can't Put My Arms Around a Memory*, a lesser Ellington tune that shows that all was not gold, old or otherwise, in the golden age of the bands and songs.

Further proof of this was offered at a session in late August or early September in Liederkranz Hall, to record a tribute to the infantry bearing the bizarre title *There Are No Wings on a Foxhole*. It contains some breathtakingly awful lines, the most mawkish being "there are no wheels on your tootsies when you march from night till the dawn." Given Woody's sardonic sense of the incongruous, his apparently sincere vocal is a triumph of acting over content. The composer of this curiosity, incredibly, was Irving Berlin.

But the session also produced an early performance of *Apple Honey*.

Ralph Burns's sojourn as the band's pianist would not last long. The burden of being pianist and principal arranger was growing heavy. He recalled:

"We'd play at night. We'd be at the Pennsylvania Hotel, or something like that. I'd play piano from maybe seven in the night to two in the morning. And then I'd take a couple of benzedrines or whatever, and stay up all night and do my writing then. There was no time to sleep. When you're that young, it doesn't affect you. But!

"Woody got the Wild Root show. I said, 'Woody, I'm doing so much writing I've got to stop playing. It was then I stopped playing for the band. I'd meet them once a week. Tony Aless came in on piano.'"[5]

Born Anthony Allesandrini in Garfield, New Jersey, on August 22, 1921, Tony would stay with the band two years, then work with various members of the Herman alumni in small groups, and with Charlie Parker, Seldon Powell, and others. Later he became a fine teacher of jazz piano in New York City.

▼   ▼   ▼

Some time during this period Woody became associated with Abe Turchen, who was to play one of the most significant roles of anyone in his life.

Abe was born in Sioux City, Iowa, in 1919, on February 12—Lincoln's birthday. He used to tell people that this was where he got the name, but it was a joke. Orthodox Jewish families—and Abe's was Orthodox—name their children after dead family members. His father, called Mose by the family, was an immigrant from Russia who made his living as a junk dealer. Abe had two brothers, Al and Max, and two sisters, Bessie and Lillian.[6]

Before World War II, Abe was a coin-machine operator with a line of jukeboxes in Iowa and South Dakota. Abe told me that the coin machine business wasn't as corrupt before the war as it became after it, but it was a tough training ground just the same. He said that when Mafia elements tried to muscle into his operations, he told them in an alley to go to hell, and after that they left him alone.[7]

Woody had known him in those earlier days. He said Abe would run into him and pull his leg, saying things like, "I got your latest record. Why don't you go into some other line of work?" Abe went into military service, serving in the famous First Marine Division at Guadalcanal, where he suffered bomb-fragment wounds so severe he spent eighteen months in hospitals, his injuries compounded by malaria. Like many veterans, Abe spoke little about the war, but he once pulled up the legs of his pants and showed me his calves, covered with brown scars from the wounds. They caused him pain at times. Abe talked like a cross between the comedian Jack E. Leonard, who was a friend of his, and W. C. Fields, a dour and jaded delivery. I once asked him, "Abe, do you still have contact with the Marine Corps, or any old friends from those days?"

"No," he said. "I don't bother the Marines and they don't bother me."

Abe was medically discharged from the Marines in 1944 and returned to Sioux City, where Woody encountered him in the lobby of a hotel. The war had created frustrating transportation problems for the bands, with shortages of gasoline and vehicles. Because Abe was a war hero, and the Navy Department wanted him kept happy, he was able to buy a Buick Roadmaster sedan when cars were all but impossible to get, and get the gasoline rationing coupons to keep it running. Woody told Abe that the band couldn't get a bus to proceed on its tour.

"An hour later, he had a bus," Woody said. "I don't know how he got it. A hot bus!"

Abe was an operator—"You know, with the wristwatches up the arm," as Red Norvo put it.[8]

Abe persuaded Woody to ride with him in the Buick and let the band travel on the bus. He said he'd spend a week on the road with Woody.

He stayed with the band three or four months, finally leaving to go home.

Woody returned to Hollywood and the Garden of Allah, where he and Charlotte were still living. The band was off for ten days while Woody struggled with his booking agency to get more money for their engagements. Hardly had he settled into his home life than Abe turned up at the door, saying he'd found he didn't have much to do and had taken a notion to drive out.

Milt Deutsch, the band's road manager, had been telling Woody that he was exhausted from road life and wanted to go home. After Abe had been in Hollywood for a few days, he and Woody were sitting in the Garden of Allah bar. Woody sipped a real drink; Abe only club soda. As far as I know, Abe didn't drink; certainly I never saw him drink. Woody recalled saying, "Milt is leaving the band . . . . You've been with me now for months for no reason, and we may as well make this some kind of a sensible business proposition. You'll travel with me and be the road manager."

After first protesting that he didn't know much about music, Abe accepted the offer. He would spend twelve years on the road with the band, coming to know seemingly every ballroom, high school gymnasium, roller-skating arena, pavilion and amusement park in America.

The band was playing about forty weeks of each year in theaters, traveling by train much of the time. Woody often said playing theaters, five or six shows a day, was a hellish life. He hated them, and would later laugh whenever someone said their passing had been unfortunate. But at least he had Abe to co-ordinate the band's movements.

Abe was affable and, in his own way, funny, and he got on well with the musicians, even though he was their paymaster. Woody said, "He got his heart broken a few times in the early stages, just like everyone else."

While he was traveling with the band, Abe met a beautiful girl named Peggy Martin, a dancer who worked with another young woman in a song-and-dance act, playing, among other things, USO shows. She had every reason to expect a bright professional future when, as she was riding on a train, the window by which she sat shattered inward. It is possible that someone threw a rock at the train. It cost her the sight of one eye and, although she remained beautiful, the injury spoiled her looks for movie closeups. Abe pressed her to marry him, and eventually she agreed. There is evidence that she was very much in love with him. Peggy Martin was from Coronado, California, then an island off San Diego, which is now linked to the mainland by a bridge.[9]

By the end of 1945, Woody had every reason to be jubilant. The war was over, and the exuberance that this engendered could be heard in the playing of his musicians. The band was almost Dadaesque, with wonderfully silly and celebrant numbers such as *Goosey Gander* and *Your Father's Mustache*, with Chubby Jackson shouting encouragement to his colleagues, and Ralph Burns, Neal Hefti, and Shorty Rogers turning in a stream of new charts that sound as fresh today as they did then.

Woody always said Shorty was one of the great unacknowledged influences in the band. Long afterwards, when Shorty was a successful composer in Los Angeles, when Woody needed a replacement in the trumpet section, he would phone Shorty to see if he were available, and if not, whether he could recommend someone. Woody was never disappointed with Shorty's recommendations.

Woody described him as a serious and yet happy man. He was also an extremely generous one. Recalling his time with the band, trumpeter Red Rodney said: "Shorty Rogers was the fourth, and the jazz chair, and my chair was the fifth chair and the jazz chair.

"Shorty was such a sweetheart. He'd write the solo on my chair—like *Lemon Drop*. I said, 'Shorty, now that's not fair. Your wrote the arrangement.' He said, 'I want you to play it. It'll be good for your career.' He put all the good solos on my chair. And it was very good for my career."[10]

Time after time musicians commented on this quality of Shorty's character. Henry Mancini described him as "a genuinely sweet man, very pure—pure of body, of heart, and of mind." When the Blake Edwards private-eye TV series *Peter Gunn* became a hit in the fall of 1958, the jazz score by Mancini was considered an important element in its success. Shorty had seen the pilot of the show. Shorty by then was a major recording artist for the RCA label, with guaranteed sales of eighty thousand per album, a large figure for jazz. One of the executives of RCA suggested to Rogers that he record the *Gunn* music. Shorty had lunch with Mancini and said, "Hank, I have no reason to record this. It has no connection with me. *You* wrote it, *you* arranged it, and *you* should record it."

Mancini said, "But, Shorty, I'm not a recording artist. I'm just a film writer, nobody knows who I am. You have a name."

Rogers was immovable. He said, "It's your baby. You should do it."

RCA finally gave in to pressure from Rogers and recorded the *Peter Gunn* music under Mancini's name. The album would sell more than a million copies and establish Mancini as a public name and a concert artist. Forever grateful, Mancini said, "I don't know what would have happened to my career if Shorty had decided that day to make the record."

In addition to Rogers's inventive work, Woody's trumpet section had the asset of the extraordinary power of Pete Candoli, who because of it became known as Superman. Pete's wife made him a Superman costume. He would leave the bandstand, change into the costume, and, returning, leap back into view playing blistering high notes. At the Paramount in New

York, he and the band carried the routine even further: he came sliding
down a wire from a high balcony to land just in time to go into the bridge of
Apple Honey.[11]

Despite a professorial mien, Bill Harris was one of the more famous
practical jokers in jazz. "Like," Woody said, "Bill Harris and Red Norvo
borrowed a couple of life-sized dummies from some girl dancers that
worked with these dummies. And they had them dressed in band uniforms.

"And Bill was more drastic in his humor than Red, I think, and Bill
would keep his dummy in the car with him. Whoever drove with him would
have to ride three in the front seat, with the dummy in the middle. We
reached the high point when we opened Tommy Dorsey's place on the
beach in Santa Monica, the Casino Gardens. And all of a sudden I realized
that we had four trombones, and the dummy was playing fourth trombone.
And then all night Bill was arguing with him. Every time there was two
bars out, here was Bill having a terrible beef with this dummy. It just held
the trombone all night. Bill said, 'Man, come in when I tell you!'"[12]

Flip Phillips said, "When the trombone section would get to play, Bill
would kick the dummy and say, 'Get up, get up!' It would just sit there.

"But the big story with that dummy, I was part of. We were in Detroit,
and Bill and I were on the fifteenth floor of the hotel, holding the dummy
in a window. The dummy was trying to commit suicide. And Sonny Berman
was down on the street. The street filled up with people. Yelling, 'Stop,
don't do it!' We were holding him back.

"Well, we threw him out the window. You should have heard the
screams. When he came down 'Bam!' Sonny Berman picked him up and
took him into the hotel. The fire department came, the police came, and
we *split*.'

"That band did crazy things like that."

Chubby Jackson said Bill Harris was incapable of walking by a novelty
store without entering and emerging with a dribble glass, disappearing ink,
a squirting flower, a rubber chicken, or worse. Chubby Jackson would
laugh helplessly during the most passionate Harris ballad performances.
What the audience couldn't see, when Harris was turned profile to them,
was that while the side of his face they could see was perfectly serious, the
other side, which Chubby could see, was performing maniacal grimaces,
with Bill's left eye rolling madly. When he would take a breath, he would
stick his tongue out of the left side of his mouth at Chubby.

Harris found some instrument maker or repairman to make him a right-
angle crook to fit between his mouthpiece and his horn. He would slip this
thing into place as he walked downstage to the microphone for a solo and

then play with his horn angled out from his right side. Woody, with his back to the audience and to Harris as he conducted, couldn't understand the audience reaction, and when he looked, he couldn't understand how Harris was playing the horn sideways.

Harris told Eddie Bert, who was in the section with him, that he wanted to have these crooks made for all the trombones, but he never did.[13] Woody not only tolerated these antic dispositions but actively encouraged them, sometimes as instigator, sometimes participant. In a theater in Passaic, New Jersey, the band worked with a slapstick comic named Don Rice. Rice worked with water props. He would say "Spitome" and someone would throw a bucket of water in his face. "Well, in the closing show," Woody said, "it got into a water fight, which ended up that I had the fire hoses out on the stage. And I think we had to give them about two thousand dollars for breakage. But it was worth it. P.S. We never played that theater in Passaic again."[14]

Woody insisted that the Adams Theater in Newark had the most unruly audiences in the country. "In the early part of the day," he said, "the audience was made up of kids. But they were a special breed of Jerseyites who came out of the rocks or something . . . . There was more action in the audience most days than on the stage. It was complete pandemonium. They had police who went up and down the aisles, and it never stopped. Way before rock and roll.

"One afternoon, my daughter came over with her mother. I think Ingie was about four at the time. She was standing backstage listening to the band. She got away from her mother and walked on stage in her little slacks and sweater or whatever she was wearing. I was just in the middle of a song. She just stood next to me for a while and gazed up completely enraptured at the whole thing.

"When I finished I said, 'What can I do for you?' And she said, 'I would like to sing a song.' So I dropped the mike and said, 'Have you anything in mind you would like to sing?' And she said, '*Jesus Loves Me.*'"

Ingrid says that at the time she had been going regularly to Sunday school and had been singing the song for weeks.

"Now with these characters in this audience," Woody said, "I didn't know if we should make a direct cut. But it was a funny thing. She got into the thing and did about four complete verses and it was so quiet you could have heard a pin drop. It was probably the first time in the history of the Adams Theater that there was any real peace and quiet. It knocked them cold."[15]

"We were a three-ring circus within ourselves," Woody said. "For instance, Chubby Jackson was doing his own number as part of the rhythm section, jumping in the air and carrying on like mad. And the trumpets used to parade on the riser, swinging back and forth. One day when Sonny Berman finished his solo and they were swinging up there with their horns, he jumped down to the next level and went right through the floorboard, and he was in wood up to his navel."

Ralph Burns said, "It was really like a football team on the road. We just charged, everyplace. Woody loved it, that's all. It was great."[16]

"Woody was a great organizer," Flip Phillips said. "And if you could play, he'd let you play. He'd never hold you back. He'd put the mike in front of you and say, 'Go ahead and blow.'

"Everybody in that band was happy. It was one of the best bands that ever was. It could shout, swing. It could play a lovely ballad."

"Woody was like one of the guys. We did things together. In Atlantic City, we had some time off. He wanted to drive to New York and he asked me to go along. The car broke down. We hailed a farmer. He drove us into New York. It was *cold*. Woody and I were under a horse blanket."[17]

The excellence of the music aside for the moment, it is this participation in the lives of his brilliant gypsy musicians, his tolerance of, indeed exuberant encouragement of, their most eccentric shenanigans, that gave Woody the most spirited, exciting, and innovative jazz band of the time, instantly recognizable on the radio. His clarinet playing had evolved enormously. The British writer Steve Voce, in a 1986 monograph titled *Woody Herman*, one in the Jazz Masters series published by Apollo Press in London, wrote:

> In the early days it was possible to tell which other players had caught his ear. Jimmy Noone, the languid and fat-toned prime mover from New Orleans, was a main influence, and Jimmy's expert use of trills remains an element in Woody's work to this day. Regardless of Woody's devotion to all things Ellingtonian, Duke's clarinet player Barney Bigard would inevitably have been a major source of inspiration for him. Barney's sound was more facile and jazz-committed than Noone's, but he had the same singing New Orleans quality. (Barney's nickname was Steps, and Woody deliberately emulates him in the Woodchoppers' record of that name made in 1946.) Apart from Bigard's specific sound, Woody made use of his methods, and his famous declamatory soaring over the final choruses on many of the Herd's performances echoes the way in which Duke used Bigard's sound to fly across the Ellington band ensemble.
>
> In the pre-forties one can hear Woody occasionally switch onto someone else's style. He was accomplished enough to do a Goodman or a Shaw or even . . . a Ted Lewis! But by 1940 the elements had come together and, although

Noone and Bigard influences were to remain discernable, Woody had blended them into his own distinctive sound. Perhaps the best example of it from this period is the 1941 *Woodsheddin' with Woody*, a fast-moving Lowell Martin chart to feature Herbie Haymer on tenor and Cappy Lewis on trumpet as well as Woody. Here also the Basie influence is revealed as Linehan, White, Yoder, and Carlson open with the familiar and tight and sparse rhythm section sound. Although he was never to emulate them in the way that the genius Barney Bigard did, Woody had achieved an ability to negotiate the breaks between the registers so that not even another clarinetist would notice them. This is a sure sign of a gifted musician, and the solo on *Woodsheddin'* might have been regarded as a virtuoso display of swinging jazz clarinet. It also held another formalized aspect of Woody's style, which was to be used to great effect in the ensuing years—the exciting growl from the throat used with random abandon by Pee Wee Russell and honed to exciting perfection by Edmond Hall.[18]

It is a very good description of Woody's playing. Though the influences of his models were evident, he was by the early 1940s a fully individual clarinetist and continued to evolve. With a full warm tone and inflection that identified him in two or three notes, his playing went to a new plateau of excellence. His alto work, rooted in Frank Trumbauer, was sensuous and lyrical, rather like the work of Hodges, but again, his own. He used alto on the ballads, clarinet on the up-tempo material. His singing was easy, in tune, natural, and as unassuming as the man himself.

If success had come gradually, he had all of it that he could have wanted, the status (in that vanished age) like that of a movie star. And his financial worries seemed to be over.

11

Ebony Concerto

The story of the commission, composition, and first performance of Stravinsky's *Ebony Concerto* is encrusted with mythology.

The title refers to the clarinet. Actually, good modern clarinets are made not of Indian or Ceylonese ebony but from grenadilla, or African blackwood, which is now becoming scarce. *The Harvard Dictionary of Music* says that the instrument "lends itself to the expression of love and passion as well as of fury and parody," and that is how Woody used it. It has been little employed since the bebop revolution because, in the opinion of Artie Shaw, it is too hard to play compared with the saxophone. This is because it overblows at the twelfth, called the second partial in the overtone series, while the saxophone overblows at the octave. Thus the clarinet has a more complicated fingering. That is to say, after you go above the twelfth, the fingering changes, whereas on a saxophone, the octave key is depressed with the thumb and the fingering in the higher register remains the same. This eases fingering for the complex chromaticism of bebop, although Buddy DeFranco—whom Woody admired—has managed to execute such figures with facility on the clarinet.

In 1945, *Down Beat* and other trade publications announced in headlines that Igor Stravinsky was going to write a piece to be called *Ebony Concerto* for the Woody Herman band. The excitement over this seeming signal honor reflected one of several complexes that afflicted jazz, this one a yearning for respectability.

Another of these was the notion that the classical and jazz worlds were irreconcilably separate, the former occupying a higher order of artistic merit—despite the fact that as far back as the 1920s, major figures in classical music, both in America and Europe, had expressed themselves privately and in print as deeply impressed by this vigorous emerging new music. Even the march king, John Philip Sousa, had praised it highly, and in the 1930s Vladimir Horowitz was known to be one of the most devout of Art Tatum admirers.

Because improvisation was considered a defining element of jazz, it was somehow assumed—even by some of the most enthusiastic supporters in the trade press—that jazz musicians were mostly self-taught and by corollary ignorant of classical music. From its very earliest days, many jazz musicians had undergone rigorous training, whether on their own initiative, with private teachers, or in universities and conservatories. Will Marion Cook had studied at the American University under Dvořák and with Joseph Joachim in Berlin. A photo of the Buddy Bolden band taken about 1905 shows Jimmy Johnson with his hand resting on the neck of his bass in the correct position used by symphony players. Don Redman, the son of a prominent music teacher, studied at the Chicago and Boston conservatories and played not only saxophone but the double-reed instruments by the age of twelve, which suggests that he might have joined a symphony orchestra had he not been black. More such examples can be cited. The great trumpeter Harry (Sweets) Edison said to me once, "Jazz is no folk music. It's too hard to play."

Nonetheless, reading was not in the 1940s an essential qualification for playing jazz. Rather a superb ear and a mind-hand co-ordination that would express a musical thought instantly and reflexively through an instrument were the first requisites. Music education in America has come an enormous distance since those days, when musicians who couldn't read, including Buddy Rich and Dave Tough, simply memorized their parts. Head arrangements, or simply heads, as they were called, were memorized collective improvisations. This undoubtedly contributed to the jazz musician's tendency to obeisance to "classical" music, which many of them who couldn't read or at least read well, listened to constantly. Bix Beiderbecke had been one such musician. Then, too, there was the American proclivity to be intimidated by European culture, particularly music.

Thus, when it was announced that Stravinsky was going to write a piece for the Woody Herman band, the jazz community, or at least its press, went into paroxysms of euphoria at this recognition of jazz by a man who by then was considered musical royalty.

It has been written that Woody got a call from Stravinsky announcing that he wanted to write a piece for the band. The publicists of Woody's label, Columbia Records, put out this version of the story, which has tended to persist:

"The famous Russian composer, long a follower of American jazz . . ."—this is doubtful—". . . became vitally interested in Herman and his band after hearing Herman's *Caldonia, Bijou*, and *Goosey Gander*. In a similar vein, unknown to Stravinsky, Woody and his bandsmen have long been fans of the Russian and his works. After hearing these recordings, Stravinsky decided that Woody's musicians would be the best media [sic] for performing his works in the proper spirit and interpretation. Hence, Stravinsky wrote the *Ebony Concerto* especially for the famous clarinetist, thus effecting one of the most extraordinary unions of two schools of musical thought—jazz and 'modern.'"

That was fabrication, record-company hokum at its worst. It suggests that Stravinsky henceforth would abandon other work to devote his career to writing for the Woody Herman band and its instrumental configuration, which was of course nonsense.

Furthermore, the publicity release and indeed almost every piece of writing about *Ebony Concerto* overlooks the fact that Woody's was not even the first American dance or jazz band that Stravinsky wrote for. He composed his *Scherzo à la russe* for a performance on the Mutual Broadcasting System by the Paul Whiteman band in 1944. Furthermore, his *Preludium* for jazz ensemble dates from 1937, while *Ragtime for Eleven Instruments* was completed on November 11, 1918. So his interest in American music, including jazz, was *not* inspired by some sort of encounter with a Woody Herman record.

Still another story at the time held that Stravinsky had to consult a saxophone player about the fingering of the instrument in order to write for Woody's band. This is almost certainly false. As Neal Hefti put it, "You don't have to know fingerings to write for an instrument." Finally, Stravinsky already had written for saxophones. His *Tango*, written in 1940, was orchestrated for strings, woodwinds, brass, guitar, piano, percussion, and saxophones. (He later re-configured the piece for more conventional instrumentation.)

How, then, did the *Ebony Concerto* come to be written? One version of the events is this:

In 1945, Woody's attorney, Howard Goldfarb, known as Chubby Goldfarb, in a conversation with a representative of a music-publishing firm, discovered that the man knew Stravinsky. Goldfarb thought it was worth at least exploring the possibility that Stravinsky would compose something for the band. The publisher was Lou Levy, from whom lyricist Sammy Cahn had once borrowed money to help keep the Band That Plays the Blues in gasoline, and his representative was Goldie Goldmark, a former bassist with the Mitchell Ayres band. Levy (no relation to the pianist who would join Woody two years after this) had built a powerful publishing operation on foreign tunes, and Goldmark apparently was seeing Stravinsky on a matter of foreign copyrights. He used the opportunity to expose the composer to some of Woody's records, particularly Ralph Burns's *Bijou*.

Stravinsky was one of a number of classical composers who had fled Europe after the rise of Hitler, among them Paul Hindemith, who was teaching composition at Yale; Béla Bartók, who struggled for survival in New York; and four who lived in California: Ernst Krenek, Ernst Toch, Arnold Schoenberg, and Stravinsky. Stravinsky had the biggest reputation in America, chiefly on the strength of his early works, including *The Firebird* (1910), *Petrouchka* (1911), and *Le Sacre du printemps* (1913); *Sacre* is a high-grade ore of ideas for movie composers though it seemed so radical when it was first heard in Paris, a few days after Woody's birth, that it caused a riot. All these pieces were written for Sergei Diaghilev's Ballet Russe. Stravinsky's later work did not achieve the popularity of these earlier pieces, but his was a big name, made only the bigger by Walt Disney's 1940 animated cartoon feature *Fantasia* in which *Le Sacre du printemps* was used not in its original context, a ballet about the spring rites of a pagan people, but as accompaniment to the dawn of the world. Many jazz musicians were enamored of Stravinsky's work, Ralph Burns and Neal Hefti citing him among their important influences. Pete Candoli sometimes incorporated fragments from *The Firebird* in solos.

Woody told the late Peter Clayton, a diligent British writer and broadcaster: "A mutual friend introduced our band via records to Igor Stravinsky in California. The man said he was going to get Stravinsky intrigued enough to do something for our band. I, of course, pooh-poohed it and thought it was ridiculous. I didn't believe Stravinsky would get involved with our kind of thing. Fortunately for me and the band, I got a wire from Stravinsky saying that he was writing a piece for us and it would be his Christmas gift to us."

Woody said that reading the telegram caused him "one of the wildest psychological moments I ever had." He said, "Having one of the world's great composers write for me was beyond imagination." He told Peter Clayton that it was "the greatest thing in this man's musical life."[1]

Ralph Burns was told that his *Bijou* was the piece that intrigued Stravinsky. Ralph said, "It sounded like Stravinsky. It was like his sound. Not a copy of any notes, or anything. It was what Stravinsky did that nobody else did. All the grunts and cheeps and everything. *Rites of Spring, Petrouchka.*"[2] It does indeed sound like Stravinsky, once your attention is drawn to its genesis. It is jagged, angular, with notes flicked into it in unexpected and asymmetrical ways.

None of these émigré composers found it easy to make a living in the United States. Stravinsky's combined annual royalties probably didn't add up to those from any two or three of Irving Berlin's songs. So, legend has it, Stravinsky's attorney called Howard Goldfarb and informed him that Stravinsky barely had enough money to live on. Woody, according to several accounts, immediately arranged to pay him a fee.

From no matter what direction it is approached, the story is unsatisfying. Stravinsky was not noted for idly commencing pieces of music for anyone, certainly not as gifts. Indeed, he is widely quoted as saying, when he was asked what inspired him to compose, "Somebody sends me a check and I start writing." The idea that he suddenly discovered the sound of an American dance or jazz band on exposure to some Woody Herman records is untenable.

"Let's face it," Ralph said. "Woody was probably paying him a fortune." This raises an intriguing possibility. Woody was always surreptitiously rescuing people, lending money to musicians, in one instance that I know coming up with mortgage money for a disc jockey about to lose his house. One wonders, in view of the sheer improbability of the *Ebony Concerto*, if Woody quietly engineered a commission for a composer he admired.

Woody's own testimony held that Stravinsky did indeed begin work on the piece without a commission. Then Woody got a call from an attorney who represented Stravinsky. He told Woody that Stravinsky didn't know he was calling. He told Woody: "Mr. Stravinsky is not a wealthy man. I think that a fee of some kind should be arranged." Woody agreed. How much the fee really was has never been determined; Woody said it was only a token sum. Some of the veterans of the band think it was much more than that.

Whatever the case, Stravinsky completed the work, which called for the addition of a harp and a French horn to the Herman band, on December 1, 1945, and sent it on to New York. The band was playing at the Paramount.

Woody hated the Paramount. "I think we all did," Neal Hefti said. "It was a hard job. You'd play from morning until midnight, between the movies."

Woody said, "It was a real hardship post because it was six or eight shows a day, starting at nine-thirty in the morning, plus it was seven days a week. The only time you'd get a rest was when you collapsed. They'd send you home for a day to recuperate."[3]

During an engagement at the Paramount, possibly that one, Woody put in a call to Frank Sinatra. At the end of it, Sinatra asked where he was calling from. Woody said, "The Paramount."

Sinatra said, "Do they still shove your food under the door?"[4]

"That's about the way it was," Neal Hefti said. "You never left the theater. They'd bring in the food, the wrapped sandwiches. Between the third and fourth show, we would tell Popsie Randolph, the band boy, who had come from Benny to us, what we wanted. Popsie would come back with baskets of sandwiches, saying, 'Who wanted no mustard? Who wanted it on white bread? Who wanted the thin milk shake? Who wanted the coffee without cream? Who wanted the coffee in a clean cup?' And that's the way we would eat.

"I was there for the start of the Stravinsky rehearsals. I left the band three or four weeks before the concert to go with Joe Marsala, but Frances stayed with the band for the rest of that engagement. The first transcript of the *Ebony Concerto* arrived. The trumpet section would go up to the rehearsal room in the Paramount and practice the trumpet parts and look at the score.

"Everybody in the trumpet section was a Stravinsky fan—Pete Candoli, Ray Wetzel, myself. By then I was being replaced, maybe by the same guy I had replaced, Cappy Lewis, then back from the war. There was a law that they had to give anyone getting out of the service his old job. Neal Reid came back, Walt Yoder came back, Sam Rubinwich came back. Conrad Gozzo came in, Marky Markowitz came in.

"We just glommed onto *Ebony Concerto*. Not the whole band, but the whole trumpet section and Ralph. The trumpet players were always quoting bits of Stravinsky in their solos. I loved that trumpet section. Of all the trumpet sections!

"But I never rehearsed that piece with the whole band, only with the trumpet section. I went with Joe Marsala, and we played right across the street from the Paramount, with Davey Tough, Chuck Wayne on guitar, Gene DiNovi on piano, Clyde Lombardi on bass."[5]

Near Christmas, Stravinsky arrived in New York, purportedly to begin rehearsing the piece himself. But that is doubtful, too; or at least this was by no means the sole or even primary purpose of the trip from California. He faced a more immediate and important premiere. His *Symphony in Three Movements* was to be performed on January 24, 1946—two months before *Ebony Concerto*—by the New York Philharmonic. And Stravinsky himself was to conduct the work, which he said was written under the impression of world events, including the horrors of the recently concluded war. He had written it between 1942 and 1945, and so presumably was working on it as he was planning or writing *Ebony Concerto*. In any event, they are coeval works.

The whole band was excited about meeting Stravinsky. Rehearsals, according to Woody, were held in a recreation room on the top floor of the Paramount. The band assembled after the first show of the morning, all of them formally dressed in suits and ties. Accompanied by his wife, Stravinsky arrived, wearing an aging sweatshirt and tennis shoes.

Ralph said, "Guys like Flip Phillips and Bill Harris could not read very well. In Count Basie's and Duke's bands, there were a couple of guys who couldn't read at all. Stravinsky never said anything, but it must have been kind of a culture shock when he brought in the piece. But we were very serious about it. Guys like Flip would go home and just learn it, note for note."[6]

Red Norvo said that because of the difficulty of the clarinet part, Woody asked him to take charge of at least some of the rehearsals, leaving him time to practice his own part. Chubby Jackson called in sick, Red said. He recalled:

"Woody said to me in the dressing room, 'Chubby's not here.'

"I said, 'He must have seen the bass part.'

"Woody said, 'Who'll we get?'

"I said, 'Get the guy who plays with Tommy Dorsey, Trigger Alpert.' Trigger came in and read the bass part off beautifully. All it took was about five days of Trigger playing the part, and Chubby came back.'"[7]

It isn't that the bass part was difficult. On the contrary, it gave Chubby very little to do.

Woody told me that the first rehearsal was hellish, and the band's nerves grew frayed. Stravinsky walked over and put his arm around Woody, saying, "Voody, you have a lovely family."

And the band relaxed a little.

The rehearsals were a strain on everyone. In those days, almost all jazz, except an occasional experimental oddity such as Fats Waller's *Jitterbug Waltz*, was in 4/4 time. The innovations of Dave Brubeck, Lennie Tristano, and others, using polyrhythms and compound time signatures, were in the future. The first attempts of jazz rhythm sections to play even a simple 3/4 were stiff, though eventually they assimilated and played easily all sorts of compound figures. Stravinsky, on the other hand, told Woody it was hard for him to write in simple 4/4, which is what jazz musicians were used to. He said it was torture for him.[8]

Woody said, "He hummed and whistled and tapped his foot while he dragged us through it. He was only interested in whether we got it, not how we got it." Woody was always amazed at his patience; Stravinsky in turn was deeply touched at how much time and care the Herman band was willing to expend to get his music right.

Stravinsky worked closely with Woody on the clarinet part. "Stravinsky sweated it out, and I did too," Woody said. "He worked with me by the hour and helped me and tried to give me confidence in the whole thing. I think he wrote it with a special purpose in mind, and I think he does this many times. I'm not a serious musician in any sense of the word. I've never spent that much time listening to serious music. But I'm sure about this one piece and I'm sure that Stravinsky has done it his whole life. He will make things awkward on the instrument with his complete knowledge of the instrument to get a sound, a particular feeling out of something. Make it very difficult."[9]

What Woody was saying in essence is this: Stravinsky didn't *want* the conventional sounds of instruments, the sounds that are easy for players to make according to the standard orchestration textbooks. He wanted them in their strain registers, wanted the difficult intervals. The brilliant Gil Evans did the same thing in jazz writing; and Gil was enamored of the Russian composers.

Stravinsky was startled to learn that the band was playing six or more shows a day at the Paramount while rehearsing the new piece. The band would rehearse with Stravinsky, then go back to play a show while Stravinsky slipped into Sardi's restaurant for a vodka or two, then return to rehearsal. The band hardly had time to eat.

Rumors about the work and the difficulties of rehearsing it were abroad in the business. Woody encountered Benny Goodman on Broadway at four o'clock one morning. Woody described the dialogue that followed:

"Hey, Pops, is that a hard part, that Stravinsky piece?"

"Is it hard?" Woody said. "It's impossible."

"Oh it can't be that hard," Goodman said with customary condescension.

Woody told him that he'd shown the part to clarinet players in the New York Philharmonic and they had attested to its difficulty.

Goodman said, "So it's a little bit difficult, but it can't be that hard."

Woody sent a miniature score of the piece to Goodman's house. On another encounter a few weeks later, Benny told Woody, "Hey, it *is* hard."

The premier performance of the work was given March 25, 1946, in Carnegie Hall. Personnel for the concert comprised, besides Woody, Conrad Gozzo, Pete Candoli, Marky Markowitz, Shorty Rogers, and Sonny Berman, trumpets; Bill Harris, Ralph Pfeffner, and Ed Kiefer, trombones; Sam Marowitz and John LaPorta, alto saxophones and clarinets; Flip Phillips and Mickey Folus, tenor saxophones; Sam Rubinwich, baritone saxophone; Tony Aless, piano; Billy Bauer, guitar; Chubby Jackson, bass; Red Norvo, vibraharp; John Barrows, French horn; and Abe Rosen, harp.

Stravinsky could not be there to conduct: he had been booked for a tour in Europe, and as he told Woody, he had to eat. The work was conducted by Walter Hendl, then assistant conductor of the New York Philharmonic.

Also on the program was a three-movement work by Ralph Burns, who recalled: "Woody said, 'We're going to give this concert. Why don't you write a serious piece?' I stayed out at Chubby's place on Long Island and wrote *Summer Sequence* in three movements. I called it that because it was summertime when I wrote it. It was written for me on piano, Billy Bauer on guitar, Chubby on bass, and the other members of the band. It was a big hit at the Carnegie Hall concert."

The concert, a sellout, was a great success, though *Ebony Concerto* undoubtedly nonplussed many members of the audience. The reviews in the New York newspapers were cautious. Barry Ulanov's in *Metronome* was not. He wrote that the piece was "more like a French imitation of Igor than the great man himself . . . . Rhythmically, tonally and melodically it is as dry as dehydrated eggs and far less palatable."

Neal Hefti, who was in the audience, said, "I loved it. Not all the guys in the band did. Their take was that it didn't swing."[10]

Ralph said, "The concert was wonderful. Then we went on the road with it, and Alexei Haieff conducted it. He was a protégé of Stravinsky, and I took orchestration lessons from him."[11]

The concert was booked into universities, where *Ebony Concerto* encountered audiences less eager to affect understanding. At a hall in Baltimore, it was booed. It got the worst reception at Purdue University. Woody said, "No matter when we performed the piece—at the start of a concert, in the middle, or at the finish—many of the audience decided that the music wasn't me, that we were insulting their intelligence."[12]

Ralph Burns said: "The record Leonard Bernstein made of it with the New York Philharmonic is probably the way it should sound. When you hear a symphony orchestra play it, to me it sounds much better. Stravinsky was out of his element, and we were out of our element. He was very nice. He tried and we tried."[13]

▼

Possibly. There is a recording of it by Sir Eugene Goossens and the London Symphony Orchestra, which is murky, lacking in the bite the piece would seem to require. In 1965, Benny Goodman made a satisfactory recording of it with something called the Columbia Jazz Ensemble, a pick-up band of some of the best New York jazz players in studio work. This performance, at least, has an edge on it, but the ensemble work is sloppy. It sounds like a read-through, not a thoroughly rehearsed performance.

In tribute to his fellow composer, Elliott Carter wrote, "Formulas, schemas and platitudes that would serve as useful padding have no place in [Stravinsky's] work . . . ."

That is not so. To be sure, all composers have their preferred devices. One can recognize a Rachmaninoff piece immediately by its harmonic vocabulary. Sibelius uses woodwinds in ways that identify him immediately. But Stravinsky actually cannibalizes his own work. In *The Song of the Nightingale*, begun in 1908 and finished six years later, the orchestral vocabulary is exactly that of *Le Sacre du printemps*: the propulsive rhythms, the banging chords underpinned by tympani, the skittering strings, the chirping woodwinds.

Stravinsky was a composer of amazing range and versatility. He was capable of a quite different kind of writing, as witness his sweepingly lyrical *Apollo*, written for string orchestra in 1928, or the beautiful *Symphony of Psalms*, as well as a more severe and ascetic kind of music. But, Elliott Carter notwithstanding, he had a habit of dipping into his old devices, and he does so in *Ebony Concerto*.

He begins it with a tiny two-note cell from trumpets in cup mutes, B-flat and A. This tells us what's coming: the whole piece is rather muted, quiet, and certainly does not take advantage of the resources of the Woody Herman band, especially that brilliant brass section. And that is puzzling, because Stravinsky liked brass. He then presents the clarinet over a French horn counterline that reminds me of *Petrouchka*. Then there is some syncopated piano that evokes *Le Sacre du printemps*, particularly the four-hands piano transcription of it. For a time the band plays tense little staccato fragments, as if the music can't get started. And then the music is allowed to flow as the harp takes up a running rhythmic figure. It's right out of *Le Sacre*.

Woody's own evaluation of the piece is interesting. Stravinsky had listened to the band, observing its wild qualities and the fierce power of its brass. "And what do you suppose this man did?" Woody said. "He wrote the quietest piece that he ever wrote in his life. The brass never gets out of the goddamn cup mutes. It's a very delicate and very *sad* piece. Sad. There's a lot of emotion, a great deal of sadness in the piece. And here we were, a wild, happy-sounding group. And this was the piece he wrote for us! But he knew that only this type of cats would make this sound the way he wanted it to. They feel some sadness."[14]

That view of the piece is puzzling. I find a great deal of humor in it. But one thing is certain: in this piece, Stravinsky did what Stravinsky did; he did not do what the Woody Herman band did. All he did was to use the instrumentation, plus harp and French horn, to his own ends. And—this is something Ralph Burns and I have discussed—give it time and that piece grows on you.

▼   ▼   ▼

After a concert in Boston at the end of March, Woody took Charlotte and Ingrid on vacation to Bermuda. According to a report in the July 8, 1946, issue of *Ebony* magazine, the musicians and members of general society with whom the Hermans associated themselves were mostly black. The magazine showed a photo of Woody and Ingrid with the caption: *Woody Herman and wife at Chrisley Hall, a Negro-owned hotel in Bermuda, at reception by Negro musicians in his honor.*

The report said, "Among the first tourists to succumb to the lure of Bermuda in her return to the position as No. 1 resort of the Atlantic was Woody Herman of swing fame." World War II had ended eight months earlier, and the Bermuda economy was just starting a return to normal. Thus the visit of a celebrity had a certain significance for the island.

"The Hermans put up for eight days at one of the pink and white lime-washed cottages of swank Cambridge Beaches guest colony in Somerset," the report continued.

"The Hermans were visitors at Cambridge Beaches and at Chrisley Hall, the West End's popular rendezvous of both Americans and Bermudians which is operated by Mrs. Clara Gordon, an accomplished musician in her own right . . . .

"Mrs. Clara Gordon entertained the Hermans, introducing to them many native musicians, members of local outfits that often entertain at the larger hotels here in Bermuda.

"It is odd to note that such an outstanding maestro as Woody Herman saw little of our white musicians and on no occasion was feted by them."

There is a tragic undertone in that report: the desperation of black

Americans, as manifest in their one big magazine, for white acceptance and respectability. The American dilemma is right there in the words. And jazz was the most healing force in American society.

▼   ▼   ▼

Plans were made to record *Ebony Concerto* at the CBS Playhouse in Los Angeles. Woody by now knew that he and Stravinsky were neighbors. Rehearsals were held in the Casino Gardens, a ballroom owned by Tommy Dorsey on the beach at Santa Monica. Woody would pick Stravinsky up and drive him to the rehearsals. He said:

"I had more wonderful hours with this man, and we had nothing in common actually. I knew nothing of his kind of living and existence and certainly he had none of mine. And we spent so many wonderful hours. We'd discuss everything in the world except music.

"We were driving to Santa Monica this one particular day and a group of dogs were crossing the street. A little pack. He said, 'Look, Voody. Dey have da life. Look. No worries on deir back, no taxes, no problems. You and me? Ve have to do better dan de last time. Top yourself. Look at dem. Dey're happy. Eat, sleep, and fuck."[15]

Stravinsky conducted the work in a performance on August 18 for the CBS radio broadcast, and again the next day for a Columbia records recording.

Later, Woody said, "Mr. Stravinsky, tell me about French clarinetists, about German clarinetists, and the difference in their performance."

Stravinsky said, "French clarinet players: very good technique, quick tongue, very small sounds. The German players: technique not so good, tongue not so good, but very big sound. But you, Vood-ee—Ah!"[16]

Woody, who was always a little intimidated by the technical brilliance on the instrument of Benny Goodman and Artie Shaw, said, "I could have kissed him."

12

Lady McGowan's Dream

Ebony Concerto added to the band's prestige, but by now it had plenty of it anyway, particularly among musicians. The extent of professional admiration for the Herd can be seen in a 1946 encounter at Eastwood Gardens, a dance pavilion in Detroit. The Glenn Miller band, which was to follow the Herd in the location, arrived a day early simply to hear Woody. Miller, Woody's friend of the GAC outer offices and that drunken party in Boston, had been killed in a plane crash over the English Channel when World War II was almost over. His postwar band was led by his star tenor saxophonist, Tex Beneke. The band's vocal group was the Crew Chiefs, who had been with Miller's air force band during the war. Its pianist, only a few months out of the army, was a young Henry Mancini.

Artie Malvin, who sang with the Crew Chiefs, remembers the encounter vividly: "The Beneke band was supposed to follow Woody. I think it was a Sunday night they were supposed to play their last dance there.

"It was a dance pavilion out under the stars. When you walked into Eastwood Gardens, you came into a long bar to the left, and to the right was the dance floor, and far away the bandstand. The bar was a covered area.

"The night we arrived, it was pouring rain. The dance floor was under water. Nobody showed up. We started to socialize with the guys in Woody's band, and we said, 'We came early specifically to hear the band.' And Woody said, 'We'll set up in the bar and play.'

"They played a complete concert for just the Beneke band. There was nobody there except the bartenders.

"And it was fantastic—that incredible band playing at their very best, just for us. I'll never forget it."[1]

Mancini, in his autobiography *Did They Mention the Music?*, gives a vivid portrait of what life was like on the road at that time:

> Nobody had even a remote idea that the age of the big bands was ending. The public still idolized leaders like Benny Goodman, Artie Shaw, Duke Ellington, Count Basie, Woody Herman.
>
> When you were on the road with a band, you lived in a capsule, a cocoon. There was no other world but the band, because you were always leaving behind the people you met along the way. The only continuity you had was with the band itself. You breathed and talked the life of the band. You could almost complete everybody else's sentences. You knew everything about each other. You were always on that bus, and you settled into a groove. Everything came down to two things: where do we eat, and what time does the job start? I was by now more than slightly interested in girls, but even they didn't enter into it that much: you were always waving good-bye to them through the bus window.
>
> I cannot remember ever finding a restaurant that was any good, nor can I figure out how we got our pressing done. We did our socks and underwear ourselves in the hotel room sink, but how we did our pressing is still a big mystery to me.[2]

It is little wonder that these men yearned for a permanent home and a stable family life, Woody among them. He was about to buy the house he would live in for the rest of his life.

▼　　▼　　▼

Ingrid Herman's first visual memories are of her parents' apartment in Jackson Heights and their bungalow at the Garden of Allah in Hollywood.

"I remember a Christmas in New York, the first Christmas that my father really had some money," Ingrid said. "I think that's when he bought my mother two or three fur coats all at one time. Both sets of grandparents came to New York. As I remember we had a white Christmas tree, the only time in our lives that we ever had a white Christmas tree. I think Otto, my father's father, set up an electric train around this little church scene that had lights flashing on and off."[3]

Woody remembered that his father had built a mechanism that would keep a Christmas tree turning. He brought it to New York for that Christmas Ingrid still remembers.

Woody told Stuart Troup, "The financial insecurity didn't have much of an effect on my marriage. Charlotte and I were both experienced with the show biz roller coaster, and we anticipated the lows even while hoping for the highs. When we were poor, we managed to button up. But when we had even moderate prosperity, we lived to the hilt.

"One way to have Charlotte share in any success was to surprise her with something expensive. After buying her a fur stole, I decided that every successful man's wife should have a natural ranch mink coat. She was flabbergasted. So were the lawyers who handled my business affairs."

And that Christmas, he bought her yet another fur. "I had noticed a certain look on her face one day when she eyed a Russian white fur in a store window," he said. "On Christmas Eve, I bought it. When she opened the box that evening, you could hear her for miles. My lawyers really flipped out."

The next residence Ingrid remembers is the house at 8620 Hollywood Boulevard in what was then an unincorporated part of Los Angeles County. It is hardly a boulevard at that point but a winding narrow road through the hills of what is now West Hollywood. Woody bought the house just before Ingrid turned five.

The band grossed more than a million dollars in 1946, a sum that may seem unimpressive in an era when CEOs take as much as a hundred million dollars a year out of their corporations. But it was a great deal of money then. Frank Sinatra made headlines when he became the first singer ever to earn a million a year. Charlotte and Woody thought it was time to buy their first, and as it turned out, last house, to invest some of their earnings. They learned that Humphrey Bogart and his wife were getting ready to sell their house on Hollywood Boulevard. "They bought it when they were married," Woody said, "and lived there for the first year of their married life. And then she decided they needed a bigger house. They were going to be entertaining."

The *Capitol*, a small magazine put out by Capitol Records, reported in its September, 1946, issue:

Take it from Mr. and Mrs. Woody Herman, Lauren Bacall is not a chick to deal with lightly. Like her husband, Humphrey Bogart, she won't be pushed around.

The Hermans learned about Bacall the hard way in Hollywood last month, a few nights before Woody's band completed four smash weeks at the Casino

Gardens. It seems that the Bogarts put their house up for sale. The Hermans heard about it. All four got together.

"The price," said Bogart, speaking from the corner of his mouth, "is seventy thousand. Take it or leave it."

The Hermans said it was a nice looking house, up on the pretty hill above Ciro's on the Sunset Strip, and that—considering inflation and such stuff— the price appeared about right.

Contracts were signed. Charlotte Herman looked at Lauren Bacall. Woody looked at Humphrey Bogart. All four of them looked at a fancy washing machine—the automatic kind—that was setting in the washroom near the kitchen.

"I presume," said Charlotte Herman, "that the washing machine . . . is included in the purchase price agreed upon."

Mr. and Mrs. Bogart looked at her sternly.

"It goes with us," said Bacall.

"We just bought your house," Woody interrupted, pointing at the washing machine. "For seventy thousand the Bendix should be happy to remain here."

"The machine goes with us, Bub," barked Bogart, a cigarette dangling from his lips just as it did when he first stumbled across Ingrid Bergman in Casablanca.

"We have a daughter," Mrs. Herman offered, "who will start regular school this month. The machine would certainly be a godsend to us."

This contretemps between one highly successful couple and another seems curious from our present perspective, particularly in view of the fact that the house was purchased furnished. But it has an explanation. During World War II, the industries of the United States and Canada were converted with incredible rapidity almost entirely to making the weapons, ammunition, and machinery of war. One of the major factors in the defeat of Germany and Japan was the miraculous rededication of North America's huge industrial power to weaponry. Automobile production came to a halt as the factories retooled to make military vehicles. The manufacture of household appliances ceased. Though the war was over when Woody bought the Bogart house, the conversion back to civilian production had just begun and it was as difficult to buy refrigerators and washing machines as it was cars. Hence Charlotte's plea that, with a child in school, the machine would be a godsend.

The appeal was to no avail. The Bendix went with the Bogarts, and Woody and Charlotte moved into the house where she would live until her death. Woody later described Bacall as "a pain in the ass."

The house, which has four bedrooms, is an odd one. It is difficult to park a car at that point on the street, which is narrow, snaking around the curves of the hillside. The house, on the south side of the street, looks like a modest bungalow. The front door is right on the street. When you enter it, you find you are on the top floor of the house. You stand on a small balcony; to your right is the kitchen and dining area; you look down into the living room, which you reach by descending a curved and steep stairway. The house had four bedrooms and three bathrooms. It was built in 1939, and the decor is vaguely art deco, rather quaint now but quite modern then. The living room is not small but not large. To the left is a den that Charlotte and Woody used as a bedroom in later years. At the left there is another stairway that descends from the living room to lowest of the three tiers of the house. The master bedroom is there. When I used to go there, all down the left wall of that staircase and on shelves were symbols and statuettes of a long list of honors Woody had received: honorary citizen of New York State, honorary citizen of Maryland, honorary Kentucky colonel, citations from jazz societies, along with the small brass gramophones of NARAS and two or three figurines from an award now forgotten, the little bemustached character Esky, the one-time symbol of *Esquire* magazine, holding a trumpet high in the air and silently blowing his brains out. But Woody was notorious for not preserving mementoes, and these were a mere representation of the awards he received.

Through glass doors to the right, the living room opens onto a patio balcony paved with flagstones. When I knew the house, you could see the skyscrapers of downtown Los Angeles rising out of a sea of small buildings and palm trees, but when Woody and Charlotte moved in, those tall edifices did not exist. And there were many clear days then; now the air is often brown. It was, Woody said many years later, "the only home I've ever really known, other than Milwaukee."[4]

At first the house frightened Ingrid. As family photos make obvious, she was an exquisitely pretty blonde little girl, quite Nordic.

"The house seemed very weird," she said. "It was done in an extreme style of the period. The bedroom had this hugely flowered wallpaper that matched this hugely flowered bedspread that matched hugely flowered things that went around the dressing table mirrors, these enormous man-eating orchid-like flowers. Very stylish for the period, but to a little kid? I thought it was scary. I found these lurid wallpaper effects in the bedroom extremely weird. I got used to it."

Things couldn't have seemed rosier, Woody told Stuart Troup. "The band was riding high, the family was ensconced in the Hollywood Hills, and we had such social neighbors as Robert Benchley and Charlie Butterworth.

Beneath the surface, however, a major problem was growing. It had begun to develop a couple of years earlier, when we were living at the Garden of Allah complex. Charlotte had begun drinking and she was taking pills . . . .

"I suppose she was influenced by the movie crowd who lived there, and my absence for up to forty weeks a year on the road contributed to her difficulty.

"I was disturbed about it, but there wasn't a great deal I could do. Like anyone with a drinking problem, she had many excuses. I even threatened to take a walk. But it was an empty gesture; we were very tight."

Ingrid said: "She was a wonderful mother, totally supportive, very warm, very expressive. But she had had a nervous breakdown when I was a little kid. When I was really small, I didn't see that much of her, because she was living my father's schedule. This is when we were spending roughly half the year, I gather, in New York and half the year at the Garden of Allah.

"When we moved up to Hollywood Boulevard, I didn't see too much of her until she started to get crazy. It was so horrible that I remember it, though it only happened two or three times. She would get zoned, from the pills or whatever she was strung out on, and would get into a fight with my nurse, who was really quite a wretched person, but I was very attached to her because she was the person who had my daily care. She slept in my room. Her name was Judy. She was there from the time I was three or so until I was about ten.

"My mother, in the course of their argument, would chase Judy into the room that we shared, yelling and saying, 'You're going to get out in the morning!' And Judy would say, 'Yeah, I'm getting out.' And I would be in tears. It was extremely traumatic for me. Then I came home one day and they said my mother was in the hospital. I didn't see her for a while.

"In those days everybody drank like fish. She was trying to keep up my father's life style. She was very tense and shy. Underneath her beautiful appearance, she was always a very shy, very sensitive, nervous person. I gather she mentioned this to a doctor she had, who prescribed sleeping pills as a tranquilizer. Not to sleep, even. Nobody told her they were habit-forming. If anybody had told her they were habit-forming, this was dope, she would have fled from it. She was really moralistic, very conservative, big on self-discipline.

"What she went through after her breakdown, to get herself back to health! She did everything the hardest way. She was one of the early victims of doctor idiocy. I'm sure she wasn't the only person who got caught up this way. That alone is enough to account for that problem.

"It was a difficult conflict for her. What are you going to do? To be with your kid at home or your husband on the road? They led such disparate lifestyles. By this time I had started school."[5]

▼   ▼   ▼

In 1946, the band won the *Down Beat, Metronome, Billboard*, and *Esquire* polls, the *Esquire* poll in two categories. By now Woody was a major celebrity. Bandleaders then, as we have noted, had the aura of movie stars. The term "groupie" would not be invented until the age of rock and roll, but groupies there always were. It is a mysterious phenomenon. There is no comparable flocking of men to famous women, but the phenomenon of women flinging themselves sexually at famous men is an old one. Franz Liszt seemingly made his way through half the noble beds of Europe, as did Niccolò Paganini.

The bands attracted vast flocks of girls. They troubled Woody. He would take them aside and talk to them, telling them to go home, occasionally appalled at their candor in confessing that they simply wanted to be band girls. One girl, in love with Ralph Burns, followed the band from the East all the way to California. Another, according to Terry Gibbs, was an habituée of the Paramount Theater in New York, who would make out with all the members of whatever band played there. The musicians called her Mattress Annie. "She was very pretty," Terry said, "and the funny part of it was that she was a very nice girl. She was just a straight-out nympho."[6]

"The way it was in those days," Chubby Jackson said, "is that when a band was leaving town, they'd tell a girl, 'Benny Goodman's band is coming in next week. Look up so-and-so.' The guys would pass them along that way."[7]

And then there was Lady McGowan. According to one often-told version of the story, she turned up with several trunks apparently filled with belongings, at the Ambassador West Hotel in Chicago. Lady McGowan was enraptured by the band, constantly entertaining it in her suite, buying it all the liquor it could drink and putting the expenses on her tab. Then she disappeared, and the management found that her trunks were empty. The hotel had been stuck with an uncollectible bill for four thousand dollars. In her commemoration, Ralph Burns wrote *Lady McGowan's Dream*.

According to Chubby Jackson, however, that is not the way it happened.

Chubby discovered her. Woody's band was playing the Panther Room of the Sherman Hotel, but Chubby was staying at the Ambassador West, sharing a room with the comedian Buddy Lester. One night Chubby ran out of cigarettes. He tried to call the desk to see if any were available and somehow got connected to a wrong number. A woman with an educated English accent answered, and after a short exchange, said to him, "I am intrigued by the texture of your voice. Please come over?" Chubby and Buddy Lester went to her suite.

"The door opened," Chubby said, "and here was this very attractive fortyish woman with a turban on, tight-fitting pants, and a huge white shawl that covered her breasts. We walked in, and this woman, Lady McGowan, was looking to have the two of us get into bed with her. She looked like she was out of history. Picture going back into the Roman era. She went to the telephone and started talking to some guy. She came back and said, 'He's coming over.' And now we thought she wanted to have a threesome."

The third man, when he arrived, shocked Chubby and Buddy. It was the comedian Professor Irwin Corey. "It got way beyond anything sexual," Chubby said. "We were throwing one-liners at each other and laughing hysterically.

"We went home. The next evening I told the guys at the Sherman what had happened. And I invited them over. There was Billy Bauer, Steve Condos, the dancer, there was Mickey Folus, there was Lord Buckley, the comedian, Flip, Bill Harris. We had Mickey Folus enter nude. Within minutes, Lady McGowan was leveling one-liners at everyone. She told Lord Buckley he was full of shit, which I thought he was. Finally she took off her robe, and she was totally bare.

"Now it's getting wilder. She gets into the bathtub. She had a lot of sour cream there. We were taking cupped handfuls of it and throwing it on her, splat! Finally we all went home. The next day we found out that the hotel management had ordered her out. She was taken away to some kind of place.

"A week goes by, and she's out on the dance floor with a guy and waving hello to all of us. We went over to the table and talked to her, and she introduced this doctor. She said, 'I've talked him into coming to live with me. He's left the hospital.'

"None of us little squirts had ever seen anything like this in our lives. Ralph Burns had written one of his gorgeous things for the band. It needed a title. He said, 'Why don't we call it *Lady McGowan's Dream*?'"[8]

This is the way Ralph remembers the encounter:

"We were playing the Panther Room at the Sherman Hotel. She was a jazz fan, she was a nut, she was a psycho, she was a very wealthy English lady. At least I thought so. At that age, if somebody tells you she's an English lady, you believe it. She used to give parties for the band. After we'd finish at the Sherman Hotel, we'd all go over to the Ambassador West. Chubby, myself, all of us. It was like a big sex orgy. She loved to have sour cream spread over her whole body and then we'd eat it off. We were a little stoned. It was a marijuana and brandy trip.

"It may have been hearsay, but I understood that Lady McGowan was in and out of a mental institution. Her family would put her there. Then they'd let her out to stay at the hotel. As far as I can remember, that was her real name. We'd play all night, and then go out and ball all night over at the Ambassador West. Lady McGowan balled practically the whole Woody Herman band."[9]

The girls, then, were around, and available.

▼   ▼   ▼

Abe Turchen told me, "Woody met Charlotte when he was seventeen. He'd never known anybody but her. And all of a sudden he was a big star, and the women were around, and he noticed."

Woody confirmed this to me in some late-night conversation years ago. Various reasons for the breakup of the First Herd had seen print. None of them was correct, he said.

Late in 1984, when Charlotte was gone, I talked to Woody on the phone, knowing how much he must be grieving for her. He asked me to come by, which I did. We sat on that flagstone balcony in the afternoon sun and talked for an hour or two. I reminded him of what both he and what Abe Turchen had told me about the marriage and the women. Woody nodded in agreement.

"Is it all right if I tell it now?" I asked.

"Sure," he answered.

And I did tell it. Because Charlotte had had reason to be troubled in those first years of Woody's success. In that earlier conversation he had said of the breakup of the First Herd, "It had nothing to do with dissension in the band or anything like that. I was destroying Charlotte.

"You start mixing Nembutol with booze, baby, and you're on your way home."

After discussing the situation with intimate friends such as Ray Sherman and Jack Siefert, Woody made the decision.

On December 10 and 11, the band recorded six sides (among them John LaPorta's *Non-Alcoholic*) for Columbia, the last ever made by that band. After a dance engagement at Indiana University, Woody announced to his musicians that he was about to disband and gave them their notices. The

First Herd played its last engagement at Castle Farms near Cincinnati on December 24. For that whole fantastic crew—Chubby Jackson, Al Porcino, Flip Phillips, Neal Hefti, Bill Harris, John LaPorta, Don Lamond—it was over. Ever afterwards the men who had played in that band would remember it as the pinnacle of their musical lives, something they would never quite get past or forget. It united them in a camaraderie rather like that of soldiers who have been through a war together. Many of them told me that nothing else in their careers ever really matched it. Barry Ulanov wrote in *Metronome*:

> Let us fold our hands, bow our heads and face to the east. The Woody Herman band is dead; it's official . . . . Only once before . . . was a band of such unequivocal standards and evenness of musicianship organized. That was the Ellington band. It still is, but Herman is not . . . .
>
> Came the post-war inflation, bands became too expensive for their leaders, the public shifted its taste just enough to make the shakier boys quiver a little more and give away a lot more. Heads fell, bands broke up. But never, we told ourselves, the giants. Not Ellington, we said, and we were right. Not Hampton or Kenton, and we were right. And certainly not Herman. And we were wrong . . . . Woody Herman's magnificent band is dead. *Requiescat in Pace*. And forgive me if I brush away a tear.

More than four decades later, composer and conductor Gunther Schuller, in his book *The Swing Era*, would come to this evaluation:

> [The band's] extensive repertory, primarily the creation of Burns and Hefti . . . has hardly dated in retrospect. It is as fresh and exciting now—even when played today by younger orchestras as "older repertory"—as it was then . . . . The reasons are obvious: the Burns/Hefti pieces were *really* new and original at the time, a striking amalgam of first-rate jazz solos (by the likes of Bill Harris, Flip Phillips, Sonny Berman, and Red Norvo, supported by a dynamic and indefatigable rhythm section), and orchestral writing derived from these very same fresh improvisatory styles. Secondly, the musicians played this material, night after night, with an infectious exuberance, an almost physically palpable excitement and a never-say-die energy. As I say, this partially represented the sheer pleasure of frolicking in such high-level instrumental virtuosity. But the band also played with a sense of pride in its individual and collective accomplishments. And it appreciated, indeed relished the newness of their style's harmonic and melodic language, the rich advanced harmonies, the lean, sleek bop lines. The musicians also knew they were playing for a leader who deeply appreciated their talents and their contribution to the cooperative whole.
>
> Some four decades later we tend to forget *how* new this all was. As a result

of the constant recycling since the late 1940s of that genre of big-band style by dozens of orchestras, we tend to take much of it for granted today. We should not forget, however, that there has been very little substantively new in big-band styling since Woody's First Herd, and that the ultimate perpetuation of that style during the last thirty years fell to Count Basie (for whom Hefti arranged for many years).[10]

Some writers date the end of the big-band era from that December when Woody closed out the First Herd, for that month the bands of Benny Goodman, Tommy Dorsey, Harry James, Les Brown, Jack Teagarden, Benny Carter, and Ina Ray Hutton also broke up.

And Woody went home. Charlotte joined Alcoholics Anonymous. "She didn't have as many problems as she thought she did," Woody said, with that kind of benign tolerance he extended to the foibles of our species. "She thought alcohol was the problem, but she was really hooked on the pills."

Ingrid said, "When she came back from the hospital, she went into a whole thing to restore herself to health. She was keeping daytime hours. She had had a terrible insomnia problem because she had been strung out on sleeping pills. So she did all this work around the house. She painted everything that could be painted. She wallpapered. She learned to shoot a pellet gun and would target-shoot for hours. She took long walks to get to where she could sleep."[11]

Charlotte gave up even wine, although in later years she would occasionally order it with dinner. Woody said, laughing, "I went to an AA meeting with Charlotte and my old band was sitting there."

Woody's decision to disband the Herd affected no one more than Abe Turchen. Out of work now, Abe Turchen settled in San Diego. He invested in real estate, and for a short time he owned a furniture store. And he became a father. In 1947, his wife Peggy presented him with a son, whom they named Michael.

13

The Second Herd

Inactivity did not sit well with a man who had been on the road all his adult life and much of his childhood. Woody sang on a California radio show called *The Electric Hour*, heard every Sunday at 4 p.m., hosted by Peggy Lee and her husband, guitarist and composer Dave Barbour, who was the bandleader. He also sang with a band assembled by Ralph Burns, and was for a time a disc jockey on KLAC, subbing on Saturday nights for his friend Al Jarvis. In April that year, 1947, he recorded a duet single with Dinah Shore, and in May he recorded a vocal album, using some of the best men in the large pool of excellent musicians in Los Angeles. With two former road managers, Jack Archer and Milton Deutsch, he started a booking office. For a short time one of their clients was the western swing band of Spade Cooley, who later went to prison for murdering his wife. But the booking business wasn't for Woody, and he dissolved the office.

That summer, Woody's childhood friend and vaudeville colleague, Dan Sherman, turned up at the Herman house. Three weeks earlier, on June 15, 1947, he had been ordained a priest, a Maryknoll father, and he was on his way to China, where he had been assigned and would remain for seven years. Thenceforth Woody and everyone else who ever knew him would call him Father Dan. Woody was thrilled to see him. He and Charlotte had been married by a justice of the peace and according to one version of the story it was Charlotte, not Woody, who said, "Father Dan, why don't you marry us? Don't you think it's time?" Yet in one of many interviews in which he mentioned this event, Woody said he was the initiator. Which-ever of them made the request, Dan Sherman was rather shocked: he'd never performed a wedding ceremony. And there was a complication. Charlotte was not a Catholic.

Father Dan, Woody, and Charlotte visited the pastor of Woody's church, St. Victor's, which is on a street a mile or two away below the house. You can almost see it from the balcony. The pastor, Monsignor Devlin, seemed stern, and Woody and Father Dan were nervous. To Woody's surprise, the monsignor said, "I read in *Variety* that you broke up the band."

He then instructed them in the proper procedure to obtain a dispensa-tion permitting Woody to marry a non-Catholic. The monsignor sent a telegram requesting documents from the church in Milwaukee where Woody had been baptized and confirmed, and he obtained the dispensa-tion.

Woody and Charlotte were married by the Reverend Dan Sherman in an evening ceremony at St. Victor's, the church Woody attended all the rest of his life. Also present were Monsignor Devlin; a Maryknoll seminarian who acted as Woody's best man; Ingrid; and her nurse, Judy. Ingrid, now near-ing six and a pupil at Buckley, an exclusive private school on Doheny Avenue, threw rice at her mother and father.

The party returned to the house and had drinks, and then Woody and Charlotte took Father Dan to see the Duke Ellington band at Ciro's. They wanted a secluded and private table, but the headwaiter seated them right in front of the bandstand. Duke, seeing them, said with his best ornate formality, "Woody, how are you? And lovely Mrs. Herman, and Reverend." And he did a low bow.

▼   ▼   ▼

Woody claimed that during this hiatus, he had no desire to stand in front of a band, but I find that hard to believe. He got interested in hockey, then in baseball, and pursued his interest in car races, always as a spectator. He said later that he went to those races every evening and on Sundays, and despite his avowed desire to spend more time with his daughter, Ingrid says she doesn't remember seeing much of him during that period. Charlotte was a serious baseball fan, and when Woody was away, she would take Ingrid to ball games.

Woody would say on occasion that he became interested in starting a new band when he visited a small nightclub near the intersection of Sunset Boulevard and Vine Street in Hollywood, where pianist Phil Moore had a

▼

group that included Ernie Royal on trumpet and his brother Marshall (later a key figure in the Basie band) on saxophone. He loved Ernie Royal's playing, he said, and wanted a band to showcase it. But there may have been a more compelling reason: money.

Woody was advised by his accountants that they had made an error in his income taxes and he owed the government $30,000. He always said that he and Charlotte knew how to live carefully when money was thin, but did not hesitate to live at the top when it wasn't. The tax bill erased his savings, and he had to borrow against future activities. He was almost sick over it.

Abe Turchen told him, "What are worrying about? I'll handle this."

Woody said, "Abe always had a little loot at home or stashed someplace, but that wasn't the point. We couldn't exist on his little nest egg. So he decided to bet west coast baseball . . . . And that's how we lived for six months—a good six months. He averaged between seven hundred and fifteen hundred dollars a week, and we split it. And he had the same bookmaker and he'd meet him in front of the ball park every night. And finally I couldn't go to the games any more. I couldn't take it, 'cause the bookmaker was always handing Abe an envelope at the end of each game. And that was about the time Buggsy Siegel got bumped off. And I used to say to Abe, 'Don't sit in front of the window tonight.'

"I was worried all the time. But I was living good! Nobody knew how we were making it, how I was living, 'cause I was still coming around in style, you know, and had this lovely home, and everything was cool. But Schwartz, or whoever the bookmaker was, was taking a lopping."

Abe's gambling, which later created a problem, at that time was a blessing to Woody and Charlotte.

I believe Woody simply missed the business during that period. Whatever the complex of reasons, the need for the pains and pleasures of the road, the love of making music, and admiration for Ernie Royal, a need for money, or simply his irrepressibly adventurous spirit, Woody started thinking about putting together a new band. Though the First Herd had been receptive to the thinking of Charlie Parker and Dizzy Gillespie, the new group would go even more deeply into bebop. And it would have a new sound.

George Simon proclaimed the new band in a piece in the December, 1947, issue of *Metronome* under the headline *Woody Returns!* The piece, characterized by Simon's enthusiasm for Woody, reads in part:

Woody's new band is going to be even greater than his last one was! It's going to blow exciting, modern jazz and it's going to have a book of wonderful, progressive arrangements. Reporter of this exciting bit of musical news is none other than Woodrow Wilson (sic) Herman himself, who recently gave up his plans to perform as a single and decided that the only way he could go on living was in front of a band.

"I'm sure we're going to make something great out of it," Woody insists with confidence. "As a band we have a wonderful future, mainly because of the fact that the guys think so much alike, at least so far as I can tell now—even more than the band I had last time."

The band Woody had last time was a great band, as everybody knows. To many it was the greatest band of all time . . . .

Ralph Burns is still setting the band's style. Gerry Mulligan, who used to write for Elliot Lawrence, and Jimmy Giuffre, a former Jimmy Dorsey saxist, are also contributing arrangements.

The concept for the sound that would eventually become known as the Four Brothers must be credited not to Giuffre alone but also to Gene Roland. Roland and Giuffre were friends and fellow Texans. They had attended North Texas State University together long before it had a jazz program. Roland had established himself as an arranger and composer through his work for Stan Kenton. He had played with Lionel Hampton and Lucky Millinder. A year before Woody began thinking about starting a new band, Roland had begun writing for four tenor saxophones in New York. In Los Angeles he played piano in a group that included Giuffre, Stan Getz, Zoot Sims, and Herbie Steward. But the four saxophonists were usually out of work. All of them, Woody said, were hanging out on the beach at Santa Monica.

John Haley Sims, at least, was at home: he was born near the beach, in Inglewood, California, just south of the Los Angeles airport, on October 29, 1925. In his youth, he recalled, the area was covered in lemon groves and Japanese gardens; it is now a huge, sprawling, mall-crowded urb with the usual quota of ill-trimmed and dusty Los Angeles palm trees. His mother and father were in vaudeville, booked as Pete and Kate. Pete Sims was from Missouri, Kate from Arkansas. Zoot grew up in poverty, with his father constantly on the road, and his mother changed domiciles when she couldn't pay the rent. He remembered that the gas and electricity were always being turned off. At one of his high schools, he was recruited into the band to play clarinet. His brother Ray was impressed on tuba, and his brother Bobby on drums. Ray later became an outstanding trombonist, best known for his association with the Les Brown band.

When John Haley was fifteen or sixteen, he joined a Los Angeles band led by Ken Baker. "He put those supposedly funny nicknames on the front of his music stands, Zoot said, Scoot, Voot, Zoot. And I ended up behind the Zoot stand, and it stuck."[1] Zoot was argot of the time for the hip, the clever, the aware, as in zoot suit. The name did stick, but many of his friends called him Jack.

When Jack Sims joined Woody Herman, he still had the Conn tenor his mother had bought him on time payments when he was in high school. But then, he was only twenty-one now. Mustered out of the Army Air Corps in 1946, he joined Benny Goodman, then Woody. "I loved that band," he told Whitney Balliett. "We were all young and had the same ideas. I'd always worried about what other guys were thinking in all the bands I'd been in, and in Woody's I found out they were thinking the same thing I was."

Herbie Steward was also an Angelino, born on May 7, 1926. He would stay with the band only a few months and be replaced by Al Cohn, who is more strongly identified with the Four Brothers sound.

Jimmy Giuffre gave full credit to Gene Roland for development of the sound. Since he had four fine tenor players to work with, Roland put together a group with himself on trumpet—he could play any instrument—and got the group a ballroom job. At the urging of Don Lamond, Woody went to hear them.

Because the sound of three tenors and a baritone saxophone was considered integral to the Second Herd, it is usually forgotten that the sax section at first had a lead alto, Sam Marowitz, whom Woody promptly contacted when he considered forming the new band. Thus that section comprised alto, three tenors, and baritone, as opposed to the more common two altos, two tenors, and baritone. Steward doubled alto and tenor. Eventually Woody would dispense with the lead alto, playing that part himself when the arrangements required it. But the Second Herd initially had a five-man sax section.

Stan Getz was born in Philadelphia February 2, 1927. Legend has it that he acquired his first tenor one day in his early teens and played his first professional engagement five days later, but the reality seems to have been not quite so spectacular. The British writer Richard Palmer, in a monograph on Getz published as one of the Apollo Press Jazz Masters series, wrote:

> At the age of twelve he started on harmonica, switching to string bass within a few months. After a further six months, Stan abandoned the instrument in favor of the alto saxophone—maybe because, as he remembers it, the family's apartment was too small for both Stan *and* the bass, and his father ruled that one of them had to go! He advanced rapidly on alto, and also studied tenor and

bassoon, tutored on the latter by Simon Korvar, whom Getz has called "one of
the greatest bassoonists of all time." By his mid-teens the young Getz was a
thoroughly accomplished and highly promising musician. . . .

He was a professional musician by the age of fifteen, and in the next few
years worked with Jack Teagarden, Bob Chester, Jimmy Dorsey, Benny
Goodman, and Randy Brooks. He was a gifted and experienced musician
by the time Woody recruited him.

But one of the legends about Stan may be true. It was widely said that
when he joined Woody in September, 1947, he played the book flawlessly
at sight and memorized his parts in the process. I asked Woody if it were
true that Stan never looked at the book again. Woody said, "If he ever did, I
never saw it." Chubby Jackson says that while the story might be exaggerated, Stan memorized the book in at most two or three readings.

"I don't know about it," Ralph Burns commented. "But I could believe it
of Stan if nobody else. He was a fantastic reader. At that time the musicianship was not the greatest in bands. When Stan came in, it was unbelievable for me as a writer: anything I could write, Stan could play immediately. The rest of them would have to woodshed it."

At this point Shorty Rogers, cast adrift by the dissolution of the First
Herd, was working in a Los Angeles group led by Stumpy Brown. It is
interesting to note that Johnny Mandel, who would write for this new
Herd, had gone to military academy in New York with Stumpy, whose older
brother, Les Brown, had attended it before them. Johnny knew the whole
Brown family. In Stumpy's group with Shorty were Stan Getz and Herbie
Steward. When Woody hired Shorty, Getz, and Steward, it more or less
finished Stumpy's group, but then his brother soon would have a band
again, and Stumpy would be a part of it.

Woody sent to Boston for Serge Chaloff to play baritone saxophone in
the new group. Chaloff, whose sound suggested Ben Webster but whose
thinking was influenced by Charlie Parker, had been with the bands of
Georgie Auld, Jimmy Dorsey, and Boyd Raeburn. Hiring him must be
accounted one of Woody's worst errors: Serge was a serious heroin addict
and, like so many of his kind, a dedicated proselytizer for the drug. He
would hook a number of the Second Herd bandsmen. As a player, however,
Chaloff is widely admired, even today.

From the First Herd alumni, Woody hired Shorty Rogers on trumpet,
Sam Marowitz on alto, and Don Lamond, who had replaced Dave Tough in
the previous band, on drums. The arrangers at first would be Ralph Burns,
Jimmy Giuffre, Al Cohn, and John LaPorta. The trumpet section would be

Rogers, Ernie Royal, Stan Fishelson, Bernie Glow, and Marky Markowitz. Earl Swope, the brilliant and innovative trombonist from Washington, D.C., one of the first to adapt bebop to his instrument; Ollie Wilson; and Bob Swift were the trombone section. Fred Otis was on piano. Walt Yoder, who had been with Woody in the Isham Jones band and indeed had recommended Woody for that band, came in on bass. Gene Sargent on guitar completed the rhythm section. The new band played its first job on October 16, 1947, at the Municipal Auditorium in San Bernardino, California, and did one-nighters up the California coast as far as San Francisco. Then it headed east for engagements in the major midwestern cities.

The AFM's James C. Petrillo was threatening another recording ban, and Woody wanted to get as much material recorded as possible. On December 22, the band recorded a Shorty Rogers composition, *Keen and Peachy*, whose title suggested its origin; it is built on the chord changes of *Fine and Dandy*, in keeping with the bebop practice of writing tunes on the changes of existing songs. On December 24, the band recorded an Al Cohn composition, *The Goof and I*, and on December 27, a piece by Jimmy Giuffre designed to exploit the sound of three tenors and baritone: *Four Brothers*. The sequence of solos is Sims, Chaloff, Steward, and Getz. The piece would ever after be as strongly associated with the band as *Blue Flame*, *Woodchopper's Ball*, and *Caldonia*.

That same day the band recorded a piece Ralph Burns had written as a sort of extension, or fourth movement, to his *Summer Sequence* suite, first performed in the *Ebony Concerto* concert at Carnegie Hall. The first three movements had been recorded more than a year earlier, on September 9, 1946. At three movements, the piece ran 8:36. Each movement had featured the band's principal players in solos.

Ralph Burns recalled: "Woody said, 'Will you write a fourth part?' because it wasn't long enough to put on one side of one of the new ten-inch LPs. Stan Getz had just joined the band, so I wrote this tenor thing because Stan didn't have anything in *Summer Sequence*. I wrote it in early autumn, so we called it *Early Autumn*. I think Woody thought of the name."[2]

Comparatively little known in the United States, *Early Autumn* is one of the most famous American compositions abroad, for this reason:

The best-known living American (except to Americans) is Willis Conover, whose Voice of America broadcasts created an audience for jazz all over the world. Many thoughtful persons believe that Conover's quiet radio penetration of the Iron Curtain countries did more to bring about the dissolution of the Soviet empire than all the armies and politicians of the

West put together. And Conover has used *Early Autumn* as the theme of his *House of Sounds* radio show seven days a week for more than ten years. Thus listeners in other countries have been exposed to the piece more than 3000 times.

The fourth movement, *Early Autumn*, recorded December 27, 1947, added 3:02 to the suite. The record of it, issued in 1948, instantly established Stan Getz as a major voice in jazz, and he would hold his pre-eminence until his death.

▼   ▼   ▼

In early 1947, the band played a long engagement at the Hollywood Palladium, then began to tour, playing at the Capitol Theater in New York in May. In October the band began a one-month engagement at the Royal Roost in New York, with most of the personnel of the Stan Kenton and Dizzy Gillespie bands in the audience.

Al Cohn had by then joined the band, replacing Herbie Steward on tenor, and Red Rodney came into the trumpet section, replacing Marky Markowitz. The band retained much of its old book.

▼   ▼   ▼

It is something of a tragedy, for Woody and for music, that Petrillo had imposed the second of his recording bans that year, and the band's work during that period is undocumented, except for radio broadcasts, a number of which emanated from the Royal Roost.

Public reception to the band was good, but there were fewer bookings than in the old days. Don Lamond said, "The Four Brothers band was the best. Maybe it wasn't quite as fiery as the First Herd . . . . But it was the best." Woody said, "The band's downfall was caused by a combination of things. But changing the sound was certainly a big factor. It was something I had to do. The audience that could understand *Apple Honey*, however, couldn't relate to *Lemon Drop* or *Four Brothers*. Musically, the bebop route was magnificent. But business-wise, it was the dumbest thing I ever did. Those pieces didn't really succeed, except with a small percentage of our listeners, until the mid-1950s. If we had just continued playing *Apple Honey* and *Caldonia*, we'd probably have had a fighting chance."[3]

In its first year, the band lost $175,000. To keep it going, Woody would take more profitable jobs with a sextet.

In later years, it became cant with certain critics who hated it that "bebop killed the big bands," though it never seemed to occur to them that bandleaders who didn't like bebop and didn't assimilate it, Benny Goodman among them, also had to give up their bands. The truth is that the combination of social and economic forces that had created the big-band era in the first place were changing.

Paul Weston said the beginning of the end came with a change of tempos. Earlier arrangements had been designed for dancing, and even the ballads moved along on a comparatively bright two-beat. Paul said, "Then the ballads became slower, to accommodate the singers, and the instrumentals became faster, to show off the soloists."

Alvino Rey told me, "And then there was the Kenton phenomenon. Stan Kenton's was not a dance band, except in the early days. When we tried to be more like it, people said, 'Why aren't you like your old self?' The bands became too symphonic. Too many chords. I was one of the worst offenders, because I loved all that stuff. And then, once the remotes went off the air, we had a real problem. Records couldn't build a band the way all those live broadcasts did."[4] In the audiences for the First Herd in 1946 were huge numbers of returned soldiers, airmen, and sailors who had been exposed to the band through its V discs, and now took their girls to see it and dance to it. But by 1948, many of them had married those girls, had taken jobs, and were forming homes. The first members of the generation that would be called the baby boomers, the future fans of Bob Dylan and the Beatles, were being born, and their young parents had other priorities for their money and their time. Babies crying in the night leave neither energy nor time for long evenings of dancing. Regular television broadcasting had begun in the United States in 1941, but it was little noticed by anyone, since few people had the sets to receive the signals. But in the late 1940s, more and more people acquired television sets, and in the early 1950s the medium was appealing to young couples who had trouble finding, and could little afford, baby-sitters.

Another phenomenon affected the bands. Since the 1930s, Harry Chandler, owner of the *Los Angeles Times* and of huge real estate holdings in the Los Angeles area, had begun stumping in his paper for the use of private cars as opposed to public transportation. In 1936 a group of corporations including General Motors, Standard (Oil) of California, Firestone Tire and Rubber Company, Phillips Petroleum, and Mack Manufacturing, maker of Mack trucks, established a company called National City Lines, which set about buying up the electric street railways of the country and converting them to bus lines. One of the public transportation systems it bought was the Los Angeles electric railway system, which at one time had more than 1000 miles of track in Los Angeles County. It deliberately debased the service of these railways. The company managed to plant some of its agents in the Public Utilities Commission of California, which, of course, then granted permission to tear up the tracks, one of which ran not far from Woody's house and would carry riders from Hollywood to Santa Monica. In 1947, when it was far too late, the U.S. Justice Department brought an antitrust suit against National City Lines and its owners, whose executives were convicted—and fined one dollar. It is a bitter irony that the City of Los Angeles, at a cost in the billions, is struggling now to replace those interurban trolleys and street railways with new electrical systems.

These interurban trolleys were the means of transportation by which young people without cars used to go to hear the bands. With the dismantling of these systems, attendance at dances in the lakeshore pavilions all over America inevitably declined.

The era was gone. To those who lived through it, those platoons of musicians traveling the American night in "big bands" seemed a part of the inevitable pattern of nature.

Wrong.

The gradual failure of pavilions and ballrooms meant that the jumps between engagements were inevitably longer. No longer could you do that month of one-nighters, close together, in Pennsylvania that Artie Shaw described. Even as early as 1946, Willard Alexander, the booking agent who had once let Glenn Miller and Woody wait in frustration in the outer office, told Mike Levin of *Down Beat*:

"Musicians are getting over twice the money in salaries they did before the war, and transportation and arranging costs are way up. But the hotels and spots which must be the home base for any new outfit have only gone up forty percent in their band bids—they literally can't afford any more."

The August 12, 1946, issue of *Down Beat* carried an interview with Charlie Barnet, who noted that the Goodman band had played an engagement in Pennsylvania with a guarantee of $2500 and then had drawn only 750 persons. Barnet said, "As far as the band business is concerned, the party is over."

In his book *Benny Goodman and the Swing Era*, James Lincoln Collier wrote:

The attitude of the musicians' union was that, yes, pay for musicians had gone up, but the increases were not commensurate with salaries in industry. Even though raising scales at a time when the band business was sinking seems in

retrospect like poor policy, it is easy to sympathize with musicians. The entertainment industry—and the arts in a more general way—has always been
dependent upon the ability of the entrepreneurs to exploit "talent." The musicians had done very well for a brief period of the 1920s, when there was a great
demand for dance music and mechanical entertainment was in its infancy. But
otherwise they were traditionally badly paid. The men who staffed the name
bands during the years before the war found it difficult to save anything at all
while they were on the road even if they were single, and impossible if they
were married, and it was the willingness of hundreds of musicians to work for
very low salaries that allowed the swing bands to exist. During the war they
had gotten used to being able to buy decent clothes, good cars when they
could find them, and to support families. But they were still running behind.
Sidemen who were paying nine dollars a night for hotel rooms insisted that
they couldn't live on the road for less than $125 a week, a reasonable claim.
But bandleaders replied that with salaries in that range they would have to
demand $1750 to $2500 in guarantees, and Harry James was actually getting
$4000. At that level, the operators had to charge two dollars to two dollars and
a half admission, and the public's response was that that was too much.

There really was no solution.[5]

Chubby Jackson thinks Woody was a naive man. So do I. His naïveté, to
be sure, was in a strange way alloyed with a native shrewdness. I never
quite figured out how it worked, but it did, and Woody was capable of
ignoring realities he didn't like. To the end of his life, he never, I think,
thought through the factors that ended the Swing Era. In 1948, he simply
ignored them.

But then, he had a problem that Artie Shaw, Benny Goodman, Tommy
Dorsey, and other parsimonious bandleaders did not. He had not accumulated money, and now his all-too-brief hour of prosperity was over.

14

The Young Turks

At this ebb in his career, Woody decided to get a new manager and signed with Carlos Gastel. The flamboyant Gastel, whose office was in Hollywood, had a taste for publicity such that he was himself something of a celebrity, his name familiar to every dedicated reader of *Down Beat* and *Metronome*. Gastel had considerable leverage with the powers who headed Capitol Records.

Peggy Lee described Gastel this way:

"He was a very large man. His nickname, which he knew—it was no secret—was the Aga Khan. He was from Honduras. That was another nickname: the Honduran. He was well educated."[1]

The key to Gastel's power was Glenn Wallichs.

Capitol had been founded in 1942, only months after the Japanese air attack of December 7, 1941, had all but eliminated the U.S. Navy's Pacific fleet and left Japan with control of the South Pacific and the islands thereof. Shellac, the principal substance of phonograph records in those days before vinyl, came from that part of the world, and as Woody had been well aware in his first years with Columbia, even the major labels couldn't get enough of it. How Capitol got the shellac to get started remained a mystery for a number of years.

The founding figure of Capitol was Johnny Mercer, who was in the opinion of many authorities, including Alan Jay Lerner, the greatest lyricist in the history of American popular music. Mercer had been a friend of Red Norvo and Woody as far back as the early days of the Band That Plays the

Blues. Mercer built Capitol Records rather the way Winston Churchill said Britain built its empire: in a fit of absent-mindedness.

Mercer used to visit a radio and record store called Music City, at Sunset and Vine in Hollywood. Johnny used to get his car radio repaired there. The store's proprietor was Glenn Wallichs. Johnny talked to him about his idea of starting a record company. He also talked of it to B.G. (Buddy) De Sylva, who, after a successful career as a songwriter and producer, became executive producer of Paramount Pictures, a position he held until 1944. Wallichs and De Sylva told Mercer they would invest in the company if he went ahead with his plans.

But where would the company find its shellac? At this point (and this is a typical Mercer story) Johnny learned that a man in San Diego had a warehouse full of shellac. And the man had an ambitious son who led an altogether dreadful dance band. Johnny signed the young man to the label, his recordings achieved a justified anonymity, and Capitol was off and running, with Johnny as its president and Wallichs as a senior executive. Johnny was interested only in the esthetics of it; Wallichs was interested in business.[2]

And Carlos Gastel had been one of Wallichs's employees at the record store. Thus from the inception of Capitol, Gastel had access to its executives. He soon acquired an impressive roster of artists, including Stan Kenton, Peggy Lee, and Nat Cole.

Peggy, always timid and frightened of performing, actually had tried to retire from the business after her marriage to guitarist Dave Barbour, whom she had met when they were members of the Benny Goodman band. She had a newborn daughter who absorbed all her time. Mercer decided to make an innovative (for its time) album called *The Capitol Jazzmen*, a package of 78-r.p.m. ten-inch singles that were pure small-group jazz. Peggy was asked to participate in the sessions, and she thought, "Well I suppose I could get a baby-sitter and go down and sing a couple of songs." The songs were *That Old Feeling* and a blues called *Ain't Goin' No Place*. They confirmed her as a star, and she was soon not only singing for Capitol but also writing songs with Barbour, including *Mañana*, a huge hit, and *I Don't Know Enough About You*, whose lyric she wrote.

The sale of her recordings and those of Nat Cole laid the foundation of Capitol's success. With a new career burgeoning, she needed a manager, and Carlos Gastel was there.

Peggy said, "Carlos had his own boat. David [Barbour] and he were drinking buddies. I used to go along with Carlos and David on the boat to protect them from burning themselves up. They had a kind of burner stove on the boat. We had one really bad fire.

"They used to call Carlos's boat, because it was a power boat, I suppose, the stinkpot. He kept it at San Pedro.

"Carlos spent most of his time at places like Scandia and Tale of the Cock."[3]

Woody's contract at Columbia had expired, and toward the end of 1947, with Petrillo's second ban now over, Gastel signed Woody to Capitol, where he had so much power. But there were inherent disadvantages in changing labels. The new company had no vested interest in the old material, the old label no interest in the current career, though of course Columbia continued to issue the recordings of the First Herd and the early work of the Second Herd. For that matter, those recordings are still selling. "Believe me, they are," Neal Hefti said. "I can tell from the royalty statements I get from around the world." Whatever the reason and perhaps with the ending of the big-band era the same thing would have happened had Woody stayed at Columbia. The new band never generated the same public excitement that the First Herd had, even though in the opinion of most musicians it was the better band.

The band recorded a new version of *Early Autumn* for Capitol. How this came about is unexplained; it was record-company practice to specify in contracts that an artist could not make a new version of any piece of material he or she had recorded for another company for five years after leaving the label. This version was recorded only a year after the first *Early Autumn*. It features a vibraharp solo by Terry Gibbs and a lovely tenor solo by Stan Getz.

In the June, 1948, issue of *Metronome*, a review of the band by the magazine's editor, Barry Ulanov, was at sharp variance with George Simon's enthusiastic report of the band's formation. His headline said: *Woody's new band gets a very fine sound but its arrangements leave a great deal to be desired, chiefly originality*. He was referring to the band book written by Rogers, Mandel, Burns, and Giuffre, one of the best in jazz history, and of a band that was startlingly original in conception and sound. Ulanov wrote:

It's hard to believe, but the characterizing quality of this latest Herman band is a cross between Fletcher Henderson and bop. In such jazz as Woody was able to play in the cold Century Room of New York's Commodore Hotel, the pattern was set with riffs and varied with flatted fifths. The manuscript is, almost all of it, dull, lackluster in idea and, to some extent, in execution. There is a poverty of head arrangements and an accompanying paucity of solos. And yet the band is very much worth hearing; it demands your attention on the strength of its personnel alone and the suggestion, only rarely more than implicit but always there, that sometime very soon the latent strength of these musicians will burst its bonds (or bondsmen) and all hell and great jazz will break loose.[4]

One wonders what Woody thought of the press at this point. A month prior to the Ulanov sigh of ennui, *Down Beat* ran a peculiar article over Woody's byline. The two-column headline reads:

HERMAN ATTACKS
MATHEMATICS IN
"PROGRESSIVISM"

The byline read: By WOODY HERMAN (as told to Eddie Ronan). The article began:

The words "progressive jazz" today are less understood by both musicians and layman alike than was the word "swing" ten years ago. Yet, everyone talks "progressive jazz." It's meaningless.

A certain cult of leaders and arrangers, admittedly schooled, but blinded by the brilliance of their own catch phrases, in the last few years have trimmed the words to their own dimensional liking. They have molded "progressive jazz" through an abstruse pattern of mystic formulae into an ethereal incantation only they are subtle enough to comprehend and adore. They have become so concentrated in the study of the structure of arranged jazz (this to them is the "progressive" approach) that they have lost all conception of the possible beauty of the natural jazz form.

In its arranged form, jazz to them has become mathematical. They arrange by slide rule. And, in following this prescribed code, they sacrifice the result for the construction.

Down Beat was not above contriving controversies for the sake of catchy headlines, and that interview had to be a fabrication by the writer, if perhaps developed from some small remark Woody had indeed made. But there is no way in this world that Woody Herman ever said "an abstruse pattern of mystic formulae into an ethereal incantation." Woodrow Herman? Boy saxophonist? High-school dropout? Down-to-earth no-nonsense old vaudevillian? Such a phrase simply wasn't in his vocabulary. And the story is clearly a not-so-subtle attack on Stan Kenton. Woody did not make it a practice to publicly attack his colleagues, least of all one who was with the same record label. One sees why Woody would get annoyed about being misquoted.

▼　▼　▼

Mary Ann McCall had rejoined the band in December, 1947, and guitarist Jimmy Raney came into it in January, 1948. A story is told among musicians that Raney bought one of the watches Abe Turchen wore on his arm. It bore the logo of one of the better brands. Later, when it needed repairs, the story holds, the watchmaker told Jimmy that its works were junk.

"I don't remember that," Jimmy said. "I do remember Abe selling watches and all kinds of junk on the bus. He seemed to be sort of a hustler, a Broadway type, the kind of character you can imagine started as a pitchman on a midway."[5]

Raney, a tall and very thin young man with a long face, would emerge in time as one of the major guitar players, one of the first to adapt the full implications of bebop to that instrument. His essentially introspective playing had a strong compositional integrity that, Jim Hall, another major guitarist, told me long afterwards, influenced him. And trombonist and composer Bob Brookmeyer acknowledges Raney as one of his influences.

Raney, born in Louisville, Kentucky, on August 27, 1927, was twenty when he joined the band, a few months younger than Stan Getz. He had gone up to Chicago from his home town to establish himself; Chicago was the hub that drew jazz musicians from all over the Midwest, from Bix Beiderbecke through Woody to Raney to many more. It still does.

"I had been playing in Chicago," Jimmy said in May, 1993. "Georgie Auld had passed through with Tiny Kahn, Serge Chaloff, and Red Rodney in the group, and they heard me. And I had met Stan Getz somehow at a jam session around that time. So when the guitar player left Woody, they called Tiny Kahn in New York and said, 'Who can we get who plays in this style?' And he said, 'There's only one guy, and that's Jimmy Raney in Chicago.' And then, I guess, Woody said, 'Anybody know who he is?' And Stan and Serge said, 'Oh yeah, get him.' They seconded the motion. That's how I got hired. I was totally unknown."

"Ralph Burns did a very nice thing for me. In those days, I wasn't such a hot sight reader. As a guitar player, I did as well as most. You never get to read notes. I was trained when I was young, but you get out of practice.

There were some parts Ralph wrote for guitar that weren't too easy, things he had written, I suppose, for Billy Bauer. I was struggling with them a little. This was very early, maybe my third day. We were in Salt Lake City, I think. Ralph said, 'Jim, I love the way you play. Would you like me to run over the things I wrote that may cause you a little problem?' He put it so nicely. I said, 'Oh, gee, I'd really appreciate it.' So we went into the ballroom. He got out the charts he'd written that had electric guitar parts. He played piano for me and helped me. And who was I? Some kid they'd picked up in Chicago. Nobody knew who I was, except the ones who'd recommended me.

"It was a wonderful band. Bebop was then new, relatively, and hadn't been translated into the big bands. That tenor lead on that Four Brothers sound was usually Stan. He could play the high register and make it sound like something, which is not an easy thing on tenor."

But Jimmy never really felt he belonged in the band. He carried two guitars, an amplified Gibson for solos and an unamplified instrument for rhythm playing. He said, "There really isn't much for a guitar player to do. Al Cohn took pity on me, and also Ralph and Shorty Rogers. They wrote me a few solos. Al Cohn replaced Herbie Steward the night after I joined the band. I played one night with Herbie Steward, and he left, somewhere in Nevada. Al and Ralph and Shorty made it a little easier for me.

"It was such a wonderful band, but the rhythm section wasn't up to the rest of it, since Walt Yoder, who was the Isham Jones bass player, was playing. He was probably not originally very good, and he was getting old. Don Lamond was wonderful, but I wasn't any big help in the rhythm section.

"Guitar became unnecessary, a fifth wheel, with bebop. I didn't like guitar rhythm behind me myself. But I had to play it because it was traditional. It was out of character with the bebop stuff. Rhythm sections had changed. They became a counterpoint of things. Guitar by then was in a class with rhythm piano."

In the fall, Jimmy gave his notice. "I joined Woody in January of 1948 and left in October of '48 and stayed in New York. I'd saved up two thousand dollars. I didn't drink. I saved my money, bought traveler's checks every week. My goal was New York, not to be a big shot but to learn, and be around the people who could play. And to play in small groups. I'm really a chamber player. Big bands are lots of fun, but they're more fun for horn players, I think.

"In New York, I could hear Charlie Parker and all those great people in person, because records are misleading. I was smart enough to know *that*. I knew Al Haig. He immediately invited me to sit in with Bird at the Royal Roost. I was never more frightened in my life. To play with God! He was very nice. So was Miles, and Max Roach, and Tommy Potter."[6]

Raney would play around New York for a few months and then, in 1949, join a new Artie Shaw band. (Five years later Shaw would retire from music forever.) Later still, he would be a member of the Stan Getz Quintet that recorded for Roulette and would make him famous with the cognoscenti if not the larger public. But it was with Woody that he got his first major exposure, as so many musicians did.

▼   ▼   ▼

Evidently Woody concurred with Jimmy about the guitar's place, or lack of it, in the rhythm sections suited to the new music, for he decided to drop it from the band. Except for brief periods, including one when Charlie Byrd was with him, he would not use guitar again.

Woody had initially used vibraphone, that of Red Norvo (with whom Raney would later play) in the Second Herd. Now Chubby Jackson drew his attention to Terry Gibbs, and with guitar gone, Woody hired him.

Born Julius Gubenko in Brooklyn on October 13, 1924 (his friends still call him "Gubenko"), Terry at seventy has so much energy that he would be exhausting were he not so stimulating and amusing. His father was a violinist and bandleader who started him on drums, tympani, and xylophone as a boy. He won an amateur contest and appeared on the then-famous radio network program *Major Bowes Original Amateur Hour*, which helped launch a great many performers, including Frank Sinatra. After three years in military service during World War II, playing drums in military bands, he worked on Fifty-second Street in New York, with Tommy Dorsey, and then in 1946 for Buddy Rich, who was a notoriously difficult employer.

"Johnny Mandel, myself, a guy called Jackie Carmen, and a guy named Frank LoPinto quit the band the same day in San Francisco," Terry said. "Johnny Mandel went to Los Angeles to get his local 47 union card. Jackie Carmen had a car. Jackie and Frank and I had to drive back to New York City. We had only a hundred dollars. Nobody could drive except Jackie Carmen. In Nevada, we decided to try to win some money, but we lost it. Frank LoPinto had to send home for some money. We had just enough money for gasoline and some salamis that stunk up the car. We got to the Lincoln Tunnel without sleeping, and the car blew up. This was eleven in the morning. You know how New Yorkers are. Everybody was honking and screaming. We had to push the car through the tunnel. Somehow I got home about one or two o'clock in the afternoon. I swore I'd never go on the road again. I got a call from Woody Herman. By three o'clock I was on an airplane, and I started that night with the band at the Blue Note in Chicago.

"Getting a call from Woody and knowing who was in that band—Stan Getz and Zoot Sims and Al Cohn!"[7]

▼   ▼   ▼

On October 24, 1948, the band opened an engagement at the Royal Roost in New York City to profuse praise in *Down Beat* by its New York editor, one of the most astute critics in its history, Mike Levin. While the band was at the Roost, Red Rodney joined it, replacing Marky Markowitz. The engagement ended November 28, and the band headed west to play at a new location in downtown Hollywood called the Empire Room. Its owners were Gene Norman and Carlos Gastel, and the room in fact had been opened specifically for Woody.

Gene Norman, then twenty-six years old, was, with Steve Allen, one of the best-known of Los Angeles jazz disc jockeys. While Steve went into television, founding the *Tonight Show* on NBC where he sometimes presented Woody, Gene became an impresario and record producer, eventually establishing his own label, GNP Crescendo. In April, 1993, Gene recalled:

"I had started in the concert business in April of 1947. I had done quite a few concerts in the first year with Nat Cole, Lionel Hampton, and other jazz groups. I had learned to buy talent. One night I was at KFWB, doing my ten o'clock till twelve radio show, and Carlos Gastel came in and said, 'Gene, Woody has no place to sit down in this town. We've got to open a nightclub.' That's how the Empire started.

"We took the room on Vine Street near Sunset Boulevard that had been Tom Breneman's restaurant. A morning network show had originated there, *Breakfast in Hollywood*, but now the room was vacant. It was owned by a man named Paul Kalmanowitz, called Mr. Paul, a Polish refugee who became Louis B. Mayer's chauffeur, got into real estate, and became a brewery king. He ended up owning Falstaff. We made a deal with him to lease the place, and we gave him a percentage. The place seated about two hundred.

"We opened with the Woody Herman band. He came in for about three weeks. We opened December 7, 1948, and went on the air coast to coast on the ABC network as a remote. Since I was on the radio and had a big following among young people, I had a gallery where for two bucks you could come in and have a seat, as at a concert, without having to buy drinks.

"After Woody, we played Billy Eckstine, Georgie Auld, Benny Goodman, Duke. Then Mr. Paul told us the building had been sold to ABC to make a studio out of it. The Empire Room lasted about eight months.

"I must tell you that I really loved Woody. He was a sweet, decent, gentle man."8

Petrillo ended his second damaging record ban during the time the band was at the Empire, and on December 29, the Herd went into the studio to record *That's Right* and *Lemon Drop*. The latter has a genuinely funny bebop scat vocal, with Terry Gibbs singing the low part, Shorty Rogers the middle voice, and Chubby Jackson the falsetto. Rogers by then was chief arranger for the band. The tune is by George Wallington; the chart is by Rogers.

On December 30, the band recorded *Keeper of the Flame*, a Rogers piece based on the changes of *I Found a New Baby*. The next night it played a coast-to-coast New Year's Eve radio show from the Empire Room.

The band left the Empire early in January, heading east for an engagement at the Blue Note, the biggest and best known of Chicago's jazz clubs. A heavy snowstorm impeded the train, which finally reached Salt Lake City. Woody went to see the disc jockey Al (Jazzbo) Collins, who was working in that city. Dizzy Gillespie, who then had his adventurous bebop big band, had arrived in Salt Lake by plane for an engagement at a ballroom that evening. His band, however, had been stranded somewhere by the storm. Woody had an idea: his band would substitute for Dizzy's, with Dizzy as the soloist. Despite the storm, there was a good crowd, and neither Dizzy nor Woody ever forgot the sheer delight of that evening.

The weather cleared, and Dizzy went on to California, where Gene Norman presented the Gillespie band in concert at the Pasadena Institute of Technology, recording an album that is perhaps the finest documentation of what that remarkable band really sounded like. Woody's band went on to the Blue Note, where it stayed for two weeks.

One of the jokes in the band involved Terry Gibbs and Shorty Rogers. Terry talked very fast, Shorty Rogers very slowly. The musicians said that when Shorty wanted to call his wife, to save money he would write out his message and have Terry talk to her, thereby reducing a twelve-minute conversation to six.

Terry, in that Brooklyn voice the years have not slowed, recalled, "I was making a hundred and fifty dollars when I first joined the band, which in those days was good money. Stan Getz was making a hundred and seventy-five. And the big salaries were Bill Harris, who came back after I joined, and Ernie Royal, who were making two hundred.

"I learned a little about the business from my father. He taught me something in Jewish. It comes out in English: Hit while the iron is hot. I sang the low voice on *Lemon Drop*. And it was a hit record. I asked for a twenty-five-dollar raise, because the record was hot. Woody said, 'I can't give it to you.' I learned something. It's almost a game. You can't go back; you've got to quit. I'd only been on the band about five months. I did not want to leave that band at all! It was the hardest thing, but I gave my two weeks' notice. A week later Woody came to me and said, 'I'll give you the money.' And then the record got hotter. All the people wanted to hear was *Lemon Drop* and *Early Autumn*. So I went to Woody again and I think I said Charlie Ventura had offered me two hundred a week. I said, 'If you'll give me the same thing, I'll stay with the band.' He said, 'I can't give it to you.' And I gave my notice again.

"And this time, two days before I was to leave, I was ready to shoot myself. I used to cry. I cried at night, because I didn't want to leave that band! He came to me two days before, and he gave me the money. My playing had nothing to do with my getting a raise. It was that dumb low voice on *Lemon Drop*."

I mentioned that Lou Levy had said that when Woody went home a little early, the band would play the charts it particularly liked. "That's right," Terry said. "But I'll tell you something about that. Once in a while, the last set, he'd maybe leave four or five tunes before the end. And we'd play what we wanted to play. And the band never sounded as good after he left that stage.

"I pride myself on having a great band with that Dream Band of mine. All over the world people talk about my Dream Band, and I appreciate it. But that Woody Herman Second Herd was one of the greatest bands of all time. Besides having so many great soloists, it was one of the greatest *ensemble* bands! And that was because of Woody Herman.

"There are certain guys who are just great band leaders. You've never heard a bad Les Brown band. You never heard a bad Count Basie band.

"Woody could play. Woody was a great alto player. He played better clarinet than he knew. He tried to play like we played, and that was a mistake. When he played like Woody Herman, and I heard him do it, he played his best. But most of all, he knew what a good band was like.

"I thank him for this. If it hadn't been for Woody, a lot of things wouldn't have happened in my life. We made six or seven takes of *Early Autumn*. Woody said, 'Okay, number six is it. And Stan Getz and I went to him. Stan had the bigger solo. I only had eight bars. We said, 'Take four was much better. We played better solos.' Woody said, 'The band sounded bad.' We said, 'Come on, Woody, our solos make the whole thing.' And he said, 'No.' And we were bugged at him.

"And the record came out and became a hit and Stan and I both won the *Down Beat* award because of it. If Woody had used the take Stan and I wanted, I'd probably still be looking for a job. Woody picked the one that he knew had the feel. Woody knew what a big band was all about it. You never ever heard a bad Woody Herman band."

"Yes I did," I said. "Once. It was probably late 1959 or early 1960 when I first went to *Down Beat*. It came into Chicago, and it was kind of sloppy. He knew it too. I went out with him afterwards and we got drunk. He broke that band up soon after that and went to a small group with Zoot and Nat Adderley and himself as the front line. A wonderful little group, very fiery, like his big bands."

Terry said, "When you were four years younger in those days, the other guy was really an old man. Everybody was really in love with Earl Swope. And Woody brought Bill Harris back into the band. The guys thought he was an old man." (Harris turned thirty-two that year.) "They thought that Earl would lose all his solos to Bill. But Bill was such a beautiful guy that they complemented each other. Bill fit into that band so well! And he was such a great, giant trombone player. Woody, once again, knew that it would work."[9]

The writing team for the band now included Johnny Mandel. Like Terry Gibbs, he had been a child prodigy. Like Terry, he was born in New York City. His birthdate was November 23, 1925. He had been part of that cadre of young musicians who hung around the apartment of Gil Evans in New York City, among them Gerry Mulligan, Miles Davis, John Lewis, and at times Charlie Parker. Johnny had played trumpet, trombone, and bass trumpet with a number of bands, including Joe Venuti in 1943, Boyd Raeburn and Jimmy Dorsey in 1945, and Billie Rogers in 1946, and Alvino Rey the same year, as well as the bands of Buddy Rich and Georgie Auld. But it was as a writer that he was beginning to electrify the business. He would be one of the first composers to bring jazz into movies, with his score for the 1958 film *I Want to Live*.

"I was sweating out my union card in Los Angeles," Johnny said. "Six months. I had to work as a shipping clerk downtown. I took the trolley. Then I was working as a soda jerk at the Thrifty drugstore at Hollywood and Ivar, right around the corner from where Woody's band played, the Empire Room.

"I'd been writing for Buddy Rich and a lot of bands. And I had a number of friends in Woody's band—Earl Swope, Terry Gibbs, Al Cohn. Woody said, 'Why don't you write something?'

"That was the monster band, the Second Herd. Al Cohn had just joined. He'd left us, in the Buddy Rich band. And then Bill Harris came back and they had four trombones. Ollie Wilson was playing lead trombone. And I wrote a number of things. I wrote *What's New?* as a feature for Terry Gibbs. I wrote a couple of things for Terry. He's always an instigator. He's probably the one who got me writing for the band.

"That Second Herd was the most brilliant band I ever wrote for. The trumpet section was as good as you ever could find. I would have been happier, quite frankly, if the band had had a guitar at that point. He needed a Freddie Green. If Woody had taken on Turk Van Lake, for instance, or Sam Herman, he'd have been in good shape. The kind of music that band played, it was not a bebop band, even though the solos were bebop solos. It was Count Basie music. The best they played was along those lines, laid down basically by the guys who came out of the Fletcher Henderson school of writing, with the exception of Ralph. I think the band would have benefited greatly by the right guitarist. Still, it was the best band I ever wrote for. It was considered old time by then to have guitar, and only later did it become appreciated when Basie started up again with Freddie Green.

"But Woody's rhythm section was so good that you got along without it—Chubby, Don Lamond, and Lou Levy.

"When I'd hear that band, my hair would stand on end. It was just that thrilling. It was just unbelievable. Mary Ann McCall was one of the most under-rated singers ever. It was just a great, great band. It was a culmination.

"The guys in that band were my generation. They started out playing in bands maybe in 1941. I came a little later, 1943. They were guys who had honed their skills. There were the Washington, D.C., guys, like Marky Markowitz, Earl Swope, Don Lamond. All the guys born in 1923, '24, '25. With the exception of Bill Harris, who was older. They'd been in the junior-league bush bands, like Buddy Rich and Georgie Auld. More good guys went through Georgie Auld's band. And Charlie Barnet. Everybody was really at the top of their game and they all came together in that Second Herd, playing the right music for the right guy."

As for the watches Abe Turchen wore up his arm, veterans of the First and Second Herds attest to the practice. "He really did do that," Ralph Burns said. Some of the musicians hated Abe; some do to this day. Others loved him. Woody remained loyal to him, eventually referring to him as "my best friend."

15

Bad Boys

 While marijuana had been in common use in the music world for a long time—and for that matter in more of American society than may be suspected—nothing stronger was much used in the jazz world until the deification of Charlie Parker. So great was the admiration for him that many of his young idolaters followed him into heroin, even though he warned them, Red Rodney and Gerry Mulligan among them, of its ravages. The master bassist Ray Brown once recalled to me the coming of smack to the jazz world.

Ray said, "A little pot, I was used to that. Then they told me, 'We've got something new. It's even better.'

"How do you take it?" Ray asked.

"With a needle in the arm."

"*Forget* it!" Ray said.

Exactly half the Woody Herman band at one point was on heroin, eight of its sixteen players: the entire saxophone section, Stan Getz, Al Cohn, Zoot Sims, and Serge Chaloff; Bernie Glow in the trumpet section, Earl Swope and Bob Swift in the trombones, and Lou Levy on piano.

The straights were Ernie Royal, Stan Fishelson, Shorty Rogers, Chubby Jackson, Don Lamond, Sam Marowitz, Bill Harris, and Ollie Wilson.

Terry Gibbs said he realized when he joined the band how seriously many of the men were strung out. "Bernie Glow was really bad," he said. "He almost died."

Ralph Burns said, "I used to visit them, because I was writing for them.

171
▼

It was pretty scary. I got a little bit into it at that time. You thought you had to take a little junk, otherwise they wouldn't play your music. It was sad. You'd go to see the band and the front line would be completely cacked out. On the stand! I don't know how Woody put up with it. And what he got out of them, in spite of it all.

"The funny part of it is they all got straight eventually."[1]

"I was so naive," Woody said once with his chuckle, "that I couldn't figure out why the guys were falling asleep on the bandstand."

"The whole front line would be nodding out," Ralph said.

Amphetamines were also in use. "That's the band," Woody once said, "where everybody was on practically everything but roller skates."

Drug use caused a social division within the band. The straights sat at the front of the bus, the junkies at the back, behind a gray army blanket that Serge Chaloff had hung across it. Serge was the band druggist, its supplier, and its worst offender, and Woody knew it.

Terry Gibbs said, "Serge Chaloff was probably the greatest liar in the world. If you checked into a hotel and Serge was on the seventh floor, you made sure you were on the sixth, because Serge would fall asleep and burn a hole in the mattress, and you wanted to be below the fire.

"Every time he would burn a hole in a mattress, the hotel manager would come up and say, 'Mr. Chaloff, you have burned the mattress.' And Serge would say, 'How *dare* you, sir? I am the winner of the *Down Beat* and *Metronome* polls!' Serge had that Bostonian, high-class way of speaking. And by the time the conversation was over, the manager would end up apologizing.

"One time the band bought air pistols, which shot pellets. They'd shoot them out the bus windows at night. They probably killed four hundred people without knowing it. Serge put a telephone book against the door in his room. He shot at it, and I don't think he hit the book once. We were checking out the next morning. I was a clothes freak. Woody put me with his tailor, and so I had, like, two suitcases. Nobody else had suitcases because they always wore the same clothes.

"As I was walking out, I heard this commotion. The manager was saying to Serge, 'You've ruined that door, It's going to cost you twenty-four dollars.' And Serge said, 'How dare you, sir, I'm the winner of the *Down Beat* and *Metronome* polls! And I've seen your kind come and go!' This manager didn't care. He said, 'If you don't give me the money, I'm calling the police.' Serge said, 'Well, if I have to pay for the door, it's mine. I want it.' And they unhinged the door and Serge and I walked out of the hotel with my two suitcases and a door."[2]

Johnny Mandel said, "I loved Serge, without ever getting into the stuff he indulged in. I remember that once I followed the band down to San Diego while I was waiting out my union card in Los Angeles. Serge, with his big mouth, succeeded in infuriating some sailors. They were going to take him apart. He called out, 'Zoot, Zoot!' Zoot was a natural athlete. He was even a great dancer. Zoot came over and cleaned up the sidewalk with those sailors."[3]

"When I was on the band," Terry Gibbs said, "Woody never fired anybody but Zoot, and the only reason he fired him is that Zoot spit at him. And he didn't really want Zoot to leave. We tried to stop it. If Zoot had apologized, Woody would have said, 'Great.' But Zoot wouldn't back down."

"I don't understand that," I said. "Because I know in later years, Zoot adored Woody."

"He adored him *then*," Terry said.

"Let me tell you," Terry continued emphatically, "Woody was the greatest bandleader I ever worked for in my life. He let you do your thing. In my younger days, I had a dumb temper. I was a boxer. I used to want to fight. It was much easier for me to fight somebody than talk to them. And Woody was the greatest to me.

"He came over to me like a father one time. I had so much energy when I was young. Today, I can play a whole thirty-two bars of melody." Terry referred to the discipline of playing melody as written, without adornment or improvisation, as contrasted with the desire of young jazz musicians to play everything they know or think they know in every chorus. "On *What's New?*" Terry said, singing the opening two notes, a rising minor second, "that's all the melody I played, and I went right into four million notes. That's how my mind worked. After about four months, Woody came over to me, very nice, and said, 'The arrangement Johnny Mandel wrote is so beautiful, it would sound great if you just played eight bars of melody.' I didn't even let him finish. I said, 'Who the hell are you to tell me how to play? You can't even play!' I jumped down his throat.

"I felt bad about that for years. It always bothered me."[4]

One of the most obnoxious members of the band was Stan Getz, whose arrogance then and for the rest of his life was as notorious as the brilliance of his musicianship. Sam Marowitz, who played lead alto in the band, later said that at an early rehearsal, Getz said to him, "Hey, you play pretty good for an old cat." Marowitz was then twenty-six.

Dick Hafer, who played tenor saxophone in a later Herd and adored Woody, said, "I met an old bandleader in Hawaii who said he saw Woody one time in a theater. He came backstage and had a couple of drinks and he cried over the way the guys were making fun of him in his own band. That was the Four Brothers band."[5]

Gerry Mulligan, who was himself addicted at the time, wrote a piece for the band and brought it to a rehearsal. He told me that the junkies had a smart attitude toward Woody, whose playing they deemed old-fashioned. "They played good solos," Gerry said. "But Woody's was the only solo that had anything to do with my piece."[6] The piece, by the way, which the band never recorded, was *Young Blood*. Gerry later sold it to Stan Kenton.

Sam Marowitz recounted that when Woody started to play at a rehearsal, Stan Getz said, "You play *the worst*." Woody said, "Of course I do, you schmuck. That's why I'm paying you to play. So keep your mouth shut."

Dick Hafer said, "They treated him badly. Neal Hefti was furious about it. He said he hated those guys for the way they treated Woody."[7]

Neal Hefti told me, "Frances and I would go to see them. Woody would be playing a solo, and they'd be making faces to each other behind his back." At that time, the young turks who had embraced bebop were a clique to themselves, marked by the hipper-than-thou attitude, an affectation of indifference and alienation, and a laconic secret-code slang designed to exclude. Woody was approaching his mid-thirties; Getz was twenty, Sims and Cohn twenty-two, and Chaloff was twenty-four, ages at which an illusion of omniscience and a condescension toward one's elders are common anyway. Finally, heroin addicts formed a subsect within the bebop clique, convinced they had found the secret of wisdom, the catalyst of creativity, and the path to nirvana, all in a spoonful of dissolved white powder. Shooting up was almost a religious ritual, and those who did not practice this communion were infidels. Some of the behavior of that group in that band was appalling. Legend had it that heroin made Zoot sick during a record date. Feeling his stomach churning, he turned his horn around, threw up in the bell, and went on playing. Years later, when Zoot had left heroin behind and emerged as the droll and immensely likable man he was inside, I asked him about it, and he confirmed the story, saying, "Yeah, there were stains on the music for years."

There is more than a little evidence that on occasion Woody would have a few drinks and sit down and cry over the contempt with which he was being treated by his own band.

The band's reputation for narcotics had spread and sometimes caused problems.

"Abe Turchen knew people from the narcotics squad in some of the towns," Terry Gibbs said. "He knew a lot of people from all over. One night we were onstage. We'd been playing about fifteen minutes. Abe took Woody over to the side. After we were done, Woody said, 'Whoever has anything, you better throw it away, because the narcotics squad is outside.' So the guys went to the bus, and nobody was going to throw anything away—right? So they took it from the top of the suitcases and put it in the bottom! Now it's funny. But when I think back, there were only about five or six by then who were straight. There were only about four of us who weren't even drinkers.

"In spite of the narcotics, believe it or not, we had a great baseball team. We played three games against Harry James' band. They won one, we won one. Harry said that if we won the third game, he'd give us a party. Harry James' band wore uniforms, with cleats on the shoes. They were dressed up. We got together in our band, and we said for this game we've got to be clean. Except Serge. Serge showed up out of his bird. Stan Getz was the pitcher. Stan was hard to hit, because he'd lob it in so easy. And the guys would try to kill it, and half the time they would strike out. He threw it so easy it was hard to hit."

"It sounds like the way he played," I said.

"That's right!" Terry said. "Well Serge was the catcher, down in the catcher's crouch. Stan threw the first lob, to warm up, and as it hit the glove, Serge fell over backwards.

"And we said, 'Oh no!' But we won that game, and Harry made us a party at the Empire Room. Harry was beautiful. He and his wife, Betty Grable. There was food, drinks were on Harry."

"Heroin was the drug of the period," Lou Levy said. "Pot was already old hat. Cab Calloway was singing songs about it and making jokes about pot. Heroin was a serious habit, but that was the drug that everybody was into at the time. I got into it.

"I remember Woody's expression. He'd just *look* at us. He didn't even shake his head. He'd just look. He never said anything to anybody that I recall.

"But the quality of the music was very important to them. They were very conscious of their image. What they were doing in their hotel rooms or on the bus or at intermissions was one thing, but on the bandstand they were real music-conscious. We'd all look for the opportunities to play. Sometimes Woody would get off the bandstand for the last set and go home. We'd drag out all the arrangements we really loved to play, like Johnny Mandel's *Not Really the Blues*, and play them. There was so much that we loved to play in the band anyway. Neal Hefti and Al Cohn stuff. The soloists were always at their best. We'd find a piano in some room down in the bowels of a theater and jam between shows. Al, Zoot, Stan, everybody. Always looking to play. Whatever else suffered, the music never did. The band sounded healthy. We may have had some unhealthy habits, but the music sounded healthy. Great vitality, great oneness, like Ellington had when that band was at its best. Or Basie. They had those magic moments. The band would come alive, and you'd feel a shortness of breath, it was so exciting. Sort of like Dizzy's band used to be to me, his young, wild, wonderful band that recorded for RCA Victor. I felt that same kind of excitement . . . .

"Oh God, what a wonderful experience! I'd love to go through it again now that I know a few things. When you're in the midst of such greatness at such a young age, I don't know if you realize what you're involved in. I was nineteen. The magnitude! I don't know if I appreciated it. I met Stan Getz in that band. I didn't know how good these guys were yet.

"One thing was made evident to me right away. Everybody in the band was crazy for Al Cohn. When he played, there was sheer reverence as every-body turned their eyes and ears toward him. When somebody else played, they just looked straight ahead. When Al Cohn played, it was always something special. You can ask anyone who's left from that band . . . . I remember in 1948 and '49, Stan would look up at Al with those blue eyes of his and just stare at him when he was playing. This is Stan Getz, and he's pretty snappy himself."

▼   ▼   ▼

Woody's disgust with Serge Chaloff led to an incident in Washington, D. C. "Can I tell that story, too, now?" I asked Wood during that conversation in 1984. We were sitting in the sun on that flagstone terrace of his, on lawn furniture made of curved steel pipe. It had probably come with the house in 1946; it was of art deco vintage.

"Sure, why not?" he said, and laughed at the memory. He'd first told me the story back in New York in the early 1960s. "But the funniest part of it is Joe Venuti's reaction," he said, and retold the story.

That night in Washington the band not only looked bad, it sounded bad. And Woody, furious at what had happened to it, had a row right on the bandstand with "Mr. Chaloff," as he called him sarcastically, emphasis on the first syllable.

"He was getting farther and farther out there," Woody said. "He kept saying, 'Hey, Woody, baby, I'm straight, man, I'm clean.' And I shouted, 'Just play your goddamn part and shut up!'

"I was so depressed after that gig. There was this after-hours joint in Washington called the Turf and Grid. It was owned by a couple of guys with connections, bookmakers. Numbers guys. Everybody used to go there. That night President Truman had a party at the White House, and afterwards all his guests went over to the Turf and Grid. They were seven deep at the bar, and I had to fight my way through to get a drink, man. All I wanted was to have a drink and forget it. And finally I get a couple of drinks, and it's hot in there, and I'm sweating, and somebody's got their hands on me, and I hear, 'Hey, Woody, baby, whadya wanna talk to me like that for? I'm straight, baby, I'm straight.' And it's Mr. Chaloff. And then I remember an old Joe Venuti bit." He referred to the incident in the New York speakeasy that Red Norvo described.

"We were jammed in there," Woody continued, "packed in, and . . . I peed down Serge's leg.

"You know, man, when you do that to someone, it takes a while before it sinks in what's happened to him. And when Serge realized, he let out a howl like a banshee. He pushed out through the crowd and went into a telephone booth. And I'm banging on the door and trying to get at him, and one of the owners comes up and says, 'Hey, Woody, you know, we love you, and we love the band, but we can't have you doing things like that in here.' And he asked me to please cool it.

"Well, not long after that, I was back here on the coast, working at some club at the beach. Joe Venuti was playing just down the street, and I was walking on the beach with him after the gig one night, and I told him I had a confession to make, I'd stolen one of his bits. Well, Joe just about went into shock. He was horrified. He said, 'Woody, you can't do things like that! I can do things like that, but you can't! You're a gentleman. It's all right for me, but not you!'"

▼   ▼   ▼

Woody told Stuart Troup:

"A lot of the players who wanted to play in the top echelon thought there was a connection with drugs.

"It was never proven. The guys who could play great could do it whether or not they were stoned. And many of them, including Charlie Parker, admitted that their playing was often inferior when they were high.

"I think they also were drawn into the bag because the salesmen were out there greeting them, like it was the natural thing to do. I saw a lot of it, the connections. I was well aware of it. I saw the guys out there trying to score. But I remained the biggest square in life.

"Some of the players used the difficulty of the road life as an excuse for drugs. But I don't think the road had a thing to do with it. They just wanted to get high, and the contacts were everywhere and still are. If a guy wants anything, he can get it anywhere at any time of the day or night.

"Mental strain has nothing to do with it either. The worst strain is when a guy decides to become a family person. And those guys rarely got into drugs . . . .

"The only other bandleader whose opinion I took stock in was Duke Ellington, who had some major druggies in his band as well. Duke thought pretty much like I did. 'If the players could play, let 'em play.'"

Terry Gibbs said, "Woody wasn't the instrumentalist that Benny Goodman, Artie Shaw, and Tommy Dorsey were, but he was the greater bandleader. He knew what a band was all about. I learned from Woody! Woody would get an arrangement, sometimes he would take a first chorus and make it a last chorus, or put it in the middle. He'd make it work. I learned how to do that from Woody. Just watching him do it.

"He advanced all our careers. *Early Autumn* made Stan Getz overnight. Everybody knew about Al Cohn and Zoot Sims from Woody's band. Bill Harris. Don Lamond. Lou Levy. Myself. All of us. Woody made us."

And they would all come running, whenever Woody called. They played in reunion bands at Monterey and Carnegie Hall. Or they would simply come to listen to his latest band and talk to him. The same young turks who had treated him so contemptuously in the Second Herd, almost to a man, came to idolize him as they grew older.

Years later, when I had come to know these musicians quite well, I did some informal research on how and why they quit heroin, in defiance of the conventional wisdom about the inevitability of heroin recidivism.

Lou Levy, a gentle and modest man, said, "I was not serious about it, not like some of the guys who aren't here any more. I got out. It took me a while. I finally just got disgusted with myself and gave it up."

Almost all heroin addicts make a break with the past, symbolic and actual, when they quit. Gerry Mulligan told me he found a doctor who was willing to risk his career to get Gerry medical morphine and remove him from furtive life in the shadow world of the junky. He simply destroyed the dark glamour of it, seeing to it that Gerry had good morphine and good needles. One night on a job in Detroit, Gerry felt overwhelmed with disgust, called his booking agency, canceled jobs, and put himself in a hospital to undergo withdrawal.

Zoot Sims told me he did it with the help of a girl he was going with at the time. He said they got into a car in New York and set off for Los Angeles, checking into motels at night. The girl did the driving, while Zoot endured the ordeal of pain, nausea, tremors, and sweats that go with withdrawal. One day it was over, he said, and he looked out the car window at the trees and green grass and glorious blue sky and at last reached California, his home.

Al Cohn told me, "I got an infection from a dirty needle. It settled in my eye, and it had to be removed. That's enough to make you quit."

Al was one of the great wits of the jazz world. Once when he started a gig in Copenhagen, he was asked if he wanted an Elephant beer, a brand sold there. "No," he said without hesitation, "I drink to forget."

A heavy drinker himself, he was sympathetic when a panhandler told him, "Sir, I'm an alcoholic, and I need a drink." Al got out some money and started to hand it to the man. Then he said, "Wait a minute, how do I know you won't spend this on food?"

Zoot was funny too. Once, years later, he was asleep in the back seat of a car as Al Cohn drove through a rainstorm. In the front seat with Al, who by then had a glass eye, was record producer Jack Lewis, who also had one eye. Zoot woke up, leaned over the back of the seat, and said, "I just want to be sure you guys are keeping both eyes on the road."

Like Woody, Al Cohn and Zoot Sims were immensely well liked in their later years. Stan Getz was not. His poignant lyricism was at odds with his character, which was devious, sometimes cruel, and completely self-centered. He was capable of immense rudeness and even cruelty. He was a cheat in his business dealings, and he subjected women to insult and emotional abuse. He destroyed his first wife—and a number of other people along the way. After he gave up heroin, he, like Zoot and Al, became a heavy drinker. Once, when Woody and I were talking about Stan (whom Woody always referred to sarcastically as "Stanley," in three syllables, Stan-uh-ly), Woody said, "I dunno. I think I liked him better when he was a junky."

A rumor once circulated that Stan had undergone open-heart surgery. When Bob Brookmeyer heard this, he said, "What did they do, take one out or put one in?" Zoot Sims made a comment that other musicians quoted with glee: "Stan is a whole bunch of interesting guys."

To which Johnny Mandel commented, "Yeah, and I knew several of them."

I have met only two musicians who liked Stan: Mandel and Lou Levy. Stan and Lou remained close to the end of Stan's life. While I admired Stan's playing, I think there is something to be said for Whitney Balliett's perception of its "whining tone of self-pity." But there was no gainsaying the brilliance of his work.

Stan had fantastic ears, enormous imagination, and a remarkable control of his instrument. Asked for his definition of the perfect jazz tenor player, he said, "My technique, Zoot's time, and Al Cohn's ideas." John Coltrane said, "We all envy Stan's tone." He was a complex and contradictory man. Ralph said that when he came into the band, "he was this nice Jewish kid. He used to bring us knishes made by his mother or his grandmother."

Richard Palmer said of his work in his 1988 monograph on Getz:

He has refined saxophone technique and mastery to the ultimate; he has achieved a corpus of work which for both supreme consistency and wide-ranging beauty can hardly be equalled, let alone bettered; and he has created a style that is inimitable in its amalgam of lyricism, fierce power and imaginative command.

Stan was still actively working at the time. Palmer concluded: "Whatever he does, it is more than likely that it will confirm Stan Getz, the man with the sound of an angel and the thrust of an aircraft engine, as one of the greatest jazzmen and among the finest artists alive."

Ralph Burns put it laconically: "Stan was a prick, but he could play."

▼   ▼   ▼

I saw Zoot in Ottawa a few months before his death, which came March 23, 1985. He was so weak that he played sitting down—and played beautifully. I talked to Al Cohn on the telephone when he was fading quickly in the hospital in New York. I'd been told that he wanted to hear from his friends. Johnny Mandel and several other of his old colleagues then living in California more or less elected me to make the call. Al's voice was feeble, but he was indeed thrilled to know we all cared about him. He died February 15, 1988, in Stroudsburg, Pennsylvania, where the Al Cohn Memorial Foundation now houses his papers.

Serge Chaloff predeceased all of them. He broke his heroin habit only to contract a spinal tumor. He played his last concert in Boston from a wheelchair and died in that city, his home town, July 16, 1957.

You can make what you wish of this statistical aberration. Of the famous Brothers, Al Cohn, Zoot Sims, Stan Getz, and Serge Chaloff, all four died of cancer. But then so did Bill Harris (on August 3, 1973, in Florida) and he didn't use heroin. So many jazz musicians have died of cancer that I have wondered what correlation there might be between the smoke they inhaled in nightclubs and the disease.

Terry Gibbs continued to be haunted by the confrontation with Woody over *What's New?* "About a year before Woody died," Terry said, "he came in to see me in a club called Light's in the Royal York Hotel in Toronto. I told the story about that tune to the whole audience. I said that I'd yelled at Woody after he'd been so nice. And I said, 'Woody, this is for you.' And I played two whole choruses of melody on *What's New?* It was my apology."[8]

16

Sidewalks of Cuba

 Carlos Gastel organized a month-long concert tour, aimed primarily at college students, to feature two of his biggest clients, Nat Cole and Woody. One of its engagements was the University of Illinois at Urbana.

Most of the band was traveling by bus, but Stan Getz and Serge Chaloff were with Ralph Burns in his new Ford. When icy roads made it impossible to proceed further, they halted in a small town and telephoned Walt Yoder, who was now the band's road manager. Yoder said he would have the express train to St. Louis stopped in the town so that they could board it. In 1987, Stan recalled the incident to Larry Kart of the *Chicago Tribune*:

"We went to the station, the train came by, they threw the flare out, and it took the train about half a mile to stop. Then as we were walking down the track, we heard sirens. . . . (and) we learned that when the express was flagged down, a brakeman on a local train got off to see what was happening, and he slipped on the ice and was decapitated by the express. Well, when I heard about that, something happened inside me. I felt so bad that I just lost heart and decided I was going to leave the band. . . . I don't know, it just did something to me."

The Cole-Herman concert played Carnegie Hall on February 20, 1949. Shorty Rogers had written a finale for the concert titled *More Moon*, based on the changes of *How High the Moon*. Nat Cole would perform with his trio early in the concert, then join the band for this final number, scat-singing the first chorus and then playing piano. Later Shorty wrote a new first chorus and the band recorded the tune. A record reviewer for England's *Melody Maker* complained of the use of the other song's changes, asking:

"What does the law say about all this? Unfortunately—nothing that helps. Neither here nor in America does the law give any indication of where originality is presumed to end and plagiarism to begin; and few have thought it wise to risk the heavy cost of attempting to get the position more clearly defined through test cases." With a certain indignant heat, he said that it was a matter "which I have long felt legislators on both sides of the Atlantic should deal with without further delay." Evidently he had not noticed how many songs were based on the I VI II V chord sequence, or for that matter how many used the changes of *I Got Rhythm*. You can't copyright titles or chord sequences.

Zoot had already left the band after the spitting incident, and as Terry Gibbs observed, the Second Herd was crumbling. In March, Getz left and Buddy Savitt took his place. Bernie Glow soon dropped out, to become one of the first-call studio trumpeters in New York, and Al Porcino joined the trumpet section. Don Lamond left to join Harry James, only to leave that band, too, and join the growing group of former band players resident in New York and working as studio free-lances. Lamond was replaced by Shadow Wilson, formerly of the Basie band. Then Al Cohn left, and Gene Ammons took his chair. Thus the band now had three black players.

One of the most interesting of small groups in jazz was that billed as Jay and Kai, founded in 1954 by trombonists J. J. Johnson and Kai Winding. In 1956 it broke up, J. J. told me, not because of dissension between the leaders but because J. J. was black and Kai white. The ordeal of finding hotel and other accommodations became unendurable.

In the 1930s, traveling black entertainers could find no hotel rooms at all. They stayed in a circuit of private homes owned by other blacks, whose names were quietly known to show business people.

Artie Shaw told me that when Roy Eldridge was with his band, the trumpeter developed a deception to get the key to his hotel room wherever the band was staying. Eldridge, who was advertised as a star with the Shaw band, would stride across the hotel lobby and announce to the room clerk that he was Mr. Eldridge's valet and would like the key to the room. And he would get it.

As hard as touring with a white band was on Eldridge, Shaw said, it was even harder on Billie Holiday when she sang with his band.

The singer Ernie Andrews once described to me what it was like when he traveled with the Harry James band. The hotel reservations would be made weeks in advance. Then the band would arrive. Ernie said, "You never go on the road without a confirmation from the hotels. When the bus pulled up, they'd start passing the rooms out. So when they called my name, they'd tell me to wait. Harry said, 'What's the problem?' I said, 'I don't know, they called my name, but I haven't got a key.'

"So Harry got up and said, 'Mr. Monty . . .'" (the reference was to Pee Wee Monty, the James band's road manager). "Harry said, "Do we have a manifest?' Harry looked at it and saw my name on it and he said to the room clerk, 'Now what is the problem?'

"The room clerk'd say something like, 'Well, we don't have a room for him here but we could put him two blocks down the street and he'd be close to the band.' So Harry would say, 'Pee Wee, go down the street and see if they can accommodate twenty-eight of us. Take the stuff out of this lobby, put it back in the bus, and let's go.' And they would say, 'Well, wait a minute,' and Harry would say, 'What are we waiting for?' And the clerk would say, 'Well, we might find something here,' and Harry would say, 'Well, find a corner room.' And they'd say, 'Why a corner room?' And he'd say, 'Because that's the biggest room. It gets plenty of air from both sides, and right now he needs it.'

"I never opened my mouth. It didn't happen often. But it happened."[1]

These pressures tended to keep bands all-black or all-white, regardless of the wishes of musicians to work together. Johnny Mandel was one of the first white musicians ever to play with the Count Basie band.

Woody had used a black arranger even before he commissioned Dizzy Gillespie to write for the band and to play with it during an engagement at the Apollo Theater. In 1940 the Band That Plays the Blues recorded *Fine and Dandy* and *Cousin to Chris. Down Beat*, in its review, said, "Zilner Randolph, the talented Negro arranger, did a great job with *Chris*."

Woody told me once that the fight to integrate bands was, in those earlier days, almost impossible to win.

The band was booked on a ten-week tour of Loew's theaters. Not long after it began, Woody received a telegram from Washington, D.C., demanding that he abide by the terms of the contract, stating that he would bring an all-white orchestra to the Loew's theater there, failing which the entire tour would be canceled. Woody needed the money just to pay the band's overhead. And the band included Oscar Pettiford, Shadow Wilson, Ernie Royal, and Gene Ammons.

"I didn't know what to do," Woody said. "I discussed it with my lawyers. So I called the guys to the dressing room and said, 'Look, if we're going to finish this tour, which I certainly have to do if we're going to continue, what I will do so I can get over this thing without getting into the papers and everything else—because it will—I will pay your salaries plus expenses to go back to New York and have a ball for a week.'

"By the time they got off the train back in New York, there was a battery of lawyers from the NAACP, and they kept them up all night, grilling them, trying to do something for their people."

The musicians went back to Woody in the morning. He told them, "Well, look, fellows, I'm not going to argue. You can do whatever you like, because it's bigger than I am. But I will tell you this: If you insist on staying here and going back to work, I'm certainly not going to prevent you. But tomorrow morning I'll be back on my hill in California, and that's the end of this."

The musicians returned to New York and then, with the exception of Shadow Wilson, rejoined Woody at the end of the Loew's tour. Shelly Manne had replaced Shadow Wilson, but Wilson, Woody said, "got zonked," and Shelly stayed on with the band.[2]

Woody's daughter, Ingrid, said: "My dad hated the South. He hated it. He just hated it. He had run into Jim Crow when he had Ernie Royal in the band. That put him off right away. He found the blue laws exceedingly annoying, when you wanted to have a drink after a gig and you didn't know whether you were in a county where you couldn't. One of the things he hated most about it was the way southern speech communicates between the lines.

"I like southern people. I lived in Nashville for several years. I like the culture. I learned to communicate with the culture. But my dad never did. He found it devious and highly annoying."

Woody said in 1957, "I never took a completely mixed group down south but once or twice. There would be maybe one person like Ernie Royal. He was a very fair colored person, and these people had the eagle eye out at all times, especially on a northern swing band, and once in a while I would receive an inquiry whether that boy up there was a Mexican. I would say, 'No, he's a Cuban.' They would say, 'He sure do blow!' At intermission time, Ernie would have a ring of people around him, slapping him on the back. He was a very impressive trumpet player, you know, with high notes. They would be just loving him, and after the gig, he would go out to his car and he couldn't buy gas or get a sandwich to eat."[3]

Despite the fuss made over Benny Goodman's hiring of Teddy Wilson in 1936, Wilson played only in Goodman's small groups, not the big band, and Goodman employed comparatively few blacks in the long run of his career. But in his bands and sextets, Woody employed probably more black

musicians over the years than any other white bandleader, among them
Nat Adderley, Joe Alexander, Keter Betts, Oscar Brashear, Joe Carroll,
Jimmy Cleveland, Rudy Collins, Albert Dailey, Jeff Davis, Ray Drummond,
George Duvivier, Harry (Sweets) Edison, Frank Foster, Al Gibbons, Dave
Gibson, Dizzy Gillespie, Harry Hall, Slide Hampton, Gregory Herbert,
John Hicks, David Hines, Major Holley, Tate Houston, Alfonso Johnson,
Gus Johnson, Reunald Jones, Rufus Jones, Russ Little, Dennis Mackrel,
Ronnie Mathews, Andy McGhee, Howard McGhee, Billy Mitchell, Monk
Montgomery, Cecil Payne, Seldon Powell, Julian Priester, Carl Pruitt,
Rufus Reid, Charlie Shavers, Byron Stripling, Buddy Tate, Lutten Taylor,
Mel Wanzo, Carl Warwick, and Frank Wess, as well as Ammons, Pettiford,
Royal, and Wilson.

And when Terry Gibbs left in February, 1949, Woody replaced him with
Milt Jackson, who would spend two years with the band.

"I had a beautiful experience with Woody," Milt said in October, 1994.
"He paid me a nice bit of money for a sideman. We had a beautiful rapport
and we got to be very close. He had a lot of respect for me and of course I
had a lot for him."[4]

Jackson would later be one of the founders of the Modern Jazz Quartet,
with which he would be associated for more than forty years, recognized as
one of the major jazz musicians.

Born in Detroit on January 1, 1923, he learned guitar and piano as a
child, then taking up xylophone and vibraharp. On this latter instrument
he would reign as a master, a player of immense invention and strength.
He already had established his name with Dizzy Gillespie before joining
Woody.

Woody used to take delight in Milt's apparently inexhaustible memory
for tunes and would try to stump him. He claimed, without much exag-
geration, that Bags—as Milt is universally known—knew every tune ever
written.

"Look here," Bags said with a chuckle, "well, you know what happened.
From the days of Miles, when we recorded together—that now-famous
album of *Bags' Groove*, with Monk on it—the challenge was that I *could*
play *anything*, that there wasn't a tune they could play that I couldn't hear
or didn't know. I was blessed with two gifts. A lot of us are blessed with
none. I was blessed with two: perfect pitch and photographic memory.

"In those days I could remember any conversation. I'll give you the best
example. In two years I stayed in Woody's band, '49 and '50, I never carried
an address book for the dates. If you gave me directions, I'd remember.

"When I got to that band, it became a challenge to Woody to the point where he went and found a tune for the band to play that he thought I didn't know or couldn't play. I enjoyed the challenge, man. It was funny to me. As a kid I sat at my piano and would just play tune after tune, merely to see how many I could play. All the tunes that were popular then and are standards today. I'd just go from one to another, without going back to the same song, and I sort of gained a reputation for that.

"Woody would stomp off a tune without telling me what we were playing. He challenged me nightly until finally he said, 'I gotcha.' He had Jimmy Giuffre write up a revised arrangement of *Stars Fell on Alabama*. That night, he gave me the part. I had a solo of course. And I played the tune. After that, he walked over to me and said, 'You know, I quit.' "

Laughing again, Bags said, "I told him, 'Woody, don't try that. It won't work.'"

There were, of course, the constant harassments faced by black musicians who worked in white bands, and for that matter whites who worked in black bands. One of these involved a car Woody bought in Chicago. Woody was going on to New York, for some reason in a hurry.

"It was a brand new '49 Oldsmobile," Bags said. "And I was going back to New York. He asked me if I would drive it for him. I stopped in Detroit. That Sunday I was on my way to take my mother to church. The cops stopped me. I wasn't speeding or anything like that. I didn't know where the registration of the car was. So they thought I'd stolen it. They took me down and were getting ready to book me. They told me to empty my pockets. I put $750 up on the counter. I'd just been paid. It was an awful lot of money then. I told them I was with Woody Herman's band, and I said, 'Man, all I can do is give you Woody's number and have you call him.'

"And they phoned him. I could hear Woody's voice across the room, giving them hell. Calling them every . . . well, I can't say it. Calling them so and so and so and so. I could hear him saying, 'Yes, he's with my band. He's a featured artist.' I guess he offered to come out to Detroit or Abe would come out to Detroit. But they believed him. They gave me my money back, with a thousand apologies of course, and they let me go."[5]

Bags became close friends with Buddy Childers, who had come into the trumpet section. "One night after the job, in Terre Haute, Indiana," Milt said, "Buddy Childers and I and the bass player were going to a nightclub. The whole band had been invited. When we got to the door, they weren't going to let me in. Buddy Childers, man, he was livid. He said, 'This man is the featured artist with the Woody Herman band. And we were all invited to this club.' The man said, 'You can't come in here.' Buddy went *off*. He said, 'Look, man, you've got a choice. You either let us come in here, or we're gonna turn this place out.'

"And I said, 'Hey, man, no, I don't want to cause trouble for the band. I'll go back across town, where the black folks are.' And then Buddy turned on me, and he said, 'Hey! Don't you move! You stay right here.' The doorman ran and got the manager. Buddy proceeded to explain to him what was happening. We were invited in. Drinks were now on the house and everything.'"

In July, 1949, the band played an engagement at Rendezvous Ballroom at Balboa, California, during which it made a short film called *Jazz Cocktail* at Universal International. Black musicians never were allowed to be seen with white musicians in films. Indeed, when Benny Carter started writing arrangements for film, he was assigned only to work with black singers. Ernie Royal and Gene Ammons were not shown in the film, and when Royal had a solo, Al Porcino had to stand up and pretend he was playing it.

On July 14, the band recorded Johnny Mandel's *Not Really the Blues*, which was a favorite of the band's musicians. Johnny said, "I wrote *Not Really the Blues* and I did *Sinbad the Tailor*, which I don't think I've ever heard. I can't remember the other things because they weren't recorded. If you hear something much later, and you never heard it played back, you don't know whether you wrote it or you dreamt it.

"I never wrote *enough* for Woody. I would like to have written a lot more. And at that time, I never got to know him very well, mostly through shyness. I got to know him later on, when I went up to the house once or twice with Pete Candoli. We sat around, and I saw what kind of a guy this was. I always knew he was great; everybody always liked him."[6]

On July 18, the band was playing softball in a ball park near Balboa. Oscar Pettiford, making a throw from left field, somehow broke his arm and had to be replaced by Joe Mondragon.

When Shadow Wilson left the band, he was replaced by Shelly Manne, one of the truly great drummers—but not the right drummer for that band. Terry Gibbs, a friend of Shelly's, said, "Every band has its drummer. And Shelly was not the drummer for that band." Johnny Mandel agrees. He said, "Shelly Manne was a wonderful drummer. But not for Woody. Buddy Rich was wonderful with Tommy Dorsey. He was wonderful with every band he played in but his own."

Said Terry Gibbs: "After Don Lamond left, we must have had six or seven of the greatest drummers, but they didn't fit. It was Don's band. Every band has its own drummer. Don fit both bands. The First Herd was more of a riff band."

The decline of the business continued. The July 19, 1949, issue of *Down Beat*, carried this bizarre headline:

SLUMP IN BIZ DUE TO
SKIRT LENGTH—WOODY

The story said, "Woody Herman has an idea. And it might cause sociologists to go scurrying around for material to write papers on. He thinks the main cause for the retrogression and slump, not only in the music business but in the whole country, can be laid to the length of women's skirts."

It quoted him as saying: "You know, when those designers in Paris decided to make skirts real long a few years ago—called it 'the new look'— they were the cause of what's happening now.

"They made styles look like styles of thirty or forty years ago and people now are thinking and acting the same way they did then.

"One thing about this 'slump' gives me a laugh. Government heads keep saying, 'It's just a little slip to help get adjusted.' Man, that pole we're slipping on is greased."

If Woody said anything remotely like that, he was pulling the reporter's leg; and Woody was not averse to the occasional put-on. He was well aware that the causes of the decline of the bands were many and complex. But he, alas, was not as prepared for it as some of his colleagues.

Benny Goodman, Tommy Dorsey, and Artie Shaw had their big successes before and during World War II. Woody's came just before the war's end and immediately after it, in the last years of the Swing Era. The successful First Herd lasted only two years; the Second Herd was largely a critical and musical, not a financial, success, and by 1949 it was finished. All of the First Herd's and much of the Second's records were on the Columbia label. They amounted to approximately a hundred sides, not including *Ebony Concerto*. It is a small canon from two of the greatest bands in the history of jazz. And now, reflecting on it, I find a melancholy irony in it, particularly since Woody, like Count Basie and Gene Krupa, was one of the few leaders whose character to this day is measured by how good he was to so many people.

Furthermore, while Duke Ellington encountered the same shrinking audiences the other bandleaders were experiencing, Ellington had the biggest body of published songs of any bandleader in American history, not excluding even Isham Jones. He had an enormous income from them.

Woody had little if anything. He was an outstanding musician, for all his own misgivings about his clarinet work; a brilliant bandleader; and an extraordinary human being. But he was a dismally inept businessman, trusting and naïve in his dealings despite an air of canny cynicism he liked to affect. In 1947, he decided to dispense with the law firm of Goldfarb, Mirenburg and Vallon as his managers, apparently thinking his contract with them had expired. A judge ordered him to pay a commission to Goldfarb for one year, which further depleted his diminishing resources. It was at this point that Woody took on Carlos Gastel as his manager.

Gastel sent Woody out on another tour with Nat Cole. In November it again played Carnegie Hall. This tour, too, was profitable, but Woody was sinking financially. The band simply couldn't last. Woody said he actually lost money on *Lemon Drop*. And it was money, not drugs, that destroyed the Second Herd.

Terry Gibbs said, "I joined Woody in 1948 and quit a year later. And the only reason I left is that Abe Turchen cut all our salaries. Abe ruined the band by being chintzy about the money. A bunch of us left because of that. He cut Ernie Royal, he cut Bill Harris. We all left at the same time."

At that time, Abe was in the throes of personal troubles. By the evidence, Abe was playing around with a lot of women, and his wife, Peggy, knew it. They separated and then were divorced. For whatever reason, Abe obtained custody of their son, Michael, and took him to Sioux City, where he would be reared by Abe's parents.

By this point the band's personnel had changed so completely that it really was no longer the Second Herd. Its body of recordings for Capitol was rather small.

Woody estimated that he had lost at least $180,000 on the Second Herd. He gave the musicians their notices, and they played their last engagement at a country club in Wichita Falls, Texas, in November. To recoup some of his losses, he assembled a septet with Milt Jackson on vibes, Conte Candoli on trumpet, Dave Barbour on guitar, Red Mitchell on bass, Bill Harris on trombone, Ralph Burns on piano, and Shelly Manne on drums. The first booking was a four-week engagement starting in early December, 1949, at an outdoor nightclub called the Tropicana in Havana.

Woody planned to fly directly from Texas to Cuba. Don Lanphere, who had come into the band on tenor; Serge Chaloff; and Earl Swope drove Woody's car back to New York.

Woody scheduled a rehearsal in a Dallas hotel where he and most of the septet were staying. Milt Jackson, needless to say, was staying in another part of town. Hotel segregation still was plaguing jazz groups in the 1960s, and this was 1949 Texas. Jackson arrived for the rehearsal.

"I got into the elevator," Milt said. "The elevator operator, who was black—I didn't realize it then, but he was frightened to take me up—said, 'You've got to take the service elevator.'

"I said, 'Why? This one doesn't run?' One word led to another, and I said, 'Well, man, I'm going up on this one. We have a rehearsal and I have to get there.' And after we got up to the floor, the elevator operator went back down.' The next thing I know the manager came up. He said, 'We don't allow blacks to ride on elevators.' I said, 'Man, I live in New York, I don't know anything about that. I have to be up here for a rehearsal.'

"And about that time, Abe Turchen walked up. Abe took him aside and explained to him. After they finished talking, we went to the rehearsal. And the manager sent up a room-service cart with all this food on it and an apology.

"But those three incidents, Detroit, Terre Haute, and Dallas, were the only incidents I had with the band. It was a happy experience with that band."

Dave Barbour and Peggy Lee were on the verge of divorce. Barbour was in an advanced state of alcoholism. Peggy was afraid he would die. Peg recalled:

"I know Woody would never do anything to hurt me. And I was told that Woody had asked Dave to go on the Cuban trip. I'm not sure it wasn't the other way around. Or possibly Carlos Gastel arranged it. It was like Carlos to send David off someplace over Christmas and New Year's. I never wanted anything less in my life than that divorce. I used to cry when I found myself getting strong on someone else's weakness. And Carlos was trying to get David for his sister, Chiqui."

The successful songs Peggy and Barbour had written together assured him a reasonably good income, drunk or sober.

"The funniest thing of all," Peg said, "is that when I finally agreed to the divorce, Carlos succeeded in getting David for Chiqui. David had no place to go. Carlos called me one night and said, 'Peg, you have to do something about David. He just hit Chiqui.'

"I said, 'I think that's your problem, Carlos.'"[7]

However it came about, Dave was with the septet Woody took to Cuba that December. The engagement was to prove a strange one. Floor shows in pre-Castro Cuba were famous for flamboyance, if not exactly for taste, and fast pace, with elaborately costumed chorus girls and Cuban bands heavily populated by conga and timbale players shouting "Arriba, arriba!" and the like.

"The Tropicana was unbelievable," Ralph Burns said. "It was the first time we were ever part of any show like that. All of a sudden a cannon would go off and a hundred doves would float up into the air. It was pretty wild."[8]

And it was an improbable booking for a jazz group. Audiences did not understand the music. Milt Jackson said, "Woody had hits on *Don't Cry, Joe* and *Happiness Is Just a Thing Called Joe*. Well down there, the Cuban people didn't know anything about an American hit. So when he would sing *Don't Cry, Joe* and get no hand, he got rather frustrated. One night I just took him aside and said, 'These people down here don't *know* those songs.' "

So Woody drew on Milt's phenomenal memory for tunes, having him play anything that sounded remotely Hispanic or that the audience just might know. For the most part, however, the group's offerings inspired silences and baffled stares. Milt said they got rained out on Christmas Eve. The club owner was taken to a hospital after a heart attack. Rain came again on New Year's Eve, normally the biggest night of the year. The job continued to be an unqualified disaster.

Red Mitchell told Stuart Troup, "Milt Jackson and I were rooming to-gether in Cuba . . . . We had cockroaches and Milt used his entire Spanish vocabulary telling the owner about the *cucarachas*. The owner just laughed. One day we got all the poison we could buy, sprays and all, and did up the apartment. When we came back, the place was crawling with dying cock-roaches. I put as many as possible out of their misery."

Finally, to compound the accumulated indignity, Ralph Burns got thrown into jail. Laughing about it now, Ralph said, "One night after the gig, we were in the bar at the hotel. There were a lot of girls around, hookers, especially late at night. Woody and I were pretty loaded. I know I was, and I think everybody else was. This girl was trying to make a deal with me. I didn't want to go upstairs with her. I said, 'No.' She called in the cops. And naturally they all spoke Spanish. None of us spoke Spanish. She told them something like, 'This man stole my fur coat.' It was some cheap old fur wrap." (Woody said it looked like an old inner tube.) Ralph said, "She was Cuban, the police were Cuban, so they believed her and they threw me in jail overnight until Woody could get me out the next morn-ing."[9]

As often happens when jazz groups return to the United States after a strange engagement in an improbable place, the band gave a collective sigh of relief. Red Mitchell said: "(Woody) had that small group for four months, and that was fun. After Cuba, we went to Philadelphia. Then we played northward, and I remember that every place we went it was twenty degrees colder. Then we went to the Midwest and to Texas and to California. It was a nice tour."[10]

Shelly Manne left the group, replaced by Sonny Igoe. The Woodchoppers played Philadelphia; Chicago, which was colder; Duluth, colder still; and Saskatoon, Saskatchewan, where temperatures at that time of year fall far below zero. At last they reached the comparatively balmy clime of foggy San Francisco, where Woody so long before had worked for Tom Gerun.

17

The Third Herd

In addition to other conditions that Woody and the other band-leaders faced as the 1940s drew to a close, two far-reaching developments were occurring that neither he nor anyone else understood. One was a profound change in the character and quality of radio broadcasting. The other was a revolution, or more exactly series of revolutions, in the record industry.

In the early days of radio, the record companies, afraid that "free" music would reduce their sales, inscribed record labels with *Not Licensed for Radio Broadcast*. The broadcasters simply ignored it. This led Fred Waring, Walter O'Keefe, Donald Voorhees, Paul Whiteman, and opera singer Lawrence Tibbett to sue a number of broadcasting corporations. In 1940, these actions were halted when the U.S. Supreme Court declined to review a decision against Whiteman and his record label, RCA Victor, by the Second Circuit Court of Appeals. In brief, Whiteman had sued the WBO Broadcasting Company, owners of WNEW in New York City.

The Court of Appeals ruling was written by Judge Learned Hand, who, despite a revered position in the history of U.S. law, revealed a deep ignorance of the nature of intellectual property. Hand wrote: "Copyright in any form, whether statutory or in common law, is a monopoly. It consists only in the power to prevent others from reproducing the copyright work. WBO Broadcasting has never invaded any such right."

To play a record on the air is indeed to reproduce it, and the ruling is nonsense. But it still stands, and it has had serious, damaging, and lasting social and aesthetic consequences.[1]

A year later, in 1941, music got another blow when the American Society of Composers, Authors, and Publishers, which collected airplay royalties for its members, sought a substantial increase in the fees paid to it. The radio stations refused, and ASCAP banned from broadcast all ASCAP material, which meant the entire body of the best American popular music, including all the songs of the great Broadway composers. The ban lasted nine months and affected 674 radio stations, which were forced to play songs in the public domain. That year Stephen Foster's *Jeanie with the Light Brown Hair* made *Your Hit Parade.*

The broadcasters were ready for ASCAP. In 1939, anticipating such a problem, they had established their own organization, Broadcast Music Incorporated, to license composers who were not members of ASCAP, and with the ASCAP ban they activated it. The ban cost ASCAP and its members $300,000 a month, and the organization capitulated to the broadcasters, not only without the raise but acquiescing in a reduction of fees from 5 to 2.5 percent of the broadcasters' advertising revenues.

A good many students of the music business blame BMI for the decline of American popular music, but if it is culpable, it is as one of many confluent factors. The next year, James C. Petrillo, head of the American Federation of Musicians, pulled the first of two recording bans, contributing to the rise of the singers, for example.

When the bands were doing their remote broadcasts from such places as the Palomar Ballroom and Frank Dailey's Meadowbrook, one of the engineers who often worked with them was a boy not yet out of his teens named Fred Hall. Hall became a disc jockey for Armed Forces Radio, broadcasting to troops in the South Pacific. After the war, he founded a series of radio stations and in 1995 has a syndicated radio show emphasizing the big-band era.

"Until the late 1930s," Fred told me, "the creative people had control of network programming. Then the advertisers took over. The agencies began to dominate. They began to package shows.

"When I got into radio, you just could not play records on the air. It was not allowed. So they made radio transcriptions, sixteen-inch discs produced especially for radio broadcast. They ran at $33\frac{1}{3}$ r.p.m. and were the predecessor of the LP.

"Then the industry just began to ignore the prohibition of records. The station I was on in Washington, D.C., WWDC, was one of the first to let us play any record we felt like. The stations, remember, were playing hits, but many of the hits were quality things. And so the disc jockeys—they weren't called disc jockeys yet, they were just called announcers—had a lot of leeway. They would pick their records from what was available, and what was available was often excellent material. A handful who were really good, such as Martin Block, were terribly influential in launching a new record, a new band. There were no industry journals, such as *Billboard*, running elaborate lists of hits and governing the selection of music by the stations. There was *Your Hit Parade*. It surveyed sheet-music sales in music stores. Sheet-music sales were still very important.

"Nobody was paying much attention to television after the war, or for that matter FM. In short order two or three thousand little radio stations went up all over the country, and many of them depended on the networks for news and drama, particularly the fifteen-minute daytime dramas. There were fewer remotes of the bands because there were fewer and fewer locations for them to play. These stations went right on playing hit records, and the hit records were for the most part still quality stuff. And gradually it began to go downhill. The networks withdrew, and withdrew, and withdrew, turning their attention to television, until all they were giving their affiliates was five minutes of news on the hour. And that left the stations to their own devices. But there were still many very innovative program directors who got deeply involved with local affairs, local programming, local news, local sports, to supplement the records they were playing.

"Then, as the small operations were bought up by large-scale operators—the group owners—the owners felt they had too little control over the stations that were far from their headquarters. So they turned to programmers. It began in the late 1950s, and by the mid-1970s, it was paramount, and today it is completely dominant. Radio became very impersonal. We got the self-styled consultants. They became the bane of the industry."[2]

To judge by a massive pile of clippings of interviews conducted in the late 1940s with such concerned bandleaders as Woody, Charlie Barnet, Les Brown, and Duke Ellington, not one of them was observing what was going on in the other entertainment industries. Nor for that matter was the trade press, including *Down Beat* and *Metronome*.

For the movie industry, the peak box-office year was 1946, when it grossed $1,692,000,000. That was the year the soldiers and sailors and airmen came home and took their girls to dance to the First Herd or to hold hands in movie theaters. A year later many of them were married and the girls were pregnant. The movie industry would not match that box-office figure until 1974 and then only with dollars worth a fraction of what they were when the war ended. Though some sort of regular television

broadcasting had gone on in New York since 1941, the large-scale manufacture of television receivers (and new refrigerators, stoves, and washing
machines) got under way in 1947. Within a year, movie receipts dropped
by a hundred million dollars. The number of tickets sold declined steadily
from 90 million a week to 20 million in the early 1980s. Even baseball
attendance was falling as the 1940s drew to a close.

As the ballrooms closed and the "remotes" that emanated from them
grew fewer, the radio stations of the United States perforce relied more
and more on records, and that dependency grew even greater as the networks turned their attention to the rapidly burgeoning television industry.
In 1947, seven TV stations began regular broadcasting to an audience
of only 14,000. In 1948, a small company called Toni Home Perma-
nents poured more than half its earnings into television advertising in
Chicago, and grew so quickly that it was soon sold at an immense profit to
Gillette, manufacturer of razors and blades. The lesson was not lost on
other corporations, who diverted some of their advertising money from
radio to television, nor on the commanders of the networks at NBC, CBS,
and ABC.

A stalwart little band of disc jockeys took a stand for good music, among
them Dave Garroway in Chicago, Fred Robbins, Symphony Sid Torin, and
Martin Block in New York, Ed (Jack the Bellboy) Mackenzie in Detroit,
Jimmy Lyons and Al (Jazzbo) Collins in San Francisco, Al Jarvis and Gene
Norman in Los Angeles, Sid Mark in Philadelphia, and Felix Grant in
Washington, D.C.

But the radio stations were only interested in cost-per-thousand, how
much it cost an advertiser to reach how many people. There was nothing to
impede them, for the United States, alone among western nations, had
declined to set up a nationally owned broadcasting system comparable to
the BBC in England. To reach the lowest common denominator of public
taste, the radio stations began emphasizing a lower quality of music, and
along with the music of the bands, the airwaves were filled with *Music!
Music! Music!*; *You, You, You*; *Wanted*; *He's a Real Gone Guy*; *Powder Your
Face with Sunshine*; *Sun Flower*; *Room Full of Roses*; *The Wheel of Fortune*, and the like. An examination of the lists of hit songs for each year
from 1945 to 1955 reveals a steady rise of meretricious novelty songs, and
a commensurate decline in good ones.[3]

Meanwhile, the record industry, with which broadcasting was linked in
an indissoluble symbiosis, was undergoing radical change.

After the rise of Benny Goodman, jazz, or the big-band form of it,
entered the main stream. "It was the popular music of the land," as Woody

repeatedly put it. But it wasn't *all* the popular music of the land at that; we still had *Bei Mir Bist Du Schoen* (1937), *Three Little Fishes* (1939), *The Hut Sut Song* (1941), and *Mairzy Doats* (1943) alongside masterpieces such as *Begin the Beguine* coming out of the Broadway musicals, whose successes, like those of the big bands, were abetted and indeed largely caused by exposure of the songs on network radio.

Records for a long time were largely distributed through furniture and department stores for the reason that these were retail outlets for the radio-phonographs on which the records were played. In brief, the record industry was an adjunct of the broadcasting and appliance industries.

In 1946, engineers began to experiment with German Magnetophon tape recorders, discovered by Allied forces at the headquarters of Radio Luxembourg. A year later, prototype stereo tape machines were demonstrated. The theory of stereo had been understood for some time, of course, and Duke Ellington actually recorded in stereo, through the use of two cutting machines, as far back as 1933. Then in 1948, CBS issued its first long-playing records, running at the 33⅓-r.p.m. speed first demonstrated by RCA Victor in 1931 and used until now only in radio transcriptions. The company also brought out an inexpensive turntable for these records, which plugged into radios. Within a year the LP, part of whose appeal was that it could present long pieces of classical music without the interruption of changing records, dominated the industry.

In 1949, the year of the Second Herd's gradual failure, RCA Victor tried to foist on the public another kind of record, the seven-inch 45 r.p.m. with a large hole in the center. The company's executives wanted to own the patent on the form of recording that dominated the industry. The sheer stupidity of this is astonishing. For the 45, as it was called, became the medium of pop "singles," while the LP was that of "serious" music. The radio-phonographs being sold had to accommodate both speeds, and some of them had two turntables. It would cost the public millions on millions of dollars in unnecessary equipment and gearing. When the first high-quality turntables went on the market, they were designed perforce to play at three speeds, 78 r.p.m. for the old records that were still being sold, 45s, and the 33⅓ LP. The gearing made the turntables less stable than those with a single drive speed.

The record industry had been an adjunct to other industries, not a major force in itself. With the coming of the 45 single, the LP, and inexpensive phonographs, that, too, began to change. Until that watershed, stars made records; after that, records made stars. How great the change would be was not apparent until the mid-1950s, but the early signs were there by 1950.

In view of the odds against the big bands, the seismic changes in the entertainment industry, and his own recent defeats, it is surprising that when the Woodchoppers reached San Francisco, Woody told Ralph J. Gleason, then writing for *Down Beat*, that he was forming a new band intended to appeal to the college crowd. He said it would have two books, one to be used for dances and emphasizing the current popular songs, the other to be played at concerts for admirers of the first two herds.

"I just love to stand in front of the sound of that band," Woody told me. But he had a more practical reason to reform at this point: a contractual commitment to play Bop City in New York with a big band. He had been working with a small group, playing saloons. He tried to get out of the commitment to Bop City, but the musicians' union ruled that he must fulfill it, and the contract called for a big band. He felt that he could not put together a good band quickly enough to play an important new jazz room, and that a poor performance would damage him. But the contract left him no choice, and so he rounded up a band of his alumni to meet the commitment. Thus, almost accidentally, the Third Herd was born.

The band he assembled comprised Bernie Glow, Paul Cohen, Conte Candoli, Don Ferrara, and Neal Hefti, trumpets; Bill Harris, Eddie Bert, and Jerry Dorn, trombones; Sam Marowitz, alto saxophone; Bob Graf, Al Cohn, and Buddy Wise, tenors; Marty Flax, baritone; Dave McKenna, piano; Red Mitchell, bass; and Sonny Igoe, drums. The band shared the bill with Sarah Vaughan.

Mike Levin again gave the band a warm review in *Down Beat*, predicting a bright future. It seems even the perceptive Levin could not see the changes occurring in the surrounding culture.

The band went on a tour of theaters, returning to New York in May, 1950, for an engagement at the Capitol. Alto saxophonist Sam Marowitz left the band. From that time to the end of Woody's life, the saxophone section consisted of three tenors and baritone, with Woody occasionally impressed into the section when an arranger wanted an alto-lead sound. Most admirers of the band liked this "Four Brothers" sound, but Johnny Mandel (who sometimes calls for six saxophones in his writing) says that he never liked it as much as the older alto-lead sound.

In June, a month after the Capitol engagement, Woody announced that he and Carlos Gastel were parting by amicable and mutual agreement. Gastel and Woody said the rupture was a matter of money. Gastel wasn't getting enough of the money; Woody said he was earning only enough to cover his payroll and his own expenses.

The rupture almost certainly had more substantial causes than that.

Peggy Lee said, "I don't like to say anything bad about anyone, but Carlos was pulling things behind the backs of all his clients, Nat Cole being one, and certainly myself. I still have some forgeries of his. He forged my signature assigning some very valuable songs of mine to a publisher without my knowledge. He was supposed to be my manager, and he was my destroyer.

"But there was another side to him, and that's why everybody stuck with him. He was funny. He was very outgoing. He was always giving you a big hug."

Could that have been a manipulative technique—projecting a sense of friendship and momentary good feeling to people in an insecure profession?

She recalled the kind of stone-age videos that were being manufactured at that time, short music movies that were shown on fairly large screens in taverns and bars. They were called Soundies. Peg said, "Dave and I did some, Nat did some, and Mel Tormé did some. And I think Woody did some. I was never paid, Mel was never paid. I don't know whether Nat was ever paid. And to this day they keep coming up in video cassettes. If Dave and I didn't get paid, I'm pretty sure Woody didn't."[4]

After parting, supposedly amicably, with Gastel, Woody told the press he would try to get along without a personal manager. He wouldn't, of course. Abe Turchen would assume the position.

Woody continued to record for Capitol. The compromised commercial nature of these records reflect his, and the company's, increasingly desperate desire to find an audience for the band. In November, 1950, he made a whistling-past-the-cemetery statement to *Down Beat*: "There's no doubt the band business is coming back . . . . The public is dance conscious now."

His two-year contract with Capitol expired at the end of 1950, and he left. In January he began recording for MGM Records, a subsidiary of the movie giant, but he was used by the company almost as he had been at Decca. With a studio pickup band, he backed singer Billy Eckstine on an album. His own band was put to work playing vapid commercial music of the time.

For all that MGM's motto was Ars Gratia Artis, its record division barely bothered to affect artistic integrity. It was hardly a good record label, and for periods of its history it was one of the most crooked, with even some of its upper executives dipping hands into the till.

Though the band was excellent, nothing it did for MGM was really memorable.

18

Scuffle Bread

The 1950s would be a bleak decade. Viewed from now, Woody is like some feral creature whose forest has been razored off by the advances of so-called civilization and who runs under an unkind sun in search of the shadows of the world he once knew. He had spent his childhood in a time before radio, then, after it arrived, had listened to Goldkette, Whiteman, and Ellington. He had watched the bands burgeon and blossom, scores of them, led by men who were mostly his friends. And most of them, Charlie Barnet among them, had quit, hung it up, had seen the future and knew there was no place in it for them. But Barnet had been born wealthy, and it was said of Benny Goodman and Artie Shaw that each of them still clasped the first dollar he had earned. Tommy Dorsey had invested shrewdly in all sorts of things, including music publishing. Woody had not. In any case, their success had come before the war. His had come after it and wasn't long. He had little money and the only world he knew was that of bands; his one surpassing asset was his ability to organize and lead one.

After the brief and demeaning passage through the MGM label, Woody was without a recording contract. And incredibly, foolishly, and doubtless because he knew nothing else to do, he formed his Third Herd and went into partnership with his friend and former press agent Howie Richmond. By 1951 Howie had established himself solidly as a music publisher, partly because he had been astute enough to evaluate accurately and early the strength of the folk-music trend. He had published such songs as *Good*

Night, Irene. The Teresa Brewer hit *Music! Music! Music!* was his copyright. These and other hits had made his company prosperous.

"Nobody wanted the Woody Herman band," Howie said. "Or any band. Artie Shaw had left the business. Larry Clinton had left it.

"Woody was at the Statler Hotel. It was the first time I had heard the band close up in years, and it was so good I was knocked out. Woody was so blue and hung up. I asked him why. He said, 'Well, we're going on the road, and I don't know how long I can keep these kids.' All he cared about was the sound. He'd worked with these guys, and the band was just super. He said, 'If we go out on the road, without making records, we're going to lose all of it.'

"So I got onto the phone to Mitch Miller at Columbia Records, and he said, 'No way, Howie, bands are not making it.' I talked to everybody in New York, the guys at Decca, everybody I knew. And they all said, 'Well it's a great band, but, y'know, nobody's interested in that.'"

In later years, Woody blamed Mitch Miller more than any other man for what went wrong with the music business. Miller had started out as an oboe player and a good one. Then he had gone into record production, where he produced hit after hit by his unflagging search for the lowest common denominator of public taste, turning out records by Guy Mitchell and Johnnie Ray. It was Mitch Miller who forced Frank Sinatra to record duets with a busty but otherwise untalented personality known as Dagmar. Paul Weston shares Woody's evaluation of what Miller did to the music business, preparing the way for the rise of rock-and-roll.

Woody said, "The pop market was rapidly changing because of people like Mitch Miller, who was running things at Columbia, feeding the nation sing-along recordings. He may have set the music business back forty years. For a legitimate oboe player, he sure caused a lot of turmoil. If he had kept playing oboe, we all would have been better off."[1]

A few years later, Miller, to the amusement of many music-business professionals, would speak out against the rise of rock-and-roll and the fall in the quality of American popular music, either not understanding or ignoring his own catalytic role in the process. But he was there at Columbia, the man in charge, and Howie Richmond and others in the business had no choice but to deal with him. Except that Miller wasn't dealing: he didn't want the band.

Howie recalled, "So I went to Woody, and I said, 'I've got one idea, I don't know if it's any good. I can't pay any money or anything, but I'll pay you union scale. I'll go to Columbia, you bring the guys, I'll get the best studio, I'll get the best engineer. For whatever Mitch is, he'll be my friend, and he'll listen.'"

Even Howie Richmond could be naïve.

"Woody said, 'Great. We'll do whatever you want.'

"The band came in and put down as much as we could. I tried to get Woody to pick the tunes, and he'd say, 'You pick 'em.' We just made some sides and we put them together in what they used to call an album of four records. There were still 78s, 45s, and ten-inch LPs. I went up to a friend in special products at Columbia. He said, 'We'll press up whatever you want.' I don't think we even got to making 45s. The records were unmarketable."

Frustrated at every turn, Howie and Woody started a record label, which they co-owned. Publishing of the new material went into Howie's company. This assured him, if only through ASCAP air play royalties for radio performances, some return on his investment in recording the band. He set out to do two things: get the records played on radio stations and get them distributed to stores. Recognizing the risk and possibly folly of what they were doing, Howie said the company was from outer space. So they named the label Mars.

When Woody asked for his advice on repertoire, Howie said: "The only thing is that I'd like to see you do *Early Autumn*."

Woody said, "I'd like to get a lyric. Maybe Johnny Mercer might do it."

Howie approached Mercer, who said he not only liked the piece but had already written a lyric for it. Johnny had a flair for attaching deeply poetic lyrics to jazz instrumentals that seemed unlikely candidates for this treatment.

Ralph Burns somewhat simplified the melody. And Mercer, whose sense of event was finely tuned, got the era exactly right in his animistic lyric: one of his most evocative and vivid. It has always seemed to me to portray the mood of men coming home from the war to find the world they knew all changed. And so it was for the band era. Howie's company, TRO—The Richmond Organization—still holds the copyright on that song.

The band's first release on the Mars label was *Jump in the Line*, backed by a Ralph Burns arrangement of *Stompin' at the Savoy*. Howie thought Woody was the best singer he'd ever heard, and at his encouragement, Woody, always the skeptic about his own ballad singing, recorded *Early Autumn* with Mercer's lyric. Bill Perkins played the tenor solo. The band recorded *Perdido* and something called *Baby Clementine*, then *Mother Goose Jumps* and *I'm Making Up for Lost Time*.

In a statement to *Down Beat* published April 22, 1953, Woody made a predictably optimistic prognosis, saying that twenty-five independent distributors had immediately taken on Mars Records, that 100,000 records had been sold in six months, and that the first LP derived from the singles had gone through three pressings in six weeks. The reality, however, was less than encouraging, and the titles of two LPs derived from the records reveal Woody's uncertainty about the band's direction. One was *Woody Herman: Dance Date on Mars*. The next, improbably, was *Woody Herman Goes Native*, in which the band played calypso, the fad of the moment.

"Man, we're jumpin'!" Woody told *Down Beat*.[2]

Not according to Howie Richmond's memory, nor for that matter Woody's later reminiscences.

The band recorded for Mars from 1952 to 1954. Mars lasted about four years. Howie found himself importuned by Tommy Dorsey and others about recording for the label. Finally Howie said, "Woody, don't send any more of your friends to me! I have to press these records!"

And Howie was learning brutal lessons about the nature of the record industry, particularly distribution, which has always been crooked. For the records to get to stores, they had to go through distributors. And even when the records had been sold to the public, distributors would resist paying the manufacturer, in this case Mars. More precisely, they would pay only when they needed more product, and the Woody Herman records were not selling sufficiently to create that demand, and so their attitude was that Woody and Howie could go whistle for their money.

One of Howie's distributors told him: "Look, the only way we would take the records is if you shipped a bunch of stuff to us and gave us some kind of deal."

Howie said, "What kind of deal?"

"We would like to get a discount," he was told. In other words, payola.

Howie said, "How about this. If you buy a box, I'll give you 10 percent free, overage."

But even when he did that, he still could not collect his money. By now Howie had 50,000 or 75,000 bucks invested in an unreturned inventory. Meanwhile, the music marketplace was changing. Singers were the now stars. "And then," Howie said, "the big corporations began devouring everything."[3]

The Mars recordings were later sold to Norman Granz, owner of the Verve label, who issued the material in LP format in an album titled *Hey! Heard the Herd?* Granz later sold Verve to MGM.

Milt Jackson left Woody to return to Dizzy Gillespie. Then in 1952, he started the Milt Jackson Quartet with John Lewis. Within a year it evolved into the Modern Jazz Quartet, with Lewis as music director, and despite periodic sabbaticals, it has continued to this day, giving Bags the perfect setting in which to display his crystalline talent.

But as always, Woody kept finding brilliant newcomers. The superb trombonists Carl Fontana, Urbie Green, and Wayne André came and went. Bill Berry, Don Fagerquist, and Al Porcino passed through the trumpet section. Chuck Flores filled the drum chair for a time, and Red Kelly came in on bass, replacing Red Mitchell, who was in hospital with a bout of tuberculosis. Thomas Raymond Kelly, born in Shelby, Montana, on August 19, 1927, had previously worked in the bands of Charlie Barnet, Herbie Fields, Red Norvo, and Claude Thornhill.

"Naturally," Kelly said, "one of the burning ambitions was to go with Woody. I was excited about it. I joined them in El Paso. We went to San Diego and on up through some one-nighters in L.A. And then Chubby Jackson wanted to come back, and so Woody said, 'Would you like to go on up to Seattle and get off there?' Because that's where I was living and my family was living.

"So I got off in Seattle. Abe Turchen called a couple of times. I said, 'No, I don't want to get all going and then Chubby will want to come back.' So finally Woody called and said, 'If you'll come, you can have it—stay till you want to leave. That was our agreement. His word was good enough for me.

"I joined the band again in Knoxville, Tennessee."

Red, who now owns a restaurant in Tacoma, Washington, remembers with wry amusement an engagement the band played in a high-school auditorium. "In 1953," he said, "the rhythm section was Art Mardigan on drums, Nat Pierce, and me. We played a show at a high school auditorium somewhere with a comedian whose name I can't remember. One of the performers was a high-school girl who did ballet. They gave this music to Nat Pierce, Art Mardigan, and myself. Between the three of us, we could almost make out the title. Reading the notes, we gave it our best shot. I'm self-taught, so reading didn't come fast at all. Nat wasn't a terrific reader, but he was better than Art and myself.

"Well, the kid's mother went over to Woody and said, 'Do you realize not one of those three people can *read*?'

"Woody said, 'Lady, I don't hire my rhythm section to read. I hire 'em to swing.'"[4]

Shorty Rogers, Bill Harris, Al Cohn, and Ernie Royal came back to the band for brief periods—as much as anything, one suspects, to help out the

Old Man. When he picked up that name is uncertain. He was not yet forty, but to anyone twenty, and Woody always had players that young or younger, anyone forty is old. Vietzeck had become the Woodchopper had become the Old Man. He would pick up one more nickname in his lifetime: the Road Father.

Woody had always relied on the judgment of his bandsmen and friends and his growing body of alumni to find new young players. And young ones he needed, because he couldn't afford the seasoned veterans. Al Cohn, for example, was busy both as a player and arranger in the New York studio world. Stan Getz was a star.

With another war under way, Dave McKenna received his draft notice and went to Korea as a cook. In the fall of 1951, at Hershey Park, Pennsylvania, twenty-six-year-old Nat Pierce, experienced in the bands of Shorty Sherock and Larry Clinton, joined Woody on piano. He also contributed a little to the band's book. Ralph Burns remained chief arranger, turning in as many as six charts a month, but he, too, was in demand elsewhere.

Nat always remembered how difficult the 1950s were for Woody and the band. He said, "Abe Turchen saved our ass many times . . . . I remember we were on TV, *The Big Show of 1952*, with people like the Mills Brothers and Dinah Washington, and then we would go cross-country for about thirty days. A lot of times we bombed out money-wise. Sometimes there wasn't enough to meet the payroll, and Abe would call some bookie in New York and ask, 'Who's playing tonight?' It could be basketball or baseball. It didn't matter what sport. He would bet on these games, and somehow by the time the night was over, he had all the money in his hands."

And Abe was still selling his watches. Dick Hafer, who joined the band on tenor saxophone in 1952, recalled:

"I bought some of those watches. I remember I bought one at the Statler Hotel in New York, for my wife. I was showing it to Woody on the bandstand. He said, 'You bought that from Abe? C'mere, give that to me.' I paid a hundred and twenty-five dollars for it. Woody made Abe give me the money back. He said to me, 'Give him twenty-five bucks, and be sure it has the insides in it that it says. It was a LeCoupre, a French watch. It was a good watch.'

"Abe had those watches to fend off the cops if he got stopped for speeding. He would go to the trunk and open up a box of watches and hand the cop a watch. A sort of a bribe. He was something. He was a real operator.

"He was a wheeler-dealer, and he was a gambler. And he was pretty good at it. When we were at the Gold Nugget in Reno, we worked strange hours, like twelve to four o'clock in the morning. Abe was playing the games. I used to watch him, because it fascinated me how he could win. He was winning a lot. One night one of the bosses took Woody aside and said, 'Who is this fatso who's hanging around the band?' Woody said, 'My manager.' And the guy said, 'Well tell him to lay off the games, because this is not for pros; this is for tourists.'

"Abe had a lot of skills with money. He could grab a handful of ones and tell you how many were in it, just by the feel of it. He was an amazing character, sort of like a Damon Runyon character.

"One night when I first joined the band, he overpaid me about ten dollars. I went back to him, and said, 'You gave me ten dollars too much.' He said, 'Well keep it, because you're honest.' He was testing me. He tested everybody to see where they were.

"Guys could get money out of him if they insisted on it and were really willing to back it up all the way. But nobody wanted to lose their job, because it was too much fun playing the music."[5]

Most of the time, that is. Woody recalled a gig in a jazz club in a shabby Philadelphia hotel called the Powelton Inn. He said, "We were in for two nights, and they had the lowest piano in the world. It was just impossible. Nat Pierce was fighting it, hitting a note here and there.

"The business was fantastic. People were waiting in line. So I told the boss, 'As long as we are going to be here tomorrow night, why don't you rent a piano? This thing is not even fit to try to play on.'

"And he said, 'Oh man, that's a good piano. Erroll Garner used it last week.'

"Erroll probably tried to commit suicide the first night if I know him.

"So along about midnight or one o'clock, and we were getting going pretty good, and the place was just jam packed, all of a sudden a deluge came down through the ceiling over the back part of the stand, where the piano was. A few guys were scurrying and leaving, trumpet players moving forward. It seemed that some broad upstairs had fallen asleep in a bathtub and it overflowed. It didn't stop until the cops got there and they sent a plumber. And we blew right through the whole mess.

"So now comes the end of the gig, and the two bosses are standing there, new at this business, and they are the happiest. They said, 'Oh, what business!' So I said, 'Now look, fellows, you're going to have to do something about this piano. Tonight. Now get it cleaned up, get some towels, get in there and wipe it up. Get a guy in there and try to repair it and if it can't be repaired, go borrow or rent. Do something.'

"Next night we came to work and here is the piano, full of water. Some more had leaked during the day. It was turning green with mold. It's the only time I've seen Nat Pierce get shook up. It finally reached his sensitivity. I sent him to a movie. I said, 'Catch a double feature and come back a little later on.' And that's the way we wound up."

▼   ▼   ▼

Woody was well aware of the problems of the men in his band in trying to maintain career and marriage. The conflict was a major cause of the turnover in his bands. Of his own marriage, he said:

"Like any two normal humans, we have our ups and downs—pretty drastic ones at times. On the whole we have been very happy, and I have to give credit where it is due, and I happen to be married to a woman who has the patience of Job.

"You know once you get older that this is the best thing for you—that it must work. We try to make up for it. When I get to a place Charlotte likes, she'll join me. If I am in Chicago and she hasn't been to Chicago for a while, sure. New York, maybe once every two years for a stay, and there's fun and kicks and then: Let me get home to my house."

Woody's own yearning for home is encountered in a recollection of the Voice of America's Willis Conover: "One time, in Washington, Woody and I went to an after-hours spot. We sat around and had a couple of drinks. I invited him to come around to my home. I remember him saying, 'No, I don't want to go to any home, I don't want to be reminded of home when I'm this far away from my home.'"[6]

Woody could not always get home for Christmas. "Sometimes," he said, "we come home New Year's Day, if it looks like a profitable holiday season. Then we celebrate Christmas a little late that year, and the tree is still up and everything is ready. We do things, a lot of times, ass backwards, but I think we have more fun in the long run than a lot of people I know.

"Sure we are gypsies, and we're kind of wild. For instance, if I am in New York working a location like Basin Street and I have Monday night off, it is very probable—I've done it many times—that I'll catch a plane to L.A., get there in the afternoon, take a two-hour nap, we'll go out some place, have a lovely dinner, come back, take a nap, get up, take a plane and go back to work. It costs money, but what are you going to do?"[7]

Charlotte's cousin Shirley had moved with her husband to California in 1952. "Charlotte and I became very, very close," Shirley recalled. "We used to go to the beach together and eventually played bridge together. She learned to play bridge and so did I. We did stained glass together. Charlotte was a very artistic woman.

"My mother and her mother were sisters. There were about fifteen of them in that family, and they were a wacky bunch. Charlotte and I had a bond because of the family situation. I knew what her mother was like because of my mother, and it was the same for her. It was a bond nobody else could experience. They couldn't know what her mother was like, and wouldn't believe it if they knew. And the same with my mother.

"But I'd got away from my mother. Charlotte was here in Los Angeles with hers, and Charlotte was dominated by her. I think it was in September just before Charlotte died, we had gone out to lunch. When she got out of the car, she said, 'Don't tell Gammy.' Here was a woman who was sixty-nine years old who was afraid to tell her mother she was out with me.

"She was very possessive of Charlotte. I'm sure she resented me too. It was very hard for Charlotte. Charlotte was a very sensitive and very timid person, the most sensitive and timid I ever met. She didn't dare cross her mother.

"Towards the last ten years of my Uncle Martin's life, Charlotte's father, they would take turns coming up to Charlotte's. My aunt would come up for a couple of days, then she'd go home and Uncle Martin would come up. Charlotte told me he said to her one day, 'Boy, she was rough today.'

"She could really raise hell with a person's emotions."[8]

Charlotte caught it from both sides: Woody's mother also made her life difficult. This absolutely exquisite woman was the object of jealousy from both her mother and her mother-in-law. "Charlotte was always so elegant," Shirley said. "Her mother-in-law had sent her a pair of the most awful looking slippers. They were quilted and came up around the ankle, and I think they had some velour or baby-fur trim. Charlotte opened the box and looked at the present and said, 'That woman hates me.'"

Woody was what she lived for. There is no question of this. "Charlotte would be a different person when Woody came home," Shirley said. "It would be like a god returning home. She'd say, 'He's *here!*' It was very sweet. They were very loving. Charlotte loved him dearly. They were lovers."[9]

Through all these years, Woody's friendship with Jack Siefert, the boy he had met when the Band That Plays the Blues was working at the Ocean Pier in New Jersey—like his friendship with the Sherman family—had grown deeper. Jack by now was a graduate engineer, still living in Philadelphia. Indeed, I have never seen more touching and devoted intrafamily relationships. The Shermans and the Sieferts *were* Woody's family. Jack Siefert and his wife, Mary, had two children. Woody had seen them come into the world. He would stay with the Sieferts whenever he was in the Philadelphia area, or when he was in the East and the band had a few days off. Sometimes Charlotte, too, stayed with the Sieferts.

A pattern developed. When Woody was scheduled to tour overseas, he would leave his car with the Sieferts, renting another to get him to the airport in New York. Jack would take Woody's car to a garage for servicing. On returning, Woody would rent another car to get him back to Philadelphia. Woody referred to the Sieferts' home as his eastern pit stop.

Mary Siefert, born April 25, 1928, a round-faced woman still strikingly attractive when she turned sixty-six in 1994 and had hair as white as paper, became very close to Charlotte. She remembered how Woody loved their summer home at Stone Harbor, New Jersey. "Woody was there many times," she said.

"He loved the beach. He would sit on the beach and people would look and whisper, 'Is that Woody Herman?' And he loved Jersey tomatoes. God, did he love Jersey tomatoes. And hamburgers with ground sirloin just charred.

"Each person perceives another person in a different way. Jack perceived Woody in an entirely different way than I perceived him. The longest he ever stayed was a week."

"Jack was working eight to five every day. Woody would finish the gig and come back to the house late."

Jack said, "At three o'clock I started caving in. I'd have to go to bed."

Mary said, "Sometimes I would stay up and talk with Woody. Or I would just go to bed. I'd say, 'Woody, I made a little tray for you,' Jersey tomatoes and cold cuts and bread. He loved Lebanon bologna. It is from Lancaster County. He'd have a Heineken beer or a little vodka. When he was ready, he'd go up to bed.

"Jack would get up at seven and go off to work. About eleven Woody would get up, and we'd have all afternoon together. The kids were in school. He'd go pick up the kids. He'd pack them and their friends into the back of a Corvette, laying on the floor.

"He didn't talk about music to me. But I don't know that much about music. He would talk about his mother and his childhood and how they lived. He was exceptionally fond of his mother. He loved his father, but his father was more a German tyrant type. His mother was soft and sweet.

"He'd chat and then he'd say, 'I have to call so-and-so.' And I'd give him pencil and pad and he'd sit at the telephone.

"He thought I could do his shirts beautifully. He'd say, 'I could take you on the road.'

"He used to wash his own socks, but at our house I'd wash his socks. He was a sweet man, a very sweet man."

Jack Siefert became, almost by default, the keeper of Woody's memorabilia. For as Ray Sherman also attested, Woody never saved anything. Ray had one of his Grammy awards, Jack had another.

Jack said, "His philosophy was, if he was asked what was his greatest band, 'The one I'm gonna have tomorrow.' He wasn't interested in anything he'd done before. He used to drop off air checks with me with no identification. I have a lot of them I have to find out about. Here I am wrapping them up in plastic and cleaning them with Ivory soap and using cactus needles! And he treated them like Frisbees!"

▼   ▼   ▼

In 1954 the band was booked for a six-week tour of Europe. One of the countries it was to visit was Charlotte's ancestral land, Norway, and she wanted to go on the trip. But she refused to fly. "My mother didn't fly if she could possibly help it," Ingrid said. So she and Ingrid, by then twelve years old and a high school student at Marymount in Los Angeles, left early; Woody, Abe Turchen, and the band, would leave later. Charlotte and Ingrid sailed on the *Stockholm*, Sweden-bound from New York City. Ingrid remembers:

"The Stockholm was a very small ship, about 12,000 tons. There was a dock strike, so it had no cargo. It was known as a rolling ship anyway. We got into the northern equivalent of a hurricane. The thing rolled mercilessly for eight days and eight nights.

"One woman fell and broke her arm. They had rails on the bed. Nobody could sleep because you were tossed around so hard. In first class, there were only about fifty people, and they were all Scandinavian, mostly Swedes and a few Danes. They prided themselves on not letting this bother them.

"As a kid, I was kind of terrified. We were on the top deck, in first class. The ship would lean over so far that water would entirely cover the porthole. I'd say, 'Mother, are we going to sink?' She was very brave and she'd say, 'Oh no, dear,' but I think she was probably scared stiff, as any sensible person would be.

"All the waiters, all the stewards, were Scandinavian, and they were totally into the spirit of this thing—Viking culture, you know.

Woody Herman as a boy in Milwaukee.
The date of the photo is unknown. The
suit was probably made by Julia Sherman.

Woody with his father, Otto Herman.

Woody is in the foreground, a child dancer in Milwaukee. The show is probably *School Days*.

Deciding to get out of "show business," Woody embraced "hot" music and took up the alto sax at the age of nine.

Young Woody became professional on the instrument almost immediately, as may be seen on the marquee of the Oshkosh theater in Milwaukee.

Woody played tenor with the Gus Arnheim band, late 1934.

With the Isham Jones band. Isham is in the middle, wearing a slight and uncharacteristic smile. Woody is kneeling, far right.

Radio actress Carol Dee, whose real name was Charlotte Neste. Woody would marry her, and she would never use the stage name again. She was probably twenty at the time of this photograph.

Publicity photo from Rockwell O'Keefe Inc., Woody's managers. It is the Band That Plays the Blues, but the billing is already Woody Herman and His Orchestra. This was the real First Herd

Woody with Charlotte and his parents. The photo was taken in the late 1930s or early '40s.

The *Caldonia* band. It was actually the Second Herd, but it became universally known as the first. From the left to right, rear: Skippy DeSair, Neal Hefti, Sam Marowitz, Conte Candoli, Mickey Folus. Next line: Ralph Keefer, Pete Candoli, Don Lamond, the band boy, Chubby Jackson. Next line: John LaPorta, Shorty Rogers, Dodo Marmarosa, Bill Harris, Billy Bauer, Flip Phillips. Front: Ed Kiefer, Woody, Frances Wayne.

Charlotte and Ingrid in 1941. *Photo by Gene Lester.*

Charlotte and Woody. She is wearing one of the fur coats he bought her when the band got hot. The dog is the infamous Freckles.

Ingrid and Woody. She was about three. And she doesn't seem thrilled by the music lesson.

Woody as a doting father.

Woody with his friend Gene Krupa. Gene was Polish, and from Chicago. Woody was half Polish, from nearby Milwaukee. They had something else in common: they were unusual among bandleaders in that they were universally, deeply, and unconditionally loved by the musicians who worked for them. *Photo by Robert Alderson.*

During a New York rehearsal, Igor Stravinsky makes a small change in the score of *Ebony Concerto* as Woody watches.

Woody with his old friend and former bandmate Tony Martin at the Hollywood Palladium in the 1940s. *Photo by Gene Lester.*

Charlie Parker (left) and Dizzy Gillespie in 1948. Gillespie wrote for Woody in 1942. Parker in later years loved sitting in with the band. *Photo by Ted Williams.*

Stan Getz, probably in 1955. Getz was one of the many stars brought to the fore by Woody. *Photo by Ted Williams.*

In Santiago, Chile, with Ingrid and Charlotte.

With Hermie Dressel. Date and location unknown.

Home for a little while. The nun is his beloved Sister Fabian Riley, guardian angel of his school days. He established a scholarship in her name.

Exhausted and in pain, he performed at the Vine Street Bar and Grill in Hollywood for a week in 1985. The engagement produced a cruel review in the Los Angeles *Times*. *Photo by W. G. Harris.*

The photos that follow are some of the alumni. Milt Jackson. (left) *Photo by John Reeves.*

Jimmy Rowles. *Photo by John Reeves.*

Shorty Rogers. *Photo by John Reeves.*

Red Rodney. *Photo by John Reeves.*

Terry Gibbs. *Photo by John Reeves.*

Johnny Mandel. *Photo by John Reeves.*

Alan Broadbent. *Photo by John Reeves.*

Ralph Burns. *Photo by John Reeves.*

Hermie Dressel.

At the St. Regis Roof in New York, August, 1972. From left to right: Johnny Mercer, who had written the lyrics to *Early Autumn;* Artie Shaw; Woody; George Simon, Woody's old friend and early champion in the pages of *Metronome;* and Woody's grandson, Tommy Littlefield. Tommy sang with the band during the St. Regis engagement.

Nashville, 1973. Woody and the band played an engagement in a tiny club for Ingrid and her friends.

Abe Turchen, receiving a Grammy on Woody's behalf. *Photo courtesy of Steven Turchen.*

"They had a dance. They stationed waiters who linked arms, like police do in Britain. It was not a ballroom, it was more like a living room. The ship would roll and people would slide into the linked arms of the waiters. They'd give you a little push and you'd slide back the other way. They even had Ping-Pong tournaments. It was totally nuts. The ship was a day or two late arriving."[10]

▼ ▼ ▼

On April 1, the band flew to Sweden. Charlotte and Ingrid met them. They took a night train to Oslo, Norway. From Oslo the band went to Stockholm, where it played a concert, then Copenhagen.

"I barely remember anything about Norway," Ingrid said. "It seems like we were there hardly any time at all. I don't think it sank in very much for my mother, either. Some years later she went there with her mother.

"Mainly it was one-nighters—long bus trips in the snow. A lot of being hustled from here to there. We played an army base in Germany. Germany was weird. It wasn't that long after World War II. There was rubble all over. I remember the cathedral in Cologne, because it was so beautiful. And I remember the plane had to fly almost straight up getting out of Berlin.

"We went to France. In Paris I ate snails and got sick and had to have a doctor. We went to England. We were there quite a few days. Everybody in all the countries was still very war-conscious.

"At some point, we went to an American base and got hamburgers. By this time everybody was dying for something American."[11]

"Abe was funny in Europe," Dick Hafer said. "I had been married in July of 1953. I took my wife along at my own expense. Bill Perkins and Cy Touff took their wives. Woody never wanted wives around the band. He liked my wife, and told her so, and he liked Cyril Touff's wife, Georgia, and told her so.

"We were all unbelievably stupid about business. Abe took money for Social Security out of our paychecks all year long. In those days the Social Security tax was very little. You had to pay only up to a point and then you didn't pay any more that year. He collected on and on and on, and pocketed it.

"Then, in Europe, when we were dealing with the exchange, he said, 'Don't worry about the exchange, guys, I'll take care of that. If you want marks or francs, just tell me.' My wife kept track of it in a book. She said, 'Hey, he's cheating you.' I'd go back and say, 'Hey, Abe, you're wrong.' And he'd say, 'Oh yeah, you're right.' It was unbelievable. He would do things like that. He'd chippy you every chance he got.

"A lot of guys drew advances. Red Kelly was notorious for it. I said, 'Why do you do that?' He said, 'It guarantees my job. They're not going to fire me if I owe them money.'"[12]

The tour covered, besides the three Scandinavian countries, Belgium, Holland, Germany, Austria, and France. The U.S. Air Force flew the band to its base at Sculthorpe, England.

"It is about a hundred and twenty-five miles from London," Woody said. "They took us to a place about twelve or fifteen miles in from Sculthorpe, where we stayed. This was quite an experience. It was on the North Sea and it was a little summer resort. A little tiny town, just beautiful in July. We were there in April, and April in Europe is still complete winter time . . . . Most of the time it's colder than hell.

"Naturally there was no heating in these places because they are summer resorts, kind of clapboard houses, and most of us stayed at this one house. And the little ladies that ran it were wonderful, and they made us breakfast and after the first night we had a big bash, 'cause all the English musicians came down from London. Everybody blew and it was a pretty big, happy affair. Ronnie Scott's group played opposite us and [drummer] Jack Parnell came down and so many guys."

Red Kelly said, "We were staying in the town, but we played at the U.S. air base at Sculthorpe. It seemed to me it was in some kind of big room. My method of traveling in those days was heavily sedated. We played a concert for air force people and their families. There were a lot of women and children there. We played and then Ronnie Scott's group played. We were all impressed by the band. The drummer was Tony Crombie."[13]

Dick Hafer remembered: "Ronnie Scott's band was so impressive. Woody's band had some dissension in it, largely over money. We weren't really playing too good, until we heard Ronnie Scott's band playing warm-up for us at that air base. It got us off our tails and we went up and started to play, because we had to."[14]

One of the members of the Scott group was Victor Feldman, a young virtuoso of drums, piano, and vibes by whom Woody was impressed.

After the session, Woody said, "when we left and drove back and got in this house, it seemed like it was forty below zero and everybody was running around in nightshirts screaming, 'You got any booze left?' So you don't freeze to death.

"They did have beautiful hot water bottles in each bed, and this was our salvation. It was fantastically funny.

"Then . . . we went up to London for a holiday for a day or two. That's when we met [bandleader Ted] Heath and got to hear his band at one of the theaters, and Heath was very warm and cordial. He had just gotten a new bus and sent that over for some of the guys, to bring them over to the theater, two different loads at two different hours . . . .

"My wife and our kid attended the concert the next day. We had lunch at Ted's house. It was a lovely house in the suburbs. The next evening we went out with Jack Parnell and had a wonderful time. He took us [to] some section of London where they had real down-home seafood. You know, I think between Jack and myself we ate about two hundred mussels. That is a conservative figure. Boy, how that cat can eat! And I didn't do bad either."

Other than the performance at the air base at Sculthorpe, however, the Herman band was not allowed to play anywhere else in England. The British writer Steve Voce, in his monograph *Woody Herman*, wrote:

> The simian thinking of the British Musicians' Union had persuaded it to ban appearances by Americans within the realm, and the *Melody Maker* resourcefully arranged two concerts by the band in Dublin, the Irish capital. They laid on flights from Britain and on Sunday 2 May, a veritable air lift of jazz fans arrived in Ireland. They were not disappointed. *Perdido, Early Autumn, Four Brothers*—the band played its heart out for them. And a man already a big favorite with the European audience, Bill Perkins, established his tradition of tenor ballad playing with *These Foolish Things* (Bill later returned to Dublin when he was with Stan Kenton and that band had to subvert the union's machinations).

Later, the British Musicians' Union demanded an exchange arrangement: an equal number of British musicians to tour the United States when American musicians visited England. The problem was that the English musicians were unknown to American jazz fans, while the major American players were famous in England. Thus a British impresario could make a good deal of money with an important American act but an American impresario could not do so with British musicians.

"Dublin was very amazing," Woody said. "We . . . had a terrible flight going in. We used a freight plane to get there and these guys had flown over the Hump regularly, but when they saw the amount of equipment and people we had, the crew had quite a discussion before we would try for a takeoff. They had instruments in the aisle. We finally got up and left Germany and got as far as north London, and we had to land at an emergency field—it was a grass field and it was pouring and muddy—to refuel because of the overweight. We finally got to Dublin about the time the concert was supposed to go on. We arrived at the airport, coming in sideways, but they were waiting with a police escort, and some of the English visiting musicians did a kind of impromptu session until we got there, and it worked out very nicely."

Red Kelly said: "I got off the plane with my bass. Always I was left in the airports with my bass fiddle and some other kind of luggage. The piano player, who is your buddy in the section, is long gone, not wanting to lug anything. Some little Irish guy grabbed my bag and said, 'Follow me, I'll be right behind you.' I thought, 'Okay, I'm home. I have met some of my people, my father's relatives. My mother's people were from there, too. They put my name in Gaelic in the program."

Woody said, "After the first concert in the afternoon, the promoter took us to the local hotel, a nice hotel, and with caterers and wine and wonderful food. It was just a wonderful party.

"And we went back into the evening concert."[15]

There was another party after the concert.

The band flew home. Charlotte and Ingrid sailed back on the Ile de France. "It was big and had an indoor swimming pool and it was very glamorous," Ingrid remembers.

A little more than two years later, in July, 1956, the *Stockholm*, on which they had made the stormy eastbound crossing, collided off the coast of Nantucket with the Italian passenger liner *Andrea Doria*. The *Andrea Doria* foundered with a loss of fifty-two lives.

19

A Bird in the Herd

Soon after that European tour, in May 1954, when the band was playing the New York nightclub Basin Street, someone, probably Howie Richmond, induced *Time* magazine to devote a column-and-a-half story to the band. It succumbed to the press agentry, saying, "Forty-one-year-old Woodrow Wilson ('Woody') Herman was back in town—and back on top of the musical heap—with his Third Herd, the most versatile band he has ever led."[1] The story got his name wrong and said nothing about the scuffling. And of course it may have been the most versatile band he had ever led—it could play calypso, after all—but it certainly wasn't his best. One of the pleasures to Woody of that engagement was that Charlie Parker would come down and sit in. Woody, who had always admired Johnny Hodges, thought the brilliance of Parker's mind and technique surpassed that of any alto player, and perhaps any musician, he had ever heard. In 1957, Woody said that "in recent years Charlie Parker was head and shoulders above anyone else, and all the ones that tried to emulate him, to me, just are kind of lost people."

Parker at the time had been dead two years. Woody said:

"I hate to hear just another imitator of Charlie Parker because he had the ability and the mind that could keep going and going and going for thoughts and silly ideas so often and beautiful ideas on other occasions. And basic ideas! In the middle of some intricate phrase, he played the lowest old-time blues lick you could think of. This showed his great breadth of outlook musically. He couldn't express it verbally, you know, but when he put that ax to his chops!

"We used to do some things in Basin Street once in a while, and there was another jazz club, Music in the Round, that we worked a few weeks in New York, and Charlie would come down every few nights, and he loved to play with the big band. And we started a little gimmick that was kind of funny. I had quite a few pretty tunes in the book where there were alto solos. And I would blow the first eight or sixteen and Charles would be standing on the side and I would say, 'Now go!' And the contrast was so beautiful that it was fantastic, hearing me with my little nothing sound playing the melody, and out of the blue, in came this whirlwind. And I just wished we had taped some of these things . . . ."[2]

Parker sometimes sat in with the band in Kansas City as well, and some of those sessions were taped. But, Woody said, no one knew what had happened to the tapes. They turned up, however, and were issued on an obscure label as an LP, a copy of which is owned by Jack Siefert. The performance, in August, 1951, is electrifying. The charts are transformed as Parker's fiercely inventive alto enters in places where you are accustomed to hearing Woody's clarinet, and he doesn't stop when the ensembles begin; he plays right through. He is at the peak of his powers of invention, and the band in turn is inspired by him. The sound, alas, is poor, and one is left with the regret that none of the commercial record companies saw fit to make an album of Bird and the Herd. Even as it is, that Kansas City session produced some of the most exciting jazz ever heard.

"Yes," Woody said, "I think he's Mr. Alto Saxophone. There is no doubt about that.

"One of my last meetings with Charlie, not too long before he died, we had a rehearsal at Basin Street and it was a very hot afternoon and the air conditioning wasn't on and we went down and we got there about three and we finally broke about 5:30. We just couldn't take it any longer. We were wringing wet, and we were struggling up the staircase and just entering out onto the sidewalk when up came, steaming and panting, Charlie. He was perspiring like mad and didn't look well at all, and he says, 'Wood, rehearsal all over?' Like it was a very important matter.

"'Yeah,' I said, 'Charlie, we got done what we wanted. It's pretty hot.'

"He said, 'Man, I've been trying to get here all day.' He was probably just making an endless search, or so it seemed. But this man had a look upon him. I can't describe it. But this tremendous perspiration and, like a struggle to get there, to a stinking rehearsal . . . ."[3]

Parker died March 12, 1955.

At the end of 1954, the Third Herd effectively ended when nine musicians gave their notices because Woody would not give each of them a ten-dollar raise. He told tenor saxophonist Dick Hafer, who was appalled that he would let them go over a paltry ninety dollars, that he simply didn't have the money. Hafer told him that in that case, money was being stolen. Woody said he knew where all the money was. "He didn't," Hafer said later.

Woody replaced the missing men and went on, returning to the Capitol label to record on June 6 and 7, 1955, fourteen tunes, many of them excellent and one or two of which hinted at the band's future direction, including a Nat Pierce arrangement of the Horace Silver composition *Opus de Funk*.

It was about this time that the twenty-one-year-old Victor Feldman, whom Woody had heard at Sculthorpe during the European tour, moved from London to New York. Born in London on April 7, 1934, Feldman had been a child prodigy on piano, drums, and vibraharp.

Nat Pierce took him to a Herman band rehearsal. Woody offered him the vibes position previously held by Red Norvo, Marjorie Hyams, Terry Gibbs, and Milt Jackson.

The hits that year included *Ain't That a Shame?*; *Ballad of Davy Crockett*; *Dance with Me, Henry*; *The Yellow Rose of Texas* (by Mitch Miller's sing-along group); *The Great Pretender*, and, most significantly, Bill Haley's record *Rock Around the Clock*. A few good songs turned up, too, but there was nothing like the glorious outpouring of major American songs of 1935. The changes in American music were obvious to all but those who refused to hear them.

Dick Hafer said, "By the end of 1954, the Third Herd had become a better band when Jerry Coker, Richie Kamuca, and Jack Nimitz joined it. We did two albums for Capitol that year. Things were really looking up, and I thought we were really going to get going financially.

"But we were still working for the same little money and working just as hard, seven nights a week on one-nighters. Nobody could get a raise. I said to Woody, 'How come we can't get any money out of this band?'

"He said, 'I don't have it.'

"I said, 'Well *somebody's* got it.'"

Woody knew perfectly well whom Hafer meant.

Nat Pierce left the band in 1955; he would return. Bill Harris returned to the band early in 1956. Later that year, Nat introduced the bassist Major Holley to Woody and the members of the band, and Woody hired him.

But in January of that year, Elvis Presley recorded *Heartbreak Hotel*. It reached the number one position on the sales charts by February 22. Before the year was out, Presley would have nineteen hits on the charts, three of which reached number one. Dick Clark's television show *American Bandstand*, which had been on the air six days a week since 1952, was now reaching an estimated audience of twenty million teenagers and, perhaps even more significantly, twenty million adults.

The April 25, 1956, *Milwaukee Journal* reported that Woody's band had "shivered the timbers at Marquette University's Brooks Memorial Union in two jazz concerts Tuesday." Marquette was the university from which some of the publicity said Woody had graduated. He never got into Marquette, much less out of it, though eventually he would receive an honorary degree there. Also on the afternoon program was the Rev. Norman O'Connor, Catholic chaplain of Boston University, a Paulist priest who was an authority on jazz. Father O'Connor, a strikingly handsome man with white hair, and an unfalteringly charming one, gave a lecture on jazz.

There to hear the band was Woody's beloved teacher Sister Fabian, by then in her early eighties. Though she was limping a little, she was in otherwise excellent health. She had brought four nuns in their twenties to hear the band, telling Woody, "I thought they might enjoy the concert."

Woody wanted to drive her back to St. John's High School in Milwaukee at the end of the evening. His current vehicle was a Mercedes sports car. Father O'Connor ran outdoors just to see Sister Fabian in her nun's garb get into the car. Woody took off, and anyone who ever rode with him can imagine at what speed. No doubt Sister Fabian's habit was whipping in the window. She said, "Say, this is *nice!*"

Five months later, on September 3, 1956, while the band was playing the Riviera Hotel in Las Vegas, Woody received a call to tell him his mother had died. The Mafia owners of the hotel would not allow him time off to attend her funeral. Nonetheless, he flew home, according to Ray Sherman, to view her in her coffin. He saw no one else, said nothing, and flew back to Las Vegas. The Milwaukee gossips made much of the fact that he did not stay for the funeral.

In January, 1958, *Variety* reported that the Al Belletto Sextet had joined the Herman band *in toto*. On March 30, the Wichita, Kansas, *Beacon* ran a picture of Woody with Belletto while the band was playing the Stardust Club in that city. The headline read: "Woody" Herman Blasts Rock 'n' Roll.

"Rock 'n' roll won't do any permanent damage to American music, according to Herman," the paper reported, showing that whatever else he was, Woody was no oracle. The story quoted Woody as saying, "It is nothing but a vulgarization of the shuffle blues, one of the simplest forms of music. It has no place in our repertoire." In the 1970s, had anyone summoned up the ghost of interviews past, he would have had to eat those words.

A little more than a month after that, in May, 1958, Vice President Richard M. Nixon visited South America, to be stoned and seriously jostled in Caracas, Venezuela, and booed and spat upon in Lima, Peru, where students held up posters saying "Nixon is a viper!" In both countries students had lined Nixon's parade routes to denounce U.S. policies in Latin America. Though there was the predictable claim that the protests were Communist-inspired, the newspaper *La Tribuna of Lima*, a moderate journal, said that Latin Americans were bitter about U.S. support for Latin American dictatorships. Nixon canceled the rest of his trip and flew to San Juan, Puerto Rico, on May 14.

In July, the U.S. State Department sent the Herman band on a tour that would take in the islands of the Caribbean as well as Central and South America. Such was the anti-American sentiment following the Nixon visit that it seemed the band was being sent into a storm. But it received such a welcome that the *New York Times*, in a story dated August 31 from Santiago, Chile, wryly reported:

Vice President Richard M. Nixon should have brought a band.

Touching at all the countries visited by Mr. Nixon in May, Woody Herman's jazz band is having nothing thrown at it but bouquets, particularly by student audiences. Local musicians have been effusively hospitable.

In Caracas, at the national university, nearly 3,000 students crowded into the auditorium to hear the seventeen-member band play. They gave a standing ovation at the end.

In Guayaquil, Ecuador, the students broke down the doors to get into a theater where a free performance was being given.

"I guess where music is concerned it's different," Mr. Herman said here during an intermission in one of the two shows the band plays nightly at the Caupolican Theater.

Electric heaters and hot coffee took some of the chill out of the unheated, cement dressing room. Mr. Herman had a wool poncho, given to him in Colombia, thrown over his shoulders.

"People have been wonderfully warm. The audiences are appreciative. They seem to like everything we play," said the band leader, a top jazz clarinetist and saxophonist for more than twenty years.

The Woody Herman band is on a 100-day tour of eleven South American countries under the sponsorship of President Eisenhower's Cultural Exchange program.

Interior State Department memoranda corroborate *the New York Times* report. From the U.S. embassy in Caracas, Venezuela, August 14, 1958:

> We cannot praise them enough for their willingness to cooperate with us, and their realization of the type of tour they are doing. We are extremely grateful for their willingness to help us in our public relations work here.
>
> The student concert was the most successful event of their Venezuelan tour. Over 1,800 students attended; the sound system and acoustics were the best available here; and the orchestra responded to the students' enthusiasm. The rector of the university who attended was highly pleased, as was the director of culture.

From the U.S. embassy in Santiago, Chile, September 12, 1958:

> The program impact of the Woody Herman band in Chile has been equalled only by *Porgy and Bess* and the New York Philharmonic Orchestra in the President's Fund program series. From USIS' [United States Information Service] standpoint, the group's success professionally and personally was beyond all expectations.
>
> Attendance averaged over 3,000 per show with 22,000 people in all. The press and critical reaction was voluminous and universally laudatory.
>
> During one of the shows the Jazz Club presented Herman with a plaque of excellence and the host group of musicians, who are local idols, came up as a man to exchange "abrazos" with the entire Herman group and publicly state that this was the greatest event ever for Chilean jazz and musicians.

And so it went, in memo after memo.

Musicians swarmed around the band wherever it went. In Montevideo, Uruguay, it outdrew the Russian Ballet, which was also performing that night. The band set attendance records in a number of locations. The press was ecstatic about the Herd.

Like almost every other artist who ever made a State Department cultural-exchange tour, Woody was critical of the way U.S. officials along the way handled it. The ineptitude of booking and the ignorance of the American culture itself seemed to surprise him, no doubt only the more so because these visits are handled through the cultural affairs officer at each embassy. My own experience in touring Latin America is that the cultural affairs officers attached to the embassies were, with occasional exceptions, astonishingly ignorant of the U.S. culture and incapable of explicating or representing it to peoples abroad. Twenty years after the tour, Woody said:

"Unfortunately our State Department people, at least during that period, were not very well equipped to get the most good out of having someone like ourselves there. They didn't really know how to approach it from an impresario [standpoint]. And so very often, we'd go for a week and maybe do one concert. However, in my estimation, it was pretty much a success because we were able to do in some cases something toward the reason we were really there." He referred to the Nixon debacle, particularly the confrontation in Caracas.

"And that's where we opened our tour. The interesting thing was that the State Department sent our band for jazz, they sent the New York Philharmonic with two conductors, Bernstein and Mitropoulos, and the San Francisco Ballet and the Catholic University drama group from Washington. And we were all at different times in different areas of South America. We covered almost all of it, and so did the other people."

The trip was harrowing, physically and emotionally strenuous and sometimes dangerous.

Coincidentally, I retraced much of the band's route three-and-a-half years later, on a State Department tour with the Paul Winter Sextet. We played many of the same theaters and university auditoriums the Herman band had played. The conditions of travel were terrifying. Major Holley said that some of the planes they flew on were so old that they could see the ground through holes in the floor. Many of the planes had been purchased very worn from North American airlines, and 1930s DC3s were common. They flew so low that in our group we used to say the pilots must think they were buses: they weren't flying the planes, they were driving them over the mountains. The winds in the mountains shook these ancient crates so severely that we thought they would come apart.

Maintenance on the aircraft was casual, to be kind about it. Once we were about to take off in a Lockheed Constellation, a considerable improvement in equipment at least. But as we taxied down the runway, our drummer, Harold Jones, later with Basie and Sarah Vaughan, looked out the window, saw gasoline sloshing over the wing near an exhaust flame, and called a stewardess. She blanched and ran to the pilot, who cut the engines and taxied back to the terminal. There a mechanic, perhaps the one who had left it off in the first place, screwed a gas cap into place and we took off.

"In Bolivia," Major Holley told Stuart Troup, "they have the highest airport in the world, and we couldn't breathe up there. They had oxygen on the stage for us."

He might have expanded on the subject. La Paz, Bolivia, is at 11,000 feet. Oddly enough, horn players have less trouble than pianists, bassists, and drummers, because they breathe deeply to perform. I can describe what the Herman band experienced leaving that city, because we went through it too.

The airport of La Paz is another 2000 feet above the city on a vast flat plateau. After our several concerts in that area, we were driven *up* to the airport, which has an extraordinarily long runway. We soon learned why. The pilot taxied for what seemed miles out to the end of it, turned around, raised the r.p.m. of the engines with locked brakes until the plane was shaking wildly, then released the brakes and raced back toward the small terminal and the precipitous slope above the city. The plane raced and rattled and shuddered, and I suddenly realized why: it had to reach a speed higher than the stalling speed for 13,000 feet before it could even lift its wheels. It was reaching the rim of the mesa. It seemed it was the pilot's intention simply to drive the plane off the edge. I think it lifted a foot or two before the ground fell away beneath us. Below us on the slope was a great white arrow; I learned later that it pointed down to a landing strip of some sort, for in case of trouble, the pilot would have no chance of getting back up to the airport. The plane went *down* from the airport, gathering speed, and then gradually arced upward. The mountains were psychedelically clear in the rarefied air.

And when at last we were airborne, heading west toward Arica on the arid coast of Chile, the plane went not over but between two volcanoes. It was explained to me later that Latin American pilots flew low like that to save fuel.

Major Holley reported similar experiences—aircraft that couldn't take off because they were overweight, flights over jungles populated by hostile Indians and deadly serpents in varieties the naturalists do not even know, vast deserts, and always the mountains. In those days you did not fly over the Andes, you flew among them, great jagged masses white with snow. Holley said that Charlotte, who liked to sit with him, was almost paralyzed with fear; she had not realized they would be flying through the mountains. And she dreaded flying even under the best of conditions.

And, Holley said, he met in some places in South America the same kind of racism he had encountered all his life in the United States. One incident happened in Brazil, which supposedly is innocent of racism. Holley said that when he entered a shop to buy gifts and a black Brazilian followed him into the place for the sole purpose of meeting him, a saleswoman called the police because she thought they were there to rob the store.

The band's road manager on this trip was Dick Turchen, Abe's nephew. In 1994, Dick remembered another incident in Brazil:

"The agent who booked us there had put us on Varig airlines. We got to the airport in Rio de Janeiro for a flight to Sao Paulo, and they tried to put us into a DC-3. We had made arrangements that we would always go into a larger aircraft because of all the baggage and people we had. We said, 'We're not going to fit in a DC-3.' They said, 'Oh yes you will.'

"They loaded us onto a DC-3, over our objections. I ended up sitting in the aisle, strapped on top of a trunk. We got to the end of the runway, and brakes slammed on and we went back to the gate. The same agent who swore up and down that we'd fit into a DC-3, with a big smile on his face, said, 'I think you're right. We'll put you into a bigger plane.' By this time Woody and his wife were very upset. Woody said, 'Charter a plane.'

"They started to put us onto a commercial airline. Major Holley had a thing about his bass not going into a luggage compartment."

The reason was that when a bass was shipped as baggage, it stood a very good chance of arriving as kindling wood.

Dick said, "We always bought a seat for his bass. Here comes Major Holley, laughing and telling jokes, with his bass strapped to his back. There were only three or four other passengers, including two little old ladies. They began a discussion with the steward and stewardess. The guy came over to Woody and me and said, 'We have a problem. These two ladies are deathly afraid of that black man. They want him off the plane.'

"I looked at Woody, Woody looked at me, and I said, 'I'm sorry, we're here on a State Department tour. If he gets off the plane, then we'll all get off the plane.' They went back and talked to the women and had a discussion among themselves and came back and said, 'Then you'll all have to get off the plane.' They were bluffing, of course. Woody and I weren't. We got up and said, 'Okay, guys, let's go.'"

"We got off the plane and chartered an airplane to take us to São Paulo.

"Another time, we flew into some country—for the life of me, I can't remember which one—and did the job and came back next day to the airport. There was nobody in the airport but a guy sweeping up the floor. And here we are with a truck loaded with equipment and a chartered bus. They're all twiddling their thumbs while I'm trying to get someone from the U.S. consulate. We find out that the flight only goes out of that airport on certain days of the week.

"Coincidentally, in came a U.S. Air Force plane that was empty. We told the crew our problem. They took us in and flew the whole band to the next country."

The band traveled 30,000 miles, visiting nineteen countries in all. It had left in July and returned to the United States in October.

After his rejection by major American record companies in the early years of the 1950s, and his own indecision about policy and direction, Woody was exhilarated by the reception in Central and South America and the Caribbean. Harrowing or not, the tour had been a triumph.

▼   ▼   ▼

Somewhere along the way, Charlotte bought Woody a little gold whistle that he thereafter wore on a cord around his neck. When during rehearsals the band got so loud that he couldn't talk to them, he would blow his whistle, like a referee calling time. He would use it at the end of an intermission to summon the musicians back to the bandstand. Or sometimes he would blow it on the stand, to add to the pandemonium of some particularly loud ending, as in *Caldonia*. Old vaudevillian that he was, ham by his own admission, he then would throw open his beautifully tailored jackets to reveal dazzling colors, as if to say these linings were the only thing in the world louder than that band.

Major Holley put another meaning on the whistle. Because of it he called Woody "the sheriff."

"Once he blew that whistle on you," Holley said, "forget it, you were out the door. I only heard him call it a couple of times on players or on situations. He also would pull off his coat and rumble with you if that's the way it was. But it was a lot of fun working with Woody. He was always on an even keel. His was the best band I was ever in."

Holley said there were no racial incidents while he was in the band. "Woody was always cool about that," he said. "He wouldn't tolerate any foolishness."

The only man I ever met who didn't speak well of Woody was the tenor saxophonist Billy Mitchell, an alumnus of the Basie band, who was with Woody for a time. Billy said that once a hotel where they worked refused to serve him dinner in its main dining room, and he didn't think Woody had made a vigorous enough protest.

But I never heard such a thing from anyone else, nor do I know anyone who has. Major Holley recalled that after the return from Latin America and a brief tour of the big band, Woody broke down to the small group, bringing in Howard McGhee on trumpet and, later, during an engagement in Las Vegas, tenor saxophonist Seldon Powell and drummer Gus Johnson.

▼   ▼   ▼

"The British Musicians' Union was moving into the twentieth century," Steve Voce wrote, "and was permitting a controlled exchange of British and American musicians."[4] In late March of 1959, Woody took a nucleus group of seven musicians to England. A band led by Chris Barber was to tour the United States, according to the exchange agreement.

Woody's contingent included Nat Adderley, cornet; Reunald Jones, trumpet; Bill Harris, trombone; Zoot Sims, tenor; Vince Guaraldi, piano; Keter Betts, bass; Jimmy Campbell, drums; and Charlie Byrd, guitar. To these were added a group of British musicians, including Les Condon, Kenny Wheeler, and Bert Courtley, trumpets; Ken Wray and Eddie Harvey, trombones; Don Rendell, Art Ellefson, and Johnny Scott, tenors; and Ronnie Ross, baritone. Actually two of them were not British. Ellefson and Wheeler were Canadians who had come to England within weeks of each other in 1952. But they were members of the British Musicians' Union. Woody called rehearsals.

Don Rendell told Steve Voce, "We thought things were going quite well, and then quite suddenly Woody stopped us. He really hammered us. He used all kinds of phrases that I can't remember, but it was to the effect that the band did not have enough balls in it." Eddie Harvey told Voce, "After the pep talk, the effect was electric, just as though Woody had turned a switch, and the band immediately played better. From that moment we never looked back."

Voce wrote: "The Anglo American Herd was one of Woody's triumphs, and for the first time a British audience was blown out of its seats by the authentic Herman sound."

It was the first time Nat Adderley had worked with Woody. Born in Tampa, Florida, on November 25, 1931, he was the brother of alto saxophonist Cannonball Adderley, who was making his name with the Miles Davis Sextet. Later Cannonball would form a quintet, and as long as he lived, Nat would be associated with him in that group. Nat had turned from trumpet to cornet, one of the few bop-influenced trumpet players to do so. He had worked with J. J. Johnson before joining Woody and the Anglo American Herd.

Nat Adderley remembered: "Kenny Wheeler was just formulating his style. He was very good, obviously." In later years Wheeler would emerge as a major and very original trumpet player and composer.

"You had all these contrasting things going," Nat continued. "Burt Courtley played a lot like Clark Terry at the time. I was a little more versatile. I had more influences going.

"Bill Harris played lead trombone and, of course, solo. Ed Harvey from England was very good.

"All of the saxophones except Zoot were British. Art Ellefson, a Canadian, could *play*.

"The rhythm section was all American. The rhythm section seemed a bit eclectic. But it was a solid rhythm section in the Woody Herman tradition.

"It was a very good, representative Woody Herman Herd. I would have compared it favorably with some other bands. The saxophone players were not the four brothers, but we did have a good strong trumpet section. And Bill Harris *is* a trombone section. No doubt about it.

"We stayed in England about three weeks. We did very well. We made an album. There are a few copies floating around."

At the end of the English tour, Woody scaled the group back to a septet that included only the Americans. Nat Adderley said:

"We went to Saudi Arabia with a small band to play for Aramco, the Arabian American Oil Company. We went to Dhahran and checked into the oil camp and played there for about a week and a half for the employees.

"I loved that little band in Saudi Arabia, because I really loved Bill Harris. He was not unsung. It's not that he was not well known. But he was one of the greats in terms of trombone playing. Because of what he played on that instrument, I think he was one of the greatest who ever lived.

"Zoot had what I would call the west coast approach. But Zoot could outswing everybody else. Zoot could *pop*. You could tell in the dressing room. We'd be standing around warming up. Zoot and I would be playing little Bird tunes. I don't think other guys who played in that style could possibly know all those things. Zoot could grab hold of a funk merchant tune, and he'd play all of *that*. Whatever there was to be played, he could play it. He was a remarkable player.

"And I really liked Vince Guaraldi. He had great success later on and I don't think that his piano playing could override the success in terms of critical acclaim and even recognition from the musicians. But at that point he had not had that success, and he was swinging away. The band was very good. It was the precursor of the group we took into the Metropole."

When the group returned to New York, Woody kept Nat, Zoot, and Jimmy Campbell with him in a sextet. Bill Harris dropped out, and the French pianist Bernard Peiffer replaced Guaraldi, and Chubby Jackson came in on bass.

That engagement remains vivid in my memory, for it was at that time that I met Woody, Nat Adderley, Zoot, and the other members of the group.

I was in New York on business for *Down Beat*, of which I had recently become editor. Marian McPartland, an old friend, and I went to hear the group. I remember being astonished that it played with the same kind of wildfire feeling that infused Woody's big bands.

Woody sat down with Marian and me at the end of a set. At some point he said, "I never was much of a clarinet player. I'm an alto player." On a stage he was a vibrant, exuberant, cocky, electrifying star; at a private table, he was a quiet, sometimes humorous, and essentially rather shy man. Later I heard him refer to "my nothing little tone" on alto, and since he produced a big warm sound on the instrument, I was puzzled by his constant self-abnegation. Possibly the Second Herd had left wounds that would not heal.

▼　▼　▼

In September of that year, Woody organized yet another band, this one to perform at the Monterey Jazz Festival. The festival's director was Jimmy Lyons, a San Francisco jazz disc jockey whose constant playing of their records had contributed greatly to the launching of the Dave Brubeck group, first the trio and then the quartet. Lyons, an astute listener with discerning taste, had worked during World War II in armed forces radio, producing shows in Hollywood, a few of which featured the First Herd. Briefly, after the war, he had worked as Woody's advance man, traveling ahead to get publicity in the newspapers and air time on radio to announce that the band was coming.

In 1958, Lyons organized the first Monterey Jazz Festival, staunchly supported by the *San Francisco Chronicle* columnist and jazz critic Ralph J. Gleason, another ardent Herman admirer. From its inception, the Monterey festival was intended to differ from the older and established Newport Jazz Festival, which its critics accused of having gone commercial. The purpose of the Monterey festival was to be the art of jazz. Skeptics thought it could not survive; in 1994, it celebrated its thirty-sixth anniversary, though by then, with Lyons retired, it had succumbed to an unembarrassed commercialism.

But in its first years, it was long on idealism, long on the enthusiasm of its organizers and the musicians who played it, and short on money. Among its advantages: it was set in a small and rustic city in Steinbeck country, the land made famous in novels and novellas such as *Tortilla Flat, The Red Pony*, and *Cannery Row*. Now the sardines have fled from Monterey Bay, the canneries are gone, the area is criss-crossed with freeways and crowd-

ed with shopping malls, the roads are jammed, and in summer tourists clog
the streets and sidewalks of once-rustic Carmel by the Sea. It wasn't that
way then.

For that 1959 festival, Woody put together a group of his veterans. By
now his alumni association had grown so large that in New York and on the
west coast, he could easily pull together a new band made of old members
who already knew the book, or most of it. The band he assembled included: Zoot Sims, Bill Perkins, and Richie Kamuca, tenors; Don Lanphere, alto and tenor; Med Flory, baritone; Al Porcino, Bill Chase, Conte
Candoli, and Ray Linn, trumpets; Urbie Green and Si Zentner among the
trombones, Charlie Byrd, guitar; Victor Feldman, vibes; and the powerful
Mel Lewis, drums. The band played in a hot afternoon sun as civilian
aircraft droned overhead; the U.S. Navy and Air Force had graciously
routed their flights away from the festival. You can hear the annoying
aircraft on the album derived from the concert.

Woody then organized a new road band, playing the first job in Mississippi. The musicians got, on an average, $125 a week, out of which they
had to pay for their hotels and food, though not transportation. The measure of change in the economics of the business can be seen in that figure;
it was the same salary Woody had received as a sideman with Tom Gerun
twenty-five years before.

The 1950s—that decade of McCarthyism, blacklists, intellectual terror-
ism, the Korean War, bad popular music growing worse, Elvis Presley, Pat
Boone, Mickey Spillane, *Peyton Place*, the rise of Hugh Hefner and Fidel
Castro, the first hydrogen bomb, Christine Jorgensen, Dacron, the execu-
tion of the Rosenbergs, Sputnik, Orval Faubus, Jack Kerouac, and the
Edsel—was over.

Woody later cast an over-the-shoulder glance back at it, saying, "Anyone
who survived it should be congratulated."[5]

20

The Metropole

The new decade began inauspiciously with Woody fronting a mediocre band, though it had some good musicians in it, including drummer Jimmy Campbell and trumpeter Don Rader. Perhaps it is more accurate, to judge by the memory of those who went through it that year, to say that it was uneven.

It played in Chicago in February, 1960. The head office of *Down Beat* was in Chicago, and I went to hear the band—as I recall, at McCormick Place, a vast cold convention center bearing the name of the *Chicago Tribune*'s late publisher. Woody remembered meeting me in New York, and afterwards he and I went up to the area Chicagoans call the Near North Side, the Rush Street neighborhood that at that time was rich in little clubs devoted to jazz and cabaret singers, the Purple Onion, the Cloister, Mister Kelly's, and more, all of them gone now. It struck me as odd that this man, one of the gods of my adolescence, had no one to talk to after the gig but me, a near stranger. We found a low-lit little bar whose jukebox contained nothing but the records of Frank Sinatra. Sinatra's pictures covered its walls. I had no idea that he was a close friend of Woody's. Woody and I sat and drank and talked until very late.

I do remember being completely taken by the man, by his gentle character, his unaffected self-deprecation, the wry smile, and his genuine interest in people. Woody had an open mind; I think he was naturally and always curious, and he had an enormous respect for the abilities of others. Was he spending the time with me because I had a job that made me useful to him? I doubt it. Woody didn't think that way. He liked those he liked, and those he disliked he disliked adamantly.

To see him fronting a band that was less than the best he had led, one that I didn't think was even very good, depressed me. And I think it depressed him, because certainly he was in a melancholy mood that night.

Or maybe he was just missing his home in California. Or maybe he had begun to worry about Ingrid.

Ingrid's childhood had been lonely. Her father, as he said, in his lifetime spent perhaps a total of three years in that house on Hollywood Boulevard. To be sure, she sometimes traveled with him on the road and had seen an astonishing amount of the world. But much of the time she was brought up by a nanny.

According to Ingrid, in 1947, when Woody and Charlotte bought that house overlooking Sunset Strip, their friends were acquiring land in the San Fernando Valley, which was still very cheap, and building there. The San Fernando Valley—The Valley, as everyone in Los Angeles calls it—at that time was farmland, miles on miles of orange and lemon groves, whose blossoms scented the wind, and Woody wanted to live there. But Charlotte had been indoctrinated by her mother with a fear, if not horror, of farm life, and she rejected the idea of what looked to her like a bucolic life; hence the decision to buy the house from Bogart and Bacall, one of those goofy Los Angeles abodes perched on a steep hillside where no sane house would ever want to be, not in that land of earthquakes and canyon fires and lethal mudslides.

Woody rationalized that its living room was good for entertaining; but he was never home long enough to do much of it. What later became a flagstone patio was at one time a garden, and during one of the more severe southern California winter rains the overflow from the garden flooded the living room. "I was seven or eight," Ingrid said.

Living in this house revealed it to be highly impractical. "It was awful," Ingrid said. The winding road at its front door, a ledge, really, carved out of the steep hillside, was hardly wide enough for two cars to pass each other, and there was no parking space. It certainly was not a place where a little girl could meet, much less play with, neighborhood children. You couldn't even ride a bicycle there.

"When I was a kid," said Ingrid, "my mother and father had a cocker spaniel named Freckles. He was awful, a miserable animal.

"We moved up to that house on Hollywood Boulevard. The Bogarts had a fenced yard for their dog; I think they had a boxer. That was already called the dog's yard. We always called it the dog's yard. My mother and father put Freckles out there. And they got another cocker, who was really quite mean, and bit people. Then they got this standard poodle named Hershey, who was great. He was kind of my childhood dog. He was sweet and I dressed him up in dresses. I was so lonesome. I'd put him in dresses and drag him around.

"They kept getting poodles. Some friend of my dad's who lived in Vegas had a miniature poodle puppy that he gave to my father. After that my mother got toy poodles."

Later on they had a poodle named Bill. Bill had a stroke and fell off the balcony. Charlotte's mother was there alone, and though she didn't drive she somehow got him to a veterinarian. Bill survived both the stroke and the fall.

"Once my mother got the small poodles," Ingrid said, "she strung this elaborate sort of fishnet-chicken wire around the balcony. The look of the house in the later years was kind of ruined by the fence."

Ingrid had little interest in jazz. On the contrary, she liked country guitar.

"When it came time to take music lessons," she said, "my father wanted me to take classical piano, which I did. I was very mediocre. I liked it all right, but it didn't ring bells. In high school I wasn't interested in any music except things like the Pretenders—teen-age love songs.

"Then in my last year of high school they opened a coffee house in L.A. called the Unicorn. That was 1957–58. I started going there. It was the first time I had ever seen beatniks or anything like that. The waitresses had long straight hair and big theatrical makeup and wore all black, and the guys had beards and wore all black turtlenecks. I thought this was the sexiest, farthest-out bunch of people I had ever laid eyes on. I was totally enamored. The doorman had a little classical guitar, and he played folk stuff like *John Henry*. And I just thought this was like seeing God."

After graduating from Marymount High School, Ingrid became an English major at the University of California at Riverside. While she was there she met a young Los Angeles printer named Tom Littlefield. She dropped out of the university after a year to marry him. That was in 1959. The first of their two children, whom they named Tom, was born on March 9, 1960, when Ingrid was still six months short of nineteen. Thus Ingrid was carrying the child when I saw Woody in Chicago.

"I'm a very stubborn man," Woody once said, "and when I get a lot of opposition, I work harder."[1]

Again he scaled back to a small group, this time a quintet. It worked as an act with tap dancer Steve Condos and pianist and singer Norma Douglas. It played for dancers at the Waldorf and at Freedomland, a minor imitation of Disneyland in the Bronx. Not long after this he began to build his next great band. Its genesis, an accident of concurring circumstances, came at a time when Woody felt depleted, perhaps even defeated. Possibly that is what I had sensed in Chicago a few months before.

The new band was built around the arranging talent and organizational abilities of Nat Pierce, who was given extensive authority and freedom, and the trumpet work of Bill Chase. Bill had changed his name from Chiaiese —his origins were Italian—and he was the latest in a long line of New Englanders who had come into the band, among them Ralph Burns and Nat Pierce.

Born in Boston in 1935, Chase was one of the new breed of musicians trained in the jazz schools that had sprung up. Chase came out of Boston's Berklee School of Music and, like so many Berklee alumni, got his first experience in the big band of Herb Pomeroy. Chase gained further experience with Maynard Ferguson's band. Chase was a remarkable trumpeter with immense stamina and an ability to play solos in all sorts of moods, including the lyrical. He could play lead. He could play jazz. His lead playing entailed, when he wanted them, high notes of extreme power and accurate intonation. Chase once said to me, "Maynard practiced with Harry James records and decided he could play higher. I practiced with Maynard Ferguson records and tried to go still higher." His high notes were not uncontrolled squeals for brief effect; Chase could really play up there. His work would add one of the major colors to the band Woody was building, for he was also an excellent arranger. Bill was tall with powerful shoulders, athletic, dark, notably handsome, polite, kind, and devoid of vanity. He was immensely likable.

Trombonist Phil Wilson would be a central figure in the new band. Because Wilson is more typical of the genesis of a jazz musician than the accepted myth, his background is worth examining. He was born of mostly Scottish ancestry in Belmont, Massachusetts, on January 19, 1937, and grew up in Exeter, New Hampshire, where his father taught history at Phillips Exeter Academy, which Phil attended. Phil studied music with Phil Viscuglia, who was later a clarinetist with the Boston Symphony. Wilson said, "In those days, he was so fearful of his job, teaching woodwinds at Phillips Exeter, that in order to play jazz with myself and few friends in the afternoon, he would pull the shades on the living room windows of my folks' house. It was freaky."[2] Wilson became capable of effortlessly hitting high C's on the instrument, well up into trumpet register. Further, he acquired the skill of rotary breathing. This ability, developed by only a very few brass and reed players, involves maintaining an outgoing pressure of air in the mouth while taking in air through the nose. No doubt there are others who can do this, but the only ones I have known are Clark Terry, the late Harry Carney, and Wilson. The skill permits extremely long uninterrupted lines.

Viscuglia sent Phil to Herb Pomeroy, who led a small group at a club in Boston called the Stables. Pomeroy asked him to sit in. Later, Phil studied trombone at the New England Conservatory, which, he says, was a complete waste of time. He really wanted to attend the Berklee School of Music, then a new and radical institution in that it taught jazz. He spent much of his spare time at Berklee, because trombonists were needed. Phil then began working in the Herb Pomeroy big band.

Pomeroy, who had himself graduated from Berklee, is an important formative force in American music because of the number of excellent musicians who performed in the band, many of them gaining their first professional experience with him, among them Bill Berry and Joe Gordon. Phil Wilson said, "I ended up in Herb's B band, along with a lot of other enthusiasts, such as Bill Chase, Jim Mosier, Bob Rudolph, Gordon Brisker, Danny Nolan, Gene Allen, Eddie Morgan, Gerry Lamy, Paul Fontaine, and Jake Hanna. We were all in that band." Charlie Mariano and Boots Mussulli also played in that band.

The key to the new Herman Herd, according to Wilson, was Chase, but in the broader sense it was Herb Pomeroy. Many of the men who were in the first two Herman herds had come out of the Charlie Barnet band. But the new Herd was made up of Pomeroy alumni. By 1961, Wilson was in the army, playing in the band of the North American Regional Air Defense command (NORAD).

Phil said, "Bill Chase had been with Woody back as far as '58, I think. He went out with a band that was terrible. God, I hated that band. They recorded a terrible album for Verve. It was just dreadful. I don't think they had much respect for him. Woody was at loose ends then." Phil was referring to the band I heard in Chicago and also disliked.

"Then Woody went down to a small group. They played at the Rooster Tail in Detroit in 1961. In that band were Bill Chase, Gordon Brisker, Jake Hanna, Charlie Andrus, and Woody. And Nat Pierce. Nat was from Boston, and most of us had known him there. I was with the NORAD band with Bobby Shew and Paul Fontaine. We were playing out at the Michigan State Fair on the outskirts of Detroit. Bill came out to see us, along with the rest of the band, because Bill and I were friends from the Herb Pomeroy band.

"Nat was trying to talk Woody back into fronting a band. It looked as if it might happen, if Nat would manage the band. Bill asked me if I would be interested. I think he also asked Paul Fontaine at that time. We were both due to get out of the army. I said, 'You're damn right, man.' Because that was the chair where the king of the trombone sat, the lead trombone, Bill Harris. And Urbie Green and Carl Fontana.

"For me to have that opportunity was just huge. I made Bill aware of my availability. Sure enough, the call came. I went back up to Exeter, New Hampshire, when I left the NORAD band, to work in a forestry crew for about four months, to lose a lot of weight that I had. I lost sixty-three pounds.

"I went with Woody around May of 1962. Twelve of us in the band had been with Herb Pomeroy. Woody now had a great band. I lived for that band. It was such an exciting experience that I've been living off it ever since. God bless him."[3]

Of the time in his life just before the birth of the new band, Woody said, "Once again I was running out of gas. I took a small group on the road." And that group was the nucleus of the new band, which had the same rhythm section—Pierce, Andrus, and Hanna—and Chase as lead trumpeter.

"It was really tough to get bookings," Woody said. "And yet, that was the beginning of the '60s band, right there. What put it together was the Metropole."

The Metropole was a rowdy cavernous bar on the east side of Seventh Avenue in midtown Manhattan. It booked small jazz groups in its upstairs room. Its main, ground-floor, room didn't even have a bandstand. Woody was asked by the management (and I never did find out who owned the place) to bring a big band into that room. But where could it play?

Behind the bar. The bar was very long, running perhaps fifty feet back into the darkness of the place. Behind the backs of the bartenders was a long platform. If a band were to play there, it would be under conditions that violated every principle of acoustics that big bands had always observed: saxes in a line in front, trombones seated behind them, trumpets behind them, on three platforms rising to the rear. Rhythm sections were placed to one side, usually stage right, audience left. The reason for this arrangement was a practical one: so the musicians could hear each other and thus play tightly. At the Metropole, if Woody brought in a big band, they would have to stand, not sit, in a straight line. Furthermore, the band would face a mirrored wall; not only would the musicians be staring at themselves, but their projected sound would come snapping back into their faces. Woody should have turned down the job; he didn't. The arrangement should have been a disaster; it wasn't.

The unorthodox formation baffled musicians who came in to listen. With the rhythm section in the middle and the saxes standing audience left, the brass audience right, the end man on the one side was a good fifty feet from the end man on the other, and the acoustic delay between the two ends of the band was considerable. How did they manage to play with rhythmic coherence? They had found an odd solution to the problem. They watched the drums in the mirror on the facing wall. More specifically they watched Jake Hanna's high hat, and played to that. And some of the band's hottest nights occurred at the Metropole.

The Metropole became the band's base of operations for the next several years. "It took a lot of responsibility off me," Woody said. "The salaries of the band and so on were paid by this place. And I was given actually a salary, that simply would take care of my immediate needs. And we could pick and choose a time. If we got some good dates, we could go out for two weeks or four weeks, and come back and go back in for two or four weeks, or whatever we wanted. It was a great place to break in a band, by sheer necessity, because you either played together or you'd never see each other again. It was like being in a police lineup above a bar and playing into a mirror for a baffle. But it really worked into a remarkably quick way to get a band in shape.

"Another thing that made it all possible was, in the midst of this whole scene, I went in with the rhythm section and did a quartet album for Philips. It was the first successful album we'd had in several years, as far as sales and [air] play went. And from that I was able to convince them, because we were now in the Metropole, that they should record a big band. They had no eyes. Most labels didn't at that period. But they went ahead with it.

"Sal Nistico, Chuck Andrus, and Jake Hanna were there, constantly, and Nat Pierce and Chase were there every night, and Nat got different trumpet players at different times. They were usually guys from Boston or the New York area. That was his department. And then the trombones. It was some time during that earliest time when we brought in a guy from Richmond, Virginia, Henry Southall."[4]

By now Abe Turchen was the band's business manager. He and Woody had taken office space at 200 West 57th Street, an outer room and then two smaller rooms, which looked north over 57th Street. At a desk to your left as you entered sat Dick Turchen, Abe's nephew, who sometimes had worked as the band's road manager; he had made the South American tour with Woody. But he now had a business of his own, Video Components, and was only peripherally involved with the band.

On the facing wall as you entered were two doors. The one on the right was Abe's. The one on the left led to a small room sublet from Abe and Woody by one of Woody's old friends, Lou Singer, an excellent orchestral composer and sometime amanuensis to composer Frank Loesser. Lou had written *Sleepy Serenade* and, after he actually heard someone make this order in a restaurant, *One Meat Ball*. That silly little song haunted him, but he was a well-trained composer, educated at Juilliard and Columbia University, who had studied with Wallingford Riegger. His office contained a spinet piano, a nondescript settee, a desk, chair, telephone, and nothing else. He was a very humorous man and kept the office bright.

The building was heavily tenanted by show-business people. Down the hall was the office of the Modern Jazz Quartet, run by their manager, Monte Kay. Elsewhere in the building was that of Woody Allen, whom Woody would occasionally encounter in the elevator, saying to the comedian, "Hi, I'm the old one."

Woody had enormous faith in Abe Turchen's acumen and gave him total control of the business. Abe, who stood about five-foot-eleven, was bulky now, his weight having risen to about 250 pounds. He always looked rumpled. Abe had married again. His second wife, Cindy Richmond, had worked briefly at the Copacabana. At the time of the marriage, she was nineteen, Abe was forty-three. She was very pretty. She and Abe had two sons, Steven, born August 3, 1957, and David, born June 22, 1959. They lived in a corner apartment on Riverside Drive at 78th Street that commanded a magnificent view of Riverside Park, the 79th Street Boat Basin, the smooth expanse of the Hudson River, and New Jersey beyond it. In the living room were a heavy and well-upholstered pale blue sofa and armchairs.

Abe Turchen had remarkable powers of persuasion and booked the band with ingenuity. At the same time, he was an indefatigable pessimist; his prognosis for almost everything was: "It'll never happen. It'll never happen." He liked show-business comics, particularly Jack E. Leonard, always called Fat Jack Leonard in the business, and I think Abe, whether consciously or unconsciously, affected Jack's misanthropic style of delivery. He tried to be humorous, with only intermittent success, his efforts to tell Jewish jokes foundering on his inability to get the hang of the accent. By contrast, Lou Singer, a native New Yorker, had the accent under perfect control, and always knew the latest Broadway jokes.

Abe would sit there every day, playing solitaire and watching sports on television, quietly placing bets on the telephone, shuffling the incredible clutter of papers on his big old wooden desk in a search for some phone number or other, and from time to time on sudden impulse or inspiration picking up the phone to place a bet or book the band into some improbable gig like the opening of a shopping mall. Meanwhile, as Woody noted to Stuart Troup, the outer office was "usually loaded with bookmakers, money lenders, and others he was doing business with." Abe, as everybody said, was a character. Anyone who could book that band and carry all the information in his head would seem a natural at counting cards, and everyone who ever saw him play in Las Vegas said he was a master at blackjack. "It's too bad he went overboard," Ingrid Herman said, "and bet on the wrong things, instead of gambling like a professional."

The new band was taking form. And because of his obvious organizational abilities, Nat Pierce was road manager. This meant he was in charge of paying the men, getting them to and from each job, and seeing that things ran smoothly.

It was at this point that I got involved with Woody and with that office.

I was editor of *Down Beat* from May, 1959, to September, 1961, when I resigned. In February, 1962, I left for Latin America with the Paul Winter Sextet. By the time we got back in July, I had translated into English some of the songs of a Brazilian composer I had met, the late Antonio Carlos Jobim. No one in New York was interested in them.

Those first months in New York were terrifying. I could not sell my writing, either my prose or my songs, and I was living at the West Side YMCA, a famous but depressing oasis for artists arriving in the city. Tennessee Williams wrote some of his early plays in that place.

I rapidly learned a dark lesson during that period. When I had been at *Down Beat*, I was useful to the record companies, and they treated me with a graciousness of which, fortunately, I was always a little suspicious. But now that I was needy, I learned quickly who my friends were. And they were the musicians. They were the ones who stood by me in a bad time, and I have never forgotten who they were. The complete list would be long, but their names include Art Farmer, Miles Davis, Gil Evans, Dave Brubeck, Paul Desmond, Bob Brookmeyer, Philly Joe Jones, Wynton Kelly, Gerry Mulligan, and, particularly, Woody Herman and Bill Evans.

Somehow or other I ran into Woody. I probably went to hear the band at the Metropole. I saw him repeatedly over the period of a month or so. And Abe Turchen said to me, "A guy like you shouldn't be living like this. Why don't you come to work for us? We can give you a small salary, and you'll have the use of the office."

"Doing what?" I asked.

"I don't know," Abe said. "Publicity. You could help us with that."

I took the offer. Later, I was talking to Nat Pierce about the time when Abe hired me. Nat said, "Abe didn't hire you. Woody told him to do it. I was there."

Thus I became one of the many souls whose lives were reshaped by Woody Herman.

▼   ▼   ▼

With what Woody was paying me, I was able to take a small basement apartment at the rear of a brownstone (actually, the stone was gray) on West End Avenue between 70th and 71st Streets. A door opened onto my own cool, shaded little courtyard that let you look up at a geometric piece of sky against which the leaves of a locust tree made patterns. Around the corner from me, in a large modern building, lived Erroll Garner, Roger Kellaway, and many other musicians. My little apartment became a meeting place of sorts. Antonio Carlos Jobim came to New York, and we wrote a number of songs in that apartment. The first of the songs I had translated in Rio, *Quiet Nights of Quiet Stars (Corcovado)*, began to be recorded, one of the first versions being by Stan Getz and Astrud Gilberto. I wrote some others with Gary McFarland.

I got used to the chaotic nature of the Woody Herman office. One day he called in from the road, seeking someone's phone number. He said, "Take a look in the files, and . . . . " He broke off, laughing, and said, "Hah! What files?"

When Woody ran out of clean shirts on the road, he simply bought more. He accumulated huge quantities of them, along with his shoes: he carried with him as many as twenty-six pairs of shoes hand-finished by his father. There was a suitcase full of shirts under a bench in the office, and more clothes in a closet. He came in from the road and said, "Have you got any room at your place for these things?"

"Yeah, I s'pose," I said.

"Would you mind taking 'em home and keeping 'em for me?" I remember that there was an excellent pair of gray slacks and a brass-buttoned blue blazer in this accumulation of unused wardrobe.

I had discovered a curious object in a drawer. Woody by then was losing his hair. It had thinned and receded from his forehead. It troubled me that he was, as it seemed to me, growing old: he was forty-nine. The object in the drawer was something hairy. I asked Abe, "What is this weird-looking thing?"

Abe said, "It's Woody's rug. He hates it. Won't wear it."

So when Woody asked me to take his clothes home, I opened the drawer, took out the toupee, dangled it between my thumb and forefinger, and said, "What would you like me to do with this?"

"Oh, that's disgusting!" Woody said. "Get rid of it!" And I tossed it into a wastebasket.

The musicians in those days in New York used to hang out in four bars, within walking distance of one another in the midtown area: Jim and Andy's, Junior's, Charlie's, and the Spotlight. Some favored one over the other, but most of the jazz musicians patronized all four. I was partial to Jim and Andy's. When Woody's band was in town, playing two or three weeks at the Metropole, its members could often be found at Jim and Andy's, Woody among them. You'd find him hanging out with his guys, listening to the woes of the younger musicians with a paternal patience. Everybody by now called him the Old Man. I do not know whether they had yet started calling him the Road Father, but that was the role he was more and more assuming: the great teacher, the one-man finishing school.

The band was becoming phenomenal, now that it had overcome the problem of being stretched out in a line. On the left were the four saxes. Then came the drummer, Jake Hanna, then the bassist, Chuck Andrus. Then Nat Pierce, seated at a small upright piano, the only man with his back to the audience, and for that matter the only man who wasn't standing, playing the charts from memory. Then came the five trumpets, and on the far right, the three trombones.

And sometimes, standing at the bar, facing them, was in effect another Woody Herman band, veterans of the earlier herds, including trombonist Willie Dennis, Al Cohn, Zoot Sims, Stan Getz, Don Lamond (busy with studio work and a regular at Jim and Andy's), and more. Sometimes, when they were in New York, Johnny Mandel and Ralph Burns would wander by. The members of that Four Brothers band who had treated him with such contempt had grown up and now treated him with reverence. It was an incredibly celebratory atmosphere, for the old hands who came in would marvel at the prowess of this new generation of players. The band played *Caldonia* at twice the speed of the original record, and when he sang it, Woody stumbled over the time, trying to keep up. When the Neal Hefti trumpet unison passage arrived, Bill Chase would jump his part an octave above the others so that the thing bordered on the frightening.

Phil Wilson recalled, "The *Tonight Show* was at the Hudson Theater. When it let out, all the guys from the *Tonight Show* were there, hanging out. And you'd have Dizzy running in and Ben Webster. I was just in heaven. Woody used to call me a stranger in paradise, with all of these people. Wow. What a time."

The band was contracted for nine weeks at the Metropole that year, and had the management been able to get more time, it would have stayed there longer. But the bookings were accruing. I was managing to place a great deal of publicity about the band, but it soon became unnecessary; the publicity was generating itself, with critics and musicians alike saying this was the best band Woody had led since the Four Brothers band. By the end of 1962, Abe had booked the band all the way into August, 1963.

George Simon wrote in the *New York Herald Tribune*:

> What is so exciting about this particular Herd?
>
> First of all, it has the almost-forgotten sort of pulsing ensemble sound that makes you want to cheer. The arrangements are exciting. The brass is brilliant. The trumpets blast as one. They blow high, but they're accurate and they get a great blend. The saxes are loose and easy. And the rhythm section—well, if there's one reason why this Herd stands out from among all the rest, it's because of the rhythmic trio's fantastic, swinging drive . . . . In Jake Hanna, Woody has the most propulsive big-band drummer to emerge on the jazz scene in years. The way he drives everything before him (with valuable assists from Chuck Andrus) is absolutely astounding.

He did not exaggerate. Quincy Jones had gone into debt trying to start a big band, and the magnificent Gerry Mulligan Concert Jazz Band could only make a living overseas. Who was responsible for this remarkable new band? The principals inclined to give rather than take credit.

Nat Pierce told me, "It's because of him—Woody. If there are so few big bands out here, it's because there are so few professional bandleaders. Woody's a pro.

"Being a professional bandleader involves knowing when to let a guy play because he's playing exceptionally well. Some leaders might not like to see their sidemen getting a lot of applause.

"Woody's delighted. Another thing: Woody's an entertainer as well as a musician. He can get away with a lot of things on the mike, quips and that sort of thing, that younger guys couldn't.

"One reason the guys love to work for Woody is that we never feel we're actually working for the man. It's more like working *with* him. He appreciates what we're doing, and he lets us know it. And the guys appreciate and respect him. So they work all the harder."[5]

One night when Al Cohn came by to hear the band, I asked him why all

Woody's groups, no matter what their size, had the same quality of fire.

"It's the way Woody rehearses a band," Al said. "He lets the guys play around with a new chart, run it down themselves, get their own feeling going on it. After that, he steps in and cleans it up. For this reason, the guys get a lot of themselves and a lot of feeling into it."[6]

Bill Chase said that it was the same now as in Al's days with the band. "We'll get a thing run down," Bill said, "and then Woody will come in and say, 'That's good, but I don't like this other thing. So go from letter K over to here, and then take it out.' And he always seems to be right.

"I'd like to make this one point, though: that quality isn't *always* there. I've been with Woody when it wasn't there. We have to have the right rhythm section. Jake Hanna is very important to the feeling this band gets."[7]

Jake said, "Woody's flexible. He goes along with the way the band feels instead of sticking strictly to the book. That makes it always interesting and exciting for us. If a man's really blowing, Woody doesn't stop him after eight bars because the arrangement says so. He lets him keep on wailing."

Woody said, "If I may make so bold, I'll compare myself to Basie and Ellington. If Duke had a whole bunch of new people tomorrow, it would sound just like Duke. The same with Basie.

"But I have to have the right kind of people. If you have people who are content in what they're doing and believe in it, you'll have a hell of a lot better result. If I haven't got the right people, I can't do it.

"I think I'm a good organizer and a good editor. I try to let the band have its head and then strengthen what they're doing.

"Mind you, for each guy I've told 'Go blow' there've been nine others I've told, 'Don't blow.' I don't mean to upset anyone's progress, but *at that point* I decide whether a guy should blow or not. For the first two weeks, I don't listen to a man. I'll hold off for a while. And then I want to hear him."[8]

Actually, the process was a little softer than that. When a new young musician would come into the band, Woody would tell him not to worry about anything, just relax and get used to the book. Then, when it seemed the young man had become familiar with it, Woody would hold up a finger and nod to the musician, meaning, "Take one chorus." If that chorus went well, he might hold up two fingers, meaning, "Take another one." And thus he would judge. He was no martinet.

But, Woody said, "we've got to have pros in this band, in both attitude and playing ability.

"A guy who's been a tremendous aid to me has been Nat Pierce—his writing, his way of encouraging others. He's got everybody in the band writing. This band has more amateur writers! I'm even writing some."

Phil Wilson thinks Woody had mysterious abilities that defied analysis. "In front of a band he was very subtle," Phil said. "He would react. He never missed a note. He listened to what everyone was doing. He *sold* the music to the public by his reactions to it. It could be the facial expression, it could be the way he moved his coat. He had a show-biz sense. He could take something outrageous that we were doing back in the band, and react to it with an outrage, much like the Marx Brothers, and a lay person who knew nothing about music—particularly the stuff we were doing, because damn! it was advanced—would get it. Woody would make light of it, make fun out of it, make pathos out of it, he would react to it so that the common man would be able to say, 'Hey, there's something going on back there.' I watched him night after night after night, wondering, 'How can I ever do that?'

"For all the freedom of the band, there was a discipline there. Very strict. We had a respect for it. And you knew it. We were in shape. You could confront Woody in the most embarrassing situations you could imagine, and he was together when he had to be—always!"

Neal Hefti thinks that Woody was intimidated by the sheer brilliance of the players he had hired for the Second Herd. Phil Wilson concurs. Phil said:

"Woody was a *great* clarinet player. The problem with him is that the son of a bitch developed to such a musical degree that he got nervous in front of his own band. If we were playing the Dallas Country Club, which we often did, and the lights were out and we were doing great old standards and nobody was clapping, boy! how he played. I'm a connoisseur of clarinet players. I look at clarinet players like I look at great wines. Woody was a giant player. But when he had a high-pressure band, he was intimidated by it. And the band I was on was high pressure.

"God, what a musical band."[9]

But mere musicality was not enough to make the band a success. The ballroom business was all but finished. Booking agencies were not interested in helping anyone build a band. The cost of transporting a band by bus had risen to fifty cents a mile—a small figure now, but not a small one then. Furthermore, booking agencies were inclined to kill a band with one-nighters. The reason was peculiar. The American Federation of Musicians allowed a booker to take 20 percent of the fee for one-night engagements, but only 10 percent for long engagements, known as locations, such as the Metropole. Further, the collective gross for a week of one-nighters ran higher than that for location jobs. So it was in the short-term financial interests of the bookers to get double the commission on a larger gross. But without being able to stay in one place at least for a little while from time to time, a band became exhausted.

Abe despised booking agents. He said in his mortuary voice, "We work with agencies but not for any one of them." And so he functioned as both manager and booker for the band, which technically was contrary to an AFM regulation forbidding anyone's filling both roles. But Abe collected only a manager's commission. His years on the road with the band stood him in good stead now that he was booking it. "For one thing," he told me, "I know every ballroom operator in the country."

And when any one market grew weak, Abe looked about for new ones. "I started the whole college market," he claimed. "I started in it in 1948 and '49. This was after we came back from Cuba and broke down to six men. The band business was down to a nub. I picked up the phone and started calling small colleges, with 1500 students and up. I'd say, 'I know you don't operate in midweek, but how'd you like to have the Woody Herman band for nothing?' "

He would let the school take its expenses for tickets and publicity off the top. Woody would then get everything up to a predetermined figure, perhaps a thousand dollars, after which the proceeds were shared by the band and the school. This ingenious but simple plan took all risk out of the venture for the schools.[10]

"Colleges were the only reason Woody survived for twelve years," Abe said.

Woody's view was different. When I told him what Abe had said, Woody said, "Abe's the reason I survived."[11]

▼ ▼ ▼

The band had one more fixture. He was a thin little man, probably in his mid-thirties, on whose stooped shoulders hung a rumpled raincoat like that worn by Columbo in the television series. He had a thin, knife-like face with hollow cheeks, and never smiled.

Night after night he would appear on the sidewalk at the front door of the Metropole and simply stand there, listening to the band and worshiping from afar. He never bothered anybody, he was just there. Somebody found out that his given name was Stanley, and Woody gave him the sobriquet Sidewalk Stanley. And thus he was ever afterwards known to the musicians. As new young musicians came into the band, Sidewalk's omnipresence had to be explained to them, although no real explanation was possible; no one knew where he came from, where he lived, or how he survived, because no one ever had a conversation with him that I know of. I never saw him inside the Metropole, only out on the sidewalk, although the band, in full roar, could clearly be heard from there.

Jack Siefert said, "Sidewalk Stanley had a cymbal that he carried around. I saw him outside Basin Street East at two o'clock one morning, just standing there in the rain, waiting to see Woody. He used to thumb his way to the various gigs and showed up in Atlantic City and at the Sunnybrook Ballroom in Pottstown, Pennsylvania."[12]

It was assumed by everyone in the band that he was retarded, but no one ever knew for sure. All anyone knew with certainty is that his devotion to Woody was total, gentle, and sad, and he became almost a mascot to the band. Eventually he was paid due tribute when Woody recorded a composition by Alan Broadbent titled *Sidewalk Stanley*.

I remember leaving the Metropole one night late with Abe Turchen and Woody and seeing the faithful Stanley standing there, asking nothing of anyone and inspiring about as much interest and attention from the passing world as a fire hydrant. Abe held out a hand, palm up, and looked aloft, as if expecting rain. "It's very Jewish out tonight," he said.

Abe continued to gamble. Nobody paid any attention.

21

Dallas November

It was in late 1962 that I first encountered—you could hardly say met, since it was on the telephone—Ingrid. It was at Woody's instigation. He put me in a very uncomfortable position. He told me that his daughter was interested in folk and what is now called country-and-western music but was then largely known as hillbilly music, sometimes even by the people who made it. Indeed, some of them referred to Kern and Gershwin and the like as "uptown music."

Woody said Ingrid was playing guitar, and something about it troubled him. Ingrid says today that she had discovered these other kinds of music and was trying to preach to him. "I can't believe," she says now, "that I had the audacity to tell my father that less is more." She told him that Lightnin' Hopkins was more profound than some of the guitarists in the tradition he admired, such as Charlie Christian.

He asked me to talk to her. Why me, I do not know to this day. Perhaps he thought that someone outside the family could communicate with her when he and Charlotte could not; or that I was more persuasive than he; or that I was nearer her age, which I was, but not that near. I was already in my thirties. I gained an impression that she was about seventeen, when she was actually twenty-one and a mother.

My end of this bizarre conversation occurred in the office on 57th Street; she must have been in San Francisco. Whether Woody called her and handed me the phone or she called him when I happened to be in the office, I no longer remember. But I found myself trying to convince her of the mediocrity of country music and guitar in particular, something I wouldn't dream of doing now, having known the late Thumbs Carllile and the late Lenny Breau. Lenny came out of country guitar to become one of the most brilliant of all jazz guitarists; and Thumbs could have had a career in jazz had he so chosen. Later I became familiar with the work of Hank Garland and others; and Chet Atkins showed me around the Nashville recording studios, where I quickly learned just how good that city's session players are (and how many of them play jazz at night in clubs).

I spoke to Ingrid of such jazz players as Charlie Christian, Jim Hall, Herb Ellis, Oscar Moore, and Jimmy Raney. All I succeeded in doing, of course, was to entrench her defensively in her own convictions, which she had every right to. I got off that telephone as fast as I could, annoyed at Woody. The conversation had been idiotic, surrealistic. Certainly there was nothing in it to suggest that Ingrid and I would someday be good friends.

More than thirty years later, we laughed about this lamentable encounter. Jazz guitar was not her favorite approach to the instrument. She thinks jazz musicians do not use its full resources, and in that she is right, although within those limitations, the best of them do brilliant work. Jazz guitar imitates horns, which is to say it largely is used for single lines. This is precisely what was admired about Charlie Christian. The only other function of guitar in jazz is to strum time in a rhythm section. The rest of the instrument's capacities were largely jettisoned in jazz, until the advent of Lenny Breau, whom she admires, along with Stanley Jordan. It is interesting that Jimmy Raney, coming from Kentucky and well aware of country guitar (I remember his choice of words when he told me he'd bought his first guitar "from a hillbilly"), didn't think guitar belonged in the Woody Herman band.

Ingrid's daughter Alexandra was born on September 11, 1961, and thus was at least a year old at that time of my conversation with Ingrid.

For a time Ingrid had gone to Los Angeles City College. She said, "I ran into a guy who gave me a few lessons. I learned *I Gave My Love a Cherry* and *Where Have All the Flowers Gone*—that kind of stuff. That's how it all started, with that folk music thing."

Her grandfather, Martin Neste, had played fiddle in what was known as a western swing band. "When I would go over to their house," she said, "they were listening to western swing. I remember *Smoke! Smoke! Smoke (That Cigarette)*. I just hated the sound of it, because I hated that non-pedal steel sound on guitar. They'd have strings and horns and the steel they used before they had pedal steel. Real high. I hated it. I still don't like it. And I don't like the mix of strings and horns.

"And my grandfather would play things for me like *Turkey in the Straw.*"

Ingrid's marriage became troubled. She was either divorced from Tom Littlefield or about to be when I "met" her. Perhaps that, too, contributed to Woody's perturbation. Woody was Catholic.

She moved up to the San Francisco area, where she met a southerner named Bob Fowler, who had a background in bluegrass music. Fowler, at twenty-three, was learning to play guitar. "He was a *good* singer," she said. They married in 1962.

"When I found grown-ups playing guitar in the way I liked," she said, "I was just crazy about it. I spent several years after that trying to learn in the midst of getting married and trying to raise kids and going through this up-and-down nonsense.

"I had a real fear of being a music widow. Had I been going with a jazz player, I would never have picked up a saxophone. But under these circumstances, I would take his guitar and follow him around and try to learn it too. I'm sure he hated it, but I didn't care. I was just driven. I was driven by fear of being left out as much as by the desire to play."

I pointed out to her that she had seen her mother left behind much of the time, a band widow all her life, and probably had heard lots of table talk about the broken marriages of road musicians.

"Oh yes," Ingrid said. "There was good reason for my fear."

Fowler became good enough on guitar to play with Bill Monroe. "He was good. He had a lot of talent," she said. "And I was going to do everything I could not to get left out.

"But it made it hard for me to learn. I was driven all the time. I panicked. I would practice and then cry if it didn't go well. I practically resented the kids because I didn't have enough time to practice. I was just sure that, since I had not grown up playing, I had a congenital lack of talent and would never be able to play, never be able to keep up."

Ingrid and Fowler and some friends formed a group called the Styx River Ferry, the first group, she believes, to play bluegrass in the San Francisco area with some measure of authenticity.

"After my grandfather's death," she said, "I was given his fiddle. It turned out to be a very good fiddle, a George Gemmunder. Gemmunder was quite a well-known maker. My grandfather, I'm sure, had no idea. He just bought it. But it was a very fine violin. And it was *loud*. And it had nice low tones, which most of them don't. I decided to learn one song on it for my grandmother for Christmas. Why I thought this would please her, as critical as she was, I have no idea.

"I found the instrument in some ways so much more imposing than the guitar. I had always felt behind the eight-ball. And here I had this big loud fiddle. I took *that* sucker and made it my own!

"Also it was a matter of fingering. I always had a pretty good ear for playing in tune, and I found the fingering so much easier than that of the guitar. It was only later that I learned how hard the fiddle really was. To this day I don't use the bow well. In fact I've been thinking of taking some lessons, because all my fears are . . . well, who cares now?

"I would get people to show me things, but I was afraid that they would think I was too slow. If it wasn't something I could grasp right away, or if it seemed too elementary, I was afraid to ask. Like, how the hell do you get this bow to go straight, instead of sliding all over the place? I wouldn't ask. I was too proud. It's too bad, really. I could have learned so much more.

"Since I didn't have a whole lot of talent, and since I started late in life, my father probably thought I was insane."

And this was the girl who could only have been rendered more insecure and defensive by that stupid conversation Woody got me into.

▼   ▼   ▼

Despite that uncomfortable memory, it was a good time in my life. The band generated a constant excitement. My friendship with Bill Evans, whose recordings already had changed the course of jazz piano and indeed jazz history, became close, and at Bill's request I wrote lyrics for his tune *Waltz for Debby*. A singer in Sweden, Monica Zetterlund, recorded it. I gave a copy of the record to the respected jazz disc jockey Mort Fega, who played it on his show—the first time, as far as I know, that a song of mine was ever heard on radio.

The next day Woody confronted me in the office. He said, "I heard a song of yours on the car radio coming into town last night. Mort Fega played it. Why didn't you tell me you could write lyrics like that?"

"You didn't ask. And it's not the kind of thing you can tell somebody, anyway," I said.

Woody picked up the telephone and called Howie Richmond, his former press agent and, later, partner in Mars Records and music publishing. Woody sent me over to Howie's office, two blocks away in the Coliseum on Columbus Circle, and within a day or so I had a songwriting contract with a regular weekly advance. I could afford a better apartment now, but I was attached to my small pad on West End Avenue and stayed there.

Bill Evans had long been struggling to overcome a heroin habit. Finally he went to Florida, where his parents were living in retirement, to try to break it. He called from time to time, and then he said he'd succeeded. Bill had recorded an album in which, by the technique of overdubbing, he'd played three pianos. It was titled *Conversations with Myself*. I wrote its liner notes. We received Grammy Award nominations, he for the album, I for the notes. Bill came back to New York from Florida. After all the critical acclaim, he didn't have a penny. Heroin had consumed all he had earned. And so for a time he stayed with me in that little pad. We took turns on who got the bed, who got the rump-sprung sofa.

Bill had an engagement, probably two weeks, at the Village Vanguard, and during that time we were to attend the Grammy Awards dinner. Bill had no appropriate clothes for the occasion. I had a thought. Though Bill was taller than Woody, he was very thin at that time. My closet was crowded with Woody's clothes. I took out Woody's beautiful blue blazer, saying, "Try this." It fit Bill rather well, and we went to the dinner. (He won.) And he played the Vanguard engagement in that blazer.

Woody came in for one of his periodic sojourns at the Metropole. Bill said he had always wanted to meet Woody. "I grew up listening to that band," Bill said. Woody wanted to meet Bill. I set up a lunch, telling Bill to meet us at the office. To my chagrin, Bill walked in through that outer office, past Dick Turchen's desk, wearing Woody's blue blazer. And instead of being cool about it, he said to Woody, "How do you like the blazer?"

"I like it *a lot*," Woody said pointedly, suppressing a grin.

Bill whipped it open to show the monogram over the inner pocket: WH. "That stands," he said, "for William Heavens." And Woody laughed aloud. Bill wore that blazer for a long time. I think he was proud of the initials in it. We all have our heroes.

I learned later that Woody was in the habit of giving clothes away. David Gale, who was in the brass section of the band at that time, told me that Woody called him to his hotel room, looked critically at David's threadbare suit, and said, "You shouldn't be going around like that, kid." And he gave David one of his own cashmere suits.

Bill and I went to the Metropole to hear the band. We sat at a table near the rear. As Woody tried to announce a tune, some drunk shouted, "Play *Woodpecker's Ball!*" Woody tried to ignore him, continuing his announcement.

"Play *Woodpecker's Ball!*" Woody tried again.

"Play *Woodpecker's Ball!*" The audience began to laugh.

"All right," Woody said venomously, "for Charlie *Pecker* over there, we're going to play *Wood* Pecker's *Ball*."

Bill, who was quite shy, always turning his bespectacled and scholastic face a little away from the audience as he hovered over the keyboard, said with admiration, "Man, that takes real hostility! If I tried that, some cat would come up on the bandstand and belt me in the mouth."

Think of Isham Jones, treating nuisances in exactly that way.

The personnel of the band in March, 1962, comprised Bill Chase, David Gale, Paul Fontaine, Gerry Lamy, and Billy Hunt, trumpets; Phil Wilson, Henry Southall, and Bob Rudolph, trombones; Bobby Jones, Noah Brandmark, Jackie Stevens, tenor saxophones; Gene Allen, baritone saxophone; with Hanna, Andrus, and Pierce in the rhythm section. Sal Nistico, the superb young tenor player from Syracuse, New York, had left the band, a serious loss to its solo strength. He would, however, return to the band from time to time.

Chase was twenty-eight. He played lead, he played solos, he worked constantly, and in his off hours he wrote arrangements and compositions for the band. "Anything that came from the trumpet section." Woody said, "was pretty much guided by where he wanted to go.

"[There were] certain similarities about us. Where Jake and some of the other people didn't want to go to a new world, Bill and I had a perfect understanding of why we had to go to the new world. That didn't make us lose our feelings for the other people, but . . . .

"We had a very close, warm association, he and I, just as guys. We had a lot of the same hobbies and enjoyed the same things. Cars, automobiles, engines, and things of that nature. And we'd both be sloshing around Europe or the United States, wherever we were, trying to catch a race or the Grand Prix or the Indianapolis or whatever. And so we spent a lot of time in that fashion, which was the first time, actually, that anybody in my band and I got that tight.

"And so we became and remained very dear friends."[1]

In addition to new pieces by Pierce, Chase, and others, the band continued to play its old repertoire, *Apple Honey, Caldonia, The Good Earth, Four Brothers*. One evening someone asked Chase if he remembered the original recording of *Sidewalks of Cuba*. He said, "No. I never heard it. I was only twelve years old when it came out."

Ralph Burns dropped by one night and said unequivocally, "This is the best brass section Woody's ever had." Don Lamond said, "I hate them! They're so young! They're so great! I *hate* them!"

The success of the Herman band inevitably inspired questions about whether the big bands were coming back. It was about then that Woody unveiled an answer he would often give to that question: "Sure, next football season."

Abe Turchen said bluntly, "No," with his Jack E. Leonard delivery. "There are too many things against the band business. For one thing, there are too many ghost bands around. I mean led by ghosts—the Tommy Dorsey band, the Jimmy Dorsey band, the Glenn Miller band. Everyone forgets that if Miller were alive, he wouldn't be playing that way. He'd have moved on with the times.

"Another thing that's against the band business is the type of music the American public is dancing to. I've watched those kids at record hops. They don't dance. They're like a flock of cattle in the stockyards trying to keep their feet out of the mud. Watch the Dick Clark show. If they play a good tune, they don't know how to dance to it.

"Then there's the problem of the ballrooms. The fact that ballrooms aren't doing business is their own fault. I haven't seen the first ballroom that's changed its sound system or lighting or done anything to improve the business. All the ballroom operators have done is groan . . . .

"The only bands who've survived are the good music bands—Basie, Ellington, Kenton, Woody. Where are all the Art Kassel-type bands today? Yet ballroom operators hire mickey bands because they like that kind of music themselves. They don't think in terms of the public's taste."

Woody said, "You can't sell a band simply by telling everybody, 'This is a great band.' For some reason there's prejudice against jazz per se. But if you disguise it and start selling them 'great excitement' instead, then I think you've got a chance."[2] It was as if he couldn't believe his own new fortune and if he did believe it, already had begun to wonder how long it could last.

Every day Abe would sit at that cluttered desk in that chaotic office, playing his solitaire, watching sports on the little black-and-white TV set that sat on top of a filing cabinet, his various friends and assorted Broadway characters wandering in and out, chatting a while and leaving, then suddenly he'd pick up the telephone and place a bet on some game somewhere and a minute or two later pick it up again and find the band a gig in some bowling alley in Visible Breath, South Dakota, or the opening of a shopping mall in Frozen Lung, Saskatchewan, negotiate the money, firm the deal, and go right on with solitaire. I never saw him write anything down, never saw him take a note, and he never forgot a thing. He carried it all in his head. Sal Nistico thought he was a mathematical genius.

One day he asked me to take his car, a Cadillac, and drive out to Lundy's, a huge and well-known seafood restaurant at Sheepshead Bay in Brooklyn. He told me to sit at the bar and wait. A man would come to me. A tough-looking man approached me and asked my name. I told him. He handed me an envelope, saying, "Count it." I counted five thousand dollars, a lot more money in 1963 than it is now.

And I took the money back to Abe. I guess he won that day.

Then occurred an incident that, in the retelling, has been distorted: the story has it that Abe gambled away a week of the band's payroll. But it wasn't Abe, it was Nat Pierce who handled that money as road manager. The band had two six-week engagements at the Harrah's clubs in Reno and Lake Tahoe. Abe was given 50 percent of the money as an advance. Nat operated with the other 50 percent, collected on the job. After work one night, Nat got drunk while gambling. He dropped between four and five thousand dollars. Sick with guilt and embarrassment, he telephoned Abe the next morning.

I was in the office when that news came in. Abe took it all very calmly and said he would find the money. Woody apparently laughed when he was told, but he wasn't laughing later when he talked to me about it. I asked him what he was going to do about the situation.

"Nothing," he said.

"You're not even going to fire him?"

"No," Woody said. "If I fire him I'll never get my money back. I'll get it out of him in charts."

And as Nat said later, "I wrote charts for years to pay that back."

There is some indication that Nat lost more than one week's payroll.

"You know where the money came from to replace the payroll, don't you?" Abe's son Steve asked in 1994. "The Mafia. My older brother Mike was traveling with my dad. They drove out to Vegas and my dad double parked somewhere, which was his wont. He told Mike to go to one of the high floors of this building and to go to this room. He said, 'A guy's going to give you something.' Mike went up there.

"The guy said, 'You Abe's kid?' and Mike said, 'Yes.' The guy gave him a paper bag full of money. That paid off the gambling debt. But then he owed them something. So if somebody didn't show up for a booking somewhere, then Woody would have to fill in and not get paid. Because they'd been paid in advance."

Nat Pierce told Stuart Troup: "A few times Abe came out (to Reno and Lake Tahoe) and played at the blackjack table. When I lost some of the band's money, I said to him, 'I need twenty-five hundred.' Then he said, 'How much more you need?' I told him, and later he called me back and gave me more. 'You got enough?' Yeah.

"They finally barred him, he was winning so much.

"In Los Angeles, we played a place called Basin Street West, where we

made the record that won the Grammy. Our engagement was an unqualified success. We came back there six or eight months later, and business
was still pretty good. But I couldn't get any money. There were these
strange people coming in and out of the club every evening. Some of them
carrying paper bags. They were apparently siphoning off the money. When
I went to get the pay, there wasn't any. Woody was up in his house, and I
called him and said, 'What should we do?'

"We bounced a few checks for gasoline money, so we could get to the
next gig in Tahoe. When I didn't have money to get us out of Tahoe,
everybody came up with a little cash to put money in the bus.

"Later on, Abe was taking all the money and I wasn't able to operate the
band. I called him from a phone booth in the desert in Texas, and told him
that if the money wasn't where we were going, we weren't going to be able
to operate. Sometimes the money was there."[3]

Evidently Abe could do some losing too.

▼   ▼   ▼

Despite these omens, the band's success continued. Woody had recorded
one album for Philips, *Woody Herman 1963*, a name it bore though it was
recorded in 1962. Now he made another. It was produced by Jack Tracy,
one of the men who had occupied the editor's chair at *Down Beat*, then
became a producer for Mercury Records, and when Philips absorbed Mercury, for the Dutch-based conglomerate. The album, which would win a
Grammy, was recorded live at Basin Street West. "The room was jammed
every night," Leonard Feather noted.

In the audience, as so often was the case, were former members of the
band, including Red Norvo and Mary Ann McCall. Singers Nat Cole, Joe
Williams, and Sarah Vaughan were there with songwriters Johnny Mercer
and Bob Russell. Nat Pierce's taste for the work of Herbie Hancock was
reflected in his chart on *Watermelon Man*, recorded that evening, along
with the frenetic new version of *Caldonia*. Sal Nistico had rejoined the
band and is heard on that album to excellent advantage. "Sal Nistico,"
Woody said, "was a dynamite player. As long as you'd give him a tempo,
he'd play it. I don't think his sensitivities were as great as some of the other
tenors we've had, but that's something else. For what he did, I don't think
there was ever anyone any better, or maybe not nearly as good."[4]

Woody Herman 1963 had been released in January. By July sales reached
an estimated 100,000, and the Columbia Record Club had added the

album to its list, assuring further large sales. Another album, *Encore*, was rushed into release within a month of being recorded and enhanced sales of the first.

Thus the success of 1962 had been achieved without a new recording in the marketplace. Woody had upset the truism that live performance attendance was dependent on record exposure. Woody had all the bookings he could handle before either LP was released, and Abe was declining offers from jazz festivals for the summer of '63 because he simply could not fit them into the schedule. Festival impresarios immediately proffered bids for the summer of 1964.

Soon the band was booked through the end of 1963, and thirty-four weeks into 1964 had been written into the route book. Nor were these the long strings of one-nighters that drain and deplete a band; they were location engagements of one to three weeks. One-nighters merely filled the holes in the band's itinerary. The situation was unprecedented. Again Woody was being asked if his success would bring back the bands. He'd reply: "We're not going to bring back the bands, we're just going to bring back this band. We're selling excitement, not nostalgia."[5] And he kept adding new material by younger writers to the band's book. At Harrah's in Reno, a listener approached him and said, "Wouldn't it be better if you played some of the old dance music the way those Glenn Miller and Tommy Dorsey bands do?"

Woody responded, "They're dead and I'm alive and as long as I'm alive we'll be playing new things. Sure, we do some of the old ones. But I don't want to go back. I want to go forward."[6]

Someone asked Al Cohn which of the several Herman Herds he considered the best. He thought a moment and said, "This one."

Ralph J. Gleason wrote in the *San Francisco Chronicle*, "The most exciting and interesting new big band I have heard in years is the Woody Herman unit." Gleason said that for weeks before the band turned up in San Francisco he had been getting phone calls from musicians and others, raving about the band.

"At the Metropole," Woody said, "we found out something. We had to play with everybody standing along in a single line. And we found that the people loved the sound that way: they could get to hear everybody individually, as well as get the effect of the whole band.

"Too loud? You're never too loud when the music is good. We worked a hotel where we played dinner music the first set. Well, we did that for a while and then I said, 'Ah, the hell with it. We might as well blow.' So we did, and after the set, the hotel owner came over and told me to go right ahead and blow. It was the best band he'd ever had in his hotel, and it was okay with him.

"I don't talk about the bands, but this one is different."

As 1963 proceeded, the band had one triumph after another, with applauding crowds everywhere. It seemed that it would gross as much as the First Herd had in 1945, though in dollars diluted by inflation.

On or just before May 16, 1963, a telegram for Woody arrived in the office. It read:

"You may be admitting it but I'm not. Happy birthday. Tony Martin."

And I realized Woody was fifty.

There is a correlation between the political and economic atmosphere of the United States and the mood of its concurrent popular music. World War I brought an outpouring of ingenuous enthusiasm for war in songs such as *Over There*. Much of the 1920s music had a bounce and a giddiness to it. After the economic crash, the music became sensitive, with emphasis on romantic love, an ideal that, the music suggested, could be attained without money. *I Can't Give You Anything but Love, Let's Have Another Cup of Coffee, Let's Put Out the Lights and Go to Sleep, With Plenty of Money and You,* and *I Found a Million Dollar Baby (in a Five and Ten Cent Store)* were typical. In a commercial marketplace, songwriters sought to capture the public mood; and the public accepted the songs that touched that mood, making them hits.

During World War II, popular music in the United States became deeply sentimental as young men went away, and songs such as *I'll Walk Alone, I Don't Want to Walk Without You, My Sister and I, Time Was, He Wears a Pair of Silver Wings, When the Lights Go on Again All over the World, I'll Be Seeing You,* and *(This Will Be) My Shining Hour*, along with such cheer-up songs as *Don't Sit Under the Apple Tree (with Anyone Else but Me)*, and *Deep in the Heart of Texas.*

During the Eisenhower years, the music became ever more banal and shallow. And then came the election of John F. Kennedy.

On the evening of January 20, 1961, as a blizzard blew outside, the Herman band played the new President's inaugural ball. For many of the young musicians in the band, the engagement would remain one of the most memorable in their lives, for the excitement and sense of history, seeing Kennedy and the First Lady enter with Vice President Lyndon Johnson and his wife.

The new administration set a style of optimism. Whatever Kennedy was or wasn't, he did generate a national mood of youth, expectancy, and idealism. I find it no coincidence that Woody's band found its new success during that administration, and the gorgeous melodies of the Brazilian bossa nova movement became huge hits in the United States. Tony Bennett, who had recorded mediocre songs in his early career, now sang superb songs from the past and present, always accompanied by good arrangements, and became one of the biggest singers in the business. Nancy Wilson was a success, Peggy Lee and Dinah Washington were big stars, and Frank Sinatra was at his peak of ability and popularity. And the Woody Herman band was roaring. We thought it could go on forever.

Late on a November morning in 1963, I wandered down to the office on West 57th Street. Woody was in town, working that day at the A&R studio on West 48th Street, next door to Jim and Andy's, recording a third album for Philips. As I entered, Dick Turchen, sitting at his desk, said, "The President's been shot." At first I took this as a setup for a joke of some sort, and then I thought I had not heard him aright, then his hushed voice told me something was gravely wrong. "What are you talking about?" I said apprehensively.

"It's no joke," Dick said. "It's on television."

I went into Abe's office and sat down in my usual chair, in front of the IBM Selectric typewriter. Abe was leaned back in his chair, looking up at the little TV set on the filing cabinet. Lou Singer was standing somewhere in the room, as mute as Abe. I looked up at the set and watched the news from Dallas and, like everyone else old enough to comprehend (or at least try to comprehend), I went into a kind of emotional paralysis.

Dick Turchen came into Abe's office, and the four of us, Dick, Abe, Lou, and I simply stared at the screen, finally learning that the doctors at Parkland Hospital had pronounced the President dead.

At last I stood up. "Wood's down at A&R?"

"Yeah," Abe said.

"I'm going down."

It was not a long walk, eleven blocks from 57th to West 48th. I stopped in at Jim and Andy's for a couple of heavy drinks, then went next door and got into the aging elevator that took you up to A&R Recorders, at that time considered the best studio in New York, despite a shabby appearance. I sat on a folding chair in the studio. Woody looked over at me. I said, "I presume you've heard the news."

"Yeah."

He looked at the band. "Okay, let's try another one," he said, and counted off. It was Bobby Scott's tune, *A Taste of Honey*. The band had apparently made several runs at it. They started playing.

Unlike classical music, jazz can reflect the moods of its time not in the weeks or months it takes to write a symphony, such as Beethoven's *Eroica*, but in hours or even, as in this case, within minutes. There is nothing especially melancholy about the chart on *A Taste of Honey*, but what came out of the band was some of the most mournful music I have ever heard in my life. I would hear the band play that arrangement many times in the future, but the piece never had the mood that it did that day in the studio or on the record that eventuated from that session. It was all in the way the band played.

The band finished the take and Woody said, "Okay, that's it. Forget it for today."

He and I and some of the band went down to Jim and Andy's. Woody had given up cigarettes a little over a year earlier, after smoking up to four packs of Pall Malls a day for years. Like so many converts, he was already pressing me to quit. He was living very moderately at the time, drinking only Heineken's. But he ordered Scotch that day, and I sat there with him in a booth, watching the television, feeling bleak and forlorn, along with the rest of the country. Finally he rose and left.

▼   ▼   ▼

The world never seemed the same after that. Woody, though he was a Democrat, was not enamored of the Kennedy family, but you didn't have to like the Kennedys to be horrified that nameless powers, or so it seemed, could remove a president from office with bullets whenever they chose.

In the office, after the execution of Lee Harvey Oswald by Jack Ruby, Abe—the midwesterner who had once had a jukebox route and who, after years in the band business, knew a lot of Mafiosi—told me he knew Ruby; he said Ruby had been a minor minion of Chicago hoodlums.

Lyndon Johnson became president, pulled his dog's ears and raised his shirt to show a new surgical scar to the press, and committed the United States ever more deeply to a war it could not win. Anger in young people rose, and popular music of the land turned increasingly ugly, with snarling, fuzz-toned guitars and squealing feedback effects expressing the collective anger and disillusion. The brief bossa nova era of exquisite melodies was over. The Beatles had arrived, demonstrating to the record industry just how much money could be made from popular music, now that every young person in the country (or so it seemed) owned some sort of stereo set and bought records. Major labels suddenly saw the possibilities of sales in the millions, with rock groups catering to the lowest common denominator of public taste. They weren't interested in paltry successes like a hundred thousand sale on a Woody Herman album.

But the band went on, drawing big crowds everywhere. In a sense, its success—like that of Basie, Ellington, and Kenton—was *the result of* this turn to the coarse and crude in popular music. These four bands had no effective competition: they were glorious dinosaurs, survivors of another age, and the only working, traveling big bands the public could get to hear.

Woody was cognizant of this. When I asked him once why he thought these four bands were surviving, he said: "Well, for one thing, I think it's because they are basically jazz bands. When styles and fads and kinds of music change, there's always a hard-core audience still there—a jazz audience. They may be a minority group, but somewhere in the world, they're waiting for you."7

▼   ▼   ▼

By now, thanks in part to Woody and to Howie Richmond, singers were recording my lyrics, among them Tony Bennett, Frank Sinatra, Peggy Lee, and Sarah Vaughan. When Woody arrived in from the road, I told him, "I have something I must talk to you about."

It was nearly noon and he said, "Okay, let's have lunch."

We went around the corner to a tavern on Seventh Avenue. "What's bothering you?" he said.

I hesitated, stumbled. "Well," I said, or words to this effect, "thanks to you, my songs are getting recorded, I've got a book coming out, I'm getting very busy, and. . . ."

"Good, then what's the problem?"

"Well, the band's doing well, you really don't need me any more. . . ."

"And what?"

"I haven't got time to work for you any more."

"So?"

"But I just hate to leave you and the band."

"Is that all that's bothering you? I'll make it real simple for you. You're fired. Now let's have lunch."

Sometimes in later years he would introduce me to people, with an impish look on his face, as the only man he ever fired. Within the band, Woody didn't have to fire anybody. When a musician wasn't cutting it, the others in the band would make him so uncomfortable that he would quit.

Such was the spirit of that band. And Woody did fire a few men over the years, including Leonard Garment, but, like Duke Ellington, he found it very hard to do.

And so I left him. But I'd still drop into the office frequently, continuing to use it as a sort of base of operations.

Howie Richmond called me from Paris to ask whether I would come over and translate some of the songs of Charles Aznavour into English. I worked with Charles for a few weeks, then headed home, stopping in London on my way. Lifting a suitcase in my hotel room, pivoting to throw it on the bed, I heard a snap and felt a pain in my knee, then found I couldn't straighten the leg. Doctors in a hospital emergency clinic told me I had torn a cartilage, which would have to be surgically removed. I decided to get it done when I got home.

But how was I going to get there? I could barely hobble, much less walk. Woody and the band were arriving in London at the end of a European tour. I changed my plane reservation and Woody and the band took me home.

When I came out of the drugs after surgery at Roosevelt Hospital, I was disoriented, not knowing where or who I was. I thought I was a boy again. And as the mist thinned a little, I saw a figure sitting on a chair by my bed with a worried expression. The man resembled Woody Herman. But what would Woody Herman be doing at my bedside? Surely it was a dream.

The mists cleared and I realized that it was, indeed, Woody Herman, watching over me as he had watched over so many young men, so many careers.

22

Death and Taxes

In August, 1965, a musician who would play an important role in the band's history joined the Herd: Bill Byrne, a trumpet player trained at the Cincinnati Conservatory and in the Naval Academy band. He would become its road manager.

The personnel changes continued on through January, 1966, when the band played an engagement at the Playboy Club in Los Angeles. The State Department had asked Woody to undertake another cultural exchange tour, this one to Europe and Africa.

The schedule for the next weeks was even more frantic than the norm. On Tuesday, March 1, the band flew to London and, after one day off, played in Croydon, Birmingham, Bournemouth, Portsmouth, Bristol, London, Brighton, Southend on Sea, London again, Leicester, and Manchester. It then flew to Spain for a one-nighter in Barcelona, followed by four one-nighters in Germany, returning to New York to work the Playboy Club from 21 through 26. During the Playboy engagement, Woody began recording an album of Al Jolson songs with modern arrangements by Ralph Burns, Nat Pierce, and Bill Holman.

The genesis of that Jolson album is worth examining. It resulted from yet another of Woody's close friendships, this one with Ken Glancy. Glancy was—he is retired now—one of the finest executives in the history of the record business, one of those most sympathetic to music and one of the most ethical men in a business not famous for this virtue. Woody had known him since the 1950s.

Glancy is a New England Irishman, born in Springfield, Massachusetts, September 13, 1924, and looks it, a stocky, handsome man with a warm sense of humor. After army service in World War II, he went to the University of Michigan to major in English literature, intending to become a teacher. But he married and needed a job, and got one with the regional distributor for Columbia Records, traveling throughout the Midwest as a salesman.

"In travel you run into people," Ken said, "especially when you're trying to kill an evening." And one of the people he ran into in the 1950s was Woody, then recording for Capitol. By the time Woody's contract with Philips expired, Ken was head of A&R at Columbia records. Glancy said:

"One night at the Metropole, I was trying to sign him to Columbia, and after the gig, we went across the street for coffee. He said, 'I'll go. But I want to do a Jolson album.'

"I said, 'Well you've got that.'

"He said, 'I want an album with all the obvious tunes, *Sonny Boy, Carolina in the Morning*, and the rest. And the whole band's gonna be screaming.' Those were his exact words.

"You know, Woody was a very good ballad singer, an under-rated one."

Why Woody had this determination to do Jolson songs, nobody knows, but he did, and work on the album began.

Then followed an appearance on the Ed Sullivan television show, a day off, and one-nighters in Rhode Island and Long Island, after which the band flew again to Paris and a one-nighter, the start of an eleven-week schedule that took it to Africa and eastern Europe.

Several veterans of earlier Herds had returned to make the tour, and when the band left on March 3, accompanied by Abe Turchen and Charlotte, its personnel included: Bill Chase, Marvin Stamm, Alex Rodriguez, and Bill Byrne, trumpets; Henry Southall, Jerry Collins, and Carl Fontana, trombones; Frank Vicari and Bob Pierson, tenor saxophones; Tom Anastas, baritone saxophone; Nat Pierce, piano; Michael Moore, bass; and Ronnie Zito, drums. Sal Nistico and Dusko Goykovich, both living in Europe, joined them when they arrived. It was an outstanding band.

The band flew from Paris to Rabat, Morocco, then played two one-nighters in Meknes and Rabat. It played Madrid on April 10 and Rome April 11 and then flew to Dar es Salaam, the capital of Tanzania, where it stayed three days, the first of which was a day off.

Bill Byrne remembers that phase of the trip vividly. He said, "Dar es Salaam is on the Indian Ocean. It's just gorgeous. It's beautiful there, a wonderful place.

"I was in my hotel room. I didn't know who was next to me. I thought it was a guy and his chick in the next room. The wall was just thick enough that I couldn't make out their voices. I couldn't get to sleep. Whoever they were, they were laughing and raising hell and having a great time. This went on until about six o'clock in the morning. The next morning I came out the door and found out it was Charlotte and Woody. They were like two little kids, romping around and laughing and having a great time.

"That was a love story."

The band was in Tanzania for eight days, from April 11 through 18. Then it flew to Kampala, capital of Uganda, for three performances. This was only months before Idi Amin took power and began his reign of bloodshed. From Uganda it went on April 11 to Elizabethville (later re-named Lubumbashi) in the Congo, which had become independent of Belgium in May, 1960—only six years earlier. The country had been swept by turmoil since then with various factions struggling for power, United Nations troops trying to bring stability, and white mercenaries further bloodying the mix. Months earlier, communications in the country had been disrupted and the destruction of crops had created a serious food shortage. UN troops had recently pulled out, and when the band reached the rear of a theater they were to play, they were startled to see a U shape of machine-gun bulletholes in the stage door.

Given Belgium's history of cruel colonialism in the region and the work of the white mercenaries, the populace had reason enough to be suspicious of whites. In the town square of Elizabethville, on April 19, the band got ready for a performance. Local officials had set up barricades around the square for the band's protection. But the crowds tore them away and surged around the bandstand. "All these people were rushing toward us," Bill Byrne said. "Everybody in the band started looking at each other. Our eyes got pretty big. We thought, Oh boy, this is it! But all they wanted to do was get closer. Woody took a little kid out of the audience and put him on his knee and sang *Sonny Boy* to him. It was pretty touching. The people loved it, smiles all over. That's the kind of reaction we got all over Africa."[1]

State Department officers had warned the band not to drink the local water. So they purchased bottles of booze at a duty-free shop and some of them later recalled the strange experience of cleaning your teeth in the morning with a toothbrush soaked in gin.

"We had a night off in Elizabethville," Byrne said. "Some of the guys were sitting around on a veranda of the hotel playing cards and drinking— Smitty the band boy, Carl Fontana, and Nat Pierce. Nat hears a boom-boom-boom-boom. He had just been drinking enough that he grabbed his tape recorder—he wanted to get some authentic African drum sounds. He flagged a taxi and said, 'Take me to the drums, take me to the drums!' Fontana stopped him. The sound was coming from almost across the street. There was a big excavation there for a building, and down at the bottom, a water pump. Nat went down into the excavation. He wanted to record it anyway. That was Nat's experience with the African drums."[2]

After six days in Elizabethville, the band went on to a four-day stay in Leopoldville, including a concert for university students. And there Woody had a medical problem. He had for some time suffered from gout. He later recounted to an American physician that after the band had been drinking heavily and just before one concert, he had a severe attack, so painful that he couldn't walk. A huge crowd had assembled, and he felt compelled to perform; he usually did. A French-speaking Belgian physician gave him an injection of colchicine, the standard prescription for the ailment, and he made the performance.

One of the stars of the tour was Marvin Stamm. Stamm, born in Memphis, Tennessee, May 23, 1939, had graduated with a bachelor of music degree from North Texas State University in 1961. On his arrival in New York, he was almost immediately recognized by fellow musicians as a superb technician on trumpet and an outstanding jazz player. Marvin said: "I don't know anybody in the band who at that point was very politically minded, including Woody. Interestingly enough, today everybody seems to take much more interest in world politics than we did then. I don't remember anybody referring to any of it as the Third World or the Emerging Nations. We didn't take much notice of any of it. We were just getting on and off the bandstand."

Soon after the band left the Congo, four government ministers were arrested, charged with treason, and publicly executed. The turmoil continued.

After the Congo, the band made a four-day visit to the Ivory Coast.

All its members were enthralled by Africa, its rich topography, its people, their costumes, and the immensely varied cuisine. "It was one of the highlights of my life," Bill Byrne said.

"It was wild," Woody said later. "We played some universities. We'd have them all cheering and stomping and flipping, reacting to the excitement. It took a while for some of our audiences to go along with us. We played a few remote spots and the people there were puzzled for a while. They'd never heard anything like our kind of music. Then we started to use some basic measures, simplified our stuff, and they really caught on, clapping and shaking and all."[3]

After a concert at the University of Abidjan in the Ivory Coast, the band flew for a night off in Nice, France, then re-crossed the Mediterranean for two nights in Algiers. From there, on May 18, it took a tortuous route via Paris and Munich to Belgrade.

There had been some question in Woody's and other minds whether Dusko Goykovich should continue on to Yugoslavia. He was born there, at Jajce, on October 14, 1931, and on reaching military age had fled the country to escape the draft, working in bands in Germany, including that of Kurt Edelhagen, before studying at the Berklee School of Music from 1961 to 1963. He had played with Woody in 1964, then returned to Germany. He was worried that if he entered Yugoslavia, he might not be allowed to leave again or, worse, could be brought up on the old draft-evading charge. Through State Department channels it was determined that he would not encounter trouble.

A huge crowd greeted the band at Belgrade airport. Woody had just commented on the warmth of the fans there only to see them rush past him to surround Dusko. Marvin Stamm said, "It was the first time Dusko had been back since he defected. There was quite a bit of tension. An incident might have caused a real uproar. When we got off the plane, there was a crowd at the airport, and a little girl came up with flowers for him. He was a returning hero. It was a pretty amazing thing to see. And Woody played it to the hilt. Who wouldn't?

"Yugoslavia was very open at that time. It was a beautiful place. We didn't have any sense of the things that are going on now. None of us even had a sense of the historical background, how Yugoslavia was formed after the war. People walked the street, the markets were open, you never had a feeling that you were being followed or anything like that. People smiled. The two towns I remember were Belgrade and Ljubljana."[4]

The band was fêted like royalty. And every evening Woody would call Dusko down from the trumpet section to tell the audience goodnight in its own language. As promised, Dusko was not impeded when it came time for the band to move on to Romania, one of the most backward of the communist countries. The band reached Bucharest on May 23, and immediately found the country hideously depressing.

"It was quite a shock after Yugoslavia," Marvin said. "Everything you had ever heard about strict communism was there. It was cold. And the people walking the streets kept their heads down and looked on the sidewalk. Nobody looked up, nobody smiled. It was like walking through a doorway when the lights go out.

"Every night, after we finished playing, the guys from the radio orchestra in Bucharest would come to our hotel. We would invite them up to our rooms for a drink or something, but they wouldn't go because, they said, 'Your rooms are bugged.' We would sit at a large table in the dining room, and when they spoke they would lean their heads real close to the table and they would whisper, because they were afraid they'd be overheard. They didn't want anybody joking about anything, as musicians are wont to do, to make fun of everything. They were quite frightened of that kind of experience.

"Woody had told us before we went in about conditions. He asked Ronnie Zito to take extra drumsticks for the musicians there. Some of the trumpet players took extra mouthpieces that we didn't want so that when we met the guys there we'd pass them to them. The saxophone players took extra boxes of reeds. The musicians there told us how difficult it was to get instruments, and once you had an instrument to get parts to repair it— everything we took for granted as musicians, that we just bought at the store, valve oil, ligatures for clarinets and saxophones, new pads, was extremely difficult for those people to get. Things like a Bach mouthpiece that we would buy for ten or twelve dollars here, over there, if they could even come across one, it would cost them two or three months' wages. Romania was back in the dark ages. It was really tough.

"When we left, some of those musicians that we had hung out with cried. They were very touched by our being there and wanting to spend so much time with them and doing all that, and giving them the few small gifts we'd been able to bring."[5]

From Romania the band went to Athens and then, on June 2, to Egypt. It played concerts there on May 10 and 11, then attended a reception given by the U.S. State Department, and played a concert on June 6 in Alexandria, followed by a performance in Cairo, the last stop of the tour.

On June 7, the *New York Times* reported on the band's performance in Cairo, a booking at the Gezira Club, "once the staid stronghold of the British during the days of empire." The band shared a program with actress Celeste Holm reading from the writings of Abigail Adams, wife of the second President of the United States, anthropologist Margaret Mead, George Bernard Shaw, and Oscar Hammerstein. Also on the bill was the Phoenix Trio, a black American vocal group singing spirituals, calypso, and folk songs. It was a curious program.

The next day, Wednesday, June 8, the band flew from Cairo to Athens to Rome to New York, arriving at 4 p.m. It spent June 9 and 10 in the recording studio, completing the *Sonny Boy* album of Jolson songs, which is now almost forgotten. Bill Byrne said, "It's too bad that band was never recorded in another album besides the vocal album."

"That band was burning," Marvin Stamm said. "That was really a good band."

There were some personnel changes. Carl Fontana and several others left and were replaced. When Woody asked Frank Foster, veteran of the Basie band and an old friend, if he could suggest a pianist to replace Nat Pierce, Foster recommended someone with whom he had worked briefly earlier that year, Kenny Ascher.

Ascher, one of many pianists inspired by Bill Evans, was born in Atlanta, Georgia, October 26, 1944. After he completed his undergraduate work in composition at Columbia University, he went home to Atlanta for the summer, planning to return to Columbia in the fall to work on his master's. (He would eventually get his doctorate there.)

Kenny, then twenty-two, had seen the Herman band when he was six years old in a basement nightclub in Chicago—probably the Blue Note— to which he had been taken by his father. He was electrified by it and grew up on its records. Abe Turchen telephoned him in Atlanta, told him of the pending busy itinerary, including a number of dates with singer Tony Bennett, and said that if he wanted the job, based on Frank Foster's recommendation it was his.

Ascher would play with the band that summer, in January of the following year for three weeks on a European tour, and in the summer of '67, three short periods. The experience is burned into his memory. Twenty-eight years later, he is a successful composer in several fields and a prominent songwriter—*You and Me Against the World*, *The Rainbow Connection*, and all the songs of *The Muppet Movie*, written with lyricist Paul Williams, are his. Kenny said: "This was a dream for me. I was playing with Woody Herman's band! I had loved the band so much. And I was going to San Francisco and Las Vegas for the first time in my life, all sorts of places I had never seen. My first night on the band was Marvin Stamm's last night. Ronnie Zito, too, had left after the African tour. I remember playing Basin Street in New York. Bill Byrne was extremely helpful, as was everybody.

"Bill Byrne is one of those people who has an integrity about him that is wonderful. I'm sure that's why he and Woody got along and why Woody trusted him to actually run that band on the road."

Woody said, "Well, he's probably the best road manager that was ever put together on this earth." He praised Byrne for infallibility in handling the payroll, arranging transportation, making reservations, and getting the band to its destinations on time. "Unbelievable," Woody said of him. "He's a very complete kind of human being . . . an impartial, selfless man."

As he did so many others, Woody encouraged Kenny Ascher to write, and by the end of the summer, Ascher had written four charts for the band, including an original he called *These Blues Were Made for Cooking*. It was eventually recorded on a Verve album, retitled *Woody's Bugaloo*. Kenny said, "It's in the album recorded in Monterey that has Bill Holman's *Con-*

certo for Herd in it. I was thrilled. That may have been my first recording of anything, ever.

"Woody was very, very kind to me, and wanted me to write. I remember how Woody would talk to me after a gig. He'd buy me a beer or we'd have a meal together. After I left the band, I ran into him in a restaurant called the Tower of Pisa in Las Vegas. He said, 'No, no, don't sit alone. I'm alone too.'"

With Ascher aboard, the band left New York. June 13 through 18, it backed Tony Bennett at a theater-in-the-round in Connecticut. On June 18 and 19, it played the Pampa Lanes in Detroit.

"In Detroit," Bill Byrne said, "Woody always headed right after the gig for the Lindell Athletic Club, about two blocks from Tiger Stadium. Musicians and athletes used to hang out there."[6] The club, founded in 1949 and one of the oldest sports bars in America, was owned by Jimmy and Johnny Butsicaris, more of Woody's friends. Woody had an accident at the Lindell A.C., as it is called in Detroit, that would eventuate in one of the most important friendships of his life, that with Dr. Stanley Levy.

Among the many athletes who frequented the Lindell was Detroit Tigers baseball star Dick Wakefield. While he was at the Lindell, Woody was stricken by a severe pain in the chest. Wakefield called Dr. Levy.

Levy was born on July 10, 1926, in Pittsburgh. He had played piano in his high school band, and he assuredly had heard of Woody Herman. Wakefield told Dr. Levy of his friend's condition. The physician told him to bring Woody to his office.

"I remember that it was a Thursday evening," Dr. Levy said. "Dick Wakefield brought him to my office. He brought Woody in the back door. Woody had his fist clenched to his chest. That usually means a coronary. I got him an EKG while I tried to take care of some other patients. They brought the EKG back, and it was OK. Woody said, 'I know what it is. There's food stuck in there.' I gave him a barium swallow and took a look with a fluoroscopic device, and he was right, there was something in there.

"I called my friend Stu Purcell, who is one of the great thoracic surgeons, and took Woody over to Sinai Hospital. That night we pulled out a piece of chicken, about as big around as a quarter. It was almost a ball, and his esophagus had spasmed. It had been there since the previous evening.

"He said that he had had these spasms in the past, and that it related to his emotional state and maybe getting upset when he was eating. Maybe it was an occupational hazard. I never did find out what triggered him off at that time. He alluded to it. Somebody came up and interrupted his dinner.

"We got the esophagus cleared, and the next day we were concerned as to why this had occurred. Did he have some intrinsic disease that could cause it? We wanted to do an upper GI. We kept him overnight. Of course he hadn't eaten. He was pretty dry and we got some intravenous food into him. The next day we did an upper GI. There was no tumor mass or anything of that nature obstructing him. That was Friday.

"That Thursday night the band was supposed to play in Midland, Michigan. The band went without him. Friday night, they were supposed to play in Chicago, I believe at the Aragon Ballroom. Woody got Count Basie to sit in for him."

On Saturday morning, Levy went to the hospital to discharge his new patient, only to find Woody had another problem: acute gout.

Levy said, "We'll have to keep you here."

Woody said, "No, no no. Just give me colchicine and I'll be out of here in fifteen minutes."

Levy protested: "You can't do that. It takes a while to be effective."

Woody said, "No no! You give it to me by injection."

"What are you talking about?" Levy said. "Nobody ever gives colchicine by injection."

Woody told him about the incident in the Congo, when a Belgian doctor had injected the drug. Woody said that fifteen minutes later, he'd been well enough to give a performance before a crowd of perhaps thirty thousand.

"Get me a shot of colchicine," he insisted. Levy gave him a bemused stare. He was then a young professor at the Wayne State University medical school, and he'd never heard of injecting colchicine. But to humor Woody, he looked it up in a book and found that, sure enough, colchicine in ampules was available. The doctor ordered it and gave Woody his injection. Fifteen or twenty minutes later, Woody left the hospital.

"So that was my first encounter with Woody Herman," Levy said.

The first of many. Stanley Levy would be Woody's physician, and close friend, for the rest of his life. Two weeks or so later, Woody called him to thank him and tell him that he was doing fine.

The band played Cincinnati, then the Miami Boat Club, which it did every year, and then two days with Tony Bennett at McCormick Place in Chicago. It accompanied Bennett again at a music tent in Warwick, Rhode Island, from June 20 through July 2. On July 3, it played from two to four in the afternoon at the Newport Jazz Festival. Zoot Sims, Stan Getz, Al Cohn, and Gerry Mulligan joined the band, with Buddy Rich on drums.

Bill Byrne said, "The next day, the Fourth of July, through the 10th, we were at a music theater in Framingham, Massachusetts, with Tony Bennett again. On the 11th we were in Rochester, New York, and on the 12th we were at the Palais Royale in Toronto for one night."[7]

23

Trouble in Mind

Toronto was always a good town for Woody. He had many friends there among critics and newspaper columnists, including Alex Barris and Helen McNamara. A particularly close friend was the late disc jockey Phil MacKellar, who had once sat in with the band on drums for a set or so and never ceased to reminisce about it. For the most part, the reception was warm, the reviews good. The exception was one written by Patrick Scott, printed in the *Globe and Mail*.

Scott was despised by jazz musicians. He hated all modern jazz, and at times it seemed he simply hated musicians.

This is Kenny Ascher's recollection of the Palais Royale engagement:

"It was such a good band! It was a poppin' band, a crackling band. The brass was sizzling. Sal Nistico and Bill Chase were still with us. What a band."

And this is part of the Patrick Scott review:

It would be nice to be able to report that the near-capacity crowd cavorting to the sounds of Woody Herman and his Sixth Rate Herd at the Palais Royale last night signified something positive, but I'm afraid all it really proved is that P. T. Barnum was right.

It also demonstrated, for anyone still naive enough to wonder if the big bands will ever come back, not only why they won't but what killed them in the first place.

This is not the worst big band I have ever heard live—Stan Kenton retains that distinction—but it comes closest to being the most difficult to dance to, which, after all, is what big bands were made for.

Admittedly, my main reason for going to hear it (besides the fact that I should have my head read) was not to dance but to investigate a suspicion I have long held that the Woody Herman band no longer exists except as a figment of Phil MacKellar's imagination. And I'm still not sure.

MacKellar himself was there, of course—all but leading the band and even holding the microphone for soloists who should not have been allowed within 10 feet of one—but I still am not convinced that Woody Herman, though I have never been his most ardent admirer, could stand there, in public, in front of a band so bad. But there was somebody up there who looked like him, and this is what made it so sad.

It's pathetic, really, to think that a 53-year-old man, who has been a bigtime bandleader for 30 years (and never led a worse one than the motley crew he has now), can't find a more honorable and respectable way to make a living at this late date.[1]

Evidently not all those who attended the performance found the music undanceable. A *Toronto Star* reporter described the audience:

Lead trumpeter Bill Chase sends a torrent of notes screaming to the slatted roof of the old barn. A middle-aged hipster near me, brown suit, gray-haired, and slightly jowly, helps the notes up with a pow of the arm. 'Wow!' he breathes.

At the back, about fifty couples are dancing on the easy hardwood floor. One lady, svelte, thirty-ish, jives through a number with the nonchalant precision of a ball bearing. Another couple frugs to the beat, and it goes, all right, but it doesn't seem to fit. And a third couple, who do the twist—THE TWIST!—are nowhere, neither from the '40s nor the mid-50s.

The Palais Royale is very definitely of the '40s. It stands, an old wooden hulk, oozing sounds . . . .

Woody told the reporter that he had never been busier, "on the move for fifty weeks a year . . . . In the past five years, we have been more active, recorded more, our records have sold better than they had for a long time."

A *Toronto Telegram* reporter wrote that same day: "When Woody Herman says he'll keep playing as long as he keeps standing, you believe him."

The prediction would prove more accurate than the reporter, Sheri Craig, could have imagined. She continued:

The man, at fifty-three one of the last of the big band leaders, is vital, all suntanned and smiling, ready to pick up tomorrow and travel to Tibet if there's a good booking . . . . The next Herman tour is already scheduled. Woody will be leaving for a four-week European jaunt in January.

Woody played the Palais Royale Ballroom last night. Today he's up in Muskoka for a one-night stand at the Bigwin Inn.

From Muskoka, Woody turns his new sports car—"with a 427-cubic-inch engine and straight pipes it develops 460 horsepower and that's a whole lot; you can quote me"—back home to Hollywood. He drives the car all over the country.[2]

Woody told the reporter: "When I was younger I used to think that at some point I'd want to quit and enjoy a life of ease. But I'm too old to change now.

"I'm not alone though. A lot of the young guys in the band talk about a better goal, staying put and not traveling all the time.

"Some of them manage to get out but I've had others in and out (of the band) five times or more. They keep on running home to settle down and first thing I know they're back again."

It was whistling in the dark. The Internal Revenue Service would never let him have peace or rest until he found it in a coffin.

▼   ▼   ▼

"I didn't think Abe Turchen's yen for gambling would get in the way," Woody said. "But there were plenty of clues if I had been more attentive." During one of the European tours, Woody had received a call from Abe, saying they would have to sell Charling Music, Woody's publishing company. Woody said, "Forget it. Charling is my legacy to Charlotte and Ingrid." The company's name was derived from the two names.

But Abe had power of attorney as Woody's business manager, and he sold the company without Woody's knowledge or consent.

"In the mid-sixties," Woody said, "I had fallen into a stranglehold from which I would never recover."[3]

In 1980, Woody told a *JazzTimes* interviewer:

"When you're out on the road, there's enough to do just making the dates and taking care of business. You can't worry about all the other things. You just can't do it all. You have to trust that people are taking care of the financial end of things.

"I never had an inkling that anything was wrong until guys in black suits and white-on-white shirts started showing up in some unlikely places and saying, 'Get up the money; we're getting tired of waiting.' "

Then the Internal Revenue Service sent Woody a letter ordering him to appear in person in its office. He arrived with Abe, and learned that not only had his own income taxes for 1964 through 1966 gone unpaid, but the withholding taxes on the musicians' salaries had not been paid. He was handed a tax bill for $750,000. With interest and penalties, the amount was $1.6 million.

"I sat there stunned," he told Stuart Troup.

"I never believed their figures. All the years in which we had big grosses—not big profits—we paid taxes to the hilt. Here I was down and out in the sixties, and the IRS was basing its estimate of my debt on years when our revenues had been high."

To this day, a measure of mystery infuses the story of Woody's ordeal with the IRS. Woody was the oddest mixture of shrewd perception and pure naïveté. He could be almost cunningly observant of people. There are those who think he was aware that Abe had siphoned off the tax money. I don't. What Woody was guilty of was not paying attention. The legacy of Tom Gerun's what-the-hell attitude was catching up with him at last.

"I never went into a state of shock over it," Woody told Stuart Troup. "I was depressed for a moment or two, but I knew that I had to get back to the business of music in order to take care of it as best I could. We worked out an arrangement to pay the government a thousand dollars a week through whoever was booking us. But we couldn't always afford it; we had to renegotiate.

"My lawyers worked hard to help get me off the hook somehow. I saw what the government had done to Joe Louis, forcing him to wind up as a handshaking shill for a Las Vegas hotel. I would have preferred going to jail than to finish like that. But I never considered imprisonment as a threat. I always figured the IRS would have less to gain with me behind bars."

In 1966, Abe and Woody had hired a young attorney, fresh out of law school, named Mayer Kanter. Like Abe, he was from Sioux City, Iowa. His mother and Abe's father were sister and brother. Kanter, now a prominent lawyer in Sioux City, said in September, 1994: "I worked for Woody in '66 and '67. Things were already going to hell. Business was bad. You'd get twenty-five hundred dollars for a Saturday night in New York City and the next night you'd be playing an Elks Club somewhere in Iowa for eight hundred dollars.

"I thought I could help, but things were too far gone. I hadn't realized how bad they were."

Abe by now was divorced from Cindy and living alone at the Park Sheraton Hotel, a block south of the office.

"I was up there on a Saturday afternoon in the fall," Mayer Kanter said. "Abe played the football games. The games were over and we were listening to the scoreboard on television. He'd bet about thirty games. Every single game. He had the sheet in front of him with the point spreads. He lost on Notre Dame, he lost on Michigan, he lost on Wisconsin. He lost on every game. There were about twenty-nine games in a row where he was a loser. And they gave the score for North Carolina State or something, and they'd won, and he said, 'What'd I tell you about that North Carolina State? I told you they'd win.'

"I always thought that would have made a great epitaph for Abe.

"That's where the money went."[4]

"For some unearthly reason," Woody told Stuart Troup, "I kept Abe on the job. But by August, 1968, I couldn't take any more."[5]

The IRS was by no means the only creditor. Debts were scattered everywhere, among them bills for the band bus. Someone was always appearing with a writ to seize something, in one case Woody's alto, and even the money for musicians' salaries, to satisfy some unpaid bill. At one point the bus company seized the music and, remarkably, the band played the book from memory until it was returned.

The incident that finally ended the relationship with Abe took place in Newport, Rhode Island. Two sheriff's deputies came to Woody in his hotel room with a warrant for his arrest over an unpaid debt to the bus company. Both officers were apologetic, since they were fans who planned to attend that night's concert. Desperate, Woody telephoned Hermie Dressel, an old friend who at that moment happened to be hanging out with the band. Hermie somehow resolved the immediate problem and in late summer of 1968 took over as the band's manager.

Woody had known Hermie since the latter had been in high school, in New Britain, Connecticut, playing in the school band with Conrad Gozzo, who would later play lead trumpet for Woody. Hermie's parents would take him to see the Herman band. Hermie had once owned a music store in Connecticut, worked as a promotion man and salesman for several record companies, and done promotion work for an artists' management agency.

Hermie would remain Woody's manager for seventeen years. He once said that he worked for the first year without pay: there was no money to get. He borrowed $20,000 from Joe Glaser, famous in the jazz world as Louis Armstrong's manager and president of Associated Booking Corporation, which was now the band's booker, to satisfy a debt in Las Vegas: Abe had signed Woody's name to a bad check.

For years Hermie had been one of the men dropping by Woody's New

York office, where he and I became good friends. We spent a great deal of time together, and we would shake our heads at the sheer sloppiness of the operation. But we were fond of Abe, as just about everyone was, and certainly did not foresee the disaster ahead.

But Hermie was not the hustler Abe was, and Woody told Stuart Troup that the reason he took on Hermie was, very simply, that no one else would take the job. Norman Granz had already declined it.

One of the brighter moments of 1968 was receipt of a Grammy award from the National Academy of Recording Arts and Sciences for an album made for the Verve label at the Monterey Jazz Festival in the fall of 1967. The work was Bill Holman's suite *Concerto for Herd*, which is widely considered to be a masterpiece marred by poor recording. It would be interesting to see what modern recording techniques could do to improve it.

Another Holman composition in that album is *The Horn of the Fish*, notable not only for Holman's predictably beautiful writing but for the fact that it is probably the first recorded example of Woody playing soprano saxophone. For a long time, the instrument was little used in jazz, except by Sidney Bechet and, to a lesser extent, Johnny Hodges. The instrument presented serious intonation problems, but manufacturers had improved the horn considerably.

John Coltrane was the proximate cause of Woody's taking up the instrument. "Coltrane was in New York, and I decided I would listen to what he was doing," he said. "I had heard some of his recordings, and I was aware of what he was into, and I also knew something about his background. We had done a couple of tours together. I knew that this man was stating a very important, beautiful case, and I wanted to become more aware of what he was doing. We were at the Metropole, and I went around the corner to Birdland, in the last era of Birdland. Coltrane did his performance of *My Favorite Things*. And he did his usual fifteen-minute version. He was one of the few people who could hold an audience for that length of time and just state his thoughts.

"I became terribly impressed, impressed enough to remember that as a boy I had once tried to play the soprano saxophone. I was about twelve, and I had a small curved one. I was willing, after witnessing his performance, to try it again . . . . I sent to an instrument company in Kenosha, Wisconsin, and they sent me one, a student model Leblanc. I still own it.

"I think I was one of the first people to really want to take a shot at it, like, the people of my ilk, at least . . . . John and I had some very meaningful talks on occasion that never lasted long. But he could never understand why I did what I did and I guess I stated the same case as far as he was concerned. I said that we had complete recognition and complete under-standing and complete belief in each other. We had a great deal of admiration and respect for each other.

"And it seemed to me best if I tried [the soprano]. It was almost sort of a different kind of challenge. I didn't want to prove anything, not at all. I knew I never could play [it] like John or anyone else played it. But maybe I could do some noises that somebody else hadn't done. And, after all, that's been my way of life."6

Woody quickly became skillful on the instrument. He had a distinct personality on soprano. He played clarinet, alto, and soprano in three different manners, and some of his most beautiful playing was on that soprano.

Willard Alexander was then booking the band but, according to Woody, had no faith in it, giving his best attention to those bands he did believe in, including Count Basie and the Glenn Miller ghost band.

Woody had twenty-two years of life ahead of him. He would never know a day of it free of worry and the harassment of the IRS. Sometimes IRS agents would show up where the band was playing and demand the money it had just earned.

By now Woody's father was in a nursing home, with Ray Sherman looking out for him and paying the bills from money Woody sent. While Woody was visiting Jack Siefert, he made a call to his father. A nurse told him, "I'm sorry, we can't rouse your father. He doesn't know who you are."

Siefert recalled that Woody had tears in his eyes as he put down the telephone.

"Dad didn't know who I was," Woody said. Then he put his arm around Siefert, who was trying to comfort him, and said, "Jack, the important thing is that I knew who he was."

Aged eighty-two, Woody's father died September 20, 1969, while the band was playing an engagement at Notre Dame University and seventeen days after Ingrid's twenty-eighth birthday.

"I lived in San Francisco from '62 until '71, when we moved to Nashville," Ingrid said. "Our group was like the first bluegrass band out there in San Francisco. We played the Fillmore, opening for somebody. We played at a San Francisco State folk festival with Merle Travis on the bill.

"We had met Lester Flatt's band when they were playing the hungry i. They were entranced with us because they had never met any hippies. And they were sure they were going to get some hippie girls if they just came with us. We took them home, we got to be friendly with them. It was like they had gone home with the Sherpas. We were the most exotic thing they had ever seen. We blew them away because we knew their repertoire. We knew every note. We had been struggling over these songs. And now to have them sitting in our living room! I can't tell you.

"They came to our house about five nights. Later on we had a chance to do a record. We were so popular in San Francisco, they were sure that if they got a record, somebody would snap us up. They should have researched it. Nobody was going to snap it up. We were just doing the most traditional stuff. There was no real market for us. They flew two of the group back from Nashville to play on our record, which was an incredible honor. We spent a lot of time with them.

"That was incredible.

"But the record never got released."

She and her husband, Bob Fowler, were living in Mill Valley, a beautiful hilly community in Marin County. Woody's grandson, Tommy Littlefield, was now ten.

Ingrid said, "Tommy started smoking pot when he was ten or eleven, with friends who were the kids of doctors, lawyers. It was a very wealthy neighborhood and his schoolmates were wealthy kids, and they were doing all manner of dope."

There would be consequences.

▼ ▼ ▼

A number of musicians found the use of rock hits diluted the band, and some of them told Woody so. But Woody stuck to his rationalization that this material was necessary if the band was to reach a younger audience. "We have to play things they know if we're going to bring some music to them," he said at the time. "It wasn't possible to do this four, five years ago, because the tunes were so bad. But they've improved enormously, and now you can find some good things. You can't ignore the young." He was wrong: the material just wasn't good enough.

But I quoted him in my *High Fidelity* magazine column in September, 1969, the month his father died. This constituted a serious change of direction. After years of denouncing rock and roll and much pop music, Woody from this time on would incorporate much of it in the repertoire.

He was about to begin recording for the Fantasy label in San Francisco, and that would be his label through much of the 1970s. He would mix rock pieces with solid jazz compositions. I discussed this body of work with Ralph Kaffel, the president of Fantasy, the only truly independent large major jazz label in America. Its catalogue is distinguished. I asked Ralph if he planned a "complete" Woody Herman reissue. He said that he didn't think that all of the material was good. And he was right. The "pop" material didn't sound good then, and it sounds bad now, very dated. But there were superb tracks from that period, including such pieces as *Naima* and *Giant Steps*, both John Coltrane compositions, and *La Fiesta* and *Spain* by Chick Corea. Alan Broadbent, who joined the band in 1969, wrote pop and jazz pieces for it.

Born in Auckland, New Zealand, on April 23, 1947, Broadbent was a pianist influenced by Lennie Tristano, with whom he studied, and by Bud Powell and Bill Evans. He had graduated with honors from the Royal Trinity College of Music in Auckland in 1962 and then received a scholarship to study at Berklee, where he stayed from 1966 to '69, when he joined Woody as pianist and arranger. He was then twenty-two.

"When I arrived on the band," Alan said, "we played at an army base in Greensboro, North Carolina. That was my first gig. I was just appalled. The drummer was turning the time around. Some of the soloists were very weak. I remember Steve Lederer, who played second tenor for Woody for a very long time, introduced himself. He said, 'Hey, I'm Steve. You've heard of the Thundering Herd? Well this is the worst you ever heard.' I wondered to myself what I'd gotten into.

"But over the course of a few months, I gravitated toward some of the good players and made friends with some of the other writers. The Blood, Sweat, and Tears things were the vogue at the time. There was a good chance for us to get Woody's interest with material like that, because we'd do proms and things. The first chart that I submitted to Woody was just a copy of a Blood, Sweat, and Tears tune called *Smiling Phases*. I did that. Tony Klatka did *Proud Mary* and some other things. We talked Woody into trying them out without a rehearsal at a prom one night. And the kids just went wild. Woody's eyebrows went up and he seemed to think 'There's something going on here,' and he had us do some other things in that vein.

"And then one night in Vegas, he asked me why didn't we try to do that on the old hit he had on *Blues in the Night*." The resultant work is a four-movement suite based on the piece. But it strains the coloristic resources of a jazz band, and Broadbent refers to it today as one of his "kitchen-sink" pieces of the period, "because every style I could think of was in there. A big conglomeration of things." The work seems very overblown when heard from a perspective of twenty-five years.

About that time Alan also composed an original piece for the band, *Variations on a Scene*. Broadbent was influential, along with some of the other young members of the band, in an area other than repertoire: per-

sonnel. Alan persuaded Woody that he should hire certain musicians he
had known at Berklee, and Tony Klatka recommended people from North
Texas State, such as trumpeter Bill Stapleton. "We always had a pretty
good sax section, thanks to Frank Tiberi's professionalism," Alan said.

In March, 1971, Woody devoted almost an entire album to Broadbent.
Titled *Woody Herman Brand New*, the album comprises nine tracks. Broadbent plays piano (mostly electric) on all of them. He composed four of the
pieces and arranged five. Nat Pierce arranged two, including the Avery
Parrish piece originally recorded by Erskine Hawkins, *After Hours*. Trumpeter Tony Klatka arranged one, *Proud Mary*. But it isn't Broadbent's album. It's Ralph J. Gleason's album.

Gleason was by now a vice president of Fantasy. Gleason, who had
become enthusiastic about developments in the rock and roll field, wrote
in the liner notes that he suggested that Woody record with guitarist Mike
Bloomfield. The result is ghastly. Bloomfield plays simplistic music with
wanton glissandi and that B.B. King-like exaggeratedly fast vibrato that
had become a fad, along with the ugliness of deliberate distortion. He is
completely out of place in a big-band context. He is heard on four tracks,
and they are uniformly awful. Woody is equally out of place singing "Rollin', rollin, rollin' on the river," in *Proud Mary*. Only two tracks of the album
come off, both of them compositions by Broadbent: *Love in Silent Amber*,
a ballad that makes lovely use of the trombone of Bob Burgess and Woody's
chalumeau-register clarinet, and a blues titled *Adam's Apple*, the only track
of the album that actually swings. That album, to my mind, is the nadir of
Woody's recording career, a compromise for the sake of seeking audience
that completely demeans the man and the music.

Broadbent stayed with the band a little less than three years, leaving in
April, 1972.

▼   ▼   ▼

Often in the summers at that period, Woody would take his grandson on
the road with him.

"I started going with him when I was eleven or twelve," Tommy told me.
"We would travel to the dates in the car. I sang with him, and when I was
about fifteen, I'd go out and be a band boy.

"When I traveled with him the first couple of summers, I would get to
stay with him in his hotels. When I was a band boy, I was a paid employee,
and I stayed in the band hotels."

"I hated singing with the band. I thought it was expected of me. It was traumatic, and yet it was fun."[7]

In August, 1972, the band played a two-week engagement at the St. Regis Roof in New York. The event was notable for Tommy's debut at the age of twelve as a band singer. The *New York Daily News* carried a photo of him with long fair hair. The paper's reporter, Patricia O'Haire, wrote:

> Young Tommy, who sings a few numbers with his grandfather, is lively, bright and disarming. He stands up there like an old pro, disdaining frills and overar-rangements. He just sings, and he does it well. He and his grandfather have something in common. They're both easy listening.

Ingrid allowed Tommy to travel with the band. "My dad gave him lessons in life," she said. "He's still using them."

Though Broadbent had left the band, Woody continued to champion his writing. In the album *Giant Steps*, recorded on April 9, 11, and 12, 1973, in New York, an exceptional album based on material by such authentic jazz composers as Thad Jones, Chick Corea, and John Coltrane, he recorded Broadbent's *Bebop and Roses*. In the *Thundering Herd* album, he recorded Broadbent's arrangement of film composer Fred Karlin's *Come Saturday Morning*.

On September 29, 1972, just after the St. Regis engagement, the band and the Dallas Symphony Orchestra gave the premier performances of two Broadbent works, *Variations on a Scene* and *Children of Lima*. Two years later, after a long concert tour accompanying Frank Sinatra, Woody and the band spent three days performing the two Broadbent pieces with the Houston Symphony. They spent a fourth day recording it.

Variations on a Scene is indeed a kitchen-sink piece, with rock rhythms churning away without swinging and a full symphony orchestra trying to match the sheer power of a big jazz band. The piece proved yet again how poorly the two types of orchestra mix. The piece, which lasts a little over eighteen minutes, seems inflated and dated. That side of the album is filled out by the modest *Children of Lima*, which shows the gentle and lyrical and much more typical side of Broadbent. It hints at the superb writing to come from him in later years.

The second side of the album uses only the band. All of the arranging is Broadbent's, including that on one of his own pieces, *Far In!*, and it is of a very high order. Broadbent has mixed feelings about his time with Woody. He speaks of his own pop arrangements and, apparently, some of the "bigger" pieces, with something less than enthusiasm: "I wish they would die and go away and just my jazz pieces would stay." And of big bands generally: "Big bands are what they are. They're very limited in terms of sonic scope and the music they play. I'm not into that any more."

But the sojourn with Woody had done for him what it did for so many others: it made him known in the jazz world, and he has since emerged not only as a magnificent arranger and composer but as one of the finest of the post-Bill Evans jazz pianists.

▼　▼　▼

Booked by the English promoter Harold Davison, the band did a tour of England with an almost entirely new personnel. Tours of the United States continued. When he could, Woody, still drove to his engagements. One of the reasons he traveled alone, he told me, is that he was feeling the growing difference of age between himself and "my young men," as he called them. Never caught in the past, Woody always wanted to push forward; but, ironically, the younger musicians always wanted to know about the past, which he was disinclined to talk about. Yet on those occasions when he did travel on the band bus, he would dip into his case of Heineken's, sitting forward near the driver, sipping on a bottle, and telling stories of the business. His young, idolatrous employees loved it.

Woody said, "You wind up a combination of Mother Superior and Father Confessor, and a bum psychiatrist, and you try to help people on occasions with their problems. And of course what makes it such a kind of a helpless thing is that 90 percent of the time the kids will listen very intently and then turn around and do what they planned to do anyway. And your advice was just a lot of wasted words and breath. But that's the way it has to be. That's the way youth is, and you learn to accept this too and you still go through the same bits.

"[Traveling by bus] is like an insane bad family, like killers! Maybe I am more extreme about this than other people, but I can't stand it. This to me is like being in stir, to have to live together on a bus. Because musicians spend too much time [together] as it is, and then to travel all together with those bad moods, like stopping for a sandwich and it takes three hours because there are twenty-some-odd people."[8]

And so he drove, alone or, sometimes, with Charlotte or Bill Chase in the passenger seat of his green Corvette.

Woody played the Palais Royale in Toronto again at the end of August, 1967, the press was beginning to sense something. A *Globe and Mail* reporter wrote: "Woody Herman, billed at the age of nine as the boy wonder of the clarinet, is plainly no longer a boy. And the wonder that remains is that, at fifty-four, Woody is still going through the grueling business of one-night stands."

Phil MacKellar caught the new mood in a story published in the *Toronto Star* on August 26. MacKellar almost certainly knew of Woody's financial problems and the harassments of the IRS. The headline on his story read:

OLD WOODY JUST KEEPS PLUGGING ON

The story, which is an interestingly dark one—and Phil had a very dark side to his character—concludes:

Woody Herman cannot exist without a band, and the band cannot exist without constant traveling. If you come down to the Palais Royale next Wednesday night to help celebrate thirty-one years of bandleading, you will have driven perhaps ten or fifteen miles. Woody Herman will have driven seven hundred from New York—and will be planning the next night's drive of three hundred.

Check in and sleep for a while, get up and play for four hours, and then jump back into the car for another. That's life for Woody Herman.

24

Abe's Odyssey

By 1970, all the great touring dance-cum-jazz bands were gone, with four conspicuous exceptions: Woody Herman, Count Basie, Duke Ellington, and Stan Kenton. In southern California, Woody's friend Les Brown kept his excellent band going on a more-or-less part-time basis, but it did not travel much, and Harry James continued to work in Las Vegas. Audiences in the East or abroad rarely if ever saw the James or Brown bands. And Benny Goodman would now and then assemble a band of old pros for short tours.

The big-band era had been over for about twenty-five years, dating from that December when Woody and so many others disbanded. It had lasted just over ten years, from the breakout of the Goodman band in 1935, to 1946; more if you date it from the 1920s to its demise about 1950.

But the rock-and-roll era, beginning with the rise of Bill Haley and the Comets in the early 1950s, was already showing signs of far greater longevity. Big-band jazz, Woody used to say, had been the popular music of America. It no longer was. Rock music was.

There had of course always been bad popular music. In the era of Jerome Kern and George Gershwin, Cole Porter and Harry Warren, when much good music was popular and much popular music was good, there were trivial little novelty songs such as *The Hut Sut Song* and *Three Little Fishes*, but no one took them seriously, no one wrote unctuous paeans of critical praise to insignificant songs proclaiming them high art, and in the rock era this had been happening for some years now. In the 1930s and

1940s, the bands could draw on this pool of superb and sophisticated popular songs and get hit records, as in the examples of Artie Shaw's *Begin the Beguine*, a magnificent Cole Porter song with an unconventional 108-bar structure, or Woody's hit with singer Frances Wayne on Harold Arlen's *Happiness Is a Thing Called Joe*. Thus in the big-band era, the bands were in a symbiotic relationship with the best popular music, brought by the likes of Porter, Arlen, Arthur Schwartz, and Hoagy Carmichael, to the level of high art, and network radio, which disseminated it to all of North America.

In the 1970s, Woody seemed puzzled in his search for a constituency; hence the kind of hybrid albums he made for Fantasy. So at times did Basie, who had recorded an album of songs by the Beatles, arranged by Chico O'Farrill. But Chico said he'd had to examine about a hundred and fifty of their songs to find ten with a sufficient melodic and harmonic value to be suitable for the Basie band. The pop music of the new era just didn't have the quality of that of the 1930s and '40s.

When musicians climbed off the band buses for the last time as the old era ended, they formed themselves into small groups and played in nightclubs. And in many cases they found highly lucrative work in the recording studios of New York, Chicago, and Los Angeles, backing singers in pop-music recordings of high quality, making jazz albums, playing on the sound-track scores of the movie industry, and making "jingles," the music of television and radio advertising. With earnings in six figures, many of them grew rich and, among those who invested it while they could, stayed that way.

"The studios" weren't as hospitable to black musicians as white, but nonetheless even many of the black players were in high demand for that work, among them Clark Terry, Hank Jones, and Snooky Young. And even those who earned their primary incomes in the studios yearned to play jazz and did so as an avocation, making records and playing in nightclubs.

The nightclubs, however, created a problem that no one at the time clearly saw. When the bands broke up and their veterans went into the clubs, their fans followed them: they were already famous. The musicians were preaching to the converted. But few converts were being made, since the natural new audience, the young, couldn't get into places where liquor was sold. And nightclubs made their money on liquor. Meanwhile, radio was playing less and less jazz and to the extent that it did, it was on specialized jazz stations that the young audience didn't listen to. Thus, as the years went on, the constituency for this music grew older.

The *lingua franca* of jazz was popular music, as we have noted. Jazz is essentially a theme and variations form, despite earnest attempts over the years to make it otherwise. For comfortable audience participation, the theme needs to be known. But the level of popular music was falling steadily. A study of *The Great Song Thesaurus*, which lists the most popular songs each year from 1226 (the estimated date of *Sumer Is Icumen In*) to the present reveals this inexorably, with the decline in quality accelerating in the first half of the 1950s.

It was useless for Woody or any other leaders, whether of small groups or big bands, to try to establish communication with the younger audience through such songs as *Happiness Is a Thing Called Joe* or *Laura*, both of which Woody recorded with the so-called First Herd. Indeed, from the time of the Four Brothers band on, he had rarely carried a girl singer. There was no point in playing the songs of Arlen or Gershwin to a young audience: they didn't know them. By the 1970s, he was wont to say that what the band was selling was "excitement." In interviews, he would even avoid the word "jazz."

Persuaded by the young members of his own band, he catered now to a generation raised on rock by playing music from that "repertoire." And to some extent it was working. Thus *Billboard* headlined in its March 26, 1969 issue:

HERMAN'S "FIRE" LIGHTS

WAY TO YOUNG MARKET

The story read:

> Los Angeles—Woody Herman's first album for Cadet, "Light My Fire," has introduced the veteran band leader to young people. As a result of air play and sales on the product after six weeks, the Herman "Thundering Herd" is now being paired with a number of pop vocalists for concerts slated to cover the summer period.
>
> These dates will help fill in the 48 weeks the band is on the road, and include eight days in New Jersey with Steve Lawrence and Eydie Gorme, one week with Johnny Mathis and 18 concerts with Dionne Warwick. The Warwick dates had been slated prior to the take-off of Herman's newest LP which seems to indicate that the jazz band can meld with contemporary arrangements.
>
> In fact a good portion of his nightclub act consists of recent hits from the pop charts. Herman gets his first major taste of playing for this young audience— which is just discovering his existence after 30 years in the business—when he plays Fillmore East May 29–31 and Fillmore West June 17–19.
>
> He has tried unsuccessfully in the past to bridge the jazz and pop cultures.

His two previous record affiliations were with Philips and Columbia, and his last disc click was "Encore 63" on Philips, released nearly six years ago.

Herman estimates that over 90 percent of today's kids have never heard a big band in a live performance. This opens a new market for the veteran musician and his 16 associates.

Domestically, 70 percent of the band's dates are for private parties, with colleges providing weekend employment. Herman remains a jazz leader but he tailors his music to the occasion, including industrial shows.

The story is revealing as much for what it doesn't say as what it does. Despite Woody's unflagging air of optimism, there is a certain desperation in the band's search for work. The dance pavilions are gone; the audience is aging and shrinking. One cannot help wondering, reflecting on those years, whether he would have retired had the IRS not been dogging him every step of his endless road.

Meanwhile, Abe Turchen was without money, ruined by his gambling addiction. For about a year he lived in the Park Sheraton Hotel. His name in the music business was now bad, and although he tried to get various things going, nothing came to fruition. There is something ironic about this. The moral climate of America was changing rapidly, and public disgrace, even a prison sentence, would soon mean almost nothing. G. Gordon Liddy would command big fees to give lectures and would appear on television talk shows and even do guest roles as an actor in movies. Richard M. Nixon would rise from ruin to be considered an elder statesman, though among his accomplishments he was the architect of small burglaries. Fired from Columbia Records on grounds that he had misused company funds, Clive Davis would find himself surrounded with offers and go on to head his own record company. And David Begelman, fired from Columbia Pictures for a similar reason, would be given a slight sentence to public service and go on producing movies. As Ingrid put it, years later, "Abe was a talented and clever man. Had he lived a little longer, he might have become one of the junk-bond kings." It was said totally without malice.

During this period, Abe apparently spent a fair amount of time with Joe Glaser. Born in Chicago of a middle-class family, Glaser early manifested a taste for association with ominous people, including bootleggers, prostitutes, and members of the mob who controlled the South Side entertainment world. Though no one ever suggested that Glaser was himself a member of the underworld, he had associations with those who were. He was, as they say, connected. Glaser drifted into booking performers and eventually founded Associated Booking Corporation, which booked bands, sometimes including Woody's. He was Louis Armstrong's manager, the white man that many black performers thought—and not without reason— they had to have to protect them if they were to succeed in the business. Woody and Armstrong had toured together on occasion. But Glaser, who given his own associations and past would hardly have been distressed by Abe's recent problems, apparently could find nothing for him.

Drawing on his own memory and that of his late brother, Mike, Steve Turchen said:

"My father was trying to find scams. He was involved with a guy who had a bookstore. I think the guy was hustling stolen airplane tickets, although I never did hear the whole story. He also had a friend named Joey. God knows what his real name was, because he used several of them, depending on how hot the police were on his trail. He was a drug addict who used to be a collector for a bookie. The bookie died, but Joey still had his collection book. He collected a couple of hundred thousand and put it all in his arm in a space of six months.

"My father and Joey were good friends. Joey was probably the best shoplifter I ever met. He once took a cash register out of a store."

The robbing of trucks was a common practice. A member of the Teamsters Union would pull up a truck to a loading dock and allow it to be stripped. He would report that the truck had been hijacked. The trucking company would report this to the insurance company and collect for the missing merchandise, which by then was on sale at discount prices all over Manhattan: raincoats, sports jackets, portable radios, TV sets, Mixmasters, you name it. Lower-echelon hustlers would visit the bars and sell the stuff to the regulars. The Damon Runyon world was very real. Since the insurance companies recompensed the original owners of such merchandise, the participants in these operations philosophized, "This way no one gets hurt." According to Steve Turchen, one of these operations yielded a truckload of expensive calculators. One of them was sold to an accountant. When it broke down, the man sent it for repair to the manufacturer, where someone looked at the serial number and said, "Wait a minute, this machine is hot." The accountant took up the matter with the district attorney's office, and inquiries were instituted.

Getting wind of this, The Boys—as the underworld is generically known in New York—got nervous and hastened to unload the remaining calculators. They gave them to Abe, saying, "Just get rid of them, we don't care, keep the money."

Steve Turchen recalled: "There were a dozen or so calculators left. My dad loaded them into the car. He took me with him. I remember we drove through a horrendous snowstorm, following the taillights of the car ahead of us. We had no problem getting across the border into Canada. We drove them to Toronto and my dad sold them to a big businessman there.

"Maybe six months later, we flew to Toronto. This time we carried cameras, Hasselblads. He gave them to me to carry. I was maybe twelve. Who's going to look in a kid's camera bag? The cameras were stuffed with diamonds. They were going to the same guy. The diamonds he'd picked up from diamond brokers. I don't think they were hot. The cameras probably were, because they were from the same guys who got the calculators."[1]

Finally, all of his options in New York gone, Abe decided to go home to Sioux City, where he could at least book acts; his name there was still untainted, that of the local boy who had gone away and made good.

"I can imagine the drive home," Steve said. "He had a car full of cosmetics that he probably bought somewhere for a penny on the dollar. I can imagine him stopping at diners along the way, tipping waitresses with them or trading them for things. He was a lifelong briber. He could charm the pants off you.

"He got to Sioux City. He still had a pretty good reputation there. He started something called the Broadway Theater League and booked Ferrante and Teicher and 'Professor' Irwin Corey and a couple more acts into a big theater in Sioux City. The idea was that he would bring this major Broadway-Vegas talent out to the sticks, and the locals would turn out and buy all these tickets. I don't know what went wrong. My older brother, Michael, was involved with him part of the time, but Michael is dead and can't tell us."

Michael had grown up in Sioux City with Abe's parents. He died in 1981 of cancer at the age of forty-four.

"My father was gambling the whole time he was in Iowa," Steve said. "Probably twice a week, he would drive to Omaha, the Aksarben track, which is Nebraska spelled backwards.

"In the summer, which is the racing season, my two brothers and I were with him. It was a track where kids weren't allowed to sit in the stands, so I hated it. I hated sitting in this caged-off area with other kids whose parents were off gambling. So I'd sit in the car and read.

"Then he'd go to a place in Merrill, Iowa, which is close to Sioux City. It had a drugstore, a five-and-dime, and a pub, with farms all around it. He would go to that pub and play pinochle at the pub six and eight hours at a time. He'd take us along. I'd bring a book and I made friends with the barmaid there. I was twelve or thirteen years old, she was as bored as I was and would indulge me in my experiments of mixing up five different kinds of soft drinks.

"I don't think there was anything going on with bookies, but there was gambling, and I'm pretty sure he was losing. Pinochle is not the kind of game you can count in.

"I remember that once we drove to Chicago. There were trotters. I think there was a dog track. Anything you could bet on in the Midwest we probably visited.

"So he wasn't spending a lot of time on his business. But he would flash these tickets around, he'd give people tickets for things that were coming up. Something happened, and he left town in the middle of the night, leaving behind a lot of debts. He told his sister Bess in 1972 that he'd climbed to the top of a four-story building, planning on jumping. To hear him talk that way was unusual. I think he wasn't making that up for effect. My guess is that he'd simply spent all the proceeds from the sale of the tickets. So he left town. And I'm sure it left a lot of bad feelings."

Abe moved to California. He was arrested in Santa Barbara on a charge involving, it is believed now, stolen travelers checks, and sentenced to jail. He apparently spent a year in incarceration, but since his health was not good, most of it was in the Santa Barbara General Hospital. Steve got letters from him there marked CDU, which he was told at the time stood for Chronic Disease Unit but now believes meant Criminal Detention Unit. Whatever happened, Abe did some time that had nothing to do with Woody's tax situation or Abe's gambling losses. And it was probably not just for his diabetes that he was hospitalized. Steve said:

"That wouldn't be for his diabetes. Diabetes they handle in jails all the time. I deal with patients in jail a lot. They're always taking overdoses in jail."

Steve has a bachelor's degree in classics, another in toxicology. He is a certified toxicologist at the San Diego Regional Poison Center. He also works as a consultant and as an expert witness in court cases.

"But," Steve said, "my father had a very unusual skin disease called epidermolitis bullosa. It's genetically transmitted. It causes you to have malformed fingernails and some other symptoms.

"Because of that and because of his diabetes and because he probably had some chronic infection that he picked up in the Pacific, he was a very interesting medical case. And he was charming. He'd charm doctors and nurses. So he probably got in there for some acute illness and got them fascinated. And you can do a lot to shelter somebody you like in that situation. They could say, 'Oh we need him for teaching,' or 'We're doing research on this,' or 'He's too unstable to transfer back.' That's my guess. I think he was in jail for a couple of months before he got into the hospital."

When he got out, he went to live with his son Michael and Mike's wife Marty. Marty recalled that Abe lived with them for about three years, working with her and Mike, selling antique jewelry, turquoise and gold at swap meets for about eight years. She remembered him with affection, as so many persons did and do. And Michael's two half brothers, Steve and David, would come out to California from New York for the summers.[2]

"My brother and I were ostensibly just coming for the summer in 1972," Steve said. "I had been begging to come out for a long time. Mike barely knew me. So it was really pretty generous of him to invite us into his house. I spent the summer there and went back to New York for a day or two, and I really couldn't take it any more, and they agreed to let me come back."[3]

With his two other sons joining him, Abe left Mike's house for an apartment of his own.

As Steve Turchen grew up, he became more and more interested in his father's past. He said, "The big villain in this was the IRS. I don't think my father would have felt as badly as he did if the IRS had come to him and taken him apart instead of Woody.

"He deeply resented the way the IRS went about it. They came into the office without a warrant and seized a lot of papers. He felt they weren't playing by their rules.

"He never felt bad that they audited him and put a lien on his earnings, though he felt the amounts were excessive, they were ridiculous. But he felt bad about what they did to Woody. He felt that it was his job to take the heat.

"My father wouldn't talk about the details of the tax problem, beyond saying that what the IRS did to Woody was outrageous."

I told Steve that no one I knew of ever heard Woody say anything against Abe Turchen. Indeed, when one young musician, new to the band, made the mistake of making a crack about Abe, Woody tore a strip off him and said, "Abe Turchen was my friend."

Steve said, "And he didn't have anything bad to say about Woody. There was some sort of understanding between them that only they understood."

I asked Steve, "Do you know if your father ever saw Woody again?"

"No, I don't. I know that my older brother Mike and his wife saw Woody several times. They saw him when he played in San Diego and in Las Vegas."

No one seems to be able to answer that question.

I found myself puzzled by something else. It had taken me a long time to track down the Turchen family. I had heard of other researchers trying to learn about the late days of Abe Turchen and encountering a solid wall of silence from the Turchens of Sioux City. Why were they so forthcoming with me, particularly Mayer Kanter and Steve?

Steve answered: "Mayer and I both loved my dad. We had a conversation about it and we feel there's nobody the truth can hurt, and from what I've read of yours in the past, you feel the same way I do about my dad. A mass of contradictions but a lovable man.

"He could persuade himself of anything, as any good con man can. He believed every lie he told."

It is said of such people that they are not liars but are fantasists.

"He had the most difficult time with things that he couldn't persuade himself he could fix," Steve said.[4]

And he couldn't fix Woody's problems with the IRS.

<h1 style="text-align:center">25</h1>

The Road Gets Rougher . . .

 In its May 11, 1970, edition, *Time* magazine carried a story about Woody under the headline:

OUT THERE FOREVER

It quoted him as saying, "If I had to play the same music in a locked-in style that I played in the forties, I would have taken the gas pipe a long time ago." Woody had his own peculiar vocabulary, and "taking the pipe" was one of his expressions.

The *Time* story continued:

> What excites Herman these days, as it does almost everyone else, is rock . . . .
> Mixing updated versions of Old Herman specialties with ear-blowing arrange-
> ments of such contemporary tunes as the Doors' *Light My Fire* and Jim Webb's
> *MacArthur Park*, the latest Herd has a rare ability to bridge pop music's gener-
> ation gap. It is equally welcome at the hip Fillmore West and Manhattan's
> touristy Copacabana, where Woody and Songstress Dionne Warwick have just
> begun a joint two-week engagement.
>
> Herman finds contemporary rock more interesting than pop music a genera-
> tion ago: tunes are longer and more complex, rhythms more diverse.[1]

That of course is nonsense. Longer and more complex compared with what? *Begin the Beguine?* I think Woody was shining *Time*'s reporter on, showing the cheerful face.

A *Down Beat* story on Woody at about this time followed much the same

291
▼

theme. Written by Jim Szantor, a trained musician who had just become assistant editor of *Down Beat*, its tone borders on the idolatrous. Woody could bring that out in people. Szantor was one of at least three *Down Beat* editors, including Jack Tracy and me, whom Woody befriended. (Szantor later became managing editor of the magazine and is now a reporter at the *Chicago Tribune*.)

Szantor covered a Herman engagement at the Holiday Ballroom on Chicago's Northwest Side. He concludes his story by saying:

> Judging by the highly favorable reaction of the huge crowd (estimated at between 1,500 and 2,000) and the quality of the band's rejuvenated book, the Herd has taken on a promising new dimension and, by all indications, has attracted a whole new generation of listeners. Though the Herman story is already an illustrious chapter in the history of jazz, many open pages lie ahead, and the future never looked brighter.

The future in fact would prove dark. And the significant thing is the size of the crowd, which Szantor described as "huge." When I, as an adolescent, used to go to hear the band, the crowds were as much as six and seven thousand persons.

With so much of his money going to the IRS, Woody was not paying his men well. There had always been considerable turnover in the band's personnel—the life on the road is hard, and for those who could get it, work in the studios, as noted, was easier and lucrative—but now the economics were even more stringent. Curiously enough, this turnover contributed to one of Woody's major historical distinctions.

Personnel of the Ellington and Basie bands was comparatively stable, its players largely veterans. Although a great many musicians passed through the Kenton band, probably no band in history, no musical organization of any kind, in America or in Europe, had employed so many young and rising musicians as Woody's. The Herman band was the great finishing school of a new breed of jazz musicians: those who had graduated from colleges where jazz was now taught as a legitimate academic study, such as the Berklee School (later College) of Music, North Texas State University (now the University of North Texas), the Eastman School in Rochester, New York, and Rice University in Houston, Texas, among them. It was from these institutions that Woody drew much of his young personnel.

But Woody was not one of the founding figures of the movement. One of the most significant was the late Dr. Eugene Hall, who established the jazz program at North Texas State. But among the working bandleaders, the most important contributor to the movement was Stan Kenton, who had been putting his band and himself in residence on campuses to conduct clinics since the early 1960s.

Woody didn't like Stan. He didn't care for the Kenton band particularly, either, finding it overblown and bombastic, which, at times, it could be: Stan loved those gigantic blazing climaxes. Woody's best friends among bandleaders were Basie, Ellington, and Les Brown. I tried without success to melt Woody down on the subject. When I asked him why he didn't like Stan, he reminded me that Stan had once married a singer much younger than he. Not long after this, he said, he was dining with Stan, who said, "Woody, you should get yourself a younger wife. It makes you young again!"

Woody was horrified by this. Then Stan said, "Do you *love* Charlotte?"

Woody said, "Love? Love? When we were young, we *loved*, and we loved very deeply. Now we're getting old, and we *understand* each other."

Then Woody asked me a question. "Has Stan ever given you one of those wet sloppy kisses on the ear?"

Stan, indeed, was prone when he had consumed enough vodka to give his friends affectionate bearhugs and kisses of the kind Woody described.

"Yes," I said. "He has."

Woody said, "Isn't that *disgusting?!*"

Red Kelly's theory of the somewhat prickly relationship between Woody and Stan is this: "They didn't trust each other. Woody didn't trust anything that didn't swing; Stan didn't trust anything that did."

But Stan did more for the jazz education movement in the United States than any other professional musician. For that alone, he was a great man.

Woody didn't venture into jazz education until 1971, when the band conducted its first clinic at Northern Illinois University at DeKalb. Jim Szantor wrote:

> Seems to me that Woody has been somewhat involved in developing young talent during his bandleading career of some 35 years . . . . But so be it. If Woody's bands have been the off-campus places-to-be for aspiring jazzmen from the 1930s on, what better place for the Herd to be in 1971 than on the campus, where jazz majors are beginning to be status symbols (but hopefully much more) and where the likes of Cecil Taylor, Donald Byrd, and Archie Shepp have taken on professorial roles.

From then on, Woody would be involved in the jazz education movement. On the Fourth of July weekend, 1972, the Kenton and Herman bands would perform in New York's Philharmonic Hall as part of the Newport Jazz Festival. Woody drew together some of his alumni for the performances, reuniting Zoot Sims, Al Cohn, and Stan Getz to play on *Four Brothers*, and bringing out Flip Phillips, Chubby Jackson, and Red Norvo toward the end.

John S. Wilson of the *New York Times* was something less than enthralled by the concert, writing:

> As for the present Herman and Kenton groups . . . it was sometimes hard to tell which was which. Mr. Herman's Herd, which periodically loses track of its roots, showed little evidence of the raw fire and excitement of his great bands.
>
> Instead, this group has taken on much of the sound of the Kenton band. And Mr. Kenton, in turn, is doing a jocular imitation of Mr. Herman as a singer and disciplinarian.

One of the pieces performed by the Herd in that concert was Alan Broadbent's *Variations on a Scene*, and Wilson's comparison of it to the Kenton repertoire was apt.

Both bands were drawing their musicians from the stage bands of the country. "Stage band" was a euphemism devised to avoid rousing the wrath of puritans on school boards when the term "jazz" was not yet respectable.

By the early 1970s, the number of these bands in high schools, colleges, and universities, had reached an estimated 35,000. Woody was enthusiastic about the new generation of college-bred players. "The caliber of young musicians is far superior today than what it was when I was a young man," he told Eliot Tiegel of *Billboard*. "They can accomplish in a couple of semesters what it took us years to learn. It's not difficult to get competent players except that some young people want to keep moving and there's a great turnover because they go with a group or try living in California or New York. The road is never conducive to relaxation."

The story's headline noted that Woody had now been on the road thirty-eight years, and Tiegel asked the inevitable question: Did he ever get tired of it? Woody said, "I've been tired of the road for fifty years but I don't know anything else. I'd rather do this than anything else. I've been on the road since I was nine years old. I wouldn't know how to live any other way." He said that in the years he and Charlotte had owned their house in Los Angeles, he had spent perhaps twenty-eight months in it. He added: "I'm exaggerating, naturally, but it isn't a hell of a lot more."[2] He told another interviewer that he had spent thirty-five months of his life in that house, but whatever the actual figure, it seems he spent less than three years of the thirty-five he had owned it in the house on Hollywood Boulevard.

One of the young college-educated players about whom Woody was particularly enthusiastic was Gregory Herbert, born on May 19, 1947, in Philadelphia. He had studied for seven years at Temple University in that city, joining Woody (he had already worked for Duke Ellington) in 1971. He is heard in Woody's Fantasy albums *The Raven Speaks, Giant Steps, Thundering Herd, The Herd at Montreux*, and *Children of Lima*. Bill Kirchner, himself a saxophonist, wrote of Herbert in *Down Beat*: "Picture, if you will, a young tenor saxophonist with the lyricism of Wayne Shorter, the gutsiness of Gene Ammons, the dazzling facility of John Coltrane and the rhythmic power of Sonny Rollins. Or better yet, listen to him. His name is Gregory Herbert and he's possibly the finest young tenor player in jazz."

"I loved him," Herbert said of Woody when he had gone on to the Thad Jones–Mel Lewis band. "It was like having my father on the road with me. He appreciated me and had as much confidence in me as a father would have. I certainly respected his singing and playing the alto every night; he's got a great feeling for music, for playing in context. And he's a great blues player. He plays what he feels and what he knows, and it sounds damned good to me—I'd rather hear that than a bunch of meaningless notes. So we understood each other musically and had a great relationship."[3]

The admiration was mutual. Woody considered Herbert a major virtuoso. He said, "He had all the attributes of every old-time saxophone player, but he never relied on it, never worked on it. He still was Gregory Herbert. And this is a thing I really demand in great players . . . . He had a giant scope. Phenomenal saxophonist, phenomenal flutist. He was one of the giants of this period in my band."[4]

Herbert stayed four years with the band, then gave his notice. He said, "I didn't want to leave, but finally I knew I had to in order to further develop myself."

Herbert played one of his last engagements with the band in Chicago. The Thad Jones–Mel Lewis band was also playing there. Thad and Mel went by to hear Woody, and learning that Herbert was leaving the band, invited him to join them. He played with their group for a time, then joined Blood, Sweat, and Tears.

In Woody's band at the same time was Nelson Hatt, who played second lead trumpet. Hatt, born on February 4, 1944, in San Antonio, Texas, was a graduate of Rice University but not in music. Although he had played in

the university band, his degree was in experimental psychology. He had
played in the Glenn Miller band directed by Buddy DeFranco and in the
Buddy Rich band.

Like so many persons over a span of three generations, Hatt became
aware of big bands in general and the Herman band in particular while he
was in high school. The first album of the band he heard was *My Kind of
Broadway*, recorded in three sessions between late November, 1964, and
mid-March, 1965.

The contract with Philips had expired, and Woody returned for a time to
Columbia Records, at the behest of his friend Ken Glancy, who was now
head of A&R. The album was a departure for Woody. It contained no
"originals" written especially for the band. Woody rarely if ever recorded
material from Broadway shows, and this one consisted entirely of such
tunes. I don't think I ever heard him play these charts in live performance.
And they are excellent: three by Nat Pierce, three by Bill Holman, three by
Raoul Romero, one by Bill Chase, one by Dusko Goykovich, and one by
Don Rader. The personnel was essentially that of the band that had recorded for Philips, though replacements were occurring in the trumpet
section. Hatt's enthusiasm for the album caused me to listen to it again,
and he's right; it's a superb album, with beautiful ensemble playing, excellent solos, and the vitality one expects of a Herman band. It is an overlooked album, almost forgotten among the Herman works. In any case, it
had such impact on young Nelson Hatt that he used to dream—literally,
he said—of playing with the band.

The band, according to Ken Glancy, made six albums for Columbia
during this period. One of them was recorded on June 28, 29, and 30,
1965, in a "live" performance at Basin Street West in San Francisco, two
tracks on October 8, another on July 7, 1966, and the last (with guitarist
Charlie Byrd a guest star) on March 23, 1967. This material was released
under the title *Jazz Hoot* in 1974.

After hearing the *Broadway* album, Hatt collected Woody's available
records. "I was mesmerized," he said, "by Bill Chase, who was playing lead
then, and when I got to see him in person, it was even more spectacular.

"What a human energy he had. His playing was one thing, but the guy
was so positive and had so much energy. I was nuts about Bill Chase.

"Bill's group, Chase, came through Houston. I had already been on the
Miller band and the Buddy Rich band. I was back in Houston, and Chase
came to play the Village Inn pizza parlor there. This was in January or
February of 1974. I was down there nine out of the ten nights. I took

pictures of them, and I hung out with them. Bill and I got along very well, talking about photography. I was so knocked out that I said, 'Bill, if there's ever an opportunity that I could play with your group, I'd be just over-whelmed.'

"They were through on Saturday night. On Sunday afternoon I played with a real hot Latin band. Bill's whole band came in. The guys I played with were blown away. Bill invited me to go to dinner. He was taking his band to a Greek restaurant. He took me aside toward the end of the night and said, 'I just wanted to tell you that you sounded great, and the next chair I have is yours.' What a trip! I was all jazzed about it."

But Hatt would never play with the Bill Chase group. A month or so after Chase left Houston, Nelson got a call from Bill Byrne, saying that Chase had spoken very highly of him. Would he be interested in joining the Woody Herman band? The split chair had become vacant, and Byrne offered him the job. The band was to play Houston in another week or so. Hatt joined them during that engagement in April, 1974.

"So," he said, "I went into the band on second lead, also known as the suicide chair, because you never quit playing. Bill Chase had the band arrangers put the high stuff on the lead book. Then he'd need to rest. One of the unsung heroes of that band was Gerry Lamy, who played second under Bill. The way the book was written, while the first lead is up there, screaming, the second is playing, and then when the first rests the split lead player has got it, and he's still playing. The second player never quits.

"I'm not a jazz soloist. So it was kind of an unsung chair. But you get a lot of playing. I didn't mind that. I was never that interested in becoming a star. I just wanted to be out there."

▼   ▼   ▼

Ingrid spent the 1970s in Nashville. The connection with members of the Lester Flatt band was one factor in the decision she and Bob Fowler made to move there, which they did in 1971. She said:

"There was this tiny handful of people in San Francisco that played bluegrass, whom we disdainfully referred to as Berkeley bluegrassers. God knows, we were bad enough, for going by the book. But these people were really stodgy.

"We got to know this guy from the navy, named Ned, who was a little North Carolina farm boy. And he *sang*! You know, those folks, if they grow up in that, they just open their mouths and it sounds like the records.

"That's what we wanted, and when we got there, Nashville was really that way. There were zillions of people everywhere who played."

Ingrid worked constantly in nightclub bands. For a time she even played in an all-girl band. And then Woody came to Nashville. She recounted:

"Four couples, people my husband and I played with, opened a little club near Vanderbilt University called the Session Inn. You can't imagine how small it was. There was never going to be any money, not with four partners in a place that seated about fifty people. I can't tell you how small it was. It had a room in the front with a bar, and the room in the back was the stage. Either room smaller than most people's kitchen.

"My father heard about it and said, 'I'll come down there with the band and we'll play, and you invite all your musician friends.'

"I said, 'Daddy, you'll never get them in here!'

"And he said, 'Bill Byrne can get the band in anywhere. Don't worry.'

"And he did, by God, and it was wonderful. That was maybe 1973, 74."

I gather, then, that Woody had reconciled himself to the career and life she had chosen.

▼   ▼   ▼

At that time I was living in Toronto. Woody and Tony Bennett were scheduled to do a concert at Hamilton Place with the Hamilton Philharmonic. The concert was to be the inaugural of the newly built and beautiful all-brick hall. Woody and Tony phoned me, asking me to come to the concert. That concert would leave me with several memories to chuckle over.

Tony arrived in Toronto early and asked me to come to Hamilton—some forty miles away—and spend the preconcert afternoon with him. We made the trip by limousine. Tony rehearsed with Woody and the symphony orchestra, at one point having me sing one of the songs while he walked around the hall to check the acoustics. After rehearsal, Tony, his pianist and conductor Torrie Zito (whose brother, drummer Ronnie Zito, had made the African tour with Woody), and I went back to Tony's hotel to hang out. My wife was driving to Hamilton closer to concert time. About an hour before concert time, in his suite at the Royal Connaught Hotel, Tony started to get ready. He went into the bathroom. I was in the sitting room reading a newspaper. Suddenly, I heard him shout, "Son of a bitch!" And since Tony normally did not use profanity, I was all the more startled. I thought he'd hurt himself and rushed into the bathroom.

"I hung my tux up to steam out the wrinkles," he said, "and it fell." He was fishing it out of a tub half filled with water. It dripped. "And I didn't bring another one!" he said. "I guess I'll have to perform in this!" He had on a brown tweed suit, and it would certainly look inappropriate with a full orchestra wearing tuxedos.

"Hey, Tony," I said, "when we were there this afternoon, I noticed that they're fully set up to do operas. That means costumes, and that means steam irons."

I telephoned backstage, where I expected that my wife would by now be, probably with Woody. I described her to whoever answered the phone, and she got on the line. I told her what had happened, and she said, "Well, Woody's got a problem, too, and he's in a rage."

"Tell me about it later. Find out about the steam irons and call me back."

She shortly reported that there were indeed irons and she had arranged for two of them. Tony, Torrie, and I went down to the limousine, with Torrie carrying Tony's dripping tux on a hanger.

I was born in that city, and so Tony planned to make a special point of singing one of my songs, *Yesterday I Heard the Rain*. I realized he had the same ability Woody did to get past small disasters in good humor. He was laughing about the accident. "I'll tell you what I'll do," he said. "When I do *Yesterday I Heard the Rain*, I'll wring out the pockets and the people will say, 'Man, that cat really gets into a song!' "

When we got there, I found out what had happened to Woody. After the rehearsal, the musicians had put their instruments back on the band bus for safekeeping. About an hour earlier, some guard had told the driver he couldn't hold the bus there; he would have to move it. The driver had driven off, and now the band had neither instruments nor uniforms and concert time was almost upon us. The Hamilton police were out looking for the bus. Woody's towering temper, the other side of his equanimity, had exploded. He called the guard, "You stupid son of bitch!" and more of the kind.

Barely in time, the bus returned, the musicians got aboard, changed clothes, and hit the stage. Meantime, Tony and my wife and I were in a dressing room with two ironing boards and two irons. Tony was standing there in black formal shoes, black stockings, formal shirt and black tie, and his underwear as we pressed his pants and jackets. Tony said, "I can do that myself."

"You have to work," I said. Finally Tony felt the jacket, which was still pretty damp, and said, "That'll do. I sweat more than that during a performance."

His segment of the concert arrived. He ran onstage, arms out wide, smiling that great smile, hit the microphone—and found that it wasn't working. The orchestra started again, and still it wasn't working.

At last the engineers got the problem straightened out, and Tony, the Herd, and the orchestra turned in a superb performance.

At the end of the evening, Tony, Woody, and the rest of us were laughing about the accidents.

▼　▼　▼

Woody would receive some severe blows in 1974.

Duke Ellington died May 24 of that year. Three months later, Woody would lose Bill Chase.

Not only were Bill and Woody close personal friends, but Bill had also shared road-management duties with Nat Pierce and been responsible for hiring the brass players. After the African tour, with Woody's blessing, he organized a jazz-rock fusion group called Chase, consisting of four trumpets, rhythm section, and a singer, the group that had entranced Nelson Hatt. Its first album, *Chase*, was a success, but later albums were not and he dissolved the group. In 1974 he reorganized it and took it out on tour.

Bill and three members of the group were killed as their plane tried to land in a storm and crashed in a cornfield near Jackson, Minnesota, on August 9, 1974. The bodies weren't found until morning. Bill was thirty-nine.

In October and December, Woody toured with Frank Sinatra, whom he had known since Sinatra's time with the Harry James band.

I moved to Los Angeles at Christmas of that year, and of course one of the first persons I called was Woody. He mentioned the recent Sinatra tour. I asked him how Sinatra had been singing. Woody said, "You know me. He can sing the phone book and I'll like it."

I remember that bar in Chicago he once took me to, with its jukebox full of Sinatra records.

26

The Fortieth Anniversary

As always, when Woody was in the East, the home of Jack and Mary Siefert was his center of operations. Sometimes Charlotte would accompany him, staying either at their home in Philadelphia or their summer place at Stone Harbor, New Jersey. Sometimes Charlotte alone would stay with them while Woody traveled. The Sieferts were as attached to her as they were to Woody.

Jack said, "Woody, Charlotte, and their grandchildren, Tommy and Alexandra, stayed with us at Stone Harbor, which is on a seven-mile barrier island. We would rent this home for six weeks each summer. Up until 1986, we summered at Stone Harbor, which Woody loved."

Mary Siefert said, "For us to know them was a little spark of show biz. We were not into that. We were regular, middle-class America. It was wonderful to be a part of it."

Jack said: "He added a whole dimension to our lives that we never would have known, and our children would never have known."

Mary said:

"Charlotte was wonderful at sewing. She sewed almost everything she wore. Every three or four years she would come east in the fall to buy her patterns. She bought them at some place in New York, and they would adjust them for her. Then all she had to do was buy her material.

"She was here one time right before Christmas, staying for a week or so.

She'd come down from New York. She fitted in nicely. She'd say, "Just go about your business. I'll take care of whatever I have to take care of." And that was fine, because I had a busy schedule. The kids were still in school and I was running here and there and everywhere.

"Charlotte said, 'Christmas is coming. Do you have any parties you're going to?' I said, 'Oh yes. There are some neighborhood parties. I don't know what to wear.'

"She said, 'Leave that up to me. Is there any place that sells materials?' I said, 'We have a couple of beautiful fabric stores in the area.'

"She took off and came back with this huge amount of red velvet. She made me the most gorgeous red velvet skirt. I wore it every year at Christmas time for about six years.

"I think I taught her to play bridge. I was going out to a bridge party one night. I said, 'Do you want to come along?'

"She said, 'I'll come along. But I don't know anything about bridge.'

"Toward the end of her life, she played a lot of bridge and was very good at it."

Jack said, "Woody invited us out to California many times. We were struggling then. We decided to go out before the kids were twelve years old because they could fly cheaper. We went out to his house and it was the greatest vacation we ever had. His grandchildren were there.

"We went down to our rooms, and there were airline tickets to Las Vegas. He was appearing at Caesar's Palace. Charlotte said, 'I want you kids to have a good vacation. So you go to Las Vegas and I'll baby-sit.'

"So she took our children down to Knotts Berry Farm and Disneyland. She loved our kids."

Mary said, "She sat on one of the wrought-iron benches just inside the entrance and gave the kids tickets. And my George, who was then just about nine, said afterwards, 'Aunt Charlotte's got a magical pocket book! We go in there and she gives us a handful of tickets and says, 'Come back when you've used those.' So we go back and she's got more! It's a magic pocketbook!'"

The tickets were employee passes. Woody played Disneyland frequently and had accumulated a load of them.

▼   ▼   ▼

April, 1975, found Woody back in Milwaukee. The *Milwaukee Sentinel* reported on Thursday, April 10:

Bandleader Woody Herman returned to Milwaukee Wednesday to pay a nearly 50-year-old debt—but the Catholic nun who helped him wasn't around any more.

Herman just missed finding her.

Sister Fabian Riley, one of Herman's teachers at St. John Cathedral High School, 830 N. Jackson St., died a month ago at age 93.

Herman, 62, had promised Sister Fabian a year ago that he was going to have his band put on a special concert here to raise a scholarship fund for Milwaukee area high school seniors.

The scholarship fund has been named after Sister Fabian.

The *Milwaukee Journal* covered the story the same day, both papers noting that during the concert Woody was presented with a Grammy award for the best big-band album of 1974, *Thundering Herd*, the second year in a row the band had won it. The *Journal*'s story said:

However, sad to say, this historic, well loved and loving jazz giant remains rather neglected in his home town. Despite heavy promotion, the concert drew just 1,287 people to a huge hall only slightly more venerable than Herman.

▼ ▼ ▼

One of Woody's peculiarities is that he rarely, and probably never, auditioned the musicians he hired. It had been this way for years. In the First Herd, for example, Chubby Jackson was responsible for much of the hiring. I once asked Wood, "Where do you find all these talented young people?"

He said, "I don't find them; they find me." But he amended that to say that he trusted the recommendations of his alumni, such as Bill Chase, who had recommended Nelson Hatt, or the current members of his band.

Jim Pugh, the brilliant trombonist then in the band, recommended a trumpet player, Allen Vizzutti, born (like Billie Rogers before him) in Missoula, Montana. "He was also recommended by Al Porcino," Bill Byrne said. "Al told me about Allen after hearing him at Eastman." Woody turned him over to Nelson Hatt for training.

Nelson recalled: "Pugh had been telling me about him, and I thought, 'Yeah, yeah, another college hotshot who either can't swing or has no soul.' Because we'd had a few of those guys through the band. When Al came on the band, I was absolutely floored by him. I think he has more physical ability on the instrument than almost anybody I ever heard. It's all-encompassing ability. He's a brilliant player of all kinds of music."

Vizzutti had in fact played in the faculty brass quintet when he was only a sophomore. Nelson and Bill Byrne had several times approached him, but Vizzutti was determined to get his master's degree from Eastman, and the school in turn was pressing him to join the faculty. But at last he gave in and joined Woody.

"Usually it was my job to break in the new lead players," Nelson said. "When Al first joined the band, I was pointing out the road maps to him." The term requires explanation. Jazz musicians use the term "charts" as opposed to "arrangements" because it covers not only arrangements but original compositions. Another term, less common than "charts," is "maps." "Road maps" thus are the charts played on the road, and they become inscrutable with penciled editing marks, revisions, coffee stains, and assorted other disfigurements. In those days before photocopying, there were no backups for the hand-copied parts.

Nelson said, "The procedures were marked on the parts. There was never time to rehearse; we had to do it as we played them. *Caldonia* was a particularly killer one. We had backgrounds written on the back of the paper, and something else in the margin, and I was telling Al, 'The tenor's going to play two or three choruses, and then you jump in here to the margin. Then jump back up here and play this one. And then on Woody's signal we've got to go down front and play the trumpet passage. Now don't worry about it the first few times. You'll eventually get it memorized. Otherwise just go down and wiggle your fingers.'

"Most of the guys that were new would be kind of shook up. 'We do what? Where? I come in where?'

"With Al, he would just nod, and say, 'Okay . . . okay.' And then he'd play the shit out of it!

"The first time we went down to play *Caldonia*, I said, 'Now when you get it memorized, on the repeat, you play it up an octave—if you feel like it.' He said, 'Okay.' He was so unassuming. I used to call him, the World's Most Unlikely-Looking Hot Trumpet Player. Thin, with glasses. Al went down front on *Caldonia*, that very first concert, and blew the shit out of it, up an octave and everything."

Vizzutti's infallibility began taking on dimensions of the awesome among the band members. It was not until his tenth or eleventh gig, during a performance of *Woody's Whistle*, that he played anything that anyone could recognize as a mistake. The whole band turned around in amazement, and Nelson told him: "Well, at least we know you're human."

Woody, that canny detector of talent in even its formative stages, was not initially impressed by Vizzutti.

"Woody would just kind of stand there and kind of stare," Nelson Hatt said. "I couldn't figure out why. He seemed unhappy. We were playing a dance. He was always pissed off on dances anyway. He wanted to play concerts. We were finishing up about the second set. He pointed a finger at me and said, 'I want to *see* you!' Al, a very perceptive, very intelligent young fellow, damn near a genius, said, 'Is that about me?'

"I said, 'Nah, I doubt it.'

"By this time I had a really good relationship with Woody. I had a great deal of respect for him. We communicated well. So I said, 'What's the problem?'

"He said, 'I'm not hearing enough balls on the lead.'

"I said, 'Well lighten up; give the guy a chance. He's trying to get used to the book. He's a *great* trumpet player, Woody.' I was afraid he'd fire him. We'd had some real dumb players, and I didn't want to lose this guy.

"Woody said, 'Well he may be a great player in front of a string orchestra or something, but I want to hear some balls.'

"I said, 'All right. Lighten up, we'll take care of it.'

"So I went to John Hoffman—who we called the Fig, for no good reason. We'd been in the Glenn Miller band together. In fact Woody hired him on my recommendation. The Fig was playing third trumpet, on the other side of Al. I and said, 'Look, Woody's on the rag. We're in danger of losing Vizzutti.' He said, 'He wouldn't fire Al, would he?' I said, 'That's what I want to make sure doesn't happen. You know what? We're just playing too loud. We're on autopilot. We're playing flat out all the time. We should be using our heads and getting underneath him, and as he gets stronger, gets used to the book, we'll boost him up. We should have been doing that anyway. It's our fault, really. We should have been using our heads.' I told Bill Byrne and I guess the Fig told Dennis Dotson. And we brought our over-all volume down and got underneath him. And the next set Woody gave me the circle, the thumb and forefinger. And afterwards, he said, 'That's better.'

"Well Al came to me and said, 'That was about me, wasn't it?'

"I said, 'Yeah, well, look. He says he wants more balls. We're playing too loud anyway, and we're going to back off and support you.'

"Al said, 'I've worked very hard for a lot of years to build up what I've got, and I just can't afford to split my lip trying to play louder. Not just yet.'

"I said, 'You're doing exactly right.' He was working his way into the book and building up his strength intelligently. We were the ones who were being dummies and not really listening.

"Woody groused for a couple more days."

At this point, Jim Pugh called Nelson to the back of the bus, where the two of them would often listen to tapes on headphones. Pugh told him he had something he wanted him to hear.

As Nelson listened to what he thought was a number of different trumpet players from both the classical and jazz fields, he grew increasingly frustrated, asking Pugh who these men were. Pugh said, 'It's all Vizzutti. That's his Eastman recital tape. He was twenty-two when he made it."

Nelson had an immediate confrontation with Woody. Woody was, as he so commonly did, driving to the next job alone. Nelson told him he had something he wanted Woody to listen to on the way. Woody guessed immediately: "What is it? Vizzutti?"

Nelson said, "Yeah, and just listen."

The night's job was in a high school. Nelson was in the band room, warming up his chops, when Woody arrived. Woody entered at the far side of the room, his suit bag over his shoulder, and seeing Nelson, stopped still in the doorway.

Nelson said, "Well? What do you think?"

Woody said, "Jesus Christ! He makes Herbert L. Clarke sound like a fag."

Herbert L. Clarke was a famous cornet virtuoso with the John Philip Sousa band. He was considered one of the great cornet soloists of all time, a peerless and powerful technician.

Vizzutti knew nothing of all this intrigue. The band played a concert. After a tenor solo, when the band normally went into the ensemble shout chorus, Woody signaled the musicians to keep it open and called out to Vizzutti. Woody had a funny way of being brusque, seeming almost annoyed, when he was about to do something very kind. I wonder if he feared seeming sentimental, or whether he maintained this air in order to retain control over a band that, after all, he ran very loosely, and it simply became a habit. And he said: "Vizzutti! Come on down here!"

Vizzutti said to Nelson, "What's he want?"

"He wants you to go down and play some jazz."

When Woody announced a player's name near the end of a chorus, that was the man's signal to stop. Vizzutti looked at Woody at the end of a chorus. Woody gave him a sign to keep going. At the end of the second chorus, he gave him the same sign. This happened repeatedly. Vizzutti played four or five choruses, and finally Woody announced his name, returning him to the brass section.

"Woody gave him at least four solos that night," Nelson remembered. "On *Reunion at Newport* he played this blinding, blazing solo. He had chops like Rafael Mendez. Amazing."

Woody immediately gained a huge respect for Vizzutti and thenceforth featured him prominently. Learning that Vizzutti could also write, he commissioned the trumpet player to compose a flamboyant showpiece for himself. Vizzutti wrote a piece called *Fire Dance*, recorded in a direct-to-disc LP. It is astonishing playing. As Bill Byrne said, "Beautiful tone, beautiful chops." The technique is amazing. Vizzutti has immense range, with altissimo playing that is effortless, impeccably in tune, and firm. His bottom register tone is huge and fat. He can be lyrical when he wants to be. There is one unaccompanied passage to which you have to listen carefully to be sure you aren't hearing a duet with another trumpet player. But no, he's alone. Nelson Hatt's admiration for him, as a fellow trumpeter, is understandable. If Vizzutti was by then the versatile trumpet master of all fields and styles of classical music that Nelson says he was, in view of his excellence as a jazz player, one is forced to the conclusion that he was already one of the greatest trumpet players in the world, possibly the best of them all. It's unimaginable that the instrument can be pushed any further than this.

▼   ▼   ▼

Hatt passed through some personal difficulties during his tenure with the band. "My then-wife was often out with the band," Nelson said. "Woody was so kind to her, the consummate gentleman. This was as opposed to Buddy Rich. I tried to introduce her to Buddy the first day on the bus, and he took one look at her and said, 'I don't want to hear any female sounds the entire trip.' Often Woody would ask us to ride with him in the car and invite us to dinner.

"I was putting her through school and she met somebody in one of her classes and she dumped me. That was pretty tough to take. I was kind of losing my focus on the bandstand. One night I was depressed, and I guess I just wasn't playing out. I looked down, and Woody was staring at me. Not exactly the Ray, just looking. And I thought, Oh oh, I'd better pay attention. And then he said, 'I want to see you in the bar.'

"I said, 'I'm not drinking, Woody.' I tried that, and it didn't work too well. He said, 'In the bar! *Tonight!*'"

Bracing himself to getting fired, Nelson entered the bar, where he found Woody waiting. Woody had saved a chair for him. Hatt sat down. Woody said, "Look, I know you're having a rough time. I've been around the block a few times. I don't want to presume anything, but if there's any way I can help you, let's talk."

When word got around that I was working on this book, several musicians, some of them strangers, called to express some variation on: Woody got me through a very rough time in my life.

▼   ▼   ▼

In December, 1975, the band played on a jazz cruise aboard the *Rotterdam*. Woody and Charlotte were talking to the late jazz critic and historian Leonard Feather and his wife, Jane. Leonard pointed out to Woody that the following November, Woody would reach his fortieth anniversary as a bandleader. Leonard said the date was embedded in his consciousness, because it fell on election day, the first Tuesday of November, when Franklin D. Roosevelt had been elected President. It had been on that date—as legend has it—that the Band That Plays the Blues had played its first date at the Roseland Ballroom in Brooklyn. Leonard suggested that something should be done to observe the occasion. Hermie Dressel, who was at an adjacent table, took note of it.

"As the months went by," Leonard later wrote, "Woody and Dressel discussed the possibility of working out [a] convocation of the Herds. The principal difficulty was the fact that, over this time span, Woody's orchestras had produced not just a few dozen but hundreds of sidemen and singers for whom the experience of working with him turned out to be a major stepping-stone."

But the project proved more and more appealing, and a concert by as many of the alumni as could be assembled seemed like the logical celebration of the event.

"Hermie and I actually started working on it about three months in advance," Woody told Leonard. "We had tentative OKs from a lot of people who wanted to make it, but for one reason or another in some cases it didn't work out. We were particularly sorry that Red Norvo couldn't get out of a commitment to a club where he was set to work.

"There was no difficulty bringing up the men who [were] now living in Florida—Flip Phillips, Chubby Jackson, Don Lamond, and Sam Marowitz. Some flew in from California. Ralph Burns interrupted a road tour with a show for which he was writing the music, and Nat Pierce was quite helpful in making some of the contracts."

Some of the older scores had to be assembled from archives at the University of Houston, to which Woody had donated them a few years earlier. They were almost illegible and had to be reconstructed and re-copied.

The work began. And Woody's old friend Ken Glancy became involved.

Glancy was now a vice president of Columbia. By then attorney Clive Davis was moving toward full power at Columbia, and Glancy was pro-moted sideways, out of the way, to head the company's British operation. Eventually he became head of Columbia for all Europe. Davis, meanwhile, had been appointed president of Columbia.

Glancy went to England in 1965 and raised Columbia's company's prof-its hugely. Whenever Woody went to England, he would hang out with Ken.

"Sometime during '66," Ken said, "Woody came over on a tour. I had gotten to know Harold Davison pretty well. We decided the company would throw a party for the business. Through Harold, we got Woody to play a one-nighter at Ronnie Scott's. We had what radio people there were, the BBC, the hacks from the press, and assorted free-loaders. It was quite an evening. That was a very good band."

Ken did so well for Columbia that RCA recruited him. From 1970 to 1973, he was head of all RCA Records operations in Europe, and did that job so well that the company brought him home to the United States as president of the company for the world. And thus, with a friend in high places, Hermie Dressel approached him about the anniversary concert, saying, "We've got to record it."

Hermie Dressel put the package together. Glancy recalled, "He even got Stan Getz, who wanted money for the gig, by the way."

The Columbia and RCA record companies had been continuous and sometimes bitter rivals since the 1930s. But one of Glancy's best friends was Bruce Lundvall, who is now president of the Blue Note division of Capitol Records, but at that time was president of Columbia Records.

Ken said, "I called Lundvall, and told him what we were going to do. I said, 'Look, before the FBI catches up with us for collusion, do you want to join in? Because you've got the historic Woody Herman material. We're gonna record the concert. Do you want to have a party for Woody and go in on it with us?' And he said, 'Sure.' So that's how it happened."

Though it was only for the purpose of throwing a party after a concert, this is the only instance I know of for such co-operation between the companies.

The next question became: where to hold this concert?

"We were trying for a date at Lincoln Center," Woody said, "because we figured we couldn't get into Carnegie Hall. But then there was a cancellation at Carnegie and it turned out to be a perfect date for us—a Saturday night. We really didn't have a staff or a lot of people working for us, and there didn't seem to be enough hours in the day to follow through on all the details. Hermie had to take the brunt of all this, trying to put it all together and hold it together. He worked so hard that during the final week he was sleeping in the office."

The office by now was at 161 West 54th Street, at Seventh Avenue, three blocks down Seventh from Carnegie Hall. Across 57th Street from Carnegie and a half dozen doors to the east, was Nola Studios, a rehearsal facility that has played a rich role in jazz history. A few days before the concert date—November 20, 1976—the alumni began checking into the nearby New York Sheraton Hotel and then assembled at Nola.

Leonard Feather wrote: "The scene in that crowded room was one that will live long in the memories of all of us who were there. Less of the first hour was devoted to playing than to renewing old friendships. Everyone assured one another how little they had changed, while members of the 1976 Thundering Herd sat bemused before trading riffs with the old masters who had played in the orchestra long before these fledglings were born."

Chubby Jackson remarked, "If this were an old-timers' ball game, people would be amazed to see a cat get to first base; but we mean business! We're here for home runs."

On election eve, Tuesday, November 2, 1976, Public Television aired a ninety-minute documentary on Woody's life. Dave Dexter Jr., writing in *Billboard*, called it "the most engrossing and entertaining special revolving around a pop music personality ever to be served up on TV."[1]

Dexter interviewed Hermie Dressel, who told him: "Woody and I made a pact when I took over his management in 1968. Neither of us would ever get old. We will age and we will die but we are young at heart and Herman's music reflects that philosophy."

And then came a dose of reality: "We must gross between $13,000 and $14,000 every week just to break even. And we do it forty-eight weeks out of the year—every year." Bill Byrne estimates that the band had to travel at least 2000 miles a week just to make its nut.

The current Herd comprised Allen Vizzutti, Nelson Hatt, John Hoffman,

Dennis Dotson, and Bill Byrne, trumpets and fluegelhorns; Jim Pugh, Dale Kirkland, and Jim Daniels, trombones; Frank Tiberi, Gary Anderson, Joe Lovano, and John Oslawski, saxophones doubling woodwinds; Pat Coil, keyboards; Rusty Holloway, bass; and Dan d'Imperio, drums.

The alumni band assembled for the Carnegie Hall concert included Billy Bauer, Ralph Burns, Al Cohn, Conte Candoli, Pete Candoli, Stan Getz, Jimmy Giuffre, Jake Hanna, Chubby Jackson, Don Lamond, Mary Ann McCall, Sam Marowitz, Nat Pierce, Jimmy Rowles, Zoot Sims, and Phil Wilson.

The old band played the old book; the youngsters played the new book. And they all came together at the end for a massed-band version of *Caldonia* with solos by Flip Phillips, Cohn, Getz, Giuffre, and the Candolis. Under Glancy's guidance, the recording of the concert was released in a two-LP package by RCA. (It has been reissued as a CD.) The concert had a kind of monumental quality.

Nelson Hatt said, "There was a guy in the front row who was just beside himself. He probably bought the first ticket that went on sale. He was in heaven. He's yelling and going nuts. He wasn't obnoxious about it, he was just enthusiastic. You can hear him on the record. While they were playing, he ran up to the lip of the stage and threw a fifty-dollar bill on the stage. Woody said on the mike, 'You cheapskate, haven't you got any hundreds?' And the guy started throwing hundred-dollar bills!"

Bill Byrne said, "The band finished playing *Four Brothers*. Zoot Sims picked up the hundred-dollar bills and took them backstage. Stan Getz and Al Cohn weren't letting him get out of their sight. All the musicians got a big laugh out of Stan and Al demanding their share of the loot."

Leonard Feather, who was the master of ceremonies, wrote in his liner notes: "I have been in music as long as Woody has been a leader, and have yet to meet a more decent, mature, and likeable human being."

After the concert came the joint Columbia-RCA party at the Essex House. Among the guests were Dr. Stanley Levy and his wife, whom Woody had flown to New York from Detroit. Levy remembers encountering Buddy Rich, standing in a corner, muttering to himself, saying, "That son of a bitch Woody Herman!" Levy said, "Before you go on about my friend and my patient, what's the problem?"

Buddy told him, "Why didn't he ask me to play in the concert? I would have played the concert with him."

Detaching himself, Levy found Woody in the crowd and told him what had happened. Woody said, "It's simple. The only guys in the concert were guys who had played in my band. And Buddy never played in my band."

That's not precisely true. Dave Tough had been too sick to play the September 5, 1945, Columbia record date that produced *Gee, It's Good to Hold You* and *Your Father's Mustache*. Buddy replaced him for that one session. And Buddy had played with the band at the Newport Jazz Festival the afternoon of July 3, 1966, soon after its African tour. Buddy also played with the band on one track of the Capitol album *The Hits of Woody Herman*, a track titled *Drums in Hi-Fly*, recorded November 30, 1955.

But Levy returned to Buddy Rich and conveyed Woody's explanation. It seemed to satisfy him. "And then," Levy said, "he turned on like a light-bulb, and he was charming."[2]

Levy had continued to treat Woody for what might be described as a concerto of ailments. "He got sick in Milwaukee on a Sunday afternoon," Levy said. "With his esophagus again. I called Jay Larkin. He and I were in the navy together at Great Lakes in the Korean War. He's an obstetrician-gynecologist. We got Woody to a gastroenterologist. We got him bailed out again. He was at the Schroeder Hotel. He played that afternoon.

"One time I was in Florida. Woody was supposed to play in Houston. He got a piece of something stuck in his esophagus at 4:30 or 5 o'clock in the afternoon. There's a doctor there named Al Levy. I got hold of him, and he tracked down a gastroenterologist. I told him he would have to esophago-scope Woody Herman, and he's not going to get paid, other than what the Blue Cross or Medicare is going to pay. And he's going to have to do it and get him out in time to play at 8:30 tonight. Al Levy's wife said, 'It'll cost you a couple of tickets.' They took him to a clinic. I told them, 'Don't fiddle around. He doesn't have a malignancy. He's got terrible blood vessels, and this has happened before.' And they pulled out the piece of food. And he went to work that night."

Woody repeatedly went back to Detroit for treatment by Dr. Stan Levy or one of his associates.

"Along the line," Levy said, "Saul Sakwa fixed a hernia, and my friend Hugh Beckman removed cataracts for him. Then there was a repair after the cataracts in the early eighties. Woody came into town in the morning and my wife and I picked him up and took him up to Beckman's office. He turned on the laser to get rid of a film.

"Then there was another hernia repair by a specialist in Los Angeles. He got into trouble with Woody's blood pressure too. He couldn't understand it, he couldn't get a pulse, he couldn't get a blood pressure, the guy should have been in shock. 'Why is that?' he asked me. I said, 'He's got terrible calcified arteries.' If you'd seen Woody's arteries on an X-ray, you'd never have believed it. They were absolutely the world's worst. You never saw anything like it."[3]

Bill Byrne recalls another instance of Levy's taking care of Woody from a distance. This one occurred in April, 1980, during a tour of Argentina. Woody called Levy to tell him of another episode of his food problem. Levy told him not to worry: he had a physician friend in Buenos Aires, a man with whom he had gone to medical school. Bill said, "An hour later Woody was in the doctor's office and Levy was advising his friend on the telephone from Detroit, 5000 miles away. He told the doctor how to get Woody fixed up in time for the concert that evening.

"Duke Ellington had his long-time friend Dr. Arthur Logan, and Woody had Dr. Stan Levy from 1966 to the end."

And by now Charlotte, too, faced a grave medical crisis. She had been diagnosed as having breast cancer. Her cousin and closest friend, Shirley Mancuso, said:

"You would never think that this beautiful woman, with so many talents, would be insecure, but her mother completely dominated her and could say the meanest things to her. The only times I ever saw Charlotte cry was when she told me she had cancer, and when her mother destroyed her with some mean little thing she said. I can't even remember what it was. But Charlotte cried at that time. She had no way to combat this old woman, because the old lady could destroy her."

Charlotte underwent a mastectomy at St. John's hospital in Los Angeles.

"Woody called me," Shirley said. "He was out of town. He asked me to pick up some things for Charlotte. This will give you an insight into her mother. I was completely dominated by this old bird myself. And I thought, 'Should I go over there or not?' And I decided, the hell with it, I'm going. And I went to St. John's. I will never forget this. I stayed with Charlotte for several hours. Charlotte was in and out of it. She always told me after that she would look over and see me sitting in the corner in a yellow dress and she would know she was still alive. Then she would turn her head and everything went dark.

"And then my aunt phoned, and she said, 'Shir, you better go home now.' She was so jealous because she wasn't there herself. Charlotte didn't want her there. She was a terrible old woman.

"While Charlotte was in St. John's Hospital, a nun told her, 'Charlotte, think about yourself. Don't think about anyone else.' And Charlotte started to assert herself. She turned against her mother. But of course by then it was too late."

Woody liked to quote his friend Igor Stravinsky saying, "Growing old is just a matter of one indignity after another." He said it so often that it has been attributed to him, but the line is Stravinsky's.[4]

27

Tommy and Charlotte

Tommy Littlefield began writing songs about the same time he began doing dope, in Mill Valley. He was not yet in high school. And he was a harbinger of the malady that would seemingly touch almost every family in America. Ingrid says firmly that her mother saved Tommy's life.

"Tommy always did music," Ingrid said. "He started writing rock-and-roll while we were in the Bay Area. He also used to sing with us at some of our gigs at places like the Freight and Salvage in Berkeley, which is still there. He knew a little guitar from an early age. My father took him on the road a couple of times. He sang with him. By the time he was in his teens he was doing rock-and-roll with some of his friends."

Tommy and his sister, Alexandra, would spend summers with their grandmother at the house on Hollywood Boulevard. Charlotte adored him.

"It was great for me," Ingrid said, "since I was not crazy about being a mother, and it gave me three months of vacation.

"It was kind of weird for them, because they'd have three months of the year with a lot of material largesse, and a lot of attention, and then nine months when the electricity was being turned off every other week and nobody paid any attention to them. That was hard on them.

"My mother and Tommy had a wonderful relationship as human beings. They were a lot alike. They had a lot of sensitivities and sensibilities in common.

"One summer I had managed to ignore the extent of his problem. I thought he smoked a little pot, and everybody did. But he was shooting up meth, and of course when I found out, I was appalled. I didn't know that until right before he was supposed to go out to California. I was at a loss as to what to do. I didn't feel that in Nashville there were the resources to deal with this properly. So I just managed to shut my eyes long enough to send him back to L.A. He was about fourteen.

"I thought, 'Well, he'll get to L.A., he'll be with my mother, and he'll cool out.'

"Well, he just had gotten so strung out.

"You know, my father was there part of the time, and he just kind of ignored it."

Woody had that ability to a remarkable degree to blinker his own vision and ignore what he did not want to think about. It was a strength, in that it permitted him to persevere through the most horrendous adversity, and it was a weakness in that it created some of that very adversity he had to endure. Even after all his experience with the Second Herd, and the loss to drugs of men he liked and respected and perhaps even loved, Charlie Parker among them, he could somehow simply ignore his grandson's entanglement in addiction.

"My poor mother was left with the problem," Ingrid said.

At one point Tommy threw his bicycle off the balcony. With dark humor, Ingrid said, "That balcony's had a lot of interesting stuff fall off it. Poodles, bicycles.

"My mother got the cops. She had Tommy toted off in a straitjacket.

"Of course my mother was horrified, more horrified because of her experience with pills. Everything in her life had prepared her for this moment. Because she felt Tom was a lot like her, this all contributed to her taking fast and deep and decisive action. And she had the resources of having a certain amount of money and being in California.

"So first she sent him to a private psychiatric hospital. They cleaned him up and kept him there for a while, but they didn't make any real inroads.

"Then she sent him to a place up in the mountains. And if people didn't do right, they shaved their heads and made them wash dishes and all that boot camp stuff.

"He was supposed to stay there eighteen months. He ran away after three. But he didn't shoot meth any more after that. Something he went through in that place made him decide not to be addicted to anything, except maybe cigarettes. Whatever they did to him at that place, he got the point, and he stopped trying to kill himself with stuff."

And of course Charlotte was fighting cancer at the time. "Yes," Ingrid said. "It made it doubly rough for him, too, because on the one hand he's having fits, and on the other he's feeling guilty. He adored her. He's well aware of what she did for him.

"He stayed with my mother for quite a while. I didn't want him back. He had threatened me. And just because he was no longer going to kill himself with dope didn't mean he was not an absolutely vile human being, and today he'll be the first to tell you: emotionally unstable, freaked out. She had to take the brunt of all that for a long time, and finally she couldn't stand it any more and she sent him back to Nashville.

"My father gave him a modest stipend, and he found a little apartment and got a job as a bus boy at Boots Randolph's club. Boots was very nice to him.

"Tom was always very explosive. He had so much rage—because of my neglect, and Bob Fowler ignoring him so thoroughly. This made it very difficult for him to keep jobs.

"But he was always writing songs. And he did extensive couch tours of Nashville and stayed with people. There are some people—and he'll tell you—he owes a lot to because they were so patient with his disposition."

Ingrid and I had come to know each other well by the time she told me all this, and I had become very fond of her. "Ingrid," I said, "you have a bizarre honesty about you."

"Bizarre?" she said, laughing.

"Yes, bizarre. Have you been in analysis?"

"No."

"Well you talk as if you had."

"It prevents the hurt," she said. "If I tell you first that I was a rotten mother, it stops you saying it to me." And she laughed at herself, and I realized how much pain there was in her laughter.

▼   ▼   ▼

While Charlotte struggled to save Tommy, Woody was still traveling. The band played jazz cruises of the Caribbean. In 1976, he took it again behind what was still called the Iron Curtain. But this trip had a special meaning: he visited Poland, his mother's ancestral homeland and that of the Sherman family. He was, he told me on his return, astounded by the reception. Polish jazz fans were utterly devoted and had mobbed the Voice of America's Willis Conover on visits there. In Woody's case, the reception had a particular passion: the fans knew about his ancestry and considered him one of their own.

The British promoter Harold Davison had booked the band on a tour of England, ending at Ronnie Scott's club in London. Then the Swedish impresario Bo Johnson booked them to tour Sweden, Finland, Poland, and Denmark. They had been playing in Europe for seven weeks when they arrived at the airport of Warsaw, where they were greeted by a delegation from the Polish Jazz Society and various fans, perhaps a hundred of them. Nelson Hatt said: "We were always treated so much better in other countries than we were in our own, and the response in Poland was so much more than we had received anywhere else. When we landed in Warsaw, there was a little Dixieland band at the airport, playing for us down on the tarmac. They had a TV crew that interviewed Woody, just off the plane.

"When we were riding into the city from the airport, on a bus, I was sitting next to a fellow who was very nice. He was in his thirties, and he spoke excellent English. He told me he was going to emcee our concerts. I said, 'Where are we playing?'

"He chuckled and said, 'You can't miss it. It's called the Congress Hall. It was built by the Russians, and it's the biggest thing in the city. They won't let anything be built bigger. It's where the Communist party meets. You'll be playing in the main hall.

"I said, 'How do you speak such good English? Did you study it in university?'

"He said, 'I learned it listening to the Voice of America and Radio Free Europe.'

"He said, 'We've been looking forward to having Woody and the band here for a long time.'

"I said, 'Is there a following here for the band?'

"He said that Woody had made a statement on Voice of America that his mother was Polish, and the Polish jazz fans immediately had adopted him.

"We were treated just beautifully by everybody."

The interpreter in question was Andrzej Jaroszewski, who remembers the encounter vividly. He still emcees the annual Jazz Jamboree.

The band played two concerts on February 25, 1976, at 6:30 and 8:30 p.m., in the auditorium of the Palace of Culture, at the center of Warsaw, dominating the city. Built with Polish labor and materials, it was the "gift" of Stalin, the largest building in the city. The Russians forbade the erection of any building larger. Its auditorium seats 3000.

"We had sellout audiences for both shows," Nelson said. "Woody was to be on TV, and it would be shown as far east as Russia, and in Hungary and Czechoslovakia, and probably Eastern Germany as well. We found out that people had come from those countries, riding a day or two on the train, to come to the concert."

Many members of the audience had paid as much as a week's salary for tickets.

"It was a gigantic hall," Nelson said, "with a lot of the interior walls and decor painted white and bright red upholstery with lacquered wood trim on the backs and the tops of the seats. It was surprisingly ornate."

Two albums from these concerts were released on the Poljazz label in Poland, and a CD derived from them was released in the United States in 1994 on the Storyville label. "The sound is lousy," Bill Byrne said. "We figured they had all the sound equipment in Poland there to record it. It was really such a poor country. They did as well as they could."

The next day the Jazz Society took the band on tours of the city. "The people went crazy," Bill Byrne said. "On the streets, when they saw Woody, they would come up to him, very loving. He knew a few words of Polish that he'd picked up around the house in Milwaukee. He bent over backwards to be nice; he was on his best behavior. The vodka was terrific, and Woody loved vodka."

Television crews were assigned to follow the band's every move, particularly Woody's. "I thought they were going to follow me into the john," Woody said.

Nelson Hatt said: "We were surprised at how pretty the women were. They look very similar to the Swedes.

"There was one awkward moment. We were sitting with the promoters at long tables in a restaurant, and John Hoffman, the Fig, mentioned something about Polish jokes. And I think it was the emcee who said, 'What are those?' We all thought, 'Oh boy, now you've stepped in it. Let's see you squirm out of this.' So he explained that these jokes were current in the States and he said it was just kind of arbitrary, and it could be any nationality, and it just kind of said that Polish people could do things that were just kind of silly or stupid. And the emcee said, 'Oh yes! We tell those jokes about Hungarians!'

"He said it was no surprise to him that we told those jokes. We said, 'Why?' He said that the people who emigrated to America at the beginning of the century were the poor and uneducated.

"They gave us one of the best tours I ever got on a trip. They took us to the Warsaw Ghetto Museum, they took us to the City of Warsaw Museum. I hadn't realized that Hitler had ordered the whole city destroyed, even though I'm a student of World War II. We saw films of German soldiers marching from house to house with flame throwers, burning the city out. And then they dynamited it. The Barbican Gate is really the only thing that was left standing."

The experience of Warsaw was emotional for the whole band, particularly Woody.

The bombing of Warsaw by Stuka dive bombers began on the very first day of the war, and appalling damage was done to the city, a treasury of ancient architecture, during the assault by German ground forces. During all the years of the occupation, the people of Warsaw were persecuted. By official Nazi doctrine, the Poles were an inferior people and were treated as such; the French, whom Hitler hoped to seduce, were treated comparatively well. Nearly a hundred thousand citizens of Warsaw were imprisoned or dispatched in summary street executions. Nearly half a million Warsaw Jews were sent to Auschwitz and death. In their effort to eradicate the Polish culture, the Germans closed all schools. Secondary and higher education were thereafter conducted by the Poles in secrecy. German troops destroyed historical monuments and closed theaters, museums, and scientific institutions.

On August 1, 1944, as Soviet troops were approaching, an underground home army and citizens of Warsaw rebelled. The Germans repressed them ruthlessly: some one hundred thousand of them murdered and countless more transported to camps in Germany. Total civilian deaths during this period are estimated to be a quarter of a million. The Germans then dynamited the royal palace, museums, churches, and libraries. By the time the Polish First Army, fighting under Soviet command alongside the Russians, freed the city in January, 1945, it was nothing but a vast expanse of shattered stones and brick.

After the war, the Poles decided to do something the people of no other country even attempted: they rebuilt Warsaw as it had been before the war. This astonishing feat was accomplished with vast amounts of donated labor and talent. Working with recovered plans, photographs, drawings, and sometimes simply the memories of survivors, they rebuilt what is now called Old Town, the oldest part of the city, with loving care.

"They were very proud of Old Town," Nelson Hatt said. "I just fell in love with Old Town. They took us to a restaurant in one corner of the square."

He referred to Rynek, or Market Square. The restaurant was the Krokodil. "It was very fancy," Nelson said. "They had waiters with little tuxedo-like waistcoats, and the napkin over the arm, and an old fellow at the door taking our coats. It was reasonably cold.

"We had this amazing dinner of roast duck and all the trimmings and ice-cold Polish vodka, Wyborowa. They served it in little thimble glasses with blinis. We had this huge meal, with great service and wines. When we got ready to pay for it, we figured out that for each one of us it was a hundred zlotys, which was about a dollar. So we called it duck for a buck, and it became one of the famous meals in the band's history.

"The dollar was precious to everyone there. We left all kinds of tips in American money on the table. The emcee had told us the average income was about thirty dollars a month. So when we were getting our coats we were leaving two and three dollar tips, and he was just about losing his mind. A half a month's or a month's earnings.

"We felt so rich there. I went into a little store off the square and started buying Christmas presents for family. I didn't even ask how much anything was. I walked out with two shopping bags that cost me six dollars and change.

"The people were wonderful."

Short though it was, the visit was a triumph, the first of a four trips to Poland. The band went from Warsaw to Copenhagen and then home.

▼   ▼   ▼

In the United States, Woody continued traveling by car as much as possible. Sometimes he would take Nelson Hatt with him, as he had previously taken Bill Chase. Mostly he traveled alone, but sometimes Charlotte was with him. Probably no man knew the roads and highways of America better than he, and he had a reputation for a connoisseur's knowledge of the best restaurants in big cities and small towns all across the United States and Canada. He would, in his endless journey, sometimes drive a hundred miles out of his way to go to a good one.

"He was a Rand McNally of restaurants," Jack Siefert said. Whenever Jack was on his way to some city or another city, he would call Woody to ask for advice on the restaurants there. And once Woody said, "Jack, the world is full of restaurants that were excellent a year ago."

Charlotte's cancer had now metastasized into the thyroid gland, and she was scheduled for another round of surgery. Probably for that reason, she was not in the car with Woody as he traveled to play a concert and give a clinic at Kansas State University in Manhattan, Kansas.

Automobile travel is one of the hazards of the life of jazz musicians. They drive too often and too long and too far—Philly Joe Jones once drove nonstop from Chicago to San Francisco to make a gig—and it is often in the night when they are exhausted after jobs. A lot of them have died in car crashes, including Clifford Brown, Richie Powell, Willie Dennis, Eddie Costa, Doug Watkins, Chu Berry, Scott LaFaro, and Stan Hasselgard. Once, when Woody and Bill Chase were on their way to the next job, a deer came through their windshield. Neither of them was hurt. Bill of course died not in a car but in a plane crash.

Inasmuch as Woody had been driving to jobs since the days when he had to sit on two pillows to do it, he had been making it to gigs by car for more than half a century. He had been in several automobile accidents since leaving Milwaukee in his Whippet to join Tom Gerun, starting with the one in which Tony Martin's car overturned on their way from San Francisco to Chicago. Yet, considering the millions of highway miles he had put in, his Corvette endlessly traversing American days, its headlights drilling tunnels through the night, it is amazing that he wasn't in more of them. Woody was a remarkably skillful driver.

On March 27, 1977, he was driving a rental car because his green Corvette was in a garage for work. (The rental agreement tells us that the car was a new two-door Thunderbird—the odometer registered 2667 miles.) The weather was warm and clear as Woody headed down the highway that morning. Feeling sleepy, he stopped and walked around the car a few times. He got back in and drove on. Around two o'clock that afternoon, on a two-lane highway—Kansas 18—about two hundred yards from the main gate of Fort Riley, he fell asleep. His car drifted across the double yellow line and crashed head on with another car. The driver of the other car was Barbara Racek, fifty-seven, of Junction City, Kansas.

Woody told friends later that what saved his life was a coincidence: an ambulance crew was parked by the side of the road. With the help of military police posted at the Fort Riley gate, they took Woody and Barbara Racek to Irwin Army Hospital, on the base, for first aid. According to the *Kansas City Times* on March 28, 1977, she was treated for abrasions and cuts. She and Woody were transferred to St. Mary's Hospital in nearby Manhattan, where she was treated further and released. Later Woody's insurance paid for the damage to her car, and she made no claim for personal injuries.

Woody had the good fortune to come under the care of a skilled orthopedic surgeon named Richard Baker. Woody's face was bruised and cut, his left leg almost demolished. And Dr. Baker encountered another problem. He telephoned Dr. Stanley Levy in Detroit.

"Woody had terrible, terrible, terrible sclerotic blood vessels," Dr. Levy said. "It would not be unusual with him that you couldn't get a blood-pressure reading. You'd put on the sphygmomanometer and you wouldn't get a reading because the blood vessels were so calcified.

"Dr. Baker was semifrantic. He was really in a bind. They didn't know what to do—whether Woody was in shock from the accident. But it didn't seem like he was in shock. I gave him my suggestions and finally they put a needle into an artery and his blood pressure was OK. They put a fair amount of hardware into his leg. Baker did a pretty decent job, considering the smashing up Woody'd had. I was in close touch with Baker. We'd talk every day or two."

The "fair amount of hardware" consisted of steel pins all the way up to the hip. Woody stayed at St. Mary's for a month before returning to California for rest and therapy. The band, meanwhile, was being led by saxophonist Frank Tiberi, who had been with it since 1969, and for some engagements, by clarinetist Buddy DeFranco.

The accident in Kansas was devastating, and there are among his friends those who think Woody never fully recovered. It is widely believed that he lost his teeth in that accident, but Ingrid said his teeth were already gone by then. He wore upper and lower plates, and false teeth present serious problems to brass and reed players.

Jack Siefert flew out to California to be with him as he arrived home. Jack and the late Wally Heider, another old friend of Woody's—he was the recording engineer on some of the Fantasy albums—came to the house. Jack said, "I asked Wally to help me carry Woody up those long winding stairs from the living room, because I had to get him to the hospital for treatment. We made a sling by crossing and locking our hands and we carried him up to the car. Woody said, 'It's nice to have some big guys around.'

"Then I drove him to the hospital. I was helping Woody through the corridors when some thoughtless woman came running around a corner and knocked Woody down. And she just kept running. She never stopped to apologize or say she was sorry. I picked him up and practically carried him to the doctor's office."[1]

Shirley Mancuso said, "Right after Woody had the automobile accident and the surgery, Charlotte had a thyroid operation. Then she had gall bladder surgery. They discovered when they opened her up that she had a growth in her intestine. So two or three days after the gall bladder surgery, which was horribly painful, they had to go back and open her up again and take out part of the intestine. She suffered terribly."[2]

"While still in the wheelchair," Jack Siefert said, "Woody flew from

California to Boston to receive an honorary doctor of music degree from the Berklee College of Music. The entire graduation ceremony was in honor of Woody. Woody was very proud of this honor. Neal Hefti and his wife, Frances Wayne, were present with other ex-members of the band."[3]

Then Woody went back on the road. He was back with the band by June, and, five months after the accident, on August 19, 1977, the *Chicago Sun-Times* reported that he was fronting it in a wheelchair. Steve Voce wrote in his monograph on Woody that he began "moving gingerly with the help of a walker, and then, incredibly, in late 1977, he was not only back with the band, but the walker became a familiar sight all over Europe as he led the band on tour."

But he soon abandoned the walker, and by the time he made his second visit to Poland, he was using only a cane. On October 22 and 23, 1977, during the twentieth Jazz Jamboree Festival, he played in Warsaw, then in Szczecin on the East German-Polish border. The reception was, if anything, even warmer than on his first visit to the country.

The Warsaw concert, which has been preserved on tape, was amazing. It opened with *Four Brothers*. Woody sang *I've Got News for You*. He sang well, with technique, range, and assurance. He was by now sixty-four, but there was no wobble in the voice; indeed, that came only near the end of his life, when he was very ill. His speaking voice, making announcements, as always giving full credits to soloists and arrangers, was strong. This was only six months after the collision in Kansas. The band was incandescent in such pieces as Chick Corea's *La Fiesta*, with some excellent electric piano by Pat Coil and the band's as-always incredible ensemble playing. In Gary Anderson's arrangement of Fauré's *Pavane*, Woody's clarinet sounded secure. The most astonishing performance of the concert was that of Allen Vizzutti in *Fire Dance*.

But the whole band comprised virtuosi, including Nelson Hatt and Dennis Dotson on trumpets, Frank Tiberi on tenor and bassoon, Birch Johnson on trombone, and bassist Marc Johnson.

The audience was on its feet and screaming after Gary Anderson's arrangement of Aaron Copland's *Fanfare for the Common Man*. Woody took the concert on out with a blues that dissolves into *Blue Flame*, and said with obvious sincerity, "Once again, I would like to thank all of you for being an extremely kind audience. And even better than that, you're extremely beautiful and kind people. And I hope that I can come back many times before the Lord takes me and visit with you all again. From the young men and me, we wish you love, and may the Lord bless you."

He would return twice more.

▼   ▼   ▼

European bookings had advantages over U.S. gigs. In the United States, the IRS was there after every American engagement with its hand out, always dangling the possibility of a jail term in front of him.

"The basic tortures of the road are still there," Woody told Herb Wong. "You don't get enough rest, you drive too far, and you don't get a decent meal. You're going to feel rotten. And that's the basic. If you can cover those two or three things, the rest will work."

Yet never once did he denounce Abe Turchen for bequeathing him this ordeal. This amazed his friends. Abe's cousin, Mayer Kanter, remained in contact with Woody. He said, "I constantly got the itinerary, and any time they were in Minneapolis, Omaha, Des Moines, I'd go to see the band and I never once heard Woody say a word against Abe."[4]

Why? Was it the memory of the time when Abe's gambling had saved him? Some have theorized that Woody was in on Abe's tax evasion. I don't think so. Neither did Hermie Dressel. Hermie several times told me of Woody's utter indifference to business and money. During the seventeen years Hermie spent with him, he never once looked at the books. Hermie told him the books were always open to him, whenever he was in New York and wanted a meeting with their accountants. Woody never bothered. He trusted Hermie, as he had trusted Abe. I told Hermie once that Wood sometimes reminded me of the fable of the ant and the grasshopper. Benny Goodman was like the ant, Woody the grasshopper that never thought about autumn. He lent money casually, gave his clothes away, and came up with mortgage money for friends who were in trouble. And he ran the sloppiest business operation imaginable.

28

Poland Farewell

On January 31, 1978, Woody suffered a loss comparable to that of Bill Chase. Gregory Herbert, one of his favorites of all the tenor players who passed through the band, was in Amsterdam, Holland, with Blood, Sweat, and Tears. He had begun experimenting with heroin, what jazz musicians call chipping, occasional rather than steady use. Someone sold him a bad dose, he injected himself, and was found dead in his hotel room. Woody was badly shaken by the news.

In April, Nelson Hatt, to whom Woody had become quite close, gave his notice. "I stayed four years, three weeks, and two days," Nelson said. "During the time I was on the band, I counted sixty people who went through it." Woody boasted during that period that his "young men" included nine graduates of the Eastman School, five of them with master's degrees. He was deeply impressed by the training of brass players at Eastman.

How could Nelson remember so precisely the length of time he was with Woody? "Because it was so hard to leave," he said. "I loved the entire time I was on the band. Woody said, 'I think you're doing the right thing in going to L.A.' The other guys were going to New York. He was Road Father incarnate. He really helped me get my head together. When I did leave, a lot of the guys that I'd been so close to, like Jimmy Pugh and Dennis Dotson, were already gone. There was a major turnover. And I was just, kind of, tired of the bus. I got off in Birmingham, Alabama, and drove across country to Los Angeles." (He still lives there.)

"I really admired what Woody stood for," he said, "and I loved him deeply."[1]

In July, 1978, Woody was back in New York to play at Avery Fisher Hall, performing a new work by Chick Corea, a twenty-one-minute *Suite for Hot Band*, highly praised in the *New York Times* by John S. Wilson, who wrote that the band was "sounding better than it has in years."

In January, 1981, Woody played his second inaugural ball, this one for Ronald Reagan, whom he had known in the past in Los Angeles. Performers do not get paid for concerts at the White House or inaugurations. The presumption is apparently that the honor of "serving" the President is reward enough. Reagan sent Woody a nice form letter, thanking him.

Abe Turchen lived out his last days on Social Security and Social Security disability payments, a Veterans Administration pension, and a military disability pension.

And in that same month Woody played Reagan's inaugural, Abe died of a heart attack, a complication of his diabetes. Steve Turchen believes Abe was born in 1914, although not even that seems to be sure. If so, he was sixty-nine. He was penniless.

Mike Turchen thought Woody should be informed. He telephoned Leonard Feather in Los Angeles. Leonard gave him a number in New Orleans, and Mike reached Woody there and gave him the news. He sounded, Mike said, saddened, and above all, he sounded tired.

October 31, 1978, found Woody and the band in Poland for the third time, playing at the Krakow Philharmonic Hall during an event called the All Souls Jazz Nights. The sponsor again was the Polish Jazz Federation.

Then, in December, 1978, and January, 1979, Woody did a series of interviews in San Francisco with Dr. Herb Wong for the Smithsonian Institution's oral history of jazz series. Dr. Wong was active with, and later became president of, the National Association of Jazz Educators (NAJE), later to become the International Association of Jazz Educators (IAJE).

It becomes evident in the course of the interview that Woody was far from enamored of the school "stage band" movement in America, despite his sometime involvement in clinics and public statements about it. The band was off for three weeks in early January, when the subject came up in one of the interviews. The band was scheduled to play the NAJE convention at 1 p.m. Sunday, March 11, at the Sheraton Hotel in Philadelphia. Woody seemed to feel—as many jazz musicians at the higher level do—that the "stage band" movement was producing cookie-cutter musicians, mechanics without individuality. As the interview progressed, Woody grew more heated. He complained about the general condition of popular music, despite earlier public statements on the value of the current pops he was incorporating into the band's book. He said of the young that "they were weaned on this and never allowed to hear anything else . . . ."

And then the tirade started.

"So, goddamn it," he said, "if somebody doesn't do anything about it, then we're dumber than I thought we were. I'd like all these big music conventions and all this bullshit that happens in America, where I've never really been, I've never been asked to attend, and I probably never will go . . . ."

Attempting to mollify him, Wong pointed out that he was going to the NAJE convention in March.

"Oh yeah," Woody said, "because we were bought to play. But I'm not going there as a person who's interested in what they're into, because I don't think they've ever come close to the real problems of the music industry, educational part of it or any part of it. They're still deciding who they like and don't like. They're doing the critique, and that's bullshit."

"Would you like to have a platform to say something about that at that convention of . . . ."

"No," Woody said, "because I don't think I want to. It's much too late for me, and I don't think they'd understand what I was talking about. I never saw such terrible egos as the few people I ever met from that organization. Sick egos."

"Is that right?" Wong said.

Woody said, "I remember when the jazz educators asked me if I was a member. I said, 'What is it?' And they told me, 'Well, if you would join, you pay the tuition or whatever it is, you can become a member.'

"I'd like for them to know about that. But I don't want to make any speech because I don't think they'd understand me."

Wong said, "No, I was just thinking about this discussion for helping them with their direction, really . . . ."

"No, I think it's too late," Woody said. "But I'll be glad if someone wanted to have a question-and-answer period. I'll be glad to answer their questions."

Again Wong tried to placate him.

"But I really have a hate thing going about it," Woody said. And, a little later, "I've done what I do because it's the only thing I like to do, and I love it. So I have no ax to grind. But I don't approve of what they're into and the way they're suggesting that we go, generally speaking, because most of it has been bullshit . . . . Do you think the educational process has been helped in the last twenty-five years by any of these groupings? I don't. I think it's been done by the educators themselves. I don't think that organization of the people that it stands for, if it stands . . . ."

Attempting to divert criticism, or at least dilute it, Wong said, "Yeah, I don't think any of these organizations in any discipline actually help that much."

Woody countered that "now we have a whole new generation of guys, they have no background, they played in stage bands in high schools. And now they're the music educator(s). . . . (And) some of them are very good, and some of them are very dumb. But that's the law of averages."

Gradually, as you read the transcript, you can feel Woody's temper cooling off. It should be noted that he *always* had the highest praise for the jazz-education programs at Berklee in Boston, North Texas State in Denton, Texas, and the Eastman School (particularly for brass players) in Rochester, New York. He got a good many of his best young musicians from those three schools. And by the 1990s, leading members of IAJE were acknowledging that much of Woody's criticism of the organization was justified. They insist that the organization is much improved and much more professional.

And Woody spoke to Wong with quiet pride of the high school scholarship fund in the name of Sister Fabian Riley in Milwaukee, saying that "once a year we show up and do a benefit concert and give away two scholarships to help the person(s) who win them in their jazz education."[2]

▼   ▼   ▼

In the summer of 1979, Woody made his fourth and final visit to Poland. The band played at Krosno, a city in the southeastern part of the country. That was on July 26.

After Woody died, a reminiscence was published in *Kurier Podlaski* of Bialystok, a little bit of writing that I find peculiarly touching. It was written by Jacek Grun, and translated for me by Irena Makowicz. It begins:

"I met Woody Herman accidentally in the southern part of Poland, in Krosno, in 1977 or 1978." The writer is in error about that; it was 1979. He continues:

> While I was at that small town, I noticed, to my amazement, posters announcing concerts of that giant of jazz and his actual big band, to be held in a small concert hall of the local school of music.
>
> Woody Herman and his young people arrived by plane from Vienna to Krakow, from where they were immediately transported by buses to Krosno.

However, a translator from Warsaw did not appear and I was asked to take over that—honorable for me—function.

When I realize how young are his musicians, I asked the Master if they indeed were his current "herd," but after the first fifteen minutes of the concert, I had the answer. They were monsters!

Each of them played in front of the orchestra and proved to be an astonishing soloist.

During an intermission, while drinking a Polish drink which he never refused, he told me that his mother was born in Poland. He did not know the exact place, only that it was in the southern part of Poland. It is possible therefore that she was a Goralka, from the mountain region, or that her roots were in Galicia.

Woody Herman knew only a few words in Polish, which he learned from his Polish friends in the United States.

Americans search for their European ancestors eagerly. But Woody was rather disappointed with his mother's homeland that day, because there was a sudden break-down in the water supply and all restaurants had to be closed. Sandwiches had to be prepared in a hurry.

The second concert, when the musicians had already had some aquae vitae in their blood, sounded different. It was just one great fun, full of musical humor, with Woody's frantic, spectacular displays as a vocalist and clarinetist, and the warm reception from the audience, sitting right at the feet of the orchestra. Woody was delighted.

During the supper I asked him how many bands like this one, considering the high level of skills of young American musicians, would he be able to form in the U.S. today? His answer was, "Probably more than ten," and later he added, "This is the clay from which a good sculptor can do whatever he wants."

The article, which concludes with a biography of Woody, presents a small problem. All other sources indicate that Woody's mother was born in Germany of Polish parents. But then the border between the two countries, disputed to deadly result over the years, has shifted. It is probably impossible to resolve the problem, but the mention of Galicia is interesting: Irena Chlecka Makowicz pointed out that large waves of immigration from Galicia hit the United States early in this century.

The Galicia of Poland is not to be confused with that of Spain. Irena told me: "The name, which older people in Poland still use, referred to the southern part of Poland under Austrian occupation during Poland's partition by the three powers, Russia, Prussia, and Austria. This may explain why they say Woody Herman's mother was born in Germany."

▼

Krosno is famous for exquisite blown glass. Bill Byrne said, "They gave Charlotte a beautiful vase that I carried all over Europe."

The next night, July 27, the band was featured in a concert at the Jazz Jantar, in the Forest Opera in Sopot, near Gdansk, on the shore of the Baltic Sea. It was. of course, at Gdansk that Lech Walesa led the Solidarity movement that eventuated in Poland's freedom from Soviet domination.

On all four of Woody's visits to Poland, Bill Byrne said, the Jazz Federation made much of Woody's Polish ancestry. And, Bill said, "Woody had a real soft spot for Polish people."[3]

In April, 1981, Woody returned to Milwaukee to play the seventh annual Sister Fabian Scholarship Fund Concert at the University of Wisconsin. Afterwards, a *Milwaukee Journal* reporter wrote:

> Somewhere deep beneath that dazzling smile there must be a hidden motivation. Woody Herman keeps coming back to his home town to perform benefit scholarship concerts in the memory of one of his high school teachers, Sister Fabian Riley.
>
> Wednesday, he dragged his sixty-eight-year-old body into the Union Ballroom of the University of Wisconsin, Milwaukee. He has just hauled his Thundering Herd by bus all the way from Arizona.
>
> There was Woody, right in the middle of the scholarship presentations, looking more thrilled about it than the high-schoolers who came up to get them. There he was, for the umpteenth time, striking up the band to swing as if it had just discovered the kick of a tricky new beat. There he was, leaning into his alto saxophone, bending plaintive notes that rise off into memory. The nun's ghost must be staring him right in the eyes . . . .
>
> What's driving this guy? Doesn't he know the big band era is over? Then I found out. It's not guilt. It's not the money or the glory. I found out why you can believe this man. He really does all this because, decades ago, Sister Fabian inspired him to a career in music.
>
> A little old lady tapped me on the shoulder and said, "I cradled Woody in my arms when he was born." I leaned over to listen, and Julia Sherman, age ninety-three, continued, "I watched him grow up. He was brought up right. His father was very strict. Woody always did the right things. He is a very good person."

More and more, the newspapers took note of his age and physical condition, the writers often marveling at his perseverance. And then, with the arrival of the 1980s, it seemed that respite was at hand; it seemed he might be able to have his own club in New Orleans, playing there for long periods of the year and largely escaping the rigors of the road.

Woody had an affection for New Orleans going back to the days when he been there with Tom Gerun. In February, 1980, the band played in the Mardi Gras parade, riding on the third float of the procession. Woody loved it, according to Bill Byrne.

The Pete Fountain band was playing at the Hilton Hotel. Shortly after the parade, Tom Gaskill, manager of the city's Hyatt Regency Hotel, approached Woody to say he would like to try something similar. He wanted to build a room adjacent to the hotel and lodge Woody's band there more or less permanently. And, he said, he had two backers to finance the project.

"It seemed like a dream idea to me," Woody said, "even a turning point for helping big bands to survive. If we were able to repeat the kind of success Pete Fountain was having, hotel people around the country might say, 'Hey, what's this?' What a way to cap off my later years.

"Best of all, it would give us a home base from which to operate and help us reduce the constant traveling. That, in turn, would cut the normal, steady turnover of young musicians. And the bonus was having the time and place to rehearse. From that base thirty-six weeks a year we could arrange tours for the other months and have our pick of the best engagements. The reason for that is that when you're not available most of the time, the demand and the price go up."[4]

Adjacent to the hotel was a 9000-foot shell that had been left unfinished, facing on Polydras Plaza. With theater seating, the club, to be called Woody Herman's, would accommodate five hundred. Though many of the fixtures and much of the lighting had not yet been installed, the room opened in late 1981.

"It was a gorgeous room, beautifully appointed," Jack Siefert said. "It was meant to be for television shows. When he wasn't there, they could use it for television shows. The acoustics were perfect. The location was great. The wall's were covered with memorabilia that I'd sent down."

In January, 1982, *Newsweek* ran a story on the event.

Even for New Orleans, it's a steamy night. Up on the bandstand, Woody Herman's Young Thundering Herd, fifteen men strong, is blistering through *Caldonia* . . . . Ta-ta-*ta*: with split-second timing, the five trumpeters, three trombones and four saxophones blast out one note each in a rapid-fire riff. In front, Herman, snapping his fingers and smiling broadly, picks up his clarinet and, head thrown back and eyes closed tight, begins plucking notes out of the stratosphere. If the band seems even more exuberant than usual, it should be. It's opening night at Woody Herman's, a sleek new club at the Hyatt Regency that, for thirty-six weeks or so a year, will be the permanent location of one of the last of the legendary big bands. After forty-five years on the road, Herman has found a home.

In July, the band went to New York to play four nights at Lush Life, a club at Thompson and Bleecker streets. In the light of later events, John S. Wilson's report in the *New York Times* July 13 has a wistful, wishful quality:

> Any time that Woody Herman has come to New York with his orchestra in the last twenty years, he has been on a trip from nowhere, on his way to nowhere—a series of one-night stands that have had no beginning and no end. In recent years he has played one night at Carnegie Hall, one night at the Bottom Line, one night at Wednesday's and one night at Jack Kleinsinger's Highlights in Jazz.
>
> But starting tonight . . . he will be making a visit under different circumstances . . . . Instead of traveling in a vacuum, the band is taking four months off from its permanent base in New Orleans, a room in the Hyatt-Regency Hotel called Woody Herman's. The band left New Orleans May 15 and will return September 15.

Wilson notes that much of the band's current book is being written by its pianist, John Oddo, and that a new album, *Woody Herman Live at the Concord Jazz Festival*, was about to be released on the Concord Jazz label. Wilson concluded:

> Next fall, when the band returns to New Orleans, Mr. Herman will start a series of radio broadcasts, five nights a week, two hours a night, originating from WWIW-AM in New Orleans and transmitted by satellite to a group of stations. According to plans, the programs will be heard on approximately fifty stations, starting October 18. In New York, where final arrangements with a station have not been completed, the program will be on Monday through Friday evenings from 9 to 11 . . . .
>
> Although Mr. Herman's New Orleans room got off to a slow start, it began to catch on during the last six weeks before the band went on the road . . . .
>
> "It took three and a half months to get anything moving," Mr. Herman conceded. "The problem was that the budget was used up just to finish the room before we even opened. So the promotion possibilities were very limited. When we go back in the fall, we should be a lot better off. We'll do a campaign and we'll have those radio broadcasts."

On August 3, 1982, the band played a gig at the Holiday Inn in Ventura, California. By now I was living near Ventura. So was Artie Shaw, with whom I was then spending a good deal of time. I asked Artie if he wanted to go to hear the band, and we went together.

The atmosphere was cordial. Charlotte was there, looking radiant and indeed showing no signs of the cancer she was fighting. She had three months to live.

A day or two later I caught it from Woody. He said, "What the hell are you doing hanging around with Artie Shaw?"

I said, "Well you know, Wood, I've got to know him pretty well in the last year or so."

"Yeah?" he said. "Well let me tell you something, pal. Just when you think you know Artie Shaw, you'll find out you *don't* know Artie Shaw."

When Woody got back to New Orleans, he found that the people who had promised the financing for the club had backed out. The place was in the same condition in which he had left it: unfinished. And, while the publicity in New York and nationally might have been good, local exposure was negligible. After playing six nights a week for months in the club, Woody said, he would encounter local friends who would ask, "What are you doing in New Orleans?"

One night Jack Siefert and Woody went to a restaurant Woody wanted to try. "We came out and grabbed a cab," Jack said. "The driver said, 'You're Woody Herman, aren't you?'"

Woody said, "Yeah."

And the driver said, "Where you playing?"

Woody looked at Jack and said, "See what I mean? There's the problem."

On November 13, 1982, the Associated Press carried a small obituary for the club:

NEW ORLEANS, Nov. 12 (AP)—A nightclub created to bring back Woody Herman and his fifteen-piece Thundering Herd to the birthplace of jazz has closed after less than a year.

"The club didn't have the funds to pay us," said Bill Byrne, a member of the band and its road manager. "Most of the guys are just going home."[5]

Charlotte's cancer had—it borders on the banal even to say so—weighed heavily on him during his absences from California. "I was on the phone with her every day," Woody said. "Not a lot of people, outside of our personal friends, knew how sick she was. She tried to cover it; she wasn't the kind of person who would have wanted anyone to know she was ill."[6] Her condition had now grown worse. She had declined further chemotherapy. She didn't want to stay in their bedroom on the bottom level of the house but spent her time on a soft leather sofa on the second floor, just off the living room.

At the airport, as he was leaving to return to California, a reporter asked about the closing of the club, then said, "What's the greatest record you ever made?"

Woody said, "I've been married and in love with the same woman for forty-six years. Can you match that record?"[7]

Shirley Mancuso said: "I thought Charlotte was the most wonderful person in the world. So warm. When she became ill, Woody was very concerned, and very sad, but there was only so much he could do. And I'll tell you, Charlotte didn't let him in. She didn't let him into her feelings. Which was too bad for Woody. Because then he would talk to others about it, and she would get very angry. I don't know whether she didn't want people to know she was so ill, or she thought Woody didn't have any business talking about it. He was sort of left out. In fact, everybody was. Charlotte didn't talk to me too much about it either, and I was about the closest person to her. We were very, very good friends."[8]

As Charlotte's condition deteriorated, Ingrid came home from Nashville. She would never go back.

Woody was at her hospital bedside when Charlotte Neste Herman slipped away on November 20, 1982.

29

Down Under

Shortly after Christmas, 1984, I telephoned Woody. I spoke briefly to Ingrid, who had suggested that it might be a good idea if I came to see him, and I could sense her concern. Later she said, with that odd and self-scathing honesty of hers: "I was really tired of what I was doing in Nashville, and knew I wasn't going to get any further. I had reached my glass ceiling. And deservedly so. I really didn't see what my dad would do without his house to come back to. I got involved in it, and decided to stay here."

She would fight to hold onto the house; and she would be with Woody for the rest of his life.

Ingrid let me in. I descended the curved stairway into the living room, and Woody shook hands with me and led me onto the terrace. We sat down on steel tubular garden furniture that looked as if it came with the house when he purchased it in 1947. He was wearing shorts and a sports shirt, and his age and fragility hurt me. I could feel within me the love that so many people shared for him, and I heard myself blurting:

"You know, you are a very great man."

"No," he said very softly. "No I'm not." And he meant it.

I asked, very gently, how he was getting along. Charlotte's absence was almost palpable. I daresay that every previous time I had been here, she had answered the door.

"It's tough at times," he said. "I'm all right as long as I keep moving."

My heart aching, I said, "Why do you keep on?"

"Two reasons," he said. "The first is my love of music. The second is that I have an overwhelming need to make a living."

"The IRS?"

"Yes."

"Are you still paying that?"

"Yes, and it gets bigger. My lawyer is trying to get a settlement for once and for all, and I am hoping he will."

"And how are you doing otherwise?"

"I'm at the stage," Woody said, "if I wake up in the morning, I figure I'm ahead of the game. I've had the flu once this year. You have to keep warm. That's when you know you're no longer a boy."

"It's crossed my mind," I said, "that if you don't make younger friends along the way, you could end up one day with none at all."

He said, "I don't have any trouble there, of course, because of the ages of the young men in the band. It keeps me in touch, and it's a stimulus. We get along just fine—as long as we stick to the subject of music. If we get on anything else, the generation gap starts to get very wide, man.

"I love bringing them along. I love seeing them develop."

It occurred to me that without the huge alumni of splendid musicians he had helped develop, music would be very different indeed.

"How do you do it, Wood?" I said. "Losing Charlotte, the road, all of it."

"Well, I was raised a Catholic . . . ."

This was the moment when I first realized this. The subject of religion had never before come up. Later, Dick Hafer told me that during his time with the band, Woody went to mass every Sunday. "He never missed," Dick said.

"Are you still?" I said. "A practicing Catholic?"

"Yes. I have my faith, and I pray. I went to church the other day."

"Was Charlotte Catholic too?"

"Yes. She was a convert."

"Is that the reason you stayed together?"

"I think the reason Charlotte and I were survivors," he said, "is humor. We could always laugh at each other." He paused, looking inward, and then said something that will tell you a lot about Charlotte, that lovely woman whose poise after the mastectomies was impressive.

"She was lying in there," he said, his hand indicating the house, "a few days before she died, and I was sitting on the bed. And what can you say to anyone in those circumstances? And I put my face in my hands and I started to cry. And she raised her hand . . . " he imitated the gesture, a slow and hesitant lift of the arm . . . "and who knows how much it cost her, and she put it on my shoulder, and she said, 'Straighten up, boy!'"

For a moment then I saw him and Charlotte as seventeen.

The day after that conversation, Woody was on the road again, playing a gig through New Year's Eve in Sparks, Nevada, with the Nat Pierce–Frankie Capp big band. Then he went on to New York for ten weeks in the King Cole Room of the St. Regis Hotel with a small group.

By now there was a new problem: Who would book the band? Four months before this, in August, 1984, Willard Alexander had died. The agency was now owned by his wife. The head of the Chicago office, Tom Cassidy, and his wife Susan, who worked in the office, decided to set up their own agency. "We started on January 1, 1985," Tom said. "Within two weeks Hermie Dressel approached us about handling Woody, and we began booking the band in April, 1985, and things started to go really well on the tours. This was the first time in ten years Woody had started to make some money."[2]

And the need for it was increasing. On March 5, 1985, while Woody was playing the St. Regis, the IRS seized his home and sold it at auction to one William Little, about whom more in due course, for $100,000, approximately a fifth of its value. The news of Woody's financial condition by now had passed beyond the tabloid press: mainstream newspapers were covering it. Little arranged to let Woody rent the house back from him and continue to live in it for a rent of $1,150 a month.

Nat Pierce recalled the St. Regis engagement. "Woody went to St. Patrick's Cathedral every Sunday," he said. "He got very serious about religion. He was lost; he was totally lost. He couldn't play. He had no teeth. His memory was gone. It was a terrible scene. We were drawing no people. It was a horror. Really bad."[3]

During the St. Regis engagement, Zoot Sims died of cancer. Zoot's funeral service, held at St. Peter's Lutheran Church, was heavily attended. Woody was one of the eulogists.

He was looking toward his own mortality: the generation of the Four Brothers band, seemingly so much younger than he when they were in the band, was passing. These considerations are inevitable as time does its inexorable work. As Artie Shaw put it to me when he reached his late seventies, "Hey, I can do the arithmetic as well as you can." The years, that once seemed to lie endlessly ahead, become numbered like those on a meter down to zero. And Woody began musing on his legacy. I suspect this is the reason he took a renewed interest in *Ebony Concerto*. If some of the members of the First Herd were not excellent readers, the young men in his current band, products of the jazz education movement in the universities, were. The problem was that he could no longer play the piece, and he never thought he had been able to play it well. But, propitiously, he met someone who could do so: the distinguished clarinetist Richard Stoltzman, who was in his early forties. And Stoltzman is of a new breed of classical musicians, those with a substantial grounding in jazz.

Stoltzman was born in Omaha, Nebraska, on July 12, 1942. He had become fascinated by jazz through his father's record collection when he was growing up in Cincinnati, Ohio. The collection included a great many Woody Herman records, and his father took him to hear the band when it appeared in that city. Stoltzman studied classical clarinet at the music school of Ohio State University, where he also played in what was in effect an underground jazz band, led by young arranger Ladd McIntosh. (They had to rehearse almost in secret, and when the band wanted to compete in the Intercollegiate Music Festival held in May, 1967, it made the trip on the members' own money. When it won in the big-band category, with attendant publicity, Ohio State authorities were actually embarrassed by this revelation that it had jazz on campus.)

"Then," Stoltzman said, "I spent ten summers at the Marlboro Music Festival with Rudolf Serkin, Pablo Casals, many of the great musicians who made me realize that chamber music is the best kind of music in the world to make. And in a sense that is what jazz is. The best kind of music is when people are communicating together and playing off each other, which is really what chamber music is. And so is jazz."

Though he became a rising star in the classical music world, a member (along with pianist Peter Serkin) of the avant-garde chamber-music group Tashi, he continued to play jazz and had performed at Fat Tuesday's in New York. He also from time to time sat in with a group in which writer George T. Simon played drums at Jimmy Ryan's on Wednesday afternoons.

Woody first became aware of him through a segment of the *CBS Sunday Morning* television show, focusing attention on him as one of the musicians interested in both jazz and classical music—a phenomenon nowhere near as unusual as the news media keep making it seem. It was probably this exposure that set Woody to thinking about *Ebony Concerto* again. He began asking around for a phone number and soon found that his old friend George T. Simon, who had first applied the term "Herd" to the Band That Plays the Blues, knew Stoltzman. Simon asked Stoltzman to come by and play at Jimmy Ryan's. He didn't tell the clarinetist that Woody Herman would be there.

Stoltzman played, and then the group left the small bandstand.

"Woody was sitting at a table in the corner," Stoltzman recalled. "I had never met him. I didn't even know what was happening. George introduced us. Woody stuck out his hand and said, kind of gruffly, 'All right. Let's talk.'"

"He then described some of the plans he had for *Ebony Concerto*, including concerts and a new recording of the work.

"I was very honored to be asked. Actually, I was completely bowled over just to meet him."

Woody arranged for Stoltzman to appear with the band, performing the work in a series of concerts.

"The band really wanted to play the piece for Woody," Stoltzman said. "I was a little apprehensive. Woody wanted me to conduct it and rehearse it with them. I was afraid, working with all these hot jazz musicians, that I was going to be out of my element. I remember the first rehearsal. Woody had that little silver whistle around his neck. I was working with them and saying things like, 'Do you think you could make this a little more staccato?' And 'The diminuendo needs a little . . . .' The guys weren't exactly tuned into all this, and comments were going around the band. And then Woody blew the whistle and said, 'This is the guy who's gonna do it; let's settle down.'

"They really were great. When I started meeting them, and riding on the bus—and we played this piece many, many times in the course of about two-and-a-half years—I realized that these guys knew their history. This piece was a big monument for them. They wanted to play it really well. They had the scores; they had studied the other recordings. And Frank Tiberi was great, because he led the sax section, and Mike Brignola, who played bass clarinet. The bass clarinet part is a bitch, and he played it great. These people were terrific.

"We had to take guitar, French horn, and harp on the road with us.

"I guess when I heard *Ebony Concerto* for the first time, it was the Benny Goodman record. I thought it was a kind of dry, academic piece. When Woody asked me to play it, I was thrilled, but I was also kind of scared. By the time I did this piece with Woody, I had played a lot of Stravinsky and had worked with a lot of contemporary musicians and I understood that contemporary music isn't necessarily dry and academic. You've got to put a lot of blood and guts into it, just like you would any kind of music. These people, these great musicians in Woody's band, they really wanted to play it well. The consequence was that I felt like it was a completely different level of playing that piece than Stravinsky got out of it in the studio.

"Some of the great artists are ahead of their time. As listeners, as we start to hear more and more strange sounds and more and more interesting combinations of instrument, we start realizing, 'Whoa! This isn't academic. This is out there.' And perhaps that's the case with *Ebony Concerto*.

"I think Woody was extremely proud of the piece. Whenever we'd play it, he would tell stories of how Stravinsky would come to the band rehearsals. Man, who wouldn't want to say that Picasso drew their picture, or Stravinsky wrote for their band? These are seminal figures of the twentieth century."

▼   ▼   ▼

Sometimes, of course, for hard economic reasons, Woody worked with small groups. In June, 1985, he put together a septet that included Harry (Sweets) Edison, trumpet; Al Cohn and Buddy Tate, tenor saxophones; John Bunch, piano; Steve Wallace, bass; and Jake Hanna, drums. Woody had been working with bassist George Duvivier, but Duvivier was fighting cancer and unable to play. (He died on July 11.) With tours of Europe, Japan, and Australia immediately ahead of him, Woody replaced Duvivier with the twenty-eight-year-old Canadian bassist Steve Wallace. Bill Byrne accompanied the group as road manager.

"The European tour started on the Fourth of July," Byrne said. "We flew to Vienna. It ended on July 24 in Valencia, Spain. Woody and I flew up to London on the 25th. He stayed a couple of nights in London, then took off for Tokyo."

Because of prior commitments, Buddy Tate and John Bunch could not make the trip to the Far East. Nat Pierce flew to Japan to replace Bunch. The group, now a sextet, played five days in Japan, ending the tour at the jazz festival in Madaroa.

Also on the tour was Dave Brubeck, whose wife, Iola, accompanied him on the trip. Dave told me: "We were in the room next to Woody at a summer festival in the mountains of Japan where it was so hot that everybody had to leave their doors open. There was no air conditioning because it was a ski resort. Woody was right next door to us. You could hear him breathing. He was on the phone all night, trying to put together the next tour—just struggling right up to the end. This was not long before he died."

Iola said, "It was so sad to think of somebody as old and sick as Woody was, who's paid all his dues, who's still on the phone trying to put together the next tour."

What the problem was remains uncertain. Bill Byrne thinks that George Wein, who had arranged the Japanese tour and accompanied it, had paid the money to Hermie Dressel. Woody, expecting the full sum, was upset when he didn't get it and screamed at George. It should be remembered that Woody's health was fading quickly now, his breathing was failing, he was often in pain, and those close to him noted that he could be unpredictably irascible.

George said there was a problem of transportation. George said, "I'd never had a bad word with Woody in my life. I loved Woody.

"He had booked these dates in Australia. They had nothing to do with us; we didn't book them. And we were trying to help him get to Australia. And something went wrong with the transportation. And he really got nasty, and I said, 'Woody, that's not fair. We have been trying to help you. I've had a person working on this for two days.' What really makes me sad is that that was the last conversation I ever had with Woody."[4]

According to Tom Cassidy, George advanced some money to Woody and Woody made more on the Australian tour. ("George Wein was always good for it," Bill Byrne said. "He never let us down. Not even when the Alexandra Palace burned down in London, and we couldn't play. He still paid us.")

One way or another, Woody got to Australia on August 8. His tour of the country was an enormous success, despite the increasingly obvious weaknesses of his own playing. On arriving in Brisbane, he was asked by a reporter why he had never before toured Australia. He said he had been waiting for thirty-five years to visit the subcontinent, but "nobody asked me."[5]

The tour opened on Friday, August 9, at the Brisbane Cultural Center, with a total of eight shows scheduled between then and Sunday, August 18, when the group was to play the Sydney Opera House. The critics gave much of their praise to Sweets Edison and Al Cohn, whose playing seemed to astonish them. After the Brisbane performance, which was a complete sellout, Neville Meyers wrote in the *Courier-Mail*:

Herman, typically, was not featured much (the 72-year-old veteran considers himself 'no great shakes' as clarinetist-singer, always preferring to spotlight his other musicians) but was in good humor, listening and cheering more than he played, guiding and inspiring the action.

There were also moments of poignancy—and I might as well say outright Herman is something of a hero of mine—to see Herman's onstage frailty as well as off-stage warmth and humility. This was especially so when, after one performance, the veteran jazz player was caught backstage in a sea of enthusiastic high-school musicians who, he told them, had 'the future of jazz in their hands.'"[6]

Dick Hughes wrote in the *Australian National Daily*:

"Just in case you thought I'd forgotten my early youth," (Herman) said towards the end of the concert, "here it is—*The Golden Wedding*." Deafening cheers were the response for this bizarre number, which has haunted Australian jazz musicians of all styles for more than 40 years. ("Hey, mate! Can you play *The Golden Wedding*?")[7]

The performances scheduled for Melbourne, Perth, and Sydney were sold out well in advance. In all the reviews, the group was enthusiastically praised; Woody was treated for the most part with a compassionate reverence. After the final performance, on Sunday at the Sydney Opera House, Joya Jenson wrote in the *Sydney Morning Herald*: "Although the warmth, showmanship and general musicality were there, his playing, with its occasional suspect intonation and other lapses, was something less than the Woody of old."[8]

One interviewer turned up an interesting and obscure bit of information about Woody's early recordings. Broadcaster Fred Somerville asked him about the quote used in the opening of *Woodchopper's Ball*. It is from *Bella figlia dell' amore*, from *Rigoletto*. Woody, typically, said he had no great knowledge of classical music and said, "I first heard that quote played by Louis Armstrong, but I can't tell you what the record was. It was one of his early ones."[9]

There was a kind of glow about that tour. The Australians wanted him back the next year. Some reporters urged him to bring the big band in the 1986-87 season. "Maybe," Woody said. "Who knows?"

It was as if they, and he, knew it would never come to pass.

▼   ▼   ▼

He flew from Sydney to Kansas City, where he was to receive an award. Tom Cassidy said: "I met him there. The award reads *From the Officers and Board of Directors for the International Jazz Hall of Fame, presented to*

Woodrow C. Herman the William J. Count Basie Memorial Award. Woody turned around and handed it to me. This was August 21, 1985, which was Basie's birthday. He was very pleased with that award." But he didn't keep it. Cassidy still has it. I remembered Ray Sherman saying, "He never kept anything." Woody had left Grammys with him, and other material with Jack Siefert, including air checks that he treated "like frisbees." I thought of the car he had abandoned on a San Francisco street so long ago, and of the clothes he was always either leaving behind or giving away.

The aftermath of the Japanese tour was that Woody let Hermie Dressel go after seventeen years. By all accounts money had been handled in a feckless way, and the embarrassment in Japan had finished the relationship. Tom Cassidy was present in the Chicago hotel room where Woody told Hermie it was over. "It was awful," Tom said.[10]

On January 7, 1986, Woody started an engagement with a sextet at the Vine Street Bar and Grill in Hollywood. It's a pleasant a little club on Vine just south of Sunset Boulevard and down the street from the Capitol Records tower. The personnel included Jack Sheldon, trumpet; Bob Cooper, tenor saxophone; Ross Tompkins, piano; John Heard, bass; and Jake Hanna, drums. I went by opening night. The club has a small band room to the rear of the main room, and I chatted between sets with Woody, Jack Sheldon, and Jake.

Woody said his teeth were hurting him, bothering him badly. The condition of the mouth is critical to any saxophonist or clarinetist because the mouthpiece is pressed against the upper teeth; the lower lip is curled back over the bottom teeth, and years of playing creates a little line of callus inside the lip. The only effective fixative for his dentures Woody had found was a product called Rigident, and for some reason the only place he could find it was a pharmacy near Jack Siefert's home. Jack bought it for him by the case. Furthermore, with his emphysema Woody no longer had the breath support he needed. It was obvious that his physical condition was deteriorating.

So was his playing. His clarinet work was weak, sometimes squeaky as he struggled against his infirmities. Oddly enough, he sang extremely well. Two days later, on January 9, a review by James Liska, then second-string critic to Leonard Feather at the *Los Angeles Times*, appeared in the paper:

> The good news is that Woody Herman is alive and well at the Vine Street Bar and Grill through Sunday night. The bad news is that at 72 Herman is but a shadow of his former musical self.

Somewhat worn out, out of tune, lacking ideas on the clarinet, and vocally void in musicianship and emotion, Herman has been reduced to an act whose every musical move can be appreciated only from a nostalgic perspective.

When protected in a big band context, Herman can keep his current weaknesses barely detectable. But in the sextet setting at the Thursday opening in Hollywood, his flaws stood out like sore thumbs.[11]

The review infuriated musicians and fans alike, because by now Woody's physical condition and tax troubles were an open secret. Everyone in the profession *knew* why he was still working. Bassist John Heard was in a rage about it. "This man is a national monument!" he said of Woody. From then on, Liska's name was anathema to many in the jazz community of Los Angeles. Eventually he left the paper to write for *Playboy*. That review is unforgotten not because it was untrue but because its tone seemed to be one almost of pleasure. Among the countless reviews of Woody Herman that I compiled in my research, I find nothing to compare to it except the manic diatribe by Patrick Scott in the Toronto *Globe and Mail*. The Australian reviews had noted Woody's musical decline and physical frailty, but without exception they were written with a tone of regret, compassion, and respect.

In April, 1986, the *National Enquirer* printed a story under the headline:

BANDLEADER WOODY HERMAN, 72, STRUGGLING TO PAY
$1.5 MILLION TAX BILL AFTER IRS SEIZES HIS HOME

The story read:

Jazz great Woody Herman owes a staggering $1.5 million in back taxes. The Internal Revenue Service has seized his home and every penny he earns after expenses goes to the government, sources reveal.

And the sad truth is it isn't even Woody's fault that he got into trouble with the IRS.

At 72, when other men his age are retired and enjoying their "golden years," Herman is still making records and performing, doing one-night stands in one-horse towns, trying to stay one step ahead of the tax man.

Woody got into trouble with the IRS many years ago when his personal manager, who handled all of the bandleader's financial affairs, failed to pay Woody's income taxes, according to sources.

"Woody's problems began in the 1940s and 1950s when his personal manager sank deeper and deeper in debt due to gambling," an insider revealed. "By the time Woody found out that the man he had trusted with every penny of his money was gambling it all away, it was too late."

The manager was jailed for eight years and later died, but Woody still owed
the tax man. By 1965 the debt was $800,000—but since then, through snow-
balling interest, it has mushroomed to $1.5 million . . . .

The dates were wrong, and Abe Turchen did not spend eight years in jail.
But more and more newspaper writers wondered at the fact that Woody
was still out there working, and more and more they commented on his
physical condition.

In June, 1986, ASMAC, the American Society of Musical Arrangers and
Composers, in a ceremony at the Castaways Restaurant in Burbank, California, gave Woody the organization's President's Award, with Les Brown,
Billy May, Ralph Burns, and other friends in the audience. The ASMAC
awards usually go to composers or arrangers, and Alex North received one
in that ceremony. The award to Woody, the inscription stated, was "For his
unqualified support of composers and arrangers and his outstanding career
as an internationally famous bandleader, instrumentalist and vocalist."

It was true. An astonishing list of arrangers and composers had written
for his bands, from the days of Joe Bishop and Gordon Jenkins on: Kenny
Ascher, Ralph Burns, Alan Broadbent, Bill Chase, Al Cohn, John Fed-
chock, Dizzy Gillespie, Jimmy Giuffre, Slide Hampton, Neal Hefti, Bill
Holman, Tony Klatka, Johnny Mandel, John Oddo, Nat Pierce, Shorty
Rogers, Bill Stapleton, and more. Even the gifted Maria Schneider, a
protégée of Gil Evans, wrote some of her first professional charts for
Woody.

Most of his old bandleading friends and acquaintances were gone.
Glenn Miller, of course, had been dead for forty-two years. Tommy Dorsey
had been gone thirty, Jimmy Dorsey twenty-nine, Duke Ellington twelve.
Count Basie had died two years earlier, on April 26, 1984, and on June 13,
three days before Woody received the ASMAC award, Benny Goodman
had died.

In early July, Woody was briefly hospitalized with fluid in his lungs. He
still would not, or more precisely, because of the IRS could not, stop
working and traveling.

30

The Last Gig

A vivid description of Woody's last days on the road was written for the *American Scholar* by Terry Teachout, a former member of the editorial board of the *New York Daily News*, a critic of jazz and classical music, and a former bassist. Teachout had studied bass in the hope of some day playing in the Woody Herman band. Now he went on the road with it for a week to observe and report on it. He wrote:

It is four minutes after noon. I am standing in the parking lot of a run-down motel on the outskirts of LeMars, Iowa. Those who eat breakfast have long since boarded the band bus. A handful of stragglers, some of whom have all too clearly just stumbled out of bed, are scrambling on board for the long haul to Kansas City, where the Thundering Herd will have a night off. Woody Herman has already left for the Sioux City airport. Too fragile to endure the day-to-day stresses of life on the bus, he will fly to the next gig. No one resents his absence. He paid his dues long before most of the musicians in the band were born.

"This is home, man," one musician says to me as we climb on board. If that is so, then the Thundering Herd is in desperate need of a housekeeper. The back of the bus, where the rowdier Herdsmen like to sit, is littered with books, pillows, and old newspapers from various cities. A huge double bass, snugly wrapped in its black canvas case, is balanced gingerly in the seat ahead of me. The overhead luggage racks are crammed with suitcases and overnight bags of every imaginable size and color. A hand-lettered sign hangs on the door of the toilet: "Contamination! Hazardous waste may be harmful to your health."

The door of the bus hisses shut and the driver pulls out of the parking lot. As the cornfields of southwestern Iowa slip by unnoticed, the players swap battered paperbacks, play Trivial Pursuit, and trade notes on the restaurants of LeMars. A cassette of the band's next album for Concord Jazz, recorded three weeks ago at a concert in San Francisco, makes the snail-like way from seat to seat. One man is banging away at a pocket calculator, working feverishly at his tax return.

I have brought along a homemade cassette of the First Herd's recordings from the forties. To my surprise, I discover that most of the people sitting around me have never heard any of Herman's early records. My interest in them strikes the tenor saxophonist in the seat across the aisle as somewhat peculiar, a mark of squareness. Why should he care about Woody Herman's old stuff? *He* plays with Woody every night. But the musicians are curious, and my cassette is soon being passed through the bus along with the rough mix of the next Herman album. "Goddamn, man, that stuff holds up *really* well," the tenor saxophonist says to me, shaking his head in amazement as Woody Herman's 1945 trumpet section wails its way through the last chorus of *Northwest Passage*.

Sitting just behind me is Mark Lewis, a slender, boyish-looking trumpeter who has played with the Thundering Herd since 1980. Cappy Lewis, his father, played with the Herman band more than forty years ago. (He plays the muted trumpet solo on Herman's 1946 recording of *Woodchopper's Ball*, one of the tunes on my homemade cassette.) "Dad took me to hear the band one night," he tells me. "We went up to meet Woody afterwards, and when Dad told him that I played trumpet, Woody said, 'So when are you going to play for my band?'"

It wasn't that simple, for Mark wasn't sure he wanted to lead the life of an itinerant musician. "The road," he says, "is the same thing every day. You don't have much time to yourself. You eat bad food a lot of the time. You're stuck in a bus eight hours a day. You wash your underwear in the sink. When you get sick, there's nothing you can do but ride the bus and play the gigs and feel rotten all the time."

In the end, Mark chose to follow his father's path and give the Thundering Herd a try. "There's freshness in our work," he explains, "that makes it worthwhile, especially when we get a young, enthusiastic crowd. That's what we look forward to. Their excitement makes us *want* to play." And, of course, there is Woody Herman, the most popular boss in the big band business. "He lets you be yourself. He keeps things relaxed. You're never afraid to go up on the bandstand with Woody. And he really loves to hear us play. That's why he's there."

Six hours after leaving LeMars, as the skyline of Kansas City begins to loom in the windows of the bus, the band members begin to discuss their plans for the evening. A rumor that a convention of beauticians is being held in our hotel ripples through the back of the bus. One group of Herdsmen wants to go out looking for some real Kansas City barbecue. All the musicians with wives or girlfriends at home decide to get together and watch a little television . . . . "Eight o'clock call, guys," says trumpeter Bill Byrne, Herman's road manager, as the bus finally pulls into the downtown Howard Johnson parking lot. A chorus of groans greets his announcement as the Thundering Herd streams off the bus for the front desk in search of room keys . . . .

At eight a.m., the same musicians who barely made it onto the bus in LeMars are barely making it onto the bus in Kansas City. The rumor about the beauticians' convention was true. As they stagger aboard, the married men quiz them closely about what else was going on last night besides *Return to Mayberry*. Ostensibly precise details are exchanged as we pull onto the highway and start our long drive across the prairies of Kansas to El Dorado, an oil town of 13,000 where Butler County Community College is hosting an afternoon clinic and an evening concert. The clinic is for the members of the college jazz band and other student musicians from the area, while the concert is open to the general public.

The afternoon clinic begins with a short performance by the Thundering Herd. About forty students, trumpets and trombones and saxophones in their laps, are scattered around the bleachers of the college gym. Many of them look skeptical. I eavesdrop and learn that a few of them have never even heard of Woody Herman. Herman knows this, too, which is why he always starts off his clinics with a few numbers by the full band. He takes his job as a jazz educator with the utmost seriousness, and he has always kept one ear open to the latest sounds . . . . But he also knows that there is only one way to make hot young guns pay attention: by being hotter than they are.

Dressed in a windbreaker and sneakers, Herman makes his slow way to center stage and offers a few terse words of greeting. The first tune, he says, will be a new arrangement of Duke Ellington's *It Don't Mean a Thing*. (How many of these rock-besotted kids, I wonder, know who Duke Ellington was?) The rhythm section pumps out a fast four-bar introduction. The saxophones enter with a crisp riff. A massive wave of sound rolls off the bandstand and washes over the bleachers. I can see that the students are surprised at how *loud* the Thundering Herd is. But it is a special kind of loudness, a kind they have never encountered before. It comes not from tall banks of shrieking amplifiers but from sixteen jazz musicians playing in bold, fat-toned unison, and it quickly sets their feet to tapping.

After the concert, the members of the band retire to separate classrooms to explain a few of the tricks of the musician's trade. Meanwhile, Woody Herman heads for the men's locker room, where a table loaded with cold cuts and soft drinks awaits the band. I have arranged to spend the next hour with him. He pours himself a glass of orange juice while I fiddle with my tape recorder. I ask him about some of his less well-known alumni from the forties and fifties. This is a gesture of homage, a sign that I have taken the trouble to learn about him, that I am a member of the fraternity of jazzmen, a respectful insider. The friendly mask and the polite, unreflective answers of a hundred hurried interviews with small-town newspaper reporters are promptly laid aside. In his soft, buzzy voice Herman begins to tell me ornate tales of epileptic drummers and heroin-soaked baritone sax players and hard times on the road. "The highways are better now," he assures me with an ironic smile, "so you get to drive farther every day."

The door opens and two nervous-looking students walk in. They are reporters from the Butler County Community College paper and they have been assigned to do a story about Woody Herman for this week's edition. It is clear to me after the first couple of questions that they have only the vaguest idea of who Herman is. I become angry for a moment, but his kindness shames me. Instead of lecturing the kid reporters, I prompt them with softball questions which Herman knocks back gracefully.

The bell rings and the two reporters, who have to go to a class, leave us alone. Why, I ask, are you still on the road after fifty years? "There's a reason for the road," Herman tells me. "As long as you're doing one-nighters and moving every day, you have the most freedom for your music. You don't have to answer to the people you worked for yesterday. You're not going to be there tomorrow night. You can play the music *you* want to play. That's why I keep going. Because it's still fun. That's the reason I'm here, and that's why all the guys are here. Sure, they gripe like hell. They go through all the motions of being unhappy people. But then they start playing, and they realize that this is the only thing they want to do. I know I can't think of anything else *I* want to do."

There is a pause. Herman is clearly eager to get back to his motel room and rest. I start to stumble over my words. Up to this moment, I have been prompting him with ease, but the thing I want to tell him most now will not come out. *My God, Mr. Herman*, I want to say, *I admire you so much. You can't imagine how hard I schemed to get to where I could sit in this dirty locker room and watch you drink lukewarm orange juice. I called my father last night to tell him about this trip. He used to drive for eight straight hours to come hear me play in Kansas City. He was so proud of me, Mr. Herman, and you did that, you and Stan Kenton and Artie Shaw and Claude Thornhill.*

"Mr. Herman," I say nervously, "do you ever play *The Good Earth* any more?"

He shakes his head. "Nope." He rises slowly to his feet. "But I'll see if I can work it in tonight."[1]

The next day, Terry flew back to New York. If he knew it, he didn't mention it: Woody's orange juice was probably laced with vodka. Nat Pierce told me that after Charlotte's death, Woody started drinking fairly heavily again, vodka and orange juice being a favorite potion.

In his article Terry said:

> As the seventies gave way to the eighties, Woody Herman's situation started to deteriorate. Charlotte, his beloved wife, died of breast cancer. Old age started to catch up with him, and his clarinet playing grew shrill and uncertain. He scaled back his solos to the barest possible minimum. From time to time, a critic would knock him in print, leaving a foaming wake of hatred among musicians who, reading the cold, tactless words, cursed the critics, cursed the IRS, cursed the idiot fate that saddled Woody with a merciless financial burden and simultaneously took away his health.

▼   ▼   ▼

Despite Woody's physical condition, plans proceeded for a celebration of his fiftieth anniversary as a bandleader on July 16 at the Hollywood Bowl. The concert was a little premature: the anniversary of that first Roseland, Brooklyn, engagement actually fell in November. But the Hollywood Bowl was available in July.

As in the Carnegie Hall celebration of his fortieth anniversary, ten years earlier, the event included two Herman bands, the current band and one made up partly of alumni, assembled by Nat Pierce. (Leonard Feather later complained in *JazzTimes* that some important veterans of the band were not included.) The late Jimmy Lyons, the former disc jockey who was the founder and head of the Monterey Jazz Festival, where Woody had played for so many years, was the master of ceremonies. Richard Stoltzman played what had been Woody's part in Stravinsky's *Ebony Concerto*, then "traded fours"—exchanged four-bar phrases—with Woody in a blues. "Herman's and Stoltzman's obvious respect for each other was quite touching," Leonard wrote.

"It was a great moment for me," Stoltzman said. He and the Herd recorded the work. (It is available on a CD from RCA records.)

After the intermission, the young band took over, emphasizing charts by trombonist John Fedchock. One of the trumpet players was Mark Lewis. Stan Getz and Jimmy Rowles, both Herman veterans, joined in.

Noting what he considered some shortcomings in the concert, Leonard Feather wrote:

> Easy though it is to split hairs about such minor flaws, the concert was an extraordinary tribute to the indomitable spirit and energy of Herman. At seventy-three, having survived a series of traumas, the worst of which is an income tax jam (not of his own making) that has him in debt to the tune of at

least $1,600,000, he still stays on the road, still keeps a first-rate band togeth-
er, still wakes up eager to go to work—and no less significantly, retains the love
and respect of the countless hundreds of musicians who have worked for him
throughout this momentous half century.

Leonard was being gentle. Some of the musicians considered the concert a disaster. And in fact Woody, the Road Father was not all that eager to
go to work. He was desperately weary, as anyone who attended the party
held after the concert that night at his house could see. There were old
friends in attendance, to be sure, including Rosemary Clooney, Benny
Carter, Leonard Feather, Jack and Mary Siefert, Tom Cassidy and his wife,
Polly Podewell, and Ray Anthony, as well as members of the current band.
But it also was plentifully attended by what show business people sometimes call "civilians"—outsiders. After too many of them asked Clooney—
with whom Woody had recorded and toured—for her autograph, she told
her escort, "Get the car."

It was about then that Woody confronted me in the living room and told
me he wanted me to write his biography. The house was crushingly crowded, not only every room of it but the patio as well. Looking lost and old and
exhausted, Woody said to my wife, "Who are all these people?"

The kaleidoscope of the crowd changed; we were separated. Woody and
my wife, I learned later, went up the stairs and settled at the breakfast nook
in the kitchen. They talked about Charlotte. The last time she had been in
this room, she and Charlotte had washed potatoes for dinner. I had called,
and found that Wood was on the road, as usual. Charlotte had invited us to
dinner. Woody smiled at her memory of Charlotte, then, looking around,
said again, "Who are all these people?"

"I don't know," my wife said. And, trying to make him laugh, she said,
"Why don't we just get out of here?"

"Where could we go?" Woody asked.

"Anywhere," she said. "Paris. The Riviera."

"No," Woody said. "I've got a better idea. Let's go to Poland. I'm very big
in Poland."

About then I found them and told her it was time to go home; we had a
long drive ahead of us. Wood said he was going to bed and stood up. I held
his hand in mine and said good night.

I would see him again only on television.

The next night he played a university engagement.

And Ingrid came to a decision: he could no longer travel without someone to watch over him. "He needed some help," she said, "schlepping

around airports and that sort of thing. It was really more strenuous for him than driving."

She had a friend named Ed Dye, an emcee, dobro player, and singer who had worked with her in San Francisco in the Styx River Ferry, and later in various groups in Nashville. "My father had always liked Ed," she said. "He'd seen us perform. He thought Ed was really a character. And Ed had it in his nature to take care of people. Just after the fiftieth anniversary concert in 1986, I asked Ed if he'd travel with my father and take care of him. After that he was with him constantly. He was with him during the hospitalization in New York at the end of '86, and he was with him in Detroit, and he stayed at the house afterwards, doing what needed to be done. He was very close to my dad until the end."

▼   ▼   ▼

In September, another of the supermarket tabloids, the *Globe*, headlined his poverty, adding to his public humiliation. The paper quoted Ingrid as saying: "Most weeks it's all he can do to pay the band and expenses and break even. Whatever's left goes to the government. All he's got are a couple of changes of clothes, three musical instruments, and his talent. Dad doesn't own a car and hasn't even got a bank account any more."

Ray Sherman corroborated this. Ray told me: "He was trying to buy a new Mercedes, and he wanted to do it on my credit card. He said, 'God damn it, I haven't got any credit!' They took away everything. He couldn't walk into a store and buy anything. He had to have cash."[2]

The *Globe*, after commenting on his feeble and failing condition, quoted him as saying: "I am not the kind of person who would try to cheat my fellow countrymen by not paying my fair taxes.

"I knew Abe Turchen was a gambler but I didn't think he'd do what he did to me. I should have seen it coming. I've got no one but myself to blame.

"I love my country and the chance it has given me to play my music. When I look at it that way, paying off this tax bill is really not that big a deal."

I seriously doubt that Woody ever said that. The whining tone is not his, and it would be the only known example of his criticizing Abe; he didn't do that even in private. It sounds like a reporter's invention.

The paper commented: "But some feel it's a bad deal and would like to see the IRS excuse the debt, as they did for former boxing champion Joe Louis, who owed $1.25 million. Among them are Senator Daniel Patrick

Moynihan (D - New York) and Leonard Garment, a former legal counsel to Richard Nixon."

Garment in fact had been contacted by Les Brown, who, like all Woody's friends, was sickened and baffled by the IRS treatment of Woody. Who, within the IRS, was pursuing this vendetta?

On July 5, 1986, *New York Newsday* printed a story about his tax troubles, quoting him as telling United Press International: "I'd like to have a justifiable settlement with the IRS so that for my last remaining breaths, the heat would be off. Once they have you, they have no pity. I keep paying and paying and paying, and nothing changes."[3]

The story noted that royalties from his albums went directly to the IRS.

▼   ▼   ▼

In October, 1986, the band played a week's engagement on a jazz cruise on the SS *Norway*. They got off the *Norway* October 18, and were joined by singer Polly Podewell for a tour of Toronto and the northeastern states.

Though Woody rarely carried a "girl singer," in the term left over from the 1940s, he had employed Podewell in the past. Podewell was born in Evanston, Illinois, March 31, 1949. She had a master's degree in early childhood development from Chicago's Erikson Institute and had worked in impoverished areas of that city, teaching classes made up of white children from Southern Appalachia, black, east Indian and native American children. But she had always sung as well, and gradually the burden of two careers had caused her to give up teaching. She went to work for Benny Goodman in 1979 and met Woody about that time. Later she worked for Buddy Rich, and from 1983 until his death was personally involved with him. "Woody loved Buddy and Buddy loved Woody," she said.[4]

Woody had hired her for a six-week engagement with a small group, starting in February, 1984, at the Rainbow Grill at the top of Rockefeller Center. Now he wanted her to tour with the full band, singing material originally performed by Mary Ann McCall and Frances Wayne.

On November 13, 1986, a day or two before the tour was to end, Woody collapsed in his room at the Sheraton Russell Hotel in New York City. He reached Bill Byrne and Ed Dye on the telephone. They immediately called Dr. Stanley Levy in Detroit. Paramedics rushed to Woody's room, and he was taken to Bellevue Hospital, where his heart stopped. The staff restored his breathing and heartbeat. He was put into a large room with other patients. Bill Byrne described Podewell as a woman "with a nurturing, mothering nature."

"It was such an awful hospital for him to be in," she said. "I had friends in New York and I stayed. I would go and visit him every day, and I was afraid to walk through the halls. It was dirty, there were drug addicts and mental patients. He was on the same ward with drug addicts. It was ludicrous."[5]

Jack and Mary Siefert arrived and found the hospital ominously depressing, with guards posted on every floor. The Sieferts were able to stay only a day because Jack had to work.

When the time for Woody's discharge from Bellevue approached, Jack Siefert urged him to come to their house. By now the Sieferts had sold the house in which their children had grown up and had purchased a large condominium on a quiet cul de sac in Lower Gwynedd, Pennsylvania, a graceful suburb of Philadelphia. On November 24, Woody left Bellevue. Frank Tiberi led the band, and Polly Podewell went home to Chicago. Woody traveled by Amtrak Pullman car to Philadelphia; Jack picked him up at the Thirtieth Street Station and drove him home. The house is airy and sunny and furnished in exquisite, quiet taste. He and Mary installed their friend in their own bedroom, since its bathroom contained a shower and Woody would not have to lower himself into a tub, and took the guest room themselves.

"He liked this place very much," Jack said. "He helped us pick it out. He was very quiet. He slept most of the time. He talked about his family. He became very sensitive. He talked about the warm love between his father and him. And he loved his mother. We went out for a night for dinner, but he was tired at the time."

Their son George, a graduate engineer just out of college, accompanied them. At six-foot-five, and weighing two hundred and twenty pounds, George dwarfed Woody, more now than ever. "He loved Woody," Jack said. "Woody had seen him grow up. In fact, he came into town when George was born and brought Mary flowers and said, 'Beautiful production, kid.'"

In the restaurant a young woman approached them and said, "Hello, my name's Charlene and I'm your waitress."

Woody gave her his best smile and said, as was his wont, "My name's Woody and I'm your customer. How's the food?"

Once, earlier, when Woody's health was already feeble and the IRS had left him with barely enough money to plod onward, Jack drove him to catch a red-eye flight home to California. Woody saw two young servicemen sitting, half asleep, in the airport. He engaged them in conversation and found that they were on their way home from overseas. He gave each of them twenty dollars and said, "Kids, get yourselves a decent meal while you're waiting."

"And he really didn't have it," Jack said. "He got on a plane. And I know he didn't have as good a dinner as he was giving those kids. That was in the early eighties. He was that considerate. He was a very warm, totally kind, compassionate, understanding individual. The more you knew him, the more you admired him."

And now, Jack continued, Woody called Charlene the waitress and gave her some money. "I don't know how much," Jack said. Woody was Jack's guest at dinner; this had been made very clear in advance. But Woody said to the waitress, indicating young George Siefert, "I want you to lay a bottle of Pouilly Fuissé on this kid. Before I blow this scene, I want him to know what a good bottle of wine tastes like."

"My son nearly cried," Jack said. "Woody was frail, and tired, but he still had that feeling for other people."[6]

▼   ▼   ▼

Incredibly, two weeks later Woody led the Herd at the Kennedy Center awards ceremony in Washington, D.C. Hume Cronyn, Jessica Tandy, Lucille Ball, and Ray Charles received the honors. Woody and Joe Williams sang blues together. On New Year's Eve he played an engagement on the *Queen Mary*, anchored permanently at Long Beach, California.

He played an engagement in Portland, Oregon. Red Kelly and his wife drove down from Tacoma to see him, sensing perhaps that this would be their last chance to do so. Red said, "We took him to dinner, and then he took us to the job as his guests. I had a chance to ask him something. I said, 'One time we were doing a clinic.' This was before clinics became popular. This college band would play. Woody would have his lead trumpet go sit with the trumpets. At one point, he stopped the band, and he went to a saxophone player and he said, 'Listen, don't pat your feet. You can't hear the rhythm section.'

"I'd never heard anyone tell horn players that. When I reminded him of it, Woody said, 'Nobody ever hires anybody to pound foot.'

"Isn't that delicious?"

Then, speaking of fame, or any of life's moments of opportunity, Woody said: "The light may never hit you, but if it does, you goddamn well better be ready."[7]

Woody continued working through 1987, the IRS always standing by, hand outstretched. With his emphysema, and when he played at high altitudes, he had serious problems breathing. Dr. Stanley Levy said:

"Woody got into trouble in Santa Fe, New Mexico. He had acute altitude sickness. Santa Fe is about 8200 feet. He called me. They got him down to 5200 feet in Albuquerque and got him on a plane and flew him to Los Angeles. As it happened, I was going to Los Angeles. I saw him there and there was no problem at that point. I went up to his house. I told them that if he was going to go to any altitudes, we'd have to get him on Diamox, a diuretic drug used in glaucoma. Then he was scheduled into Aspen.

"He was instructed to use the Diamox before, during, and after exposure to high altitude. He did that for several days as he worked his way up from Los Angeles to Aspen. He continued the medication. He came down to Denver and then went to Nebraska, and he stopped the medication. He went back into Colorado and got altitude sickness, then went to Minnesota, where he had an irregular heartbeat."

The Minnesota engagement, March 23, 1987, was at Grand Meadow High School. It had been arranged by Nathan Davidson, band director of the high school and himself a saxophonist. Davidson had been a Herman fan since he heard the band for the first time in LaCrosse, Wisconsin, when he was nineteen. He had built a rich collection of memorabilia on Woody over the years. "This man has literally shared his whole life with the world and here he is coming to Grand Meadow," Davidson said, adding that for him, to present Woody Herman in concert at the high school, was "a musical dream come true."

Ticket prices were five dollars for students, seven for adults, and six for senior citizens. Grand Meadow, in the southeastern corner of the state, is a town of about a thousand persons, but the crowd that turned out numbered 950. A newspaper headlined:

WOODY HERMAN
STILL VIBRANT AT 73.

The story said otherwise: "Although Herman, seventy-three, moved around slowly and looked somewhat feeble, he put on an enthusiastic performance, playing several instruments, singing a song, directing the band, introducing the members, telling a couple of jokes and even dancing the conga."

Another newspaper, the *Post-Bulletin*, was more direct: "Herman was visibly uncomfortable with what was said to be abdominal and respiratory ailments."

Both newspapers carried pictures, one of Woody playing clarinet, the other with a microphone in hand, talking or singing. By now he had grown a beard, which was white. He had long since gone bald.

Grand Meadow was the last gig of Woody's life. If Woody had played that first engagement at Roseland Ballroom the evening before the election of 1936, his career as a bandleader had lasted fifty years, four months, and twenty-one days. He had seven months left to live.

The next day, March 27, he was in Chicago. He called Polly Podewell. She remembered: "We went out to the Jazz Showcase. It was a lovely evening but I was worried about him. He didn't look good. He went into the men's room and was there an awfully long time. I finally had to ask someone to go in and see if he was all right."8

Woody called Stan Levy. "He said he wasn't too well. I told him to come on over to Detroit," Dr. Levy said. The doctor put him under coronary and pulmonary intensive care in Mt. Sinai Hospital. "There were times," Dr. Levy said, "when his lung disease changed his blood gases, and he'd get disoriented. Remember, he'd played in nightclubs all his life."

So disoriented was he that he didn't know who he was. "I tried to fly up to see him as often as I could, but I couldn't afford to go up that much," Podewell said. "Woody just lost contact with reality. He started hallucinating.

"He said he was going to be the next president of the United States and replace Ronald Reagan. He was going to give everybody in the United States a raise and there would be no income tax and everybody would live a hundred and fifty years. He would be number one in the government and Frank Sinatra would be number two. And I was going to be First Singer. He was really out of it. He wasn't lucid.

"But sometimes he would talk sensibly. It was in and out. He had lost a lot of weight. He was undergoing physical therapy for breathing and swallowing."9

"How did he keep going?" I asked Dr. Levy.

"Well, we worked very hard at the hospital. And he was very seductive. He could read the nurses and get them to help him. He was very good at that. A patient can make a lot of difference in the quality of care he gets.

"By the way, while he was at Sinai, Dizzy Gillespie called him almost every other day. And there were several times when I was in the room and I talked to him. He was always very amiable and outgoing."10

Woody telephoned Buddy Rich, who was in UCLA Medical Center in Los Angeles with a brain tumor. On his admission, Buddy made a remark that lives in the legends of jazz. A nurse asked, "Mr. Rich, are you allergic to anything?"

"Yes," Buddy said, "country-and-western music."

Buddy died a few days later, on April 2.

Several of Woody's friends, including Podewell, stood by at Sinai. Jack Siefert flew to Detroit to be with him. Woody's grandson, Tommy Littlefield, came to see him. Woody went into cardiac arrest, then rallied yet again and on May 16 celebrated his seventy-fourth birthday at Sinai. In June, the entire band came to the hospital, then, under the direction of Frank Tiberi, left on a European tour.

One of Woody's seemingly endless army of friends is Midge Ellis, of Livonia, Michigan, who produced a jazz series there over a period of ten years. Woody played it many times.

"When he was in Sinai that last year, Ed Dye and Dr. Levy would call me to come down to cheer Woody up," Midge said. "Sometimes Woody would think he was the president or the king of some country and would expound on how he was going to change things.

"Once, when Ingrid was there, a third-grade class at one of the Detroit schools wrote letters to Woody. Ingrid was reading them to him and he was getting a real charge out of them. One young man wrote, 'Are you related to Pee Wee Herman?' Woody thought that was hilarious, and said, 'Send that kid a Selmer!'

"One day I was sitting there and I asked Woody. 'If you could have anything in the world you wanted right this minute, what would it be?' Without hesitation he said, 'Booze. No question about it—booze!'

"Then one day, my heart nearly broke when he said, 'Midge, I want to go home.'

"Big tears welled up in his eyes and his voice broke.

"'I want to sit on my porch and look at L.A. just one more time, Midge,' he said. 'I want to go home.'

"I decided that he surely would go home. I talked to Dr. Levy about his surviving the trip. Stan was worried about him being at home without hospital facilities close at hand, but agreed that if he could get home, he certainly should do so. But it would require a hospital plane with nurses and the breathing apparatus he needed.

"I started calling around about the cost. It was out of the question for Woody. Uncle Sam had all his money. I'd know that little tax collector in hell if I saw him there. He used to come backstage and take the check or money. I think he was a Herman fan and used the IRS to get to hear the band and then collect the money!

"I spoke to Merilee Trost, vice president of Concord Records. I told her I had found a hospital plane that was going to L.A. to pick up a patient and that the cost to Woody would be considerably less if we could send him on that plane, about $8,000 instead of $15,000. She said she would talk to Carl Jefferson, the owner of Concord, about paying for the plane against whatever royalties the IRS allowed Woody to keep from his recordings for the company. God bless Carl! He agreed to do it, though the royalties were practically nil.

"I'll never forget the look on Woody's face when we told him he was going home. He was like a little kid at Christmas. Ingrid called Polly Podewell in Chicago. Polly flew to Detroit and spent the night with me. We had to be at the hospital early to have Woody ready for a 6 a.m. ambulance pickup.

"The nurse was so glad to see us. She said he had not shut his mouth all night, he was so excited about going home.

"His clothes were about three sizes too big for him. I asked him what he wanted to wear. He said he wanted his pinstriped suit. I found it in the closet. He picked out a red silk shirt and a white tie. We told him he looked like the Godfather. I found some red bikini underwear and held it up to tease him about it. He said, 'I want to wear those!'

"Polly was one side of the bed and I on the other. He was so frail I could easily raise him while Polly slide the underwear on him. He had his arm across my shoulder and started to laugh that wicked Herman chuckle. He said, 'Here I am with two beautiful blondes dressing me and I can't get it up.' We all laughed until the tears flowed.

"We finally got him into the clothes he chose. No one else was around, so we were waiting for the ambulance personnel to arrive with the gurney he would ride to L.A. He didn't have any shoes on. He had been wearing old, dirty tennis shoes whenever he was in the wheelchair in the hospital. He said the outfit called for his black patent-leather shoes. I found them. He took one look and said, 'No, I'll just wear my tennies.' So here was Woody Herman all dressed up fit for a gig at the White House and those old dirty tennis shoes!

"He was a sight to behold, being wheeled out of that hospital to the ambulance with his clothes sort of lying on his frail body and those tennis shoes sticking out of that black pinstriped suit.

"But the smile on his face and the big wave and an airborne kiss as the doors of the ambulance closed will live in my memory forever.

"I never saw him again."

The flight took place June 18.

"I flew back to California with him," Podewell said. "The plane was small. Woody and I and a nurse were the only passengers. He went to Century City Hospital."

Ingrid had to pay the hospital cash to admit him. He was there two days.

"He came home June 20," Podewell said. "We had no help then. It was just Ingrid and I. He was hard to control and he wouldn't stay in bed. He was very disoriented and didn't know where he was. It was really bad. We had to call a doctor, who gave him a sedative.

"June 25, he went to Cedars-Sinai. He was there till July 23. Then he came home, and went back August 12. On August 17, he suffered yet another heart attack and was placed in the intensive care unit, coming out of it on August 19. I got a VCR for his room. The guys in the band were great. They sent him videos of the band. They sent audio tapes with messages. And guys from the earlier days, like Chubby and Shorty, put messages on the tape, just to cheer him up."[11]

Woody was allowed to go home on August 25. The medical bills kept mounting, including those for bottled oxygen and around-the-clock nurses. Ingrid was unable to keep up with the rent. Shortly before the 1987 Labor Day weekend, the landlord, William Little, served Ingrid with an eviction notice. The sheriff's department was to remove her and her father from the house at 5 p.m. on the Tuesday, the day after Labor Day. Woody lay all but helpless in his bed. An attending nurse was watching television. A news item described the pending eviction. Woody heard it. He ordered the nurse to take him in his wheelchair out of the bedroom, and as they came into the living room, reporters and cameramen surrounded him.

Within hours, his image was on the television channels. Bearded and skeletal, he smiled and waved a feeble hand at the cameras. He looked awful, simply awful. This vibrant, this feisty, independent, exuberant man had been reduced to a kind of senile infancy. As Ingrid put it, he had gone "from indestructible to immobile."

31

The Last Days

The failure of the IRS to make a settlement with Woody left not only his friends but members of the legal profession baffled. "It's amazing how the IRS went overboard on this case," Mayer Kanter said.

An IRS spokesman named Lowell Langers told Leonard Feather, who reported it in a *Los Angeles Times* story, "His employees' money was not forwarded to us. It wasn't just a question of his own personal taxes.

"It's not just a sudden thing. We're talking twenty years later. The fact that an individual may be a public figure, and well loved, can't figure in our considerations. The code is specific and we're required to collect the taxes." Langers told Feather that when taxes are delinquent, the government can seize any money or property to pay off the taxes.

The statement is disingenuous. There are large accounting firms, some of whose officers are former IRS people—some of them even advertise on television—whose sole and full-time work is negotiating large tax debts down into small ones with the IRS. Some of them cite settlements of as little as ten thousand dollars on a half-million-dollar lien when there is no hope of getting more from a ruined debtor. And the line between payroll income taxes and personal taxes would seem to be a fine one.

Langers's statement reveals just how aware the IRS was of Woody's public position. But because of the worldwide admiration for jazz, the IRS got perhaps more publicity than it anticipated. The Leonard Feather story appeared in syndication not only around the United States but turned up in the *International Herald Tribune* under a four-column head and thus was read all over Europe. And the situation was extensively reported in other languages. The German magazine *Jazz Podium* carried a full-page story under the headline *Woody 'n' You*, under an overline: *Worldwide campaign.* It ended its article with a plea for money.

One of the most disturbed observers was Woody's old friend Les Brown. "I couldn't understand it," Les said. "So I made a call to a prominent Republican acquaintance of mine in Washington."[1] The acquaintance was Leonard Garment (who later told me that he was actually a lifelong independent). After his years as White House counsel to Richard Nixon, he was back in private practice, white-haired and distinguished—the hesitant and self-deprecating young tenor player Woody had let go in the formative phase of the First Herd. In September, 1994, Garment recalled:

"Les told me, 'This house is all Woody has, and he loves it, and he wants his daughter to have it after he's gone.'

"I had some tax lawyers in my firm check. We went up to see some of the people in the Treasury to see if we could get some indulgence. But they're very stubborn on things like that. Dick Fairbanks, a former ambassador to the Middle East, was a partner here in Washington of a Los Angeles law firm, Paul, Hastings, Janofsky and Walker. I said, 'Can you get someone on the west coast who can help out pro bono for Woody Herman?' And he said, 'Well there's this young, very talented trial lawyer who does tax work, Kirk Pasich.'

"We talked on the phone and it turned out he was the head of a local jazz club and a great fan. He went to work on it, and he worked miracles. He was just terrific. And a fellow who should get a lot of credit is Myron Mintz, who was the co-ordinator. He and Kirk worked out a set of theories that this was a rinky-dink operation."[2]

Pasich, then an associate of Paul, Hastings, Janofsky and Walker, was given the firm's permission to take Woody's case pro bono. Pasich and six other lawyers from the firm would eventually donate $100,000 worth of legal services. Pasich recalled:

"Len Garment called Wednesday evening, and I got back to him Thursday. I had done a lot of litigation, and I also did a lot of entertainment work.

"We spent Thursday afternoon and Friday getting a declaration from his doctor that to move Woody would kill him and explaining that he had chronic everything."[3] The physician was Dr. Ronald Sue, an internist trained at Stanford University and Tufts University School of Medicine. Sue had become Woody's doctor in June, after Woody had been brought home from Detroit. In detached medical language, Dr. Sue's declaration to the court recounted Woody's recent medical history, concluding:

> Mr. Herman was discharged from Cedars-Sinai on or about August 25, 1987. Since then, he has remained at home, where he is confined to a hospital bed, receives continuous oxygen and respiratory therapy, and receives twenty-four-hour nursing. This twenty-four-hour nursing is essential to Mr. Herman's feeding, administration of medication, bathing, and care of his bladder and bowel function.
>
> At this time, Mr. Herman is suffering from end-stage congestive cardiomyopathy with a left ventricular ejection fraction of less than twenty-five percent and is status-post recent subendocardial myocardial infarction. A list of Mr. Herman's major medical problems includes congestive cardiomyopathy, severe peripheral vascular disease, protein-calorie malnutrition, and multifocal subcortical white matter disease involving his brain as a complication of his vascular disease and multiple cardiac and respiratory arrests.
>
> The prognosis for Mr. Herman is as follows; by strict criteria, given his multiple medical problems, Mr. Herman has a projected mortality of eighty to ninety percent within six months, extending to ninety percent within one year. In short, Mr. Herman has a life expectancy of six to twelve months under optimal medical conditions.
>
> If Mr. Herman is evicted from his residence, where I understand he has resided for most of his life, it is likely that there will be an increase in his morbidity and mortality. Mr. Herman's clinical status is tenuous. Any interruption will exacerbate his existing lung disease, which will create added stress and strain on his heart, increasing the risk of another heart attack. Furthermore, as a result of the multiple insults to his brain and body, Mr. Herman is suffering a degree of underlying dementia and depression. In my opinion, if Mr. Herman is removed from the familiar surroundings of his home, his disorientation will increase, which will adversely impact his depression. This in turn will likely aggravate his underlying cardio-pulmonary disease. In other words, if Mr. Herman is evicted from his home, his life expectancy will be shortened and his life may be jeopardized.

Pasich continued: "I wanted the judge to know exactly who he was dealing with. And so I went through Woody's track record of hits in the forties and fifties, comparing it with groups like the Beatles and the Beach Boys and the Rolling Stones. I felt that if you did that comparison, Woody would qualify as one of the true legends of music, just based on something as simply objective as sales figures and how high his songs got on the charts" that measured records' popularity.

Poring over records dating from the start of the century, Pasich extrapolated some startling figures. He compared the hit charts for the peak years of Woody's career, from 1937 to 1956, with those of famous rock groups. He found that Woody had more hit records during those nineteen years than the Rolling Stones in thirty or the Beach Boys in twenty-eight. (See Appendix 2.)

"Everybody had heard of the Beatles," he said. "But Woody is in their class in the number of hits. If you define it as top forty or top twenty hits, he is in their class. He has a longer chart span than the Beatles, and he was right up there behind Presley, even with the Beatles and ahead of the Rolling Stones. I took the chart information starting in the late thirties and moving it forward.

"I put that in the declaration so the court would know that we were dealing with someone of that stature. It's easy to lose sight of that fact. He was in the 1940s that level of superstar. I felt that by giving him a popular counterpart in the Beatles or Presley or whoever, most people of this generation who don't know who he is, don't recognize his contribution, would get the picture. I wanted to give the judge the flavor of what we were dealing with.

"The primary purpose for us was to get the doctors' declaration and then to attack the way the procedure had been set up. Woody was getting evicted without being tried. I don't think he ever should have been in that position. But when we were brought into the case, there had been agreements reached in earlier proceedings, and we had to get it back to square one, where we had a chance to fight the eviction. So on that Friday afternoon, we made the judgment call that it might be possible to get some favorable publicity.

"We got a lot of stuff on William Little's past history and what the results were. He appeared to have more cases pending in Los Angeles Superior Municipal Court than anybody, and he had used the same procedure in other cases, and that procedure had been rejected by a Court of Appeal. We wanted the judge to know who he was and who Woody was."[4]

A year after these events, the *National Law Journal*, a publication widely read by lawyers, carried an extensive story on the case. It noted:

According to a 1985 state appellate court ruling, in one 16-month period Mr. Little had filed some 264 eviction notices in Los Angeles Municipal Court. And the opinion appeared to bar the very procedure Mr. Little used with Ms. Herman: rental documents that stipulated to the landlord's right to immediate repossession without notice or hearing in the event of arrearage. *Little vs. Sanchez*, 166 Ca. App. 2d 501 (Ct. App., 2d District.)

Reporters found their own treasure trove. Mr. Little's one-two punch of foreclosure purchases and rentals to former owners had earned him a reputation with the Legal Aid Foundation of Los Angeles. "He became a self-made millionaire on the broken backs of a lot of little people," Legal Aid's Gary Blasi said.

To draw attention to the case, Pasich telephoned the *Los Angeles Times*. "They didn't think it was a story," he said. "So I then called the *Los Angeles Herald-Examiner*, and they ran it as a front-page lead story.

"I was inundated with telephone calls. I'm the only Kirk Pasich in the phone book. I got calls at home, at the office. The office receptionist was going nuts, because we had something like a hundred and fifty calls.

"After I'd received the first half-dozen or so calls, I decided I'd better see what the *Herald-Examiner* had said. I was going to go to the back section, and it was on the front page. Then everyone picked it up. I remember Dan Rather mentioned it on the news that night.

"The *Los Angeles Times* then wanted to follow up.

"By the time Tuesday afternoon came around, and there'd been follow-up stories and radio coverage. Chuck Niles"—a well-known and widely respected Los Angeles jazz disc jockey—"was on the air at KKGO, speaking about it.

"I went down to court with Ingrid. Joan Collins had a case going at the same time. One of the associates of my firm, who was there on another matter, saw all this press, lots of TV cameras, newspaper reporters, and they all rushed toward the escalator. He said he knew this was going to be his chance to see Joan Collins. And he said he was most disappointed when I got off the escalator. That was one of the more surreal experiences I've had as a lawyer. And I've dealt with the press before.

"But the judge admitted a pool camera into the courtroom. He took us into chambers, me and the lawyer for William Little. And he said, 'Okay, here's what I'm going to rule. Let's run through it. Let's do a dress rehearsal so we can do it right in front of the camera.' I thought to myself, 'This is really strange.' But we did it. We did a dress rehearsal.

"There was the one camera, and we went through what we had rehearsed with the judge. He did it, he ruled our way. And William Little said he'd had no idea who Woody Herman was and was unaware of his medical condition.

"We took the agreement we'd drafted, essentially letting Woody stay in the house the rest of his life. We had a little press conference. We let William Little say his piece for the camera, and we gave KKGO the credit it deserved for the launching of its trust fund efforts."

Little told reporters, "I don't create the problem that leads to the sale," and again said he had been unaware that Mr. Herman was ill. He had agreed to accept the overdue rent and allow Woody and Ingrid tenancy through January 1989. Pasich had chosen that date because doctors said that Woody had six months left, if that.

"I think the publicity helped," Pasich said. "It gave the case a lot of attention. It was hotter than I thought. We had an Australian cable TV company who flew somebody in. We were interviewed by a Japanese company. I remember the Wednesday morning after the hearing, at six o'clock my phone rang. I was asked, 'Is this Kirk Pasich?' And then the guy said, 'Hi! We're live on the air with Kirk Pasich.' It was a Detroit radio station."[5]

Two days after the court hearing, the *New York Times* carried a story on Woody's tax troubles, under the three-column heading

EVICTION OF WOODY HERMAN AVERTED.

The jazz clarinetist and bandleader Woody Herman, who is ill and destitute, was spared eviction today after a jazz radio station agreed to pay $4,600 he owed for rent.

Mr. Herman, 74 years old, had fallen four months behind in the rent he owed to the man who bought Mr. Herman's house in a 1985 tax auction.

The paper quoted Pasich as saying that Woody owed a nursing service $18,000 in addition to his doctor and hospital bills.

Meanwhile, fans from around the world were sending donations to help. The IRS insisted that this money was also the government's. Representative John Conyers, Democrat of Michigan, declared that the Herman case was typical of "the tawdry treatment given jazz musicians in this country."

But Pasich had outmaneuvered the IRS. He said, "We set up a trust, because if the money went to Woody, the IRS would grab it. We structured it in such a way that they couldn't, and he would get the benefit of it. It worked out well for everybody. At that point, the IRS was catching, I think, considerable heat.

"The attention from the press and, more importantly to me, the outpouring of affection for Woody in the letters, was amazing. I believe the average contribution was five to ten bucks. And to get two hundred thousand dollars! Yes, we got contributions of from five to ten thousand dollars from Clint Eastwood and others. But the bulk of the contributions were the small ones. People saying how they'd met to his music, former GIs remembering him, kids sending in their allowances. And this went for his ongoing medical care. Something in the proximity of two hundred thousand dollars of his medical bills were paid by these contributions."

KKGO, which was then a jazz station—it now plays only classical music—paid Woody's back rent. Besides Clint Eastwood, Tony Bennett, Frank Sinatra, Rosemary Clooney, and other celebrities donated money. Howie Richmond is believed to have made the largest contribution.

The letters containing donations that so touched Kirk Pasich came from around the world. One fan wrote a brief note to Woody that read: "In remembrance of a teen-ager's before-noon excursions to the Paramount and the Strand. The world was kinder then. I wish that kindness to you."

Another wrote saying that he had been ten when he first saw the band in 1944, the so-called First Herd. "I remember my first glimpse of Woody Herman—with that slightly malevolent smile that suggested things were going to happen that weren't necessarily what the church had in mind."

▼   ▼   ▼

Woody stayed in his home until October 1, 1987. Early on the morning of that day, an ambulance picked him up. "The ambulance," Polly Podewell said, "had just pulled away from the house and an earthquake started, the worst since 1971, I was told. And it was as though God was upset by the turn of events. Or as one person put it, 'It was the big bandleader in the sky.'"

At 8:15 a.m. Woody was readmitted to Cedars-Sinai Medical Center in West Los Angeles. All the rest of that month, musicians across the country held benefit concerts to raise money for him, one of them sponsored by KKGO.

Nat Pierce had been to the hospital several times. He told me on the telephone, "They've got him hooked up to the Frankenstein machine, all those tubes and wires. It's awful."

On the morning of Thursday, October 29, 1987, Ingrid visited him in the hospital. She said, "I told him, 'You know I really love you,' but I didn't know whether I was getting through to him. He had a full-time nurse that I'd hired. But I was gone and he was alone when he passed."[6]

At 2:45 in the afternoon, Woody died of cardiopulmonary arrest.

Terry Teachout wrote:

> I was alone in my office when the news came over the wires. As I read the bare words on the bulletin, I thought of a scene from my first night on the road with the Thundering Herd. It was 12:40 in the morning. The dancers were gone,

the albums sold, the autographs signed. The pianist and bassist were jamming together on *Willow, Weep for Me* as the other musicians, tired and bedraggled from another long night's work, knocked down the music stands and took apart their instruments. Woody was standing alone near the bandstand, listening to the music, idly snapping his fingers to the beat. He picked up his clarinet and tossed off a low, breathy chorus of *Willow Weep for Me*. Then he put it down, did a stiff little dance step, and slipped out of the room without a word. Homeless and wifeless and futureless, Woody Herman was still taking what little pleasures he could find. His music had sustained him through five decades, and it would comfort him until the very end.

The Requiem Mass, conducted by Monsignor George J. Parnassus, began at 10 a.m. on the morning of November 2, 1987, at St. Victor's Catholic Church in West Hollywood, where Woody and Charlotte had taken their wedding vows before Father Dan Sherman so long ago, and from where she had been buried five years earlier. There were perhaps two hundred people at the service.

Jack Siefert delivered the eulogy, which he had written longhand on the plane on his flight out from Pennsylvania. He said: "Woody, the one word that means so much to so many. As a bandleader, he defied the laws of physics because of his unique talent of being able to make the whole greater than the sum of its parts. He was an inspiration to those who were gifted, a launching pad to success for those who were gifted, and he was a source of comfort to those who may have been less fortunate. Above all, he was a role model for the young people of today, for he proved that you can still reach your artistic goals and be a nice guy . . . . We have just lost the greatest pied piper that American music has ever produced, and I have just lost the greatest friend any man ever had."

Dapper to the last, Woody lay in the coffin in a white silk suit and a Gucci cravat. Polly Podewell put a copy of the lead sheet to *Happiness Is a Thing Called Joe* in the coffin along with a photo of Woody and Ingrid. Ed Dye put a half-pint of vodka in the casket.

One of the pallbearers was Woody's grandson, Tommy Littlefield, then twenty-eight years old. After the service, clusters of Woody's friends stood around in the sunlight in front of the church, talking quietly. Among them were Howie Richmond, Ralph Burns, Jimmy Rowles, Nat Pierce, Bill Holman, Bill Byrne, Ross Tompkins, Bill Perkins, Cappy and Mark Lewis, Mary Ann McCall, John Fedchock, Terry Gibbs, Pete Candoli, Don Rader, and Ginny and Henry Mancini, who had met Woody when Hank was the pianist with Tex Beneke's postwar Glenn Miller orchestra and Woody's band had played that a private concert for them in the rain in Detroit. There with Ingrid was her grandmother, Inga Neste, now almost ninety.

It occurs to me that one man who wasn't there was little faithful Sidewalk Stanley. I wonder if he's still alive, and how he took the news wherever and whenever he heard that Woody was gone. Woody was his life.

The pallbearers put the coffin in a gray hearse and closed its rear door. It drove off, bearing the Road Father on his last journey. Jack Siefert said later, "I think Woody would have been proud that his funeral procession had an escort of twelve motorcycle policemen who blocked intersections en route to the cemetery. We went through Los Angeles at speeds up to fifty miles an hour."

The coffin was placed in a crypt beside Charlotte's in Hollywood Memorial Park.

In his 1986 monograph *Woody Herman*, English critic Steve Voce had commented, "It is a sad commentary on the American way of doing things that an honorable man should be hounded and his last years over-shadowed by reprisals for something that was not of his doing."[7]

As we watched the vehicle drive off, one of the musicians—I no longer remember who—took note of all that Woody had done to enhance the image of his country and generate goodwill toward it in tours to Latin America, the Iron Curtain countries, and Africa and said that for that alone his debt to the IRS, mostly penalties and interest anyway, should have been written off.

Another man put it even more harshly. He said, "The government of Finland gave Sibelius a pension for life. Our government persecuted Woody Herman to the grave."

32

Legacy

The IRS kept after Woody even after his death, confiscating his royalties wherever they could find them.

Kirk Pasich was involved in three aspects of the case: representing Woody and Ingrid in resisting eviction; setting up the trust funds, both a KKGO trust and a separate Woody Herman trust, to handle donations that came in to pay for his ongoing medical expenses and keep this money out of the hands of the IRS; and, later, to represent Ingrid in a lawsuit to get her share of Woody's house back, after it had been sold by the Internal Revenue Service.

Pasich said, "William Little paid somewhere under a hundred thousand dollars for it. He was willing to give half of that to her. We got a decision by the court that the IRS sale was unconstitutional in that it violated Ingrid's due process rights. To the extent that it was purporting to sell her mother's interest in the house, which had been a gift to Ingrid, it violated her rights to due process, and the sale was not valid as to her. We got the relief we wanted.

"After that, under court order, the house was resold at auction for a substantially higher price, I believe in the vicinity of half a million dollars. She got half of it.

But the IRS was still confiscating Woody's royalties. Pasich said:

"We deposed the guys at the IRS. We deposed fairly high-level IRS people out here about why they did what they did and whether or not they'd accept an offer of compromise. We never got anywhere with an offer

of compromise. I think there were a couple of reasons behind that. One is
that with Woody, he did have a continuing income stream. Even though he
had no money, he had an income stream, a royalty chain. The basic situation with offers of compromise is that the IRS will accept them if there are
questions about liability, and if there is a question about ever having an
ability to pay.

"The liability issue was essentially resolved twenty-five years ago, against
Woody Herman in the sixties, when they came after him. As far as I can
tell, there was little in the way of defense actually put up to contest it. If
you look at the hundreds of thousands that he was assessed, the simple
fact is that in the 1960s Woody Herman was on the road three hundred
days a year, but jazz and big bands and the Herd style of music were not
popular. If you take traveling on the road with fifteen musicians, travel
expenses and all that, there is absolutely no way in the world that the tax
deficiency could be a couple of hundred thousand bucks for a given year.
It's just . . . not . . . possible.

"So there seems to have been a presumption by the IRS as to how much
money he was making. And the bulk of that at the time was failure to
withhold payroll taxes during a three-year period. Now if you take a three-
year period as a failure to withhold a couple of hundred thousand bucks
here and a couple of hundred thousand bucks there, my recollection is that
it ended up to be somewhere between five and six hundred thousand.

"That band didn't make a million dollars a year in those days, not after
travel and all the other expenses. Thus on an objective, global view, it
wasn't possible to have that size of deficiency. The problem is that when
you look at it later—we looked at it—how do you prove to the Internal
Revenue Service that the liability did not exist?

"We didn't have the specific tax records, we didn't have itineraries. We
actually came up with declarations from a couple of people who had been
involved in the band who testified about how much money the band would
make and how its travel schedule was. But it would be, in all likelihood, the
estate's burden of proof, and we could never get the IRS to take a look at it.

"And frankly I don't know that we ever had enough specific stuff, twenty-
five years later, to disprove the liability. That was one part of the problem.

"The other part of the problem was that with the royalty stream, there
was money. And the only way to cut off the money—and we took a run at
the money—was to tell them, 'Look, Ingrid has no reason to go out and try
to enforce the collection of royalty streams. We think there are a number
of royalty streams out there that aren't being paid that he's entitled to get.'

"And we also said, 'Why in the world should she stay in ASCAP and have the IRS get the money?' So we pulled her out of ASCAP. Now here's our bargaining position: 'You guys are leaving a lot of money on the table. *We* can get the money. But we're not going to do it if we don't get it. So why don't we cut a deal where there's a certain amount of liability? Because at that point there was still $1.2 million owed on what started out as $1.2 million.

"The guy works his entire life, gets his house sold out from under him, doesn't own a car, gets gate receipts seized, and when he dies, which is roughly twenty years after he got hit with all this stuff, he owes essentially to the penny what he owed twenty years earlier.

"Now I have a problem with that as a concept. Let's assume that the government has a legitimate basis that Woody is responsible. And ultimately it was his responsibility. He may have delegated it, but ultimately in the eyes of the law he's the person responsible for making sure the payroll taxes were paid. Whether they were the right taxes is another question.

"Years later, the leverage we had was: We don't have to get the royalties. We don't have to go out there and investigate and find out what's unpaid. We can back out of ASCAP and other places. And the IRS doesn't get it and we don't. So what we want to do is compromise. Either fix the amount or, better yet, agree to some sort of split with us. We'll both come out ahead.

"As I recall, we didn't get a positive response on that. There was no interest.

"And now I think most of the liens have now expired. They have set periods of time and they have to renew and do certain other things. There's a question of whether you can lien future royalties. You can do it if there's a present right, but if the right hasn't arisen, then you can't do it if the lien has expired. I think the position is that whatever the last liens were that were in effect, those were the last liens. So Ingrid ought to be okay on a going-forward basis."[1]

But Ingrid faced further problems. She put her grandmother, Charlotte's mother, into a nursing home and supported her. Ingrid and I took her to lunch one day, and I saw then what Shirley Mancuso would later describe to me: a self-importance and a kind of narcissism such that even at that age, she kept turning the conversation back to herself. I wanted to ask questions about Charlotte's youth, but in her senility, she could no longer distinguish between herself and her daughter. Inga Neste, who had made her daughter's life hell when she could, had outlived everyone. She died in 1994, just past her ninetieth birthday.

Ingrid, a skilled editor, set up a little business operation charmingly titled As You Like It Computer Service. She does a great deal of manuscript work for a wide variety of clients, including lawyers. She works incessantly and hard.

Ingrid, like her mother, contracted breast cancer. Left with almost no money by the ongoing IRS confiscations, she sold the band and its library to a Denver businessman named Stu Jackson. It does not work as steadily as it did when Woody was alive, but it does make appearances, usually under the direction of Frank Tiberi. By all reports that I have heard, it often sounds very good. And it serves to extend Woody's legacy a little further.

His direct family legacy, of course, are his grandchildren, Alexandra and Tommy. She is a skilled teacher, working on her bachelor's degree after a bad marriage. Tommy Littlefield is happily married. He is a Nashville songwriter, working in the country-and-western, rock, and rhythm-and-blues field. Like his mother, he is literate and articulate. For a time he led and performed in a small band, a quartet, called the Questionnaires. For the most part now he concentrates on writing songs, under a contract arrangement with Polygram Records. His group recorded two albums for EMI.

Tommy said, "We were about to sign when my granddad was dying. In his more lucid moments, he knew about it. I felt a lot of pride about that.

"But I also felt a lot of guilt and sadness that my grandmother didn't see me live to be something more than a fuck-up.

"She was very warm, very funny. That's how I think of her. I love her probably as much as anyone could."

Of his relationship with his mother, he said, "Quite a few years ago, we reconciled. I stopped resenting her and I think she feels a lot less guilty about it. We've developed a really good friendship. I enjoy her as a friend more than a mom. But sometimes she has come and helped me as a mom would."

Are people aware of his family history?

"Sometimes when people ask me about my background," he said, "I have to bring it up. The younger the people are, the less aware of him they tend to be. But then there are young people who are into what he did.

"I'm extremely proud of it, because I know what his place is in the pantheon of popular music. And it's a very important place.

"His singing when he was a younger man was just incredible, which I didn't find out about until recent years. And I really liked his alto saxophone.

"I always thought I was a pretty lousy bandleader with my little band. I learned how hard it is dealing with three people, much less fifteen. What amazed me was the way he maintained the quality of musicianship all those years. Every time I saw the band in the last years, it was still cookin'."

That's the family legacy. What of the professional and historical legacy?

In the past, great art survived because great artists and critics and other connoisseurs deemed that it should. We have the music of Bach and Mozart because a brilliant nineteen-year-old musician named Felix Mendelssohn read it, understood it, and revived it in concert when it was at risk of being forgotten. On the other hand, the music of Louis Spohr, a major celebrity in his lifetime, is now largely ignored because most musicians don't find it very interesting. This was long the way in the arts: time and the mind of man filtered out the meretricious and assigned it to obscurity; the good survived.

But this has changed in the age of the motion pictures, recorded sound, and conglomerate ownership of the means of communications. This is affecting all forms of art, including literature. "What we're heading for," said Jim Sitter, executive director of the Council for Literary Magazines and Presses, "is a publishing company run by a movie company run by a cable company run by a telephone company with a bunch of computer subsidiaries."

Alberto Vitale, president of Random House, put it nakedly: "We don't publish for the literary community; we publish for the public. The literary community is only a small part of that."[2]

So there, folks.

The companies—Time Warner, Viacom, Paramount—that own most of the book-publishing and movie industries also own most of the record business, and the "product" that interests them most is not the best music but that which sells the most. If *She Was Only a Bird in a Gilded Cage* and *Father, Dear Father, Come Home with Me Now* once fell from public favor because of their sheer lachrymose absurdity, more recent decades have seen a growing tendency to glorify cultural trash. This phenomenon dates from the 1960s, when newspapers began hiring rock "critics" to treat soberly pop music of numbing superficiality and declining harmonic and melodic interest. There is nothing so trivial that someone, somewhere, will not take it seriously.

With the rise of telemarketing and the power of television to sell apparently anything, the major record companies found it profitable indeed to repackage and sell not only the most banal of rock-and-roll records but even the worst of the music of the 1940s. When, a few years ago, writer Fred Binkley approached Columbia Records (now Sony) to ask if they would let him produce a package of all the Benny Goodman records on that label, he was asked what he thought it might sell. He guessed that the figure might run as high as 200,000. He was told, "We're just not interested in anything that small."

In 1963, Columbia issued some of the work of the First and Second Herds, forty-five of the hundred sides Woody recorded for the label, in a three-LP package. But for much of the time in the years since then, the work of those bands has been out of print, and seventeen of those hundreds of sides have never been issued at all. Yet there has never been a moment in which Elvis Presley has not been relentlessly marketed; his home has become almost a religious shrine. If you want it, you can buy through television such songs as *Dance with Me Henry*. We used to abandon our cultural offal. Most of the worst of nineteenth-century music is forgotten. But we trudge toward the twenty-first century dragging the most banal of our popular music with us.

It is entirely possible that work of Woody Herman will be forgotten in this tide of musical flotsam.

In a story published in *Newsweek* November 25, 1982, when Woody Herman's opened in New Orleans, a writer named Annalyn Swan said:

> Where would jazz be without Herman? It's not that he's a sensational musician: he plays a so-so sax, is a mellow clarinetist and sings the blues with a certain gruff flair. He's not a great innovator, like Duke Ellington or Louis Armstrong. Except during the 1940s, he has never even been especially popular. Nonetheless, he is one of the most durable figures in jazz and one of its uncelebrated heroes. Since Herman . . . first began leading his own band . . . in 1936, an astonishing 2,000 jazzmen have passed through his string of ever-renewing orchestras.[3]

This condescension toward Woody's playing might not have been possible without his own constantly self-effacing statements. "It seems," he said in 1957, "if I have any natural ability, it comes out in the saxophone, because I can pick up a baritone or a tenor or an alto or even a soprano and get a pretty decent sound out of it, and yet I'd fought for years and years and years to get a really nice clarinet sound, and it still escapes me. I have this old clarinet mouthpiece maker, a little old Italian man in Youngstown, Ohio, and each time I break a mouthpiece or something happens, and when he sends me a new one, it's with the closer facing, hoping to get me to eventually have a legitimate embouchure." The facing is the distance between the reed and the mouthpiece.

In an interview with broadcaster Fred Hall, Woody said, "Well, I never have really been a fan of my singing at all. I do it if I feel I can read a lyric and get something from it, or enhance what we're doing musically, but it's not because I think I can sing at all."[4]

The best evaluation of Woody's work, both as instrumentalist and band-leader, is that of composer and conductor Gunther Schuller in his *The Swing Era*. There is no book on jazz like it. Though it has minor shortcomings in terms of historical detail, it provides incomparable analyses of music of the era, not particularly for laymen, since it presupposes a considerable technical knowledge of music and the ability to read it. No one else in the history of jazz has brought to bear in jazz analysis Schuller's knowledge, musicianship, and exceptional powers of hearing. He said that Woody has never been given his proper place in jazz history by most of the music's critics and historians. He continued:

> Woody has rarely been accorded appropriate recognition for his consistently fine work as a clarinetist, as an alto saxophonist, and as a singer—he is generally dismissed as beneath discussion in these three areas—and even the many fine orchestras Woody has led through the years, his First Herd included, have been treated—at least until recently—rather casually by most jazz historians. Somehow his accomplishments are not deemed quite central to the main tradition(s) of jazz and therefore of minor consequence.
>
> The fact is that Herman is an excellent, at times superior clarinetist/saxophonist/singer—certainly never less than professional—and that his 1944-46 band was as exciting and influential an orchestra as jazz has seen is generally ignored or suppressed. Had Herman and his orchestra been black, the verdict would be quite different . . . .
>
> Herman belongs to that category of musicians who are not creative in the larger sense, who are not capable of being "unique" or "original," but who nevertheless succeed at very high levels of technical perfection, taste, and musical integrity . . . .
>
> Certainly, he derived the essentials of his clarinet style from Goodman and one of Goodman's own major influences, Jimmy Noone. And yet Herman's clarinet playing is immediately identifiable as *his*, by the warmth and expressivity of his tone, by the distinctive turn-of-phrase he favors, and by the modest role he assigns himself in any orchestral or ensemble context.
>
> Similarly, Herman's adulation of Johnny Hodges can be heard in all of his alto work. And yet there is an intensity and personal warmth beneath the outward manner in Woody's alto-playing that is undeniably his own.
>
> His work as a singer is perhaps the least appreciated of his performing roles. This is all the more remarkable since Woody sings extremely well, indeed better than the vast majority of those who think of themselves as professional

singers. Again, Woody makes no pretenses as a vocalist, but the fact remains that in three particular vocal idioms—ballads, blues, and novelty songs—Woody has few equals. Listening to his ballad-singing on records, especially in the 1930s and 1940s, one is constantly surprised to find that we aren't listening to some famous established singer but simply to Woody Herman. His control of pitch, timbre, diction, and phrasing is never less than commensurate to the assignment at hand, and often seems quite inspired and original . . . .

But clearly Herman's greatest contributions to jazz are as an orchestra leader, in 1945 producing one of the finest orchestras jazz has ever known and through it causing the creation of a body of work that stands to this day as classics of the Post-Swing Era.[5]

Writing in the London *Times* on July 8, 1990, Robert Cushman referred to "the greatest leader, if not player, of them all—Woody Herman." And time seems to be producing a growing concurrence on that point.

A year after Woody's death, in Cleveland, Donald Erb—one of the most respected of contemporary classical composers and the most widely performed—wrote a four-movement piece for solo clarinet simply entitled *Woody*. It received its premiere at the respected Cleveland Institute of Music, where Erb has for some years been composer in residence. Erb says that Woody had a profound impact on his life and his music.

Born in Youngstown, Ohio, on January 17, 1927, Erb started music at the age of six, learning cornet from a great aunt. By the time he was twelve, his family had moved to Cleveland, and, fascinated with Coleman Hawkins's record of *Body and Soul*, he began trying to play jazz, and within a few years was doing so professionally.

"I played jazz quite seriously until my middle to late twenties," Erb said. "I was okay at it, I could have made a living at it, but I picked up a pencil one day and that was my undoing. I became interested in other aspects of music.

"I guess I heard the First Herd when I got out of the navy in 1946. Like a lot of kids, I became absolutely enthralled by it. It was the drive, the exuberance, the excitement, the musicianship, the professionalism. And those tunes! *Northwest Passage, Caldonia, Goosey Gander*. They were so original. It was the most original band of that time, with the possible exception of Ellington.

"All the big bands used to come through Cleveland, and I used to jam with a lot of the players from those bands. The Herman band was the most interesting, to me. And that music sounds as fresh now as it did then.

"If he wasn't a *great* clarinetist, he certainly was a good one. But the thing I think was remarkable about him was the spirit. It was a musical spirit so open-minded. The enthusiasm about his music-making sticks out all over the world. He simply was in another world than most of his colleagues, another league altogether. So when he died, I wrote a piece.

"The first performance was given at the Cleveland Institute of Music by Richard Stoltzman. The performance on the record is by Ross Powell, a wonderful clarinetist in Dallas. It's been played by quite a few clarinetists already.

"I draw on my early experiences in my writing. So the first movement of the piece is called *Melody*. The second is called *Jazzy*, and it's played with jazz inflection, which of course all clarinetists don't do equally well. The third is called *Cadenza*, and it's a pretty elaborate thing. And the last movement comes from my childhood. It's called *Blues Shout*."

I told him of Woody's tendency to self-deprecation, particularly about his playing, and above all his clarinet playing. Erb said: "That's often the case. You have no idea how many people in our business die thinking they've failed. And I think I know the root of it. A lot of times people who've done well have what I call expectations—things that they think they should have done or, sometimes even recognition they should have had that they didn't get. And so they think they have failed. It's a sad thing. Ravel apparently died thinking he'd failed. They're the things you wake up at night thinking about."

Said Richard Stoltzman: "I listened to some of his earlier recordings when we were getting ready to do the record of *Ebony Concerto*. I listened to *Igor*." It was a piece by Shorty Rogers and Red Norvo, recorded by Woody and the Woodchoppers in Chicago on May 20, 1946. "It was some very, very tasty clarinet playing, very fine playing. I don't get it. If he was putting himself down, maybe he thought he should be a copy of Benny or Artie Shaw. The thing that made Woody great was his time. When he played the clarinet, even later on when he didn't have his chops, he put the notes in places that really meant something.

"Clarinetists are impressed by technique. The public is impressed by sound and emotion, and Woody certainly had those."[6]

At his opening at the St. Regis in 1985, with Benny Goodman in attendance, as Woody later told a reporter, "I made it clear that Benny was the innovator. What's more important is there were several of us who owned clarinets but Benny *played* the clarinet. Even Benny was blushing with that one; I put it on pretty heavy. But it was correct."

When you examine Woody's statements over the years about himself and

his abilities, his reference to "my nothing little sound" on alto, his deroga-
tion of his clarinet tone, his reference to himself as a "little creep" in
comparison to the tall musicians like Neal Reid who surrounded him, you
start to get an impression. On another occasion he described himself as "a
shriveled-up little guy" when he met Charlotte. I think about the young
boy who thought his nose was too big. Above all I remember his response
when I told him he was a great man: "No I'm not." It wasn't an affectation
of modesty. In my mind's ear, I can still hear the tone in which this belief
was expressed, gentle and soft and sad. He meant it. He really meant it.

"He had a way of keeping things to himself," Ingrid said. Was all that
exuberant onstage cockiness a professional guise, a costume to be donned
when the time came? It is not unusual to encounter in performers a
profound shyness that suddenly, miraculously, vanishes when the lights go
on and the audience roars. And gradually, as I have in these past several
years examined the life of this man I knew and loved, I have concluded that
he was essentially a shy man. The evidence has confirmed an impression
that I came to rather quickly when I first knew him.

Shyness may not be a liability in a biologist or astronomer or a cardiolo-
gist. In those lines of work, it is enough that you be known and respected
among your professional colleagues. But the arts are different, particularly
the performing arts. Every one who enters upon these pursuits knows,
whether consciously or intuitively, that it is absolutely essential that he or
she gain a public reputation on a major scale, in other words, fame. He
may not want it. He may even be uncomfortable with it. But he or she must
have it if that person is going to get the opportunity to practice the craft.
Fame is a tool of the trade. And if that person is shy, it is essential that he
or she learn to hide it. For confidence, or, lacking it, the illusion of confidence, is requisite to the work.

In early 1979, Woody said: "The highest compliment of my entire life
was from a nightclub operator in Buffalo, New York, a real dese and dem
and dose guy. And he still tended bar in his own club, so you knew he was a
down-home cat. And I came off the bandstand and the place had a tin roof
and it sounded terrible. And he was in a trance, and he said, 'Wood, that's
the best band I ever heard in my life. Man, too much.' He said, 'You da
Vince Lombardi of de bands.'

"And that to me was the epitome of everything that anyone could say.

"The second-best compliment I ever received in my life was just this past
year, when the bus pulled up to a truck stop to let the guys out to get
whatever they needed, a hamburger or whatever . . . .

"But right across the road was a McDonald's and I had never really been in a McDonald's, and I thought, 'Well, now's the time to case a McDonald's, and I'll try a hamburger.'

"And I went in, and I was waiting in line to get my hamburger. And a little girl about thirteen or fourteen was the cleanup girl. She got a little broom and a little thing and picks up dirty paper dishes and so on. And she came over and she gave me a very strange look and then she went over and did a little more, and then she came back and watched out of the corner of her eye, with a funky little attitude.

"And finally looked around, and she came over very close and she said, 'Are you Woody Herman?' And I said, 'Yeah.' And she said, 'Wow!' and split.

"That was the second highest compliment of my life."[7]

The story is funny and poignant and indicative of the man. Chubby Jackson, too, thinks he was shy.

I don't wish to overstate the case. Woody had fun on stage, he loved that music, and he loved performing. But there was that other side of him, and as a player and performer, Woody Herman never gave Woody Herman the respect that Woody Herman deserved.

One musician after another will make assessments about Woody's abilities as a player that are far above his own. And Woody had something that Gerry Mulligan accurately assessed: an ability to play solos pertinent to what the band was playing rather than bravura displays of himself. In this he was like his friends Count Basie and Duke Ellington. They, like him, have been underestimated as instrumentalists in that they sublimated their own playing to the needs of the band. One must listen to very early Ellington and Basie to realize what excellent pianists they were. As time went on, Basie abandoned the driving and facile stride style he had developed, devoting himself to a delicate and perfect placement of his little fills and plinks in the air spaces in the music of his band. So, too, Ellington. And like Ellington and Basie, Woody made the band his true instrument.

Woody's "young men" were extensions of himself. In this he was utterly unlike Goodman. When a soloist got too much response from the audience, Goodman would cut down his time or even remove the number from performance, and it is still widely said that he fired Big Sid Catlett because the drummer's flashing technique and humorous displays inspired too much applause. Goodman's band was about Benny Goodman, as Artie Shaw's was about Artie Shaw. But Woody's was about itself, and it was the most fiercely fiery orchestra of the entire big-band era.

The era is gone. The formation it developed—saxophones, trumpets, trombones, rhythm section—lingers on in local rehearsal bands and some,

like that of Rob McConnell's Boss Brass, with a more or less continuing
identity. The situation is rather better in Europe, with such big bands as
the UMO orchestra in Helsinki, the West Deutsch Rundfunk band in
Cologne, and others employed by European radio networks. And of course
there are those thousands of "stage bands" in the high schools and universities of America. Like the string quartet and the symphony orchestra, the
"big band" is an instrumentation that works and for just that reason will no
doubt persist for at least a while longer.

No one did more to establish that formation than Woody.

The band's quality reflected the man. Remember, he was a pretty wild
little kid, once upon a time, sitting on pillows to see over the dashboard
and drive himself to jobs, off on his own and getting shot in the leg when
he was only seventeen. That quality never left him. He was impish, imper-
tinent, irreverent, laughing, lyrical, and endlessly colorful (even in
speech), and that band was his mirror image.

One of the most perceptive evaluations of Woody to come from any
musician I have talked to is that of Nat Adderley. Nat is a compact, rotund,
and deceptively slow-spoken man. He has a soft southern accent. Like his
late brother, Cannonball Adderley, he has a strong academic side, and his
words are always thoughtfully measured. Nat said:

"To this day, I think Woody was the best *leader* that I know. He wasn't the
best clarinet player or the best alto player, but in terms of leading a band
and being a controller of men, and having the respect and regard of *all the
men all the time*, nobody was better than Woody. Of course, I loved my
brother, and I think Cannonball was a great leader of small bands. But in
his entire life, Cannonball didn't deal with fifteen musicians as a leader.
Woody dealt with *hundreds*. The man certainly was a bandleader par excellence. I feel that way from the bandleaders I've played with and what I
know *of* other bandleaders. And that covers a lot of territory. And I won't
name names after that point.

"But Woody!

"Someone asked Woody in an interview who would be in his all-time
best band. It could be anybody from any band he'd had. And I was *in it*! I
was so proud! Doug Mettome and I were two of the five trumpets. And I
said, 'Well I'll be damned. I never knew that Woody had that kind of regard
for my playing.' And he had what I think are some really seriously bad
dudes in his trumpet sections.

"I was so proud! I *taped* that thing."[8]

Somebody was always asking Woody to make up these all-star lists. I
discovered that in one of them, to include even musicians who hadn't

played with him, Woody had named Dick Nash for the trombone section. I sent a transcript of the interview to Dick. Dick left a frantic message on my answering machine: "You haven't made my day, you've made my *decade!*"

Tom Cassidy said: "I don't see Woody's life as sad. He was a pretty happy guy at the end. He laughed at life. After that accident in Kansas, he flew everywhere. He was flying every day, getting on these little puddle jumpers and flying around the country. It seemed like the smaller the plane, the better he liked it. He'd call me every day when he got to where he was going and talk about the storm he'd been in, and how great it was and how they almost crashed and he'd laugh at it. He was a riot. I could hardly wait for the phone call every day. He wasn't afraid of dying, he just wasn't afraid of it at all. He loved life, and he was enjoying every minute of it."[9]

Ingrid generally agrees with that assessment. She said, "No, he wasn't afraid of dying. He'd been through so much and he was in such poor health, and he wasn't afraid of stuff like that. He was religious. I don't really know how much bearing that had on it, because we never talked about it. I don't know if he thought there was a heaven or a hell or that he was going to see his loved ones."[10]

As I write this, Woody has been gone just over seven years.

The government long continued to confiscate Woody's royalties from records and publishing. One IRS agent told Ingrid bluntly that he considered that they belonged to the government in perpetuity. But the liens have now expired, and Ingrid should at last receive some money from Woody's estate.

He was, as I finally was able to tell him to his face, a great man. But he was more than that. The Irish have a word for it. He was grand.

Woody had a little expression, something he used to say to audiences at the end of the evening:

"Love, take it easy, God bless you, and see you around."

Ojai, California, February 8, 1995

Appendix 1

The Woody Herman Alumni

It is probably impossible to compile a full list of the alumni of the Herman bands. A partial list runs the risk of serious oversights. Nonetheless, such a list is helpful in assessing Woody Herman's ear for talent. Some of those in the list had significant reputations before joining the band. Most did not; their tenures with the band made them famous. This is a partial list:

Trumpet: Nat Adderley, Sonny Berman, Bill Berry, Lynn Biviano, Oscar Brashear, Bill Byrne, Conte Candoli, Pete Candoli, Buddy Childers, Burt Collins, Dick Collins, John Coppola, John Crews, Dennis Dotson, Glenn Drewes, Don Ellis, Rolf Ericson, Don Fagerquist, Don Ferrara, Stan Fishelson, Paul Fontaine, Larry Ford, Luis Gasca, David Gale, Greg Gisbert, Gary Grant, Bernie Glow, Dusko Goykovich, Conrad Gozzo, Tim Hagans, Tom Harrell, Ziggy Harrell, Steve Harrow, Nelson Hatt, Neal Hefti, John Hoffman, John Howell, Frank Huggins, Billy Hunt, Roger Ingram, Tony Klatka, Gerry Lamy, Cappy Lewis, Mark Lewis, Ray Linn, Marky Markowitz, Sal Marquez, Billy May, Doug Mettome, Brian O'Flagherty, Chuck Peterson, Al Porcino, Tom Porrello, Jim Powell, Buddy Powers, George Rabbai, Don Rader, Red Rodney, Billie Rogers, Shorty Rogers, Ernie Royal, Dick Ruedebusch, Charlie Shavers, Bobby Shew, Dave Stahl, Marvin Stamm, Bill Stapleton, Danny Stiles, Ron Stout, Byron Stripling, Nick Travis, Ray Triscari, Allen Vizzutti, Carl Warwick, Ray Wetzel, Kenny Wheeler, Diane White.

Bass trumpet: Cy Touff.

Trombone: John Allred, Wayne André, Joe Barati, Eddie Bert, Will Bradley, Bob Brookmeyer, Bob Burgess, Billy Byers, Jimmy Cleveland, Sonny Costanzo, Hal Crook, Jim Daniels, Willie Dennis, Donald Doane, John Fedchock, Carl Fontana, Bruce Fowler, Nelson Hinds, Jack Gale, Harold Garrett, Jimmy Guinn, Urbie Green, Slide Hampton, Bill Harris, Randy Hawes, Ed Kiefer, Dale Kirkland, Dick Kenny, Dante Luciani, Mark Lusk, Tom Malone, Keith Moon, Ira Nepus, Ralph Pfeffner, Gary Potter, Julian Priester, Jim Pugh, Frank Rehak, Tommy Pedersen, Neal Reid, Henry Southall, Earl Swope, Rob Swope, Bart Varsalona, Bill Watrous, Ollie Wilson, Phil Wilson, Kai Winding, Sy Zentner.

Saxophone: Joe Alexander, Gene Allen, Gene Ammons, Tom Anastas, Danny Bank, Bob Belden, Al Belletto, Pete Brewer, Mike Brignola, Nick Brignola, Gordon Brisker, Ernie Caceres, Jay Cameron, Serge Chaloff, Pete Christlieb, Al Cohn, Jerry Coker, Ronnie Cuber, Skippy DeSair, Billy Drewes, Joe Farrell, Herbie Fields, Med Flory, Frank Foster, Stan Getz, Jimmy Giuffre, Bob Hardaway, Dick Hafer, Gregory Herbert, Bruce Johnstone, Richie Kamuca, Ralph Lalama, Don Lanphere, John LaPorta, Steve Lederer, Joe Lovano, Willie Maiden, Herbie Mann, Saxey Mansfield, Steve Marcus, Lou Marini, Sam Marowitz, Arno Marsh, Warne Marsh, Andy McGhee, Paul McGinley, Jay Migliore, Dick Mitchell, Pete Mondello, Vido Musso, Roger Newman, Jack Nimitz, Sal Nistico, John Nugent, Cecil Payne, Roger Pemberton, Bill Perkins, Flip Phillips, Ray Pizzi, Seldon Powell, Les Robinson, Joe Romano, Raoul Romero, Billy Ross, Zoot Sims, Gary Smulyan, Sam Staff, Herbie Steward, Buddy Tate, Joe Temperley, Frank Tiberi, Phil Urso, Frank Vicari, Mark Vinci, Frank Wess.

Piano: Tony Aless, Kenny Ascher, John Bunch, Ralph Burns, Alan Broadbent, Uri Cane, Pat Coil, Albert Dailey, Harold Danko, Vince Guaraldi, John Hicks, Pete Jolly, Dave Lalama, Andy Laverne, Lou Levy, Tommy Linehan, Lyle Mays, Dave McKenna, John Oddo, Nat Pierce, Jimmy Rowles, Joel Weiskopf, Brad Williams.

Bass: John Adams, Jay Anderson, Chuck Andrus, Harry Babasin, John Beal, Dave Carpenter, Keter Betts, Monty Budwig, Dave Finck, Lou Fisher, Arnold Fishkin, Major Holley, Chip Jackson, George Duvivier, Chubby Jackson, Alfonso Johnson, Marc Johnson, Red Kelly, Dave Larocca, Tony Leonardi, John Lietham, Red Mitchell, Gordon (Whitey) Mitchell, Joe Mondragon, Monk Montgomery, Michael Moore, Oscar Pettiford, Rufus Reid, Mike Richmond, Lynn Seaton, Dave Stone, Steve Wallace, Walt Yoder.

Guitar: Billy Bauer, Charlie Byrd, Jimmy Raney, Gene Sargent, Chuck Wayne, Hy White.

Drums: Jimmy Campbell, Frank Carlson, Dan D'Imperio, Evan Diner, Chuck Flores, Panama Francis, Dave Gibson, Paul Guerrero, Jimmy Hamilton, Jeff Hamilton, Jake Hanna, Jeff Hirshfield, Steve Houghton, Sonny Igoe, Gus Johnson, Rufus Jones, Tiny Kahn, Joe LaBarbera, Don Lamond, Cliff Leeman, Dennis Mackrel, Shelly Manne, Art Mardigan, Dave Miller, Dave Ratajczak, John Riley, Jim Rupp, Ed Soph, Dave Tough, John Van Ohlen, Shadow Wilson, Ronnie Zito.

Vibraharp: Eddie Costa, Victor Feldman, Terry Gibbs, Marjorie Hyams, Milt Jackson, Red Norvo.

Arrangers and composers: Gary Anderson, Kenny Ascher, Joe Bishop, Alan Broadbent, Ralph Burns, Bill Chase, Al Cohn, Chick Corea, Richard Evans, John Fedchock, Frank Foster, Dizzy Gillespie, Jimmy Giuffre, Dusko Goykovich, Slide Hampton, Bill Holman, Gordon Jenkins, Neal Hefti, Tony Klatka, Johnny Mandel, Joseph Mark, Dave Matthews, Lyle Mays, Jiggs Noble, John Oddo, Nat Pierce, Jim Pugh, Don Rader, Ted Richards, Shorty Rogers, Raoul Romero, Maria Schneider, Bill Stapleton.

Vocalists: Joe Carroll, Blossom Dearie, Carolyn Grey, Dolly Houston, Carole Kaye, Gilda Maken, Jerry Nye, Mary Ann McCall, Anita O'Day, Polly Podewell, Billie Rogers, Lynn Stevens, Terry Swope-Leonard, Virginia Verrell, Frances Wayne.

Appendix 2

Chart of Hit Records
Compiled by Kirk Pasich.*

Artist	Period Songs Charted	Total Years Songs Charted	No. of Top 40 Hits	No. of Top 20 Hits	No. of Top 10 Hits	Total No. of Charting Songs
Woody Herman	1937–1956	19 years	53	39	19	55
Beach Boys	1962–1989	28 years	36	25	15	57
Beatles	1964–1986	23 years	49	40	33	69
Michael Jackson	1971–1993	23 years	32	28	25	38
Rolling Stones	1964–1993	30 years	41	30	23	54
Supremes	1962–1976	15 years	33	24	20	45

*Through 1993. Based on *Billboard* chart data, copyright © 1955–1993 by BPI Communications, SoundScan, Inc., and Broadcast Data Systems. Compiled in *Joel Whitburn's Top Pop Singles 1955–1993*, copyright © 1994 by Record Research, Inc.

BIBLIOGRAPHY

Whitney Balliett, *Night Creature*. New York: Oxford University Press, 1981; *American Musicians*. New York: Oxford University Press, 1986.

Laurence Bergreen, *As Thousands Cheer*. New York: Viking Press, 1990.

James Lincoln Collier, *Benny Goodman and the Swing Era*. New York: Oxford University Press, 1989; *Jazz: The American Theme Song*. New York: Oxford University Press, 1993.

Leonard Feather, *The Encyclopedia of Jazz*. New York: Horizon Press, 1960.

Roland Gelatt, *The Fabulous Phonograph* (revised). New York: Macmillan, 1977.

Nat Hentoff and Nat Shapiro, *Hear Me Talkin' to Ya*. New York: Dover Publications, 1955.

Richard Palmer, *Stan Getz*. London: Apollo Press, 1988.

The New Grove Encyclopedia of Jazz. London: Macmillan Press, 1988.

Gunther Schuller, *The Swing Era*. New York: Oxford University Press, 1989.

George T. Simon, *The Big Bands*. New York: Macmillan, 1967.

Stuart Troup and Woody Herman, *The Woodchopper's Ball*. New York: E. P. Dutton, 1990.

Steve Voce, *Woody Herman*. London: Apollo Press, 1986.

NOTES

The following abbreviations are used in these notes.

GL indicates an interview, in some cases many interviews, with the author. **RJG** refers to the interviews with Ralph J. Gleason, the transcript of which is in the possession of Ingrid Herman. **HW** indicates the Herb Wong interviews for the Smithsonian Institution, now at the Institute of Jazz Studies at Rutgers University, Newark, New Jersey. **ST** stands for Stuart Troup and refers to his book in collaboration with Woody, *The Woodchopper's Ball*, published by E. P. Dutton, New York, 1990.

1. Milwaukee

1. GL.
2. GL.
3. HW.
4. GL.
5. HW.
6. HW.
7. *The Illustrated History of Wisconsin Music*, compiled by Michael G. Corenthal. Milwaukee: MGC Publications, 1990.
8. RJG.
9. GL.

2. School Days

1. ST.
2. GL.
3. RJG.
4. GL.
5. *The Illustrated History of Jazz in Wisconsin.*
6. *Milwaukee Sentinel*, 4/10/75.
7. Ibid.

3. On the Road

1. *The Illustrated History of Jazz in Wisconsin.*
2. GL.
3. RJG.
4. *Chicago Sun-Times,* 8/19/77.
5. RJG.
6. *Chicago Sun-Times,* 8/19/77.
7. GL.
8. RJG.
9. RJG.
10. Whitney Balliett, *American Musicians.* New York: Oxford University Press, 1986
11. GL.
12. GL.
13. GL.
14. GL.
15. RJG.
16. GL.
17. GL.
18. GL.
19. GL.

4. Life with Isham

1. GL, interview with James T. Maher.
2. Isham Jones liner note by James T. Maher.
3. Ibid.
4. Letter to the author from James T. Maher.
5. James Lincoln Collier, *Jazz: The American Theme Song.* New York: Oxford University Press, 1991.
6. Letter to the author.
7. Ibid.
8. Gunther Schuller, *The Swing Era.* New York: Oxford University Press, New York, 1989.
9. Ibid.
10. GL.
11. ST.
12. RJG.
13. HW.
14. GL.
15. Ibid.

5. *The Band That Plays the Blues*

1. James Lincoln Collier, *Benny Goodman and the Swing Era*. New York: Oxford University Press, 1989.
2. RJG.
3. GL.
4. GL.
5. ST.
6. RJG.
7. ST.
8. George T. Simon, *The Big Bands*. New York: Macmillan, 1967.
9. ST.
10. RJG.

6. *The Summer of '37*

1. Roland Gelatt, *The Fabulous Phonograph* (revised). New York: Macmillan, 1977.
2. GL.
3. GL.
4. *New York Newsday*, 2/24/85.
5. ST.
6. HW.
7. RJG.
8. *New York Newsday*, 2/24/85.
9. GL.

7. *Woodchopper's Ball*

1. John S. Wilson, *New York Times*, 2/3/72.
2. GL.
3. RJG.
4. GL.
5. GL.
6. RJG.
7. GL.
8. HW.

8. *Birth of the Herd*

1. GL.
2. HW.
3. GL.

4. GL.
5. GL.
6. GL.
7. Gene Lees, *Singers and the Song*. New York: Oxford University Press, 1987.
8. GL.

9. *Wild Root*

1. GL.
2. Whitney Balliett, *American Musicians*. New York: Oxford University Press, 1986.
3. HW.
4. GL.
5. GL.
6. GL.
7. Whitney Balliett, *American Musicians*. New York, Oxford University Press, 1986.
8. GL.

10. *Making It*

1. GL.
2. GL.
3. RJG.
4. GL.
5. GL.
6. GL.
7. GL.
8. GL.
9. GL.
10. GL.
11. HW.
12. HW.
13. Bill Crow, *Jazz Anecdotes*. New York: Oxford University Press, 1990.
14. HW.
15. RJG.
16. *New York Newsday*, 2/24/85.
17. GL.
18. Steve Voce, *Woody Herman*. London: Apollo Press, 1986.

11. *Ebony Concerto*

1. Steve Voce, *Woody Herman*. London: Apollo Press, 1986.
2. GL.

3. *New York Newsday*, 2/24/85.
4. RJG.
5. GL.
6. GL.
7. GL.
8. ST.
9. RJG.
10. GL.
11. GL.
12. ST.
13. GL.
14. RJG.
15. RJG.
16. ST.

12. Lady McGowan's Dream

1. GL.
2. Henry Mancini and Gene Lees, *Did They Mention the Music?* Chicago: Contemporary Books, 1989.
3. GL.
4. HW.
5. GL.
6. GL.
7. GL.
8. GL.
9. GL.
10. Gunther Schuller, *The Swing Era*. New York: Oxford University Press, 1989.
11. GL.

13. The Second Herd

1. Whitney Balliett, *Night Creature*. New York, Oxford University Press, 1981.
2. GL.
3. ST.
4. ST.
5. Gene Lees, *Singers and the Song*. New York: Oxford University Press, 1987.
6. James Lincoln Collier, *Benny Goodman and the Swing Era*. New York: Oxford University Press, 1989.

14. The Young Turks

1. GL.
2. Gene Lees, *Singers and the Song*. New York: Oxford University Press, 1987.

3. GL.
4. *Metronome*, June 1948.
5. GL.
6. GL.
7. GL.
8. GL.
9. GL.

15. Bad Boys

1. GL.
2. GL.
3. GL.
4. GL.
5. GL.
6. GL.
7. GL.
8. GL.

16. Sidewalks of Cuba

1. GL.
2. HW.
3. RJG.
4. GL.
5. GL.
6. GL.
7. GL.
8. GL.
9. GL.
10. ST.

17. The Third Herd

1. Gene Lees, *Singers and the Song*. New York: Oxford University Press, 1987.
2. *Gene Lees Jazzletter*, January 1992.
3. *Singers and the Song*.
4. GL.

18. Scuffle Bread

1. ST.
2. *Down Beat*, 4/22/53

3. GL.
4. GL.
5. GL.
6. GL.
7. RJG.
8. GL.
9. GL.
10. GL.
11. GL.
12. GL.
13. GL.
14. GL.
15. RJG.

19. A Bird in the Herd

1. *Time*, 5/51/54.
2. RJG.
3. RJG.
4. Steve Voce, *Woody Herman*. London: Apollo Press, 1986.
5. HW.

20. The Metropole

1. HW.
2. GL.
3. GL.
4. HW.
5. GL.
6. GL.
7. GL.
8. GL.
9. GL.
10. GL.
11. GL.
12. GL.

21. Dallas November

1. HW.
2. GL.
3. ST.
4. HW.

5. GL.
6. GL.
7. GL.

22. Death and Taxes

1. GL.
2. GL.
3. *Toronto Telegram*, 7/30/66.
4. GL.
5. GL.
6. GL.
7. GL.

23. Trouble in Mind

1. *Globe and Mail*, Toronto.
2. *Toronto Star*.
3. ST.
4. GL.
5. ST.
6. HW.
7. GL.
8. RJG.

24. Abe's Odyssey

1. GL.
2. GL.
3. GL.
4. GL.

25. The Road Gets Rougher . . .

1. *Time*, 5/11/70.
2. *Billboard*, 5/4/74.
3. *Down Beat*, 6/2/77.
4. HW.

26. The Fortieth Anniversary

1. *Billboard*, 11/13/76.
2. GL.

3. GL.
4. GL.

27. Tommy and Charlotte

1. GL.
2. GL.
3. GL.
4. GL.

28. Poland Farewell

1. GL.
2. HW.
3. GL.
4. *New York Times*, 7/13/83.
5. Associated Press, 11/13/82.
6. ST.
7. Jack Siefert to the author.
8. GL.

29. Down Under

1. GL.
2. GL.
3. GL.
4. GL.
5. *Gold Coast Bulletin*, 8/13/95.
6. *Courier-Mail*, 8/13/94.
7. *Australian National Daily*, 8/12/85.
8. *Sydney Morning Herald*, 8/20/85.
9. *Music Maker*, October 1985.
10. GL.
11. *Los Angeles Times*, 1/9/86.
12. GL.

30. The Last Gig

1. *American Scholar.*
2. GL.
3. *New York Newsday*, 7/5/86.
4. GL.
5. GL.

6. GL.
7. GL.
8. GL.
9. GL.
10. GL.
11. GL.

31. *The Last Days*

1. GL.
2. GL.
3. GL.
4. *National Law Journal*, August, 1988.
5. GL.
6. GL.
7. Steve Voce, *Woody Herman*. London: Apollo Press, 1986.

32. *Legacy*

1. GL.
2. *Christian Science Monitor*, 9/25/94.
3. *Newsweek*, 11/24/82.
4. Fred Hall, *Dialogues in Swing*. Ventura, California: Pathfinder Publishing, 1989.
5. Gunther Schuller, *The Swing Era*. New York: Oxford University Press, 1989.
6. GL.
7. HW.
8. GL.
9. GL.
10. GL.

INDEX